WITNESSES TO A VANISHING AMERICA

1. James Mooney, "Hopi Kachinas of the Powamu or 'Bean-planting Ceremony,'" Walpi Pueblo, Arizona, 1893. Photograph. The National Anthropological Archives, Smithsonian Institution.

WITNESSES TO A VANISHING AMERICA

THE NINETEENTH-CENTURY RESPONSE

LEE CLARK MITCHELL

PRINCETON UNIVERSITY PRESS

Published by Princeton University Press, Princeton, New Jersey
In the United Kingdom: Princeton University Press, Guildford, Surrey

Library of Congress Cataloging in Publication Data will be
found on the last printed page of this book

Publication of this book has been aided by a grant from
the Paul Mellon Fund of Princeton University Press

This book has been composed in linotype Baskerville

Clothbound editions of Princeton University Press books
are printed on acid-free paper, and binding materials are
chosen for strength and durability

Printed in the United States of America by Princeton
University Press, Princeton, New Jersey

Designed by Laury A. Egan

For my mother and father

YONNONDIO*

Walt Whitman, 1883

A song, a poem of itself—the word itself a dirge,
Amid the winds, the rocks, the storm and wintry night,
To me such misty, strange tableaux the syllables
    calling up;
Yonnondio—I see, far in the west or north, a limitless
    ravine, with plains and mountains dark,
I see swarms of stalwart chieftains, medicine-men, and
    warriors,
As flitting by like clouds of ghosts, they pass and are
    gone in the twilight,
(Race of the woods, the landscapes free, and the falls!
No picture, poem, statement, passing them to the future:)
Yonnondio! Yonnondio!—unlimn'd they disappear;
To-day gives place, and fades—the cities, farms,
    factories fade;
A muffled sonorous sound, a wailing word is borne
    through the air for a moment,
Then blank and gone and still, and utterly lost.

* The sense of the word is *lament for the aborigines*. It is an
Iroquois term; and has been used for a personal name.
[Whitman's note]

CONTENTS

LIST OF ILLUSTRATIONS

PREFACE

[Travelers] never describe things as they
really are, but bend them and mask them
according to the point of view from which
they see things.
  —*Montaigne, Essays*

Everything is extraordinary in America.
  —*Alexis de Tocqueville*
  Democracy in America

Propelled across the continent by notions of "rugged individualism,"
"course of empire," "inexhaustible resources," and "manifest destiny,"
pioneer Americans soon discovered that such slogans masked the other
side of progress: empire building required the destruction of a wilderness. In the nineteenth century, that devastation proceeded at a
rate alarming enough to arouse growing apprehensions about America's westward mission itself. Optimistic catch-phrases could hardly
calm the suspicion that much, perhaps too much, was being sacrificed
to the future. Was the promise of empire worth the price? Concern
for the vanishing wilderness would ultimately lead Americans to
question their culture itself. The following pages explore this critical
attitude as it emerged, paradoxically, from the continental conquest
meant to redeem that culture.

A wide variety of documents reveals, in ways never before made
clear, that the prospect of a vanishing "wilderness" provoked nineteenth-century Americans to commitments of astonishing diversity,
energy, and consequence. Diaries, novels, and reminiscences; letters
and all-too-conventional poems; newspaper essays, artists' journals,
and scientific notes and reports—all hint at a deep sense of foreboding. This feeling in turn inspired projects aimed at forestalling the
effects of westward "progress." Grasping as they did at America's
promised future, countless Americans nonetheless attempted to preserve its landscape in words, oils, and photographs. Quickly tamed
pioneer life elicited a similar response, as citizens strove to capture
their own evanescent histories. Others focused on Indian Tribes, recording alien images and cultures before the inevitable changes that

white encroachment would bring. This undercurrent of apprehension touched even those who did not go west. Local drives for historical societies, city parks, and woodland conservation spurred broad support among citizens all across the nation into awareness of the toll exacted by America's supposedly manifest destiny. Similar concerns sparked national movements in literature, painting, and photography, as well as in archaeology and anthropology.

These interrelated developments call for a revision in our notions of American history by revealing the ambivalence felt among even those who participated in the nation's triumphant conquest of the wilderness. The reassessment required by this view, however, also compels a reassessment of ourselves. Issues that we assume are modern— conservation, protection of endangered species, native rights, and questioning of the price of progress—actually originated early in the nineteenth century. As such, they form a uniquely American legacy.

To provide a context for understanding the emergence of these alternative attitudes, the opening chapter reviews common American assumptions about nature and culture. Chapter Two then assesses the growing number of laments over the passing of America's wilderness. Manifested most simply as nostalgic regret, the impulse to fix a record spread with astonishing rapidity—as rapidly as landscape seemed to alter and wild game to disappear. Explorers, frontiersmen, and scientists, settlers and tourists all came to feel that the "West" they preserved on paper was being diminished in more profound and troubling ways than it was being developed. Some even came to view the land as valuable in itself and worth holding intact. Federal park and conservation movements of the late nineteenth century expressed an active national commitment to issues once endorsed only by isolated individuals.

Americans' desire to capture the quickly passing moment of untamed wilderness focused first upon the plains, forests, mountains, and wildlife of the West. But a vanishing wilderness included more than topography, flora, and fauna, however exotic. Chapter Three examines those who came to prize human activity not merely as a picturesque embellishment on the natural landscape, but for its own sake. Seemingly overnight, settlements grew into towns and cities, as pioneer histories and frontier folkways passed into memory. Before too much was thus lost to recollection, many felt impelled to preserve their firsthand experiences, the lore quickly acquired of necessity and as soon outmoded by "progress."

The most compelling actor in the wilderness—indeed, the human symbol of that evanescent experience—was the Indian. Americans committed to rendering accounts of native life for the sake of future generations clearly realized that they were in a race against the destruction of their subjects—if not by outright extinction, then by more insidious white influences. Chapter Four traces the career of George Catlin, the first person to devote a full career to preserving in paint and words an exhaustive record of the Indians. The strength of his lifelong dedication, the trenchancy of his insights, and the quality of his completed record make him a major representative of the themes we are examining. Chapters Five and Six consider the historical context for Catlin's singular energies, surveying the painters and photographers of threatened Indian life and reviewing the work of nineteenth-century ethnographers. First attracted to the West by notions of the exotic and colorful, all of these chroniclers completed their records out of serious apprehensions about the impact of white expansion on native tribes.

Curiosity about Indian cultures often led beyond respect, and those willing to shake off preconceptions sometimes felt a wistful envy. Herman Melville's experiences in Polynesia during the 1840s helped him to anticipate a melancholy question toward which others would struggle in the next half century: Could native cultures, nonwhite and heathen, provide a richer life for their members than that which was replacing them? Chapter Seven, on Melville's sophisticated reading of Polynesian life, enters directly into the suggestive possibilities of that question.

Chapter Eight traces the series of increasingly complex responses to indigenous tribes that Melville had anticipated. Painters, scientists, and others began by merely hoping to record one moment in history; yet contact with alien peoples often educated them to the mysterious intricacies and emotional satisfactions of cultures they knew were doomed. For the more sensitive, study of native tribes finally meant probing, sometimes radically, the idea of culture itself. Absolutist notions of the superiority of Western civilization eroded before evidence demanding more sympathetic and relativisitic interpretations. Once again, "wilderness" connoted far more than mere landscape, and nineteenth-century Americans gradually became aware of ever more complex experiences associated with that word—experiences imperiled by the westward expansion of white Americans.

The Conclusion describes the self-conscious assessments of Western civilization that resulted from admiration for tribal life. In addition, it pursues well into the twentieth century the themes raised in earlier chapters. Without consciously doing so, Americans fostered a dialogue challenging to the very premises of their own way of life. The dialogue continues today, though of course its terms have shifted and the voices have grown more strident. Yet we too often comfort ourselves with the rather threadbare blanket of modernity; Americans have ventured neither as far nor as willingly as most assume concerning issues of conservation, endangered wildlife, and native American rights. Nor have the more humane attitudes suddenly emerged from nowhere. Our nineteenth-century predecessors swaggered with less thoughtless confidence than the accepted historical record suggests, and we need to view them as aware of, even puzzled by issues that now trouble us—to recognize that they could be nearly as troubled as we are. Accepting such a heritage should help us to discern a more complex American character than that suggested by slogans blazoned across consciousness and continents.

A WORD of caution: anyone familiar with the criticism will realize that my readings of Cooper, Melville, and Mark Twain are hardly new. They are not meant to be. The newness here lies in depicting the world from which they emerged. As a graduate student, I was fascinated by these writers' criticism of their westering culture, the collective "No, in thunder" with which they repudiated popular clichés. Increasingly, however, I came to see them as less isolated in their resistance than they, their critics, or I had assumed. The place of these writers here, then, is not as uniquely perceptive figures but as spokesmen for a broad intellectual movement shared with their many less articulate contemporaries. Instead of illuminating independent texts from a new vantage, I want to place familiar works in a surprisingly more sympathetic historical context.

To the extent that scholarly books represent joint projects, this one is more so than most and has incurred for me a long and fortunate series of debts. At the University of Washington, Martha Banta helped to shape its first dissertation stages, and I continue to be grateful for her generous advice. At that same time, Ann Meyrich shared my enthusiasm for ideas still disturbingly vague. That she may not immediately recognize them in this, their final form cannot diminish the fact that they would not first have seemed worth engaging without her calm encouragement.

Others have since read intermediate drafts, interrupting harried schedules to help me map a tangled intellectual landscape. Carlos Baker, Frank Bergon, Alfred L. Bush, Emory Elliott, Douglas Gordon, William L. Howarth, Bruce Johnson, A. Walton Litz, Jr., Richard M. Ludwig, Jarold Ramsey, and Harold Simonson—all have variously altered my ideas, in the process steering me from hidden pitfalls and toward untested possibilities. Even while dissenting, I rarely failed to learn from them. Or from Susan McCloskey, who was at first unfamiliar with the wilderness I was struggling to order. She nonetheless turned a keen eye and exacting ear to the project, affirming throughout her undiminished confidence in the writer and the work. I hope this book fulfills some part of the promise she saw.

More than to anyone else, however, this book owes its existence to Howard C. Horsford. He first suggested the idea, and from early dissertation drafts to final page proof has read nearly every word. That I have subbornly refused his advice means that I must alone claim responsibility for its flaws. But the debt goes deeper than this book. A dozen years ago, he taught me to see in the academic profession more than a worthy vocation. The very example of his unregenerate curiosity, rigorous standards, and wry patience has been for me, as for many other students and colleagues, the finest model of how to engage life.

Fellowships awarded by the American Council of Learned Societies and the Surdna Foundation freed me to write, and I am grateful for their generosity. I would also like to thank the Princeton University Committee on Research in the Humanities and Social Sciences for extending funds to cover costs of travel and typing. The staffs at various libraries, including those at the University of Washington, Princeton University, the American Antiquarian Society, and the Huntington (and there, in particular, Virginia Renner), made my research far more of a pleasure than I could have hoped. Miriam Brokaw and Gail Filion first took an editorial interest in this book, and it has clearly benefited from their attention. I have been especially fortunate in both my copyeditor, Gretchen Oberfranc, whose blue pencil rarely errs, and in my research assistant, Kathryn G. Humphreys, who skillfully helped to prepare the index. Under the pressure of assorted deadlines, Helen Wright silently corrected flawed grammar and erratic footnotes, producing fair copy out of drafts barely readable to their author. I can only add my heartfelt appreciation to that of many others associated with her through the American Studies Program at Princeton.

Finally, the dedication confirms my fullest, least redeemable debt. This is a study of the offering presented by preceding generations to their successors—"a gift to posterity," as it was for a time entitled. To register here my father's reverence for American landscape and my mother's Quaker faith in unstated truths is to identify only part of what I cherish in them. Yet by attending to these considerations in the following pages, I want to offer my own small gift in return for all they have given me.

CHAPTER ONE

FROM LANDSCAPE TO CULTURE, PRESERVATION TO CRITIQUE

Let us conquer space.
—*John C. Calhoun*, 1817

The wonders of inanimate nature leave [Americans] cold, and, one may almost say, they do not see the marvelous forests surrounding them until they begin to fall beneath the ax. What they see is something different. The American people see themselves marching through wildernesses, drying up marshes, diverting rivers, peopling the wilds, and subduing nature. It is not just occasionally that their imagination catches a glimpse of this magnificent vision. . . . it is always flitting before [their] mind.
—*Alexis de Tocqueville*
Democracy in America (1835)

T HE NEW WORLD has long fascinated the Old by seeming to promise regeneration to a civilization tired of itself. That America was as old as Europe geologically; that its native population was as large and, in places, as concentrated; that its civilizations claimed illustrious pedigrees—these facts mattered little against such a powerfully attractive conception.[1] The land could hardly resist. Its assumed physical newness meant that for as long as territory lay open, a setting might be found for every sort of utopian second chance. Popular belief went so far as to ascribe rejuvenating powers to the very soil itself.[2] If Europe seemed religiously, politically, or economically stale, its institutions unresponsive to individual needs, the New World represented an opportunity to create a more nearly perfect society amid fresh surroundings.

John Winthrop's projected "city on a hill," J. Hector St. John de Crèvecoeur's celebrated American farmer, Thomas Jefferson's yeoman, Benjamin Franklin's autodidact, Ralph Waldo Emerson's self-reliant Yankee, and Frederick Jackson Turner's frontier democrat—the model holds a stalwart pose under dramatically varied trappings. In each instance, the pose proclaims: We have abandoned tradition-clogged societies to embrace a new, a free, a far richer life. America's wilderness seemed to provide a physically limitless and ahistorical setting in which men and women could imagine their finest self-conceptions fulfilled. The powerful fascination of that hope entwines more than three centuries of colonial and national experience.[3]

[1] Wilbur R. Jacobs, in calling for more attention to "what might be called the Indian point of view," has confirmed these historical actualities. See especially his "The Indian and the Frontier in American History—A Need for Revision," *Western Historical Quarterly*, 4 (January 1973), 43-56, and "The Tip of an Iceberg: Pre-Columbian Indian Demography and Some Implications for Revisionism," *William and Mary Quarterly*, 3d ser., 31 (January 1974), 123-32.

[2] Gilbert Chinard, "The American Dream," chap. 15 of Robert E. Spiller *et al.*, eds., *Literary History of the United States: History*, 3d ed. rev. (New York: Macmillan Co., 1963), pp. 195ff.

[3] The cultural context within which these assumptions emerged as effective symbols has been amply documented, most notably by: Perry Miller, "The Romantic Dilemma in American Nationalism and the Concept of Nature," *Harvard Theological Review*, 48 (October 1955), 239-53; Henry Nash Smith, *Virgin Land: The American West as Symbol and Myth* (New York: Random House, 1950); R.W.B. Lewis, *The American Adam: Innocence, Tragedy, and Tradition in the Nineteenth Century* (Chicago: University of Chicago Press, 1955); Howard Mumford Jones, *O Strange New World—American Culture: The Formative Years* (New York: Viking, 1964). See also John Conron, *The American Landscape: A Critical Anthology of Prose and Poetry* (New York: Oxford University Press, 1974), p. xviii; Loren Baritz, "The Idea of the West," *American Historical Review*, 66 (April 1961), 618-40.

What might be termed the "idea of America" integrated a set of apparently untroubled assumptions about nature, progress, and the past. However inconsistent, these assumptions nonetheless induced belief through the constant lure of a fresh start. America would foster the new citizen in a new society without materially diminishing the newfound world. Far from fearing the effects on the land, most commentators stressed its promised transformation. Even by the end of the nineteenth century, few Americans understood Thoreau's eccentric plea for wildness as the preservation of the world.[4] The continent's natural plentitude seemed inexhaustible, yet its true value could not be realized while the land remained uncultivated. The "virgin land" would find fulfillment in marriage to the plow, not in unproductive spinsterhood. So European tools conquered the continent, and the land came to serve a technological progress based increasingly on American notions of advancement. How could a democratic republic fail to thrive in the economic soil of freehold agrarianism or, later, of laissez-faire capitalist industrialism?[5]

Assumptions about natural plentitude and cultural progress combined to encourage a fierce rejection of older values. At the same time, the westward trek to a better American future signaled escape from a desultory history of economic trial and social error that most observers wanted to associate peculiarly with Europe. America offered "a new field of opportunity," in Frederick Jackson Turner's conception, and presented "a gate of escape from the bondage of the past."[6] American frontiersmen exuberantly rejected tradition, if for no other reason than that it was traditional. Customs, laws, manners, and governments all were suspect. It was necessary to adopt a new life. In the most celebrated definition of what it meant to be an American, Crèvecoeur evoked qualities that seem appropriately baptismal: "*He* is an American who, leaving behind him all his ancient prejudices and manners, receives new ones from the new mode of life he has embraced, the new government he obeys, and the new rank he holds."[7]

Yet such proud exuberance is deceptive. From this early passage, Crèvecoeur's narrative moves steadily, letter by letter, toward despair-

---

[4] Henry David Thoreau, "Walking," in *Excursions* (1863; rpt. New York: Corinth Books, 1962), p. 185.

[5] See Smith, *Virgin Land*, p. 138.

[6] Frederick Jackson Turner, "The Significance of the Frontier in American History" (1893), in Turner, *The Frontier in American History* (New York: Henry Holt, 1921), p. 38.

[7] Michel-Guillaume St. Jean de Crèvecoeur [J. Hector St. Jean de Crèvecoeur], *Letters from an American Farmer . . .* (1782; rpt. New York: E. P. Dutton, 1957), p. 39.

ing disillusionment with the new world. However much Americans think they can abandon mistakes, however completely one's past seems mere encumbrance, that past has at least the virtue of familiarity. Marcus Cunliffe sharply qualifies Crèvecoeur's embrace of his new life, detecting "an almost inherent American tendency to believe that one has been cut off decisively from the past as if by a physical barrier . . . [that] has, understandably, revealed itself in regrets and neuroses as well as in pride and exuberance."[8] Juxtaposed against America's cheering connotations as a land of hope and progress, freedom and opportunity, this statement may seem overly pessimistic. Nonetheless, it helps to clarify Americans' paradoxical melancholy, anxiety, and restlessness "in the midst of their prosperity,"[9] which Alexis de Tocqueville so presciently observed. Cut off from the past, even by an act of free will, one is compelled to view the present as equally imperiled by a deracinating future. Of course, if the breach is not self-willed, it may prove yet more unsettling.

Expounded by such orators as Daniel Webster, Henry Clay, and Thomas Hart Benton, the official faith of nineteenth-century America remained floridly optimistic, in tune with the formal symbol America represented. Yet spread-eagle rhetoric does not altogether mask a strain of misgiving, and many historians have identified what one calls an "apprehension of doom" characterizing nineteenth-century statements.[10] Such foreboding was widespread, provoked at least in part by the westering process itself. For example, the prospect loomed vague but insistent that American expansion might destroy those aspects of

[8] Cunliffe, "American Watersheds," *American Quarterly*, 13 (Winter 1961), 489.

[9] De Tocqueville, *Democracy in America* (1835), trans. George Lawrence, ed. J. P. Mayer (New York: Doubleday, Anchor Books, 1969), p. 535. See also Jones, *Strange New World*, pp. 379, 383-86; David Lowenthal, "The Place of the Past in the American Landscape," in David Lowenthal and Martyn J. Bowden, eds., *Geographies of the Mind: Essays in Historical Geosophy* (New York: Oxford University Press, 1976), pp. 89-117.

[10] Miller, "Romantic Dilemma," p. 251. See also Curtis Dahl, "The American School of Catastrophe," *American Quarterly*, 11 (Fall 1959), 380-90; Leo Marx, *The Machine in the Garden: Technology and the Pastoral Ideal in America* (New York: Oxford University Press, 1964); William R. Taylor, *Cavalier and Yankee: The Old South and American National Character* (New York: Braziller, 1961), esp. p. 98; Marvin Meyers, *The Jacksonian Persuasion: Politics and Belief* (Stanford: Stanford University Press, 1957); Fred Somkin, *Unquiet Eagle: Memory and Desire in the Idea of American Freedom, 1815-1860* (Ithaca: Cornell University Press, 1967); Roderick Nash, *Wilderness and the American Mind*, rev. ed. (New Haven: Yale Univeristy Press, 1973); Neil Harris, *The Artist in American Society: The Formative Years, 1790-1860* (New York: Simon and Schuster, 1966), pp. 158-59, 166-67; Jay Martin, *Harvests of Change: American Literature, 1865-1914* (Englewood Cliffs, N.J.: Prentice-Hall, 1967), pp. 85-86; Klaus J. Hansen, "The Millennium, the West, and Race in the Antebellum American Mind," *Western Historical Quarterly*, 3 (October 1972), 376.

frontier life that had first attracted pioneers; that material progress would introduce serious new social and psychological pressures; that America was developing according to a cyclic pattern of rise and fall characteristic of other celebrated empires; or even that a culture could be advanced without being white, Christian, or industrial. Few in the nineteenth century could comprehend these as intellectual propositions; fewer still could ignore them. By mid-century a young whaler's fictive nightmare epitomized the vague anxiety that a considerable segment of American society was beginning to feel about its flight from the past into the future. "Uppermost was the impression," Melville's Ishmael reflects, "that whatever swift, rushing thing I stood on was not so much bound to any haven ahead as rushing from all havens astern. A stark, bewildered feeling, as of death, came over me."[11] Those unenthusiastic about America's "progress" usually expressed themselves less severely. Nonetheless, as slight, isolated, unimaginative, or inconsistent as their expressions so often prove to be, they occur with remarkable frequency in nineteenth-century writings.

Among the unwelcome prospects mentioned above, the first excited greatest distress: that national expansion might diminish as well as develop the landscape. America had been imagined from the beginning in terms of timeless space, as a vacant land awaiting the starter's gun of history. Once the historical race began, the continent lent itself readily to the uses of progress and civilization. The first systematic mappers early in the nineteenth century preceded the immigration of millions committed to removing native tribes, hunting vast quantities of game, clearing forests for farms, erecting cities on open plains, and finally, crossing the continent with rails. The land would pass from Indian to trapper and prospector, from frontier trader to urban businessman, from homesteader to corporate farmer. All of these actors in the national drama clearly anticipated the landscape's transformation. Given the formulistic text of the "official faith," however, most never questioned the process, much less resisted it.

LANDSCAPE, PRESERVATION, AND DOUBTS

In the 1820s and 1830s, Americans felt vaguely uncertain about, and sometimes cringed mentally at, their altering of the land. They had begun to recognize that the continent was not merely a vacant landscape awaiting axes and plows but possessed intrinsic delights, values,

[11] Herman Meville, *Moby-Dick; or, The Whale*, ed. Harrison Hayford and Hershel Parker (New York: W. W. Norton, 1967), p. 354.

and order.[12] Of course, they were not conservationists, certainly not as we know the term. Those few who suggested preserving as they were the Indian or the buffalo or the forests were considered mere fools. Yet many ruefully anticipated the passing of the wilderness, and thousands hastened westward to see it while it lasted. "We are prone to speak of ourselves as the inhabitants of a *new* world," wrote Orsanus Turner near mid-century, "and yet we are confronted with such evidences of antiquity! We clear away the forests and speak familiarly of subduing a 'virgin soil';—and yet the plough up-turns the skulls of those whose history is lost! We say that Columbus discovered a *new* world. Why not that he helped to make two *old* ones acquainted with each other?"[13]

One reason "why not" concerned prevailing public opinion. Ready-to-hand clichés, including "virgin soil," "new world," and "course of empire," substituted for incisive assessments of specific local relationships between man and nature. "The westward-making Americans had no instructed image of the land they were bent on possessing," Bernard DeVoto has concluded. "Manifest Destiny was blindfolded."[14] The first to raise their blindfolds expressed only tentative doubts, if any, about what they saw, and public constraints drove even these expressions into various forms of private writings. Like nuggets of placer gold, they turn up not in the mainstream of books and speeches but in the side currents of prefaces and conclusions, in the eddies of allusions, dropped comments, and sometimes merely suggestive phrasings. Frontier journals, diaries, travel books, editorials, exploration accounts, and letters home by people of all classes and occupations reveal increasing apprehension.

Of course, far from a majority of those who crossed the continent had second thoughts. Nor could many anticipate the effects of their westering society. Lewis Mumford has nicely characterized the settlement of America as "a large-scale mushroom hunt: in the pursuit of a single object, urban sites, coal mines, gold, or oil, every other attribute of the landscape was neglected."[15] Even for those not quite so single-minded, the "mushroom hunt" seemed both inevitable and right.

12 See Barbara Novak, "On Divers Themes from Nature: A Selection of Texts," in Kynaston McShine, ed., *The Natural Paradise: Painting in America, 1800-1950* (Boston: New York Graphic Society, 1976), p. 60.

13 Turner, *Pioneer History of the Holland Purchase of Western New York* (Buffalo: Jewett, Thomas and Co., 1849), pp. 18-19.

14 DeVoto, *Across the Wide Missouri* (Boston: Houghton Mifflin Co., 1947), p. 397.

15 Mumford, *The Brown Decades: A Study of the Arts in America, 1865-1895* (1931; rpt. New York: Dover Publications, 1955), pp. 67-68.

Yet if they rarely questioned the transition, a considerable number felt impelled to document the "West" before it vanished.

That impulse may at first seem little more than an antiquarian quirk. However, Marcus Cunliffe's description of the American as one who believes himself "cut off decisively from the past as if by a physical barrier" challenges such a dismissive view by placing recorders of the passing frontier within a larger context. They accomplished the very objective to which most nineteenth-century American artists aspired: to arrest in realistic terms an accurate view of nature.[16] In literature, painting, and photography, work after work during this period concentrates on accurate observation and detailed rendering of the physical world. As the youthful Thoreau declared, "Nature will bear the closest inspection."[17] Landscape and genre paintings, novels and even poems declare themselves to be honest transcriptions not merely of nature but of specific locales. Perhaps it is true that "people robbed of their past seem to make the most fervent picture takers."[18] American enthusiasm for realism, whether in photography or in other art forms, certainly seems to derive from an all-encompassing historical concern. From transcendentalist essays to luminist canvases, in the Leatherstocking tales and *Moby-Dick* as in the landscape photographs of Carleton Watkins and William Henry Jackson, the finest American art maintains what has been elsewhere characterized as "a vested interest in the preservation of the fact."[19]

Throughout America and western Europe, change seemed far too rapid in the nineteenth century. Americans, however, had forsaken traditional institutions that might have insulated against the shock of change. Pioneers traveled west to escape their pasts, moving spatially, as it were, to escape time. But one truly escapes time only by arresting it, as art fixes an image. Thus, the later chroniclers who hurried west to document a vanishing world were propelled by the same impulses that had moved earlier immigrants, who, buffeted by change, had begun to regret their lost pasts. All wanted at least to ease uncertainty by holding on to the landscape of an ephemeral present.

Whatever its causes, this impulse toward preservation ramified within a definite historical frame, commencing in the 1820s. Perhaps

---

[16] See John Ewers, *Artists of the Old West* (Garden City, N.Y.: Doubleday and Co., 1965), p. 7; Donald A. Ringe, *The Pictorial Mode: Space and Time in the Art of Bryant, Irving, and Cooper* (Lexington: University Press of Kentucky, 1971), p. 1.

[17] Thoreau, "A Natural History of Massachusetts" (1842), in *Excursions*, p. 42.

[18] Susan Sontag, *On Photography* (New York: Farrar, Straus and Giroux, 1977), p. 10; see also pp. 9, 62-63, 76.

[19] Barbara Novak, *American Painting of the Nineteenth Century: Realism, Idealism, and the American Experience* (New York: Praeger, 1969), p. 59.

the new technology's awesome capacity to destroy the landscape first spurred those anxious about its disappearance.[20] Or perhaps such anxiety grew from other causes: from the sense of nationhood that first emerged after the War of 1812; from resistance to the swelling emigration to the trans-Appalachian west; or from dismay at an ideology affirming inexhaustibility even as land was visibly impoverished and wildlife decimated. Perhaps such concern grew, ironically, in response to proliferating documents themselves, which finally fixed landscapes, wildlife, and Indian tribes on record. As Susan Sontag asserts, "our oppressive sense of the transience of everything is more acute since cameras gave us the means to 'fix' the fleeting moment."[21] For whatever reasons, people did not begin to express their apprehensions until after 1820. Tentatively stated at first, by the end of the century the issues were headlined in popular magazines, and government officials were formulating responses in terms of national policies.

The shift in public attitudes occurred less uniformly than this review may suggest. In the 1870s, worried observers of an altering landscape unknowingly repeated the caveats spoken and implied half a century earlier. On the other hand, those who in the seventies began vaguely to question white civilization's alleged superiority to indigenous cultures had few precursors. Tacking into strange seas of cultural thought, they deserve consideration less for their numerical strength than for their intellectual daring. The most important insights they provided struck at the heart of assumptions about civilization itself. Whites for the first time looked closely at native cultures and came to appreciate their extraordinary diversity, intricacy, and autonomy —even their values. Though treated as one for centuries, Indian tribes shared far fewer characteristics than European nations; at last, the diversity of their histories and cultures began to be recognized.[22]

Whites returning from more objective studies began to reassess assumptions about progress. Evidence suggested that so-called primitive tribes, far from lacking institutional controls, were structured by social codes sometimes more complex and frequently more fulfilling

[20] For general background see Richard Lillard, *The Great Forest* (New York: Alfred A. Knopf, 1947), esp. pp. 138-208; Stewart L. Udall, *The Quiet Crisis* (New York: Avon, 1963), pp. 67-68. John William Ward, in *Andrew Jackson: Symbol for an Age* (New York: Oxford University Press, 1955), p. 45, has observed the effects of this increasing conflict during the 1820s between the claims of technology and those of the wilderness.

[21] Sontag, *On Photography,* p. 179.

[22] See Wilcomb E. Washburn, *The Indian in America* (New York: Harper and Row, 1975), p. xvi. See also William Brandon, *The Last Americans: The Indian in American Culture* (New York: McGraw-Hill, 1974), p. 20.

than those of white society. Was progress an absolute conception? Were cultures only relative conditions? More and more persistently, the study of native tribes sparked questions to trouble Americans' complacency about themselves and their mission westward.

LITERARY BOOKENDS

At the same time that ethnographers began to develop greater respect for the intrinsic value of native cultures, paintings of Indians changed more in perspective and content than ever before. Nevertheless, two literary works offer the most vivid illustration of these changing attitudes toward native Americans. St. John de Crèvecoeur's *Letters from an American Farmer* (1782) and Willa Cather's *The Professor's House* (1925) explore problems of contemporary society and the possibilities posed by native life in nicely contrasting terms. Standing outside the historical limits of this study, they conveniently summarize the cultural expectations that dominated the respective ends of the century.

Crèvecoeur's letters hymn the virtues of America's freehold, agrarian society. The yeoman working his own land is an enviable social model: both temporally and spatially, he is the perfect median between the extremes of barbaric frontier freedom and decadent European tradition. The system affords him maximum economic incentive with minimal social constraints. "This formerly rude soil has been converted by my father into a pleasant farm," Crèvecoeur's Farmer James declares, "and in return it has established all our rights; on it is founded our rank, our freedom, our power as citizens, our importance as inhabitants of such a district."[23] This "devout agrarianism"[24] depends on two dovetailed assumptions: that the land exists to be cleared, plowed, and planted, and that it belongs to those best capable of making such a transformation. Few eighteenth-century Americans would have disagreed.

Crèvecoeur revealed his essentially conventional perspective more tellingly in the claims that Farmer James makes for the northeastern Indian tribes. Despite the Frenchman's firsthand knowledge of native life, his descriptions merely depict the noble savage of Enlightenment discourse—indistinguishable tribe from tribe, person from person. Native societies apparently lack all social forms and restrictions. Viewing the increased dangers of life on the frontier that the forthcoming war with Britain would bring, Farmer James philosophically contemplates the prospect of life among the Indians:

[23] Crèvecoeur, *Letters from an American Farmer*, pp. 20-21.
[24] Henry Nash Smith, *Virgin Land*, p. 16, uses this phrase to refer to Jefferson's similar economic philosophy.

As soon as possible after my arrival, I design to build myself a wigwam, after the same manner and size with the rest, in order to avoid being thought singular, or giving occasion for any railleries. . . . I shall erect it hard by the lands which they propose to allot me, and will endeavour that my wife, my children, and myself may be adopted soon after our arrival. Thus becoming truly inhabitants of their village, we shall immediately occupy that rank within the pale of their society, which will afford us all the amends we can possibly expect for the loss we have met with by the convulsions of our own.[25]

Crèvecoeur sounds as if he thought Farmer James were moving cross-town instead of cross-culturally. Far from being genuinely interested in a specific Indian tribe, he invokes the subject solely as an excuse for reflection about his own society: "Thus shall we metamorphose ourselves, from neat, decent, opulent planters, surrounded with every convenience . . . into a still simpler people divested of everything beside hope, food, and the raiment of the woods." As did Rousseau before and Thoreau after, Crèvecoeur finds that primitive society offers him an opportunity intelligently to simplify his life: "Rest and peace of mind will make us the most ample amends for what we shall leave behind."[26] For Crèvecoeur, as for most of his contemporaries, European values represented an absolute cultural standard, and tribal life constituted merely the negation of supposedly "civilized" ways. The idea that "primitive" societies might perfect virtues to which Europeans and Americans gave only lip service or which their civilization actually subverted was beyond contemplation.[27]

A century and a half later, these unsettling ideas had become commonplace, even as the transformation from an agrarian economy to an urban and industrial one had given them a more complex edge. The dazzling array of comforts offered by nineteenth-century technology could not ease that technology's disproportionate costs, and the sober recognition of this contributed to the *fin de siècle* malaise of Henry and Brooks Adams, Mark Twain, and William Dean Howells. Even for those less thoughtful, the game did not seem worth the candle. The enthusiasm with which late-nineteenth-century

---

[25] Crèvecoeur, *Letters from an American Farmer*, p. 215.

[26] Ibid., p. 218. See Roy Harvey Pearce, *Savagism and Civilization: A Study of the Indian and the American Mind*, rev. ed. (Baltimore: Johns Hopkins University Press, 1965), pp. 139-41.

[27] For one possible exception in Crèvecoeur's prose to this state of mind, see his *Journey into Northern Pennsylvania and the State of New York* (1801), trans. Clarissa Spencer Bostelmann, 3 vols. in 1 (Ann Arbor: University of Michigan Press, 1964), p. 11.

Americans devoted their energies to progressive social and political movements was generated in part by a feeling that technological advancements had undermined traditional values.[28] As Felix Frankfurter later noted about the leader of the Progressive party: "Behind the diverse and discordant movements for reform to which [Theodore] Roosevelt gave voice lay the assumption that the traditional hopes of American democracy had been defeated by social and economic forces not contemplated by the founders of our nation."[29]

In Willa Cather's *The Professor's House*, young Tom Outland keenly inveighs against these changes. Visiting Washington, D.C., with grand enthusiasm early in the twentieth century, he leaves the city without regret:

> How it did use to depress me to see all the hundreds of clerks come pouring out of that big building at sunset! Their lives seemed to me so petty, so slavish. The couple I lived with gave me a prejudice against that kind of life. . . . They asked me not to mention the fact that I paid rent, as they had told their friends I was making them a visit. It was like that in everything; they spent their lives trying to keep up appearances, and to make his salary do more than it could. When they weren't discussing where she should go in the summer, they talked about the promotions in his department; how much the other clerks got and how they spent it, how many new dresses their wives had. And there was always a struggle going on for an invitation to a dinner or a reception, or even a tea-party. When once they got the invitation they had been scheming for, then came the terrible question of what Mrs. Bixby should wear.[30]

Obviously, in this bleak urban landscape the promise of Crèvecoeur's fresh green world has disappeared as even an imaginative desire. Themes of corruption, crass commercialism, and unintended betrayal interweave throughout Cather's novel, reinforcing an image of American society beyond possible redemption. Technology has prostituted America's integrity. Underscoring the theme, Cather's central character, Professor Godfrey St. Peter, concludes a class with the sardonic request: "You might tell me next week, Miller, what you

[28] See, for example, Herbert Croly, *The Promise of American Life* (1909; rpt. New York: Bobbs-Merrill, 1965).

[29] Cited by John William Ward in his introduction to Croly, *Promise of American Life*, p. viii. This quotation is from an article written by Frankfurter for *New Republic*, July 16, 1930, p. 247.

[30] Willa Cather, *The Professor's House* (New York: Alfred A. Knopf, 1925), p. 232. All subsequent references will be to this edition.

think science has done for us, besides making us very comfortable"
(69).

Against this despair over modern technology's joyless comforts,
Cather contrasts the imagined cultural richness of an ancient race of
cliff dwellers. Outland, Professor St. Peter's former student, discovers
while patiently excavating an abandoned mesa village that only an advanced culture could have erected such a stunning, yet functional,
complex. Father Duchene, a friend more experienced in archaeology,
concludes, " 'your tribe were a superior people. Perhaps they were
not so when they first came upon this mesa, but in an orderly and
secure life they developed considerably the arts of peace. There is
evidence on every hand that they lived for something more than food
and shelter' " (219). Examining this evidence with care, Father Duchene imagines how Tom's tribe "humanized" the mesa:

> "I see them here, isolated, cut off from other tribes, working
> out their destiny, making their mesa more and more worthy to
> be a home for man, purifying life by religious ceremonies and
> observances, caring respectfully for their dead, protecting the
> children, doubtless entertaining some feelings of affection and
> sentiment for this stronghold where they were at once so safe
> and so comfortable, where they had practically overcome the
> worst hardships that primitive man had to fear. They were, per-
> haps, too far advanced for their time and environment." (220-
> 221)

Crèvecoeur might have found little to disagree with in this description. The measure of how far attitudes had altered lies rather in the
contrast between his bland conception of native life as a mere escape
from contemporary political convulsions and Cather's portrayal of a
tribal culture as a rich improvement upon modern life. Thoreau
followed Crèvecoeur in ironically juxtaposing the frame house of
Concord against the Indian wigwam to illustrate the issue of economy.[31] Far more than money and man-hours of labor were at issue for
Cather.

In almost every respect, Crèvecoeur and Cather brought quite
different associations to essentially similar symbols. Farmer James
escapes to the frontier to avoid temporary social distress, not to em-
bark upon permanent cultural change. He neither embraces a particular Indian tribe nor considers abandoning his fixed agrarian
values. So easy an escape was not possible for Cather; social philoso-

[31] Thoreau, *Walden*, ed. J. Lyndon Shanley (Princeton: Princeton University
Press, 1971), pp. 27ff.

phers and anthropologists had radically altered the terms. Supposedly absolute cultural norms had been reduced to a conditional status, ranked according to their cumulative humanizing effect. A culture might be evaluated according to the sense of participation shared by its members in conceiving and achieving their destiny. The extinct southwestern culture uncovered by Tom Outland provides—in sharp contrast to Crèvecoeur's unnamed northeastern tribes—a telling critique of American and European civilization. The passage cited above goes on to suggest the symbolic link between Washington bureaucrats who allow the mesa ruins to be ravaged and a supposed Navaho horde that may have slaughtered the cliff dwellers. Progress forecloses as well as fulfills possibilities; material comforts may diminish as well as enrich individual lives.

SUBDUING THE LAND

Before Americans came to question progress in terms of Indian cultures, they found themselves first questioning their assumptions about nature. Those assumptions concerned not only particular aspects of the natural landscape but also man's relationship to the earth, to the North American continent, and to the technology he applied to it. At an elementary level, most believed that the earth was created for man's use. Textbooks repeatedly invoked Genesis 1:26-28, describing God's gift of "dominion" and his command to Adam and Eve to "subdue" the earth.[32] Such a perspective tacitly acknowledges an impersonal relationship to nature by conceiving of man as disconnected from the physical world and of God as independent of both. Of course, technological advance itself demanded these "scientific" premises. Only a civilization imbued with such thinking could have achieved the expertise Americans enjoyed in the nineteenth century. On the other hand, only such a civilization could have devastated the landscape as Americans did or exterminated so many indigenous peoples. It is one irony among many that Indians never quite comprehended those who, precisely because they conceived of God, nature, and man as independent, could acquire the power to destroy them.

[32] See Ruth Miller Elson, *Guardians of Tradition: American Schoolbooks of the Nineteenth Century* (Lincoln: University of Nebraska Press, 1964), pp. 16-40; Wilbur R. Jacobs, *Dispossessing the American Indian: Indians and Whites on the Colonial Frontier* (New York: Charles Scribner's Sons, 1972), pp. 19-25; Roderick Nash, *Wilderness and the American Mind*, esp. pp. 19, 31, 59, 104-5, 193; Nash, *The American Environment: Readings in the History of Conservation*, 2d ed. (Reading, Mass.: Addison-Wesley, 1968), pp. 3-4.

Notwithstanding the special symbolic status of the New World as a new beginning, America had seemed a physical, and thereby cultural, extension of Europe ever since its discovery. In one respect, however, this was not true: the Europeans' hard-won respect for the land never took root in American soil. Enclaves of German farmers practiced Old World conservation in their new Pennsylvania communities, but they were exceptional in a country where land had always been cheaper than labor. Whether one interprets Americans' careless use of the land in social, religious, psychological, or even sexual terms—as, say, a compensation for lapsed faith, or a ravishing of the feminine earth—the fact remains that an astonishing portion of the American forest was destroyed. In the seventeenth century it covered half the continent; by the end of the nineteenth it had been burned over, logged, and cleared to only one-fifth the original acreage. Abundance may at first have encouraged myths of inexhaustibility. Eroded lands, flooded fields, stump-spotted forests, and ruined prairies too soon stood in silent judgment of those who had acted so irresponsibly.[33]

In part, this exuberant irresponsibility testified to Americans' characteristically progressive rather than conservative perspective. Wild nature represented promise, not fulfillment, and the continent presented a vividly physical challenge to white energies. At the same time that Americans eagerly accepted that challenge, new patterns undermined their confidence in their westward mission. Tourism and pleasure traveling, for example, were activities restricted to the rich in 1800. By 1900, when they had become popular pastimes,[34] people could see for themselves the magnificence, and the devastation, of their continent.

Belief in the unhealthiness of urban life also contributed to a heightened appreciation for landscape. This romantic bias against

[33] For background information on these developments, see: Paul W. Gates, *The Economic History of the United States*, vol. 3, *The Farmer's Age: Agriculture, 1815-1860* (New York: Holt, Rinehart and Winston, 1960); Clarence J. Glacken, "Changing Ideas of the Habitable World," in William L. Thomas, ed., *Man's Role in Changing the Face of the Earth* (Chicago: University of Chicago Press, 1956), pp. 70-92; Russel B. Nye, *This Almost Chosen People: Essays in the History of American Ideas* (East Lansing: Michigan State University Press, 1966), pp. 256-304; Udall, *Quiet Crisis*, esp. pp. 31-81. See as well, for revisionist assessments of some of these judgments: Gordon M. Day, "The Indian as an Ecological Factor in the Northeastern Forest," *Ecology*, 34 (April 1953), 329-45; Daniel Q. Thompson and Ralph H. Smith, "The Forest Primeval in the Northeast—A Great Myth?" in *Annual Proceedings: Tall Timbers Fire Ecology Conference, No. 10* (Fredericton, New Brunswick: Tall Timbers Research Station, 1970), pp. 255-65.

[34] See Earl Pomeroy, *In Search of the Golden West: The Tourist in Western America* (New York: Alfred A. Knopf, 1957).

cities—found even in grammar school texts as early as 1813—acquired powerful reinforcement as reformers publicized the obvious human costs of industrialism. The various epidemics that periodically plagued the antebellum East further confirmed the impulse.[35] As well, Americans began to take pride in what was now their land. Emerson touched a resonant chord in his "American Scholar" address (1837) when he called for an art that glorified indigenous themes. Reviewers encouraged American writers and painters to take pristine nature as their subject; those who resisted did so at peril of losing public favor. Against the dominant commitment to conquer the continent, then, a vigorous celebration of its untransformed virtues thrived.

However inconsistent this conjunction of ideas, virtually everyone conceded a corollary: the continent, whether put to the axe or not, belonged to those who knew how best to use it. Crèvecoeur voiced this assumption, and nineteenth-century school texts reflect its general acceptance.[36] Though Americans may have occasionally confessed injustices toward Indians, they fell back on the right of usage, which abrogated all other rights of even the most peaceable tribes when challenged by white farmers. By whatever terms the issue may have been defined—communal versus private ownership, red skin versus white, hunting versus agrarian exploitation—the native claim seemed inferior. It could hardly have proved otherwise.

During the last third of the century, this cast of thought acquired even more extreme coloration. Social Darwinism offered "scientific" confirmation to those who believed that the less fit ought to suffer extinction, and Americans generated greater support for the theory than any other nationality. Against Europeans who responded sympathetically to the Indians' plight, Americans countered that the Old World could hardly afford to do so, having only just shaken off centuries of mistreating Africans, Asians, and Latin American Indians. Moreover, Europeans, according to Americans, retained only faulty appreciation for the requirements of turning native soil into national homeland.[37]

Europeans and Americans together were blind to the virtues of tribal cultures, largely because of irreconcilable epistemologies. In

[35] Elson, *Guardians of Tradition*, pp. 25-35. For an exemplary study of the costs of and attitudes toward disease in nineteenth-century America, see Charles E. Rosenberg, *The Cholera Years* (Chicago: University of Chicago Press, 1962).

[36] Elson, *Guardians of Tradition*, pp. 65ff.

[37] See Hugh Honour, *The New Golden Land: European Images of America from the Discoveries to the Present Time* (New York: Pantheon, 1975), pp. 219ff.; Richard Hofstadter, *Social Darwinism in American Thought*, rev. ed. (Boston: Beacon Press, 1955), pp. 82ff.

nontechnological societies, natural cycles connect man with the phenomenal world. His culture serves at every point to ensure an integrating harmony; goodness and God exist in the complete immersion within natural cycles, whether ethical, aesthetic, or economic. The tribal individual cannot conceive of himself *as* an individual, somehow isolated from a world resonating with religious significance. By contrast, technological societies render the world in physical, not moral, terms. Nature is to be dominated first for man's welfare, perhaps later for the glory of God. Instead of "family" or "tribal" individuals, technological societies assume the existence of "universal man," the "reasonable" individual who acknowledges social and political codes as absolute as those that govern his science.[38]

Native tribes could do little to halt the crusade of white America westward. The fine, pragmatic turn of mind that had produced their technological marvels, and in the process made them awesomely destructive, also blinded whites to the merits of native societies. All their standards confirmed the Indians' inadequacy.[39] Nor could the Indians understand what strange compulsions drove on their invaders. Washington Irving reported the wry response of one Sioux to a missionary imploring "the necessity of industry, etc., to happiness": " 'Father, I don't understand this kind of happiness you talk of. You tell me to cut down tree—to lop it—to make fence—to plough—this you call being happy—I no like such happiness.' "[40] In terms far more profound than this rejection of the work ethic, natives came sadly to recognize the indifferent universe that whites inhabited. Committed willy-nilly to the intellectual imagination, its technological tools and purely abstract codes, whites seemed starved in every other important

[38] For more precise discussion, see Gary B. Nash, "The Image of the Indian in the Southern Colonial Mind," *William and Mary Quarterly*, 3d ser., 29 (April 1972), 197-230; F.S.C. Northrop, "Man's Relation to the Earth in Its Bearing on His Aesthetic, Ethical, and Legal Values," in Thomas, ed., *Man's Role in Changing the Face of the Earth*, pp. 1052-67; Robert Redfield, *The Primitive World and Its Transformations* (Ithaca: Cornell University Press, 1953).

[39] See Gary B. Nash, "Image of the Indian," pp. 197-211; Nash, "Red, White and Black: The Origins of Racism in Colonial America," in Gary B. Nash and Richard Weiss, eds., *The Great Fear: Race in the Mind of America* (New York: Holt, Rinehart and Winston, 1970), pp. 1-9; Philip Borden, "Found Cumbering the Soil: Manifest Destiny and the Indian in the Nineteenth Century," in ibid., pp. 72-88; Louise K. Barnett, *The Ignoble Savage: American Literary Racism, 1790-1890*, Contributions in American Studies, no. 18 (Westport, Conn.: Greenwood Press, 1975), pp. 100ff.

[40] *The Western Journals of Washington Irving*, ed. John Francis McDermott (Norman: University of Oklahoma Press, 1944), pp. 103-4. For an excellent objective analysis of the historical effects of such a conflict of cultures, see Anthony F. C. Wallace, *The Death and Rebirth of the Seneca* (New York: Alfred A. Knopf, 1970), esp. pp. 184ff.

respect—emotionally, aesthetically, and spiritually. Some intellectuals had already begun to consider issues from this perspective. Experiencing the contrast of Indian life itself, however, helped others to reconsider the toll their civilization was taking. As well, it opened them to novel assessments of the very concept of culture.

THE MEANINGS OF CULTURE

Few words have enjoyed so striking a transition in meaning as *culture*. Prior to the nineteenth century, western Europeans rarely doubted that their civilization embodied the preeminent social qualities. Noble savages existed in a precivilized state, with both its virtues and puerile vices. Like children, they lacked social graces. Human nature being everywhere the same, however, they could appreciate the force of reason whether or not they lived by its dictates. Even Caliban might learn table manners.[41]

Increasing contact after 1800 proved that tribes did not warrant this easy dismissal. At the same time, European society was in upheaval, violently challenged by forces unanticipated only a few decades earlier. Civilization itself appeared to be under attack, perhaps even breaking down. The response to this turmoil was a more exacting assessment of the social contract that most had until then taken for granted. Thomas Carlyle, John Stuart Mill, John Ruskin, and Matthew Arnold studied the web of their society in ways that suggested its conditional status, while later cultural evolutionists, drawing on Darwin's work, posited developmental stages in social history. Implicit in all these normative analyses, however, was the familiar notion of absolute progress with European civilization epitomizing its direction. In contrast to Enlightenment assumptions about the noble savage, however,

[41] For a general history and discussion of the meaning of the word *culture* and of the noble savage see: A. L. Kroeber, *Anthropology: Race, Language, Culture, Psychology, Prehistory*, rev. ed. (New York: Harcourt, Brace and Co., 1948), pp. 265-66; Julian H. Steward, "Evolution and Process," and David Bidney, "The Concept of Value in Modern Anthropology," in A. L. Kroeber, ed., *Anthropology Today: An Encyclopedic Inventory* (Chicago: University of Chicago Press, 1953), pp. 313-26 and 686-99; David Bidney, "The Idea of the Savage in North American Ethnohistory," *Journal of the History of Ideas*, 15 (April 1954), 322-27; Henri Baudet, *Paradise on Earth: Some Thoughts on European Images of Non-European Man* (1959), trans. Elizabeth Wentholt (New Haven: Yale University Press, 1965), esp. pp. 5-29; George W. Stocking Jr., *Race, Culture, and Evolution: Essays in the History of Anthropology* (New York: Free Press, 1968), pp. 36-40, 69-132; Karl J. Weintraub, *Visions of Culture* (Chicago: University of Chicago Press, 1966); David M. Schneider, "Notes toward a Theory of Culture," in Keith H. Basso and Henry A. Selby, eds., *Meaning in Anthropology* (Albuquerque: University of New Mexico Press, 1976), pp. 197-220.

nineteenth-century evolutionists recognized that the moral values of so-called primitive cultures functioned like those that framed their own society. This was a radical turn of thought. Indeed, by conceding that every society, no matter how alien or seemingly savage, possesses an institutional structure with its own integrity, evolutionists made modern anthropological study possible.[42]

The hard-won recognition that there exists no such universal as "human nature" gained acceptance only slowly. Sympathetic anthropologists, much less the general public, had to struggle to accept the fact that cultures, all cultures, form necessary contexts for becoming very different kinds of human beings. Even today, the acknowledgement of other cultures as intrinsically worth respect does not draw wide support. On the other hand, this relativism implies a supposed detachment from one's deepest cultural assumptions, a detachment as delusive as any belief in Enlightenment absolutism. For better or worse, all individuals are bound by their societies; they can never be neutral. To claim to be free from arbitrary mores, perhaps out of respectful tolerance for other modes of behavior, is self-deceptively to ignore that tolerance itself is an arbitrary cultural more.[43] Properly employed, relativism leads not to a blithe stepping aside from one's culturally defined cast of thought but to a growing recognition that it is neither biologically nor racially determined. "So-called primitive societies," according to Claude Lévi-Strauss, ". . . have specialized in ways different from those which we have chosen. Perhaps they have, in certain respects, remained closer to the very ancient conditions of life, but this does not preclude the possibility that in other respects they are farther from those conditions than we are."[44]

The possibility that different societies provide appropriate satisfaction of their members' needs or that the histories of various cultures might complement rather than duplicate one another derives from recent studies, many of which focus on native American tribes. Only at the turn of the century did the American anthropologist Franz Boas define these premises as basic axioms of professional anthro-

[42] Raymond Williams has best defined the emergence of the distinct idea of culture in western European intellectual history; see his *Culture and Society: 1780-1950* (New York: Harper and Row, 1958). According to Williams, the concept of culture did not begin to emerge until the end of the eighteenth century; see pp. 59-60.

[43] The most cogent discussion of issues raised by culture and cultural relativism is contained in Clifford Geertz's *The Interpretation of Cultures: Selected Essays* (New York: Basic Books, 1973), to which much of this discussion is indebted.

[44] Lévi-Strauss, Inaugural Lecture, Collège de France, January 5, 1960, published as *The Scope of Anthropology*, trans. Sherry Ortner Paul and Robert A. Paul (London: Jonathan Cape, 1967), p. 46.

pology.[45] But even earlier, those who helped to create a context for Boas's breakthroughs, who roughly anticipated some of his conclusions, were Americans with firsthand experience of native tribes. They had come to appreciate the vital autonomy of those tribes and found unacceptable the normative ideals of evolutionists, especially since Western civilization served so inadequately as a measure by which to judge Indian tribes.

Conventional strains of thought could not help but distort even firsthand observation, however. Roy Harvey Pearce notes these incongruities in discussing Henry Rowe Schoolcraft's work on Indian tribes:

> The complexity of Indian customs and traits, the richness of Indian legend and belief, the stubborn self-sufficiency of Indian cultures, are embodied in his six volumes, as they are, if one looks hard enough for them, in most earlier works on the Indian. In the *Historical and Statistical Information* [1851-1857], we can see how data deny conclusions—how, for example, Schoolcraft's Indians do find in their religious meanings and rewards, motives for living and dying, which he cannot be satisfied with and so cannot see for what they are.[46]

The failure of these early studies lay in the ethnologists' condescending perspective. Yet native materials collectively belied such interpretations and sometimes converted those less single-minded than Schoolcraft to a broader view of cultural possibilities. Even those far more casual than he began during the middle part of the nineteenth century to see native cultures for what they in fact so often were—rich, vital, autonomous, and severely threatened.[47]

To trace the exact development of such patterns of thought is impossible, like trying to fix on a color spectrum the point at which yellow turns to green. Still, amid the diverse influences shaping popular thought there emerges an intellectual sequence uniquely American: widespread concern for recording a threatened wilderness landscape created a context for anxious ethnographic efforts. To some extent, of course, anthropology always springs from the impulse to preserve human cultures from the ravages of time, to fix them descriptively in order to understand them.[48] But this admission hardly places the ideas traced here in a less distinctly national perspective. Instead,

[45] For a discussion of Boas's transformation of the concepts of culture, see Stocking, *Race, Culture, and Evolution*, pp. 133-307.
[46] Pearce, *Savagism and Civilization*, p. 127.
[47] Ibid., p. 129.
[48] See Lévi-Strauss, *Scope of Anthropology*, p. 51.

it clarifies a pattern linking the concern for a vanishing wilderness with that for cultural pluralism, a pattern that uniquely characterizes an era in American history.

No other country or historical period has experienced the complex undercurrents examined here. In Africa, South America, and Australia, landscapes and native peoples suffered at the hands of invaders in ways strikingly similar to those in America. For a number of reasons connected with settlement patterns, however, the invaders' perceptions of their own impact were never as conflicted. In South America, the Spanish and Portuguese clung to the coast; Africa saw only transient exploiters, except in the south, where natives nevertheless far outnumbered colonists; in Australia, conversely, the aborigines were few, and settlements remained coastal. What follows in these pages, then, is not a comparative study but a more precise examination of the conflicting impulses that Crèvecoeur, De Tocqueville, and many since have found so fascinating and bewildering in the American character.

CHAPTER TWO

THE VANISHING
WILDERNESS

And change with hurried hand has swept these scenes:
The woods have fallen, across the meadow-lot
The hunter's trail and trap-path is forgot,
And fire has drunk the swamps of evergreens;
Yet for a moment let my fancy plant
These autumn hills again . . .
   —Frederick Goddard Tuckerman
   Sonnet XVIII (ca. 1854-60)

  The notes of a single observer, even in
a limited district, describing accurately
its features, civil, natural and social, are
of more interest, and often of more value,
than the grander view and broader gen-
eralizations of history.
—Anonymous epigraph to Bela Hubbard
* Memorials of a Half-Century* (1887)

AFTER LIVING happily abroad for seventeen years, Washington Irving (1783-1859) sailed home in the spring of 1832. During those years, he had garnered an illustrious reputation as America's first internationally acclaimed writer. Sophisticated, cosmopolitan, fully at ease in the best European court circles, Irving was returning at the height of his powers. For months beforehand, the New York City press heralded the arrival of the man who to most Americans personified success. Yet he also represented a silent, possibly reproving, judgment of his countrymen's sometimes rude Jacksonian virtues. Others crossing the Atlantic to view the young "democratic experiment" had frequently damned it with faint praise, when they praised it at all. Only a few years later, James Fenimore Cooper would return from a much shorter sojourn abroad to flay his countrymen and their institutions. If Americans felt uncertain about Irving's long-delayed return, however, they praised generously and held their questions.[1]

Irving's motives were in fact quite mixed. Nearly fifty years old, without a position, and having just lost his publisher, he shrewdly hoped to capitalize on an American reputation grown larger than his European prospects. He had a ready-made audience in America, one eager to offer approval. As well, he felt genuinely curious about his country. Reports abroad challenged memory and quickened his long-standing resolve to write on native themes. Irving worked best when he traveled, and he knew that his writing depended upon an accurate evocation of place. Perhaps the change of scene would rekindle a literary imagination temporarily gone cold.

On shipboard, Irving befriended two men who helped him to decide his itinerary: a Swiss count named Albert-Alexandre de Pourtalès and his older English companion, Charles J. Latrobe. Latrobe had been hired by the Pourtalès family to counsel the young libertine in sowing his wild oats abroad, and their joint enthusiasm for seeing the frontier soon inspired their new American friend. After

---

[1] This material on Irving and that to follow relies on the three standard modern biographies: Stanley T. Williams, *The Life of Washington Irving*, 2 vols. (New York: Oxford University Press, 1935), esp. 2:1-90; Edward Wagenknecht, *Washington Irving: Moderation Displayed* (New York: Oxford University Press, 1962); and Johanna Johnston, *The Heart That Would Not Hold: A Biography of Washington Irving* (New York: M. Evans and Co., 1971), esp. pp. 323ff. See also William Charvat, *The Profession of Authorship in America, 1800-1870: The Papers of William Charvat*, ed. Matthew J. Bruccoli (Columbus: Ohio State University Press, 1968), pp. 9-46.

arriving in New York, the trio made several short summer excursions up the Hudson River into the Green Mountains. In late August they struck out for the West. The measure of how powerfully the American wilderness gripped the imagination may be inferred from the eagerness with which these sophisticated gentlemen put aside more conventional pleasures to see it.

As they were traveling across Lake Erie toward Detroit, the friends met one of the new government commissioners for western tribes, Henry Leavitt Ellsworth. Once again, Irving caught another's enthusiasm for travel. Ellsworth persuaded the friends to accompany him to Arkansas, and in a letter to his brother later that year, Irving explained his own motive for risking the formidable hazards of such a venture: "The offer was too tempting to be resisted: I should have an opportunity of seeing the remnants of those great Indian tribes which are now about to disappear as independent nations, or to be amalgamated under some new form of government. I should see those fine countries of the 'far west,' while still in a state of pristine wilderness, and behold herds of buffaloes scouring their native prairies, before they are driven beyond the reach of a civilized tourist."[2]

Professional habit invariably compelled Irving to record his experiences. On this trip, however, his recognition of the transiency of wilderness reinforced habit to ensure an accurate account of what was already quickly receding. Although the resulting book, *A Tour of the Prairies* (1832), represents little other than a polished journal of a trip remarkable more for initial motive than for either itinerary or informed commentary, the trip profoundly influenced Irving's career. Stimulated by what he had seen, he spent the next five years in documenting aspects of his own and others' western experiences.

The separate accounts written by Irving's fellow travelers offer similar rationales for having accepted Ellsworth's invitation. Ellsworth himself showed no awareness of a threat to the wilderness. Latrobe's motives, on the other hand, matched Irving's. He too hoped to see Indian tribes and buffalo herds while they still freely roamed the plains, but like Irving, he ventured little beyond conventional predictions and laments in his completed book.[3] Only Latrobe's young charge exhibited a sophisticated understanding of their experiences, though he did so in a rather unorthodox fashion. Pourtalès's eagerness to learn the Osage language, for instance, fails to withstand close

2 *The Western Journals of Washington Irving*, ed. John Francis McDermott (Norman: University of Oklahoma Press, 1944), p. 10.

3 Charles Joseph Latrobe, *The Rambler in North America: 1832-1833*, 2 vols. (London: R. B. Seeley and W. Burnside, 1835), esp. 1:6, 166-67, 203, 2:172.

scrutiny, particularly in light of his successful seductions of native girls. Yet intimacy may curiously have shaped an exemplary insight. The vigorous count achieved a respect for the Osage as individuals and a sympathetic concern for their threatened way of life far deeper than that of his more primly buttoned companions.[4] Searching as the comments in his journal and correspondence appear, however, they fail to form the basis for an extended examination of the Osage or of the passing West. Only Irving found himself reverting again and again to the topic.

In *Astoria* (1836), Irving compiled what he hoped was the definitive history of western riverboatmen and fur traders. As in *A Tour of the Prairies*, he wrote with one eye to the expectations of a reading public addicted to frontier subjects and sentimentalized themes. John Jacob Astor had entreated him to use the voluminous manuscripts in his private collection to complete a popular, authoritative history, and the book is an important document because it includes paraphrases of manuscripts that have since disappeared. More important, asides throughout the narrative indicate Irving's awareness that his subject itself was vanishing. "It is the object of our task," he initially claims, "to present scenes of the rough life of the wilderness, and we are tempted to fix these few memorials of a transient state of things fast passing into oblivion."[5] Irving never questions the effects of the fur trade on indigenous populations. Though he openly sympathizes with their decline, his object was to document not the Indians but a distinct mode of white frontier life that was passing unrecorded.[6]

The Adventures of Captain Bonneville, U.S.A. (1837), the last work in Irving's western series, suffers from many of the weaknesses that flaw *Astoria*, including a too scrupulous attention to details copied from journals and interviews and an inability to report without sentimentality or cliché. Irving's special affection for a book that is little more than a miscellany of information on the West has never been shared by readers. Yet his intentions for the book, best revealed in its conclusion, bear close examination:

> We here close our picturings of the Rocky Mountains and their wild inhabitants, and of the wild life that prevails there; which we have been anxious to fix on record, because we are aware that

[4] Pourtalès, *On the Western Tour with Washington Irving: The Journal and Letters of Count de Pourtalès*, ed. George F. Spaulding (Norman: University of Oklahoma Press, 1968), esp. pp. 19, 21-22.

[5] *Astoria, or Anecdotes of an Enterprise Beyond the Rocky Mountains*, ed. Edgeley W. Todd (Norman: University of Oklahoma Press, 1964), p. 14.

[6] Ibid., esp. p. 517.

this singular state of things is full of mutation, and must soon undergo great changes, if not entirely pass away. The fur trade, itself, which has given life to all this portraiture, is essentially evanescent. . . . The mad carouse in the midst of danger, the night attack, the stampado, the scamper, the fierce skirmish among rocks and cliffs—all this romance of savage life, which yet exists among the mountains, will then exist but in frontier story, and seem like the fiction of chivalry or fairy tale.[7]

This passage suggests better than almost any other single quotation the kind of concerned commitment, at various levels of intensity, manifested in countless works on the West during this period.

FIXING A RECORD

People "anxious to fix on record" their "picturings" of the West almost literally elbowed each other aside. John James Audubon, for instance, returning from one of his painting expeditions, traveled aboard the same Mississippi steamboat that carried the Irving entourage.[8] Also during the summer of 1832, George Catlin visited the same dwindling Osage tribe whose language Count Pourtalès so closely studied. These men differed little from their countrymen in anticipating the dramatic changes soon to occur and in expressing the need to record an image of the original. The question then arises: Why should such feelings have appeared so early? The continent was still largely unmapped and unstudied, its resources still largely undiminished.

The answer may be found in part in a vague, but widespread, anxiety that scholars have only recently detected both in America and abroad. Granted, the psychological condition of any nation resists diagnosis; a constellation of variables keeps social complacency and unrest in constant flux. Nevertheless, nineteenth-century Americans appear to have had more cause than most nationalities for strains of uncertainty. The insidious psychological pressures predictable in a society claiming no impediments to success, the social upheavals brought about by new urban and industrial patterns of life, and the growing regional dissension over racial and economic issues form only a partial listing of causes to account for the recurrent images of apocalypse and catastrophe, the camouflaged themes of decline and doom that characterized Jacksonian American rhetoric. Anxiety about

[7] *The Adventures of Captain Bonneville, U.S.A., in the Rocky Mountains and the Far West*, ed. Edgeley W. Todd (Norman: University of Oklahoma Press, 1961), p. 372.

[8] Williams, *Washington Irving*, p. 43.

the wilderness gusted fitfully in this turbulent national atmosphere. By the time Americans considered their republic more than an experiment, around 1820, they had already long been abandoning worn-out farmland and unproductive plantations along the east coast. The very prevalence of this pattern was portentous. How could one assuage the suspicion that Indian extermination and then land exhaustion would transform the West as they had the East? Would not the cycle be successively repeated across the continent?

That Americans experienced such doubts should cause less surprise than that they felt them so early. Unlike Europeans in Africa or Australia, Americans felt more than a proprietary interest in the continent. True, they too had been colonials, with primary allegiance to the mother country. Following the Revolution, however, the continent connoted far more than, say, India would to the British or Mexico and Peru to the Spanish. Once entirely their own, the land formed a kind of collective self-extension, defining Americans even as it continued to be defined by them. In a country that had changed so rapidly, the salvaged record offered sole evidence of the earlier definitions. It alone could testify to the natural delights that had first attracted the pioneer. Few challenged the tenets of their progressive faith, caught up as they were in building new lives. Yet more than a few attempted to capture a permanent view that would form the sole content of another generation's knowledge of its heritage.

Among the myriad reasons given by those who would record their experiences, many reflect no specific urge to preserve a wilderness vision. On the other hand, certain people clearly felt so impelled, and yet failed to articulate that feeling. The impulse is sometimes evidenced in the very paintings and photographs they produced, in the ethnological or archaeological work they pursued, or in the commitment they made to collecting for museums and to establishing local and national preserves. Toward the end of the century especially, people apparently took for granted an understanding of their sometimes frenetic exertions. This chapter, however, concentrates on people who explicitly and self-consciously voiced apprehensions about the continent. In prefaces, allusions, asides, and occasional direct avowals, they committed themselves to detailing an accurate portrait of the wilderness, its forests, wildlife, scenic wonders, and Indians.

In their simpler forms, these expressions hardly cut very deep. An inescapable sense of loss is at times registered in tones of vague regret, more frequently as mild bewilderment. Some express a kind of anticipatory nostalgia for that which, however threatened, had not yet passed. They lamented what still stood in front of them. Voices were raised energetically in hymns of progress; but the more thoughtful found in the refrain "how the times have swept us by" sufficient cause to sing in a minor key.[9]

This lamentation for something departing also helps to account for the plethora of travel journals and diaries, what one scholar has termed "the characteristic literature of the period."[10] Permanent frontier settlers and travelers who, like Irving, Latrobe, and Pourtalès, hurried west to see it still undiminished wrote accounts intentionally to preserve their firsthand impressions. They appreciated their timely good fortune. Already by the 1830s and early 1840s, these varied observers included: the trapper Osborne Russell, one of the early visitors to the Yellowstone region; western judge and popular novelist James Hall; Indian captive Oliver M. Spencer; rifleman and later regimental General Thomas James; and the famous chronicler of the Santa Fe Trail, Josiah Gregg.[11] All these men shared an attitude composed of contradictory impulses, best described by a fellow spirit nearly half a century later: "In ten or fifteen years more, perhaps, this cannot be said, but as yet we may still feel a delight, keen as a woman's in the possession of a rare jewel, in the scene which surrounds us and which so few others have enjoyed."[12] Hesitation, a sense of imminent foreclosure, coupled with the immediate pleasure evoked by the wilderness—these elements characterize many of the explanations given for recording firsthand impressions.

[9] Jeremiah Church, *Journal of Travels, Adventures, and Remarks, of Jerry Church* (Harrisburg, Pa.: n.p., 1845), p. 72.

[10] William Goetzmann, *Army Exploration in the American West, 1803-1863* (New Haven: Yale University Press, 1959), p. 471.

[11] Osborne Russell, *Journal of a Trapper* . . . , ed. Aubrey L. Haines (Portland: Oregon Historical Society, 1955), esp. pp. 4, 112, 123, 138, 143-45, 154; James Hall, *Legends of the West: Sketches Illustrative of the Habits, Occupations, Privations, Adventures and Sports of the Pioneers of the West* (1832; rpt. Cincinnati: Applegate and Co., 1857), pp. v, xii-xiv; Oliver M. Spencer, *Indian Captivity* (1835; rpt. Ann Arbor: University Microfilms, 1966), pp. 11-12; Gen. Thomas James, *Three Years among the Indians and Mexicans* (1846; rpt. Chicago: R. R. Donnelley and Sons, 1953), pp. xx, 17, 93-94; Josiah Gregg, *Commerce of the Prairies* (1844), ed. Max L. Moorhead (Norman: University of-Oklahoma Press, 1954), pp. 369-70, 396; William Cullen Bryant, *Letters of a Traveller; or, Notes of Things Seen in Europe and America* (1850), 4th ed. (New York: G. P. Putnam and Co., 1855), pp. 79, 302; Peter Skene Ogden, *Traits of American-Indian Life and Character by a Fur Trader* (London: Smith, Elder and Co., 1853), p. xi; John Treat Irving Jr., *Indian Sketches Taken During an Expedition to the Pawnee Tribes [1833]* (1835), ed. John Francis McDermott (Norman: University of Oklahoma Press, 1955), p. 22; George Frederick Ruxton, *Life in the Far West* (1848), ed. LeRoy R. Hafen (Norman: University of Oklahoma Press, 1951), pp. 100, 106, 112.

[12] S. C. Robertson, "An Army Hunter's Notes on Our North-Western Game," *Outing*, 11 (January 1888), 305.

People otherwise confident about the westward progress of white settlement often betrayed deep resistance to the devastation thereby entailed. They felt alternately proud of their settlements and disoriented by the rapidity with which these were axed out of the wilderness. Praising America in the abstract, they shrank from the actual wounds inflicted on the land. Descriptions belie their complacency: "magnificent forests which the axe has not yet despoiled"; "innumerable spots where nature is invulnerable"; "while the wilderness still glowed in its pristine luxuriance."[13] The *yets* and *stills*, the hesitations and exceptions, the rhetorical graspings for a land slipping away proliferate in western accounts. Bayard Taylor, that American Marco Polo who enthralled his countrymen with descriptions of faraway lands, never jeopardized his popularity or royalties by challenging popular assumptions. Yet even he felt dismay at how far below his American dream fell the vulgar reality. Returning to California ten years after his first visit in 1849, he sadly observed in an account that otherwise continually soothes American ambitions: "Nature here reminds one of a princess fallen into the hands of robbers, who cut off her fingers for the sake of the jewels she wears."[14]

Ambivalence about this American experience characterizes much travel writing of the century, until elegy gives way to concern and then consternation in ever clearer tones.[15] From private diarists to

[13] The quotations, respectively, are from: Timothy Flint, *Recollections of the Last Ten Years Passed in Occasional Residences and Journeyings in the Valley of the Mississippi* . . . (Boston: Cummings, Hilliard, and Co., 1826), pp. 27-28; John A. Butler, "Some Western Resorts," *Harper's New Monthly Magazine*, 65 (August 1882), 326; and Benjamin Drake, *The Life and Adventures of Black Hawk* (1838), 7th ed. rev. (Cincinnati: E. Morgan and Co., 1850), p. 256. See also Rev. James Wallis Eastburn, *Yamoyden, A Tale of the Wars of King Philip: In Six Cantos* (New York: n.p., 1820), pp. 3-4, 27-29; Henry Marie Brackenridge, *Recollections of Persons and Places in the West* (Philadelphia: James Kay, Jun. and Brother, 1834), pp. 71-72; Robert Montgomery Bird, *Calavar; or, The Knight of the Conquest: A Romance of Mexico* (1834), 2d ed., 2 vols. (Philadelphia: Carey, Lea, and Blanchard, 1835), 1:v; James H. Lawrence, "Discovery of the Nevada Fall," *Overland Monthly*, 2d ser., 4 (October 1884), 371.

[14] Taylor, *At Home and Abroad: A Sketch-Book of Life, Scenery, and Men*, 2d ser. (New York: G. P. Putnam, 1862), p. 155. See Kevin Starr, *Americans and the California Dream, 1850-1915* (New York: Oxford University Press, 1973), pp. 174-75, for discussion of widespread sympathy with Taylor's attitude among California tourists.

[15] For an apt illustration of this transition, see: Timothy Dwight, *Travels in New-England and New York*, 4 vols. (London: William Baynes and Son, 1823), 1:vi; Sarah Kemble Knight, *The Journal of Madam Knight* (Boston: Small, Maynard and Co., 1920), p. xii; William C. Spengemann, *The Adventurous Muse: The Poetics of American Fiction, 1789-1900* (New Haven: Yale University Press, 1977), p. 45. See also Gabriel Franchère, *Narrative of a Voyage to the Northwest Coast of America in the Years 1811, 1812, 1813, and 1814; or The First American Settlement*

famous writers, housewives to professional journalists, the intent altered little: "to picture a fleeting phase of our national life"; "[to hand] down to posterity a faithful record"; "to delineate the character, customs and habits of the Indian tribes, who have passed, and are passing, so fast away, that little more will soon be left of them to sight or memory." Decidedly, "he who would write of the 'wilds of the West, beyond the bounds of civilization' must write quickly."[16] Some surely hoped to chart the national progress by defining initial conditions—intent, as it were, on taking a "before" picture in what they expected would make a dramatic "before-and-after" sequence. Yet the attention of later nineteenth-century picture takers seems less calmly focused in proud expectation. Their prose acquires a shrill tone and a more agitated rhythm, punctuated by expressions of mild regret.[17]

Perhaps the clearest insight into this rough transition in public attitudes can be gained by assembling a series of statements made during the course of the century. Far from reflecting a uniform shift

on the Pacific (1820), trans. and ed. J. V. Huntington (1854), reprinted in vol. 6 of Reubon Gold Thwaites, ed. Early Western Travels: 1748-1846, 32 vols. (Cleveland: Arthur H. Clark Co., 1904-07), p. 175; John Burroughs's introduction to Robert Buchanan, Life and Adventures of Audubon the Naturalist (1868; rpt. New York: E. P. Dutton, 1913), p. vii.

16 The quotations are from: Albert D. Richardson, Beyond the Mississippi: From the Great River to the Great Ocean . . . (Hartford, Conn.: American Publishing Co., 1867), p. i; Caroline Matilda Kirkland, A New Home—Who'll Follow? or, Glimpses of Western Life (1839), 3d ed. (New York: Charles S. Francis, 1841), p. 7; George H. Colton, Tecumseh; or, The West Thirty Years Since. A Poem (New York: Wiley and Putnam, 1842), preface; I. Winslow Ayer, Life in the Wilds of America, and Wonders of the West in and beyond the Bounds of Civilization (Grand Rapids, Mich.: Central Publishing Co., 1880), p. 15.

17 Those intent on a "before" shot while still possible include: Charles Loring Brace, The New West: or, California in 1867-1868 (New York: G. P. Putnam and Son, 1869), p. iv; Fortescue Cuming, Sketches of a Tour to the Western Country, Through the States of Ohio and Kentucky . . . 1807-1809 (1810), reprinted in vol. 4 of Thwaites, ed., Early Western Travels, p. 23; Joseph Henry Taylor, Sketches of Frontier and Indian Life (Pottstown, Pa.: n.p., 1889), pp. 6-7. Those intent merely on salvaging some accurate record include: Frances Chamberlain Holley, Once Their Home; or, Our Legacy From the Dahkotahs (Chicago: Donohue and Henneberry, 1890), p. 18; Emerson Hough, The Way to the West (Indianapolis: Bobbs-Merrill, 1903), p. 423; Bela Hubbard, "Ancient Garden Beds of Michigan," American Antiquarian, 1 (April 1878), 1; Humphrey Marshall, The History of Kentucky (Frankfort: n.p., 1824), introduction; Charles Alston Messiter, Sport and Adventures among the North-American Indians (London: R. H. Porter, 1890), pp. v-vi; John Lewis Peyton, Over the Alleghanies and Across the Prairies: Personal Recollections of the Far West (London: Simpkin, Marshall and Co., 1869), p. xi; Gilbert Malcolm Sproat, Scenes and Studies of Savage Life (London: Smith, Elder and Co., 1868), p. 10. See also Annette Kolodny's reference to William Gilmore Simms in The Lay of the Land: Metaphor as Experience and History in American Life and Letters (Chapel Hill: University of North Carolina Press, 1975), p. 104.

in public opinion, these statements serve rather as a paradigm for the history of an idea. The first statement was delivered in 1834 by the leading citizen of a burgeoning Cincinnati. Lecturing the city's finest on their "history, character, and prospects," he observed: "Thus the teeming and beautiful landscape of nature fades away like a dream of poetry. . . . Before this transformation is finished, a portrait should be taken, that our children may contemplate the primitive physiognomy of their native land, and feast their eyes on its virgin charms."[18] As if to reinforce this suggestion, he called attention to the recent disappearance of local game and encouraged the collecting of fossil remains and Indian artifacts before they were plowed under.

Near mid-century a less well-known resident of western New York State wrote a number of volumes on pioneer life and Iroquois traditions. Introducing one of them, he reflected wryly, "strange as it may appear, the history of this important country . . . will only attract the attention it demands, in the remote periods of future ages. The records of memory are fast fading away. The remnant of a once mighty nation is rapidly disappearing. Indian tradition, with all its vivacity and interest, is fearfully becoming extinct. A few short years and nothing new can possibly be gleaned."[19]

More than twenty years later, an antiquarian prefaced his collection of pioneer accounts by way of both apology and exhortation. "It is a great pity that the simple and unlettered actors in the rude and eventful old Border days recorded so little. . . . It is now, alas! almost too late. What can yet be done, however, should speedily be done to rescue from oblivion the evanescent memories of days that are past; to supply existing deficiencies; to correct the many errors which prevail; and to restore some degree of order to the great confusion existing among Border Chronicles and Traditions."[20]

The three statements share a similar concern, but they also suggest distinct differences in the quality of that concern as it developed over a forty-year period. Their common subject elicits a successively more intense emotional engagement. The conditional future perspective of the 1830s ("a portrait should be taken"), glowingly elaborated and calmly confident in its linked clauses, gives way in the second quotation to a reflection phrased in more agitated syntactic units. Parti-

[18] Daniel Drake, M.D., *Discourse on the History, Character, and Prospects of the West* (1834; rpt. Gainesville, Fla.: Scholars' Facsimiles and Reprints, 1955), p. 17; see also pp. 16-21.

[19] Joshua V. H. Clark, *Onondaga; or Reminiscenses of Earlier and Later Times* . . . , 2 vols. (Syracuse: Stoddard and Babcock, 1849), 1:xiv; see also 1:xiii, 77.

[20] Charles McKnight, *Our Western Border . . . One Hundred Years Ago* (Philadelphia: J. C. McCurdy and Co., 1875), p. x, also p. xi.

ciples seem to teeter on the fulcrum of tense, present and past; the sentences shrink, increasingly isolated, as each becomes more simply declarative, less structurally related to its predecessor. The style, that is, reflects an underlying sense of loss. Although the final statement may not seem to move as dramatically along the spectrum of attitudes, its combination of resignation and determination, its almost business-like assessment of missed opportunities and remaining possibilities nevertheless defines the kind of response many finally made in recording the vanishing appearance of the frontier. Of course, the rhetorical differences detailed here may illustrate stylistic idiosyncrasies as well as historical changes in response. Still, quotations similar to these can easily be replicated, alternating between assurances that there is "still time" and regrets that it is "too late."

For the most part, those concerned about the threatened landscape lacked the training in art, the professional experience as writers, or the unsparing commitment that might have shaped full careers in documenting the West. Though sharing a common historiographic bond, they usually acknowledged it only once, in diaries, essays, or illustrations that stand as unique efforts, not as part of lifelong missions. Most exceptions to this pattern, predictably, were trained artists or scientists, often members of government-sponsored surveys of the Far West. They devoted years, even decades, to preserving records of a wilderness threatened by the very opportunities revealed in their reports, whether for potential railroad routings or possible settlement locations.

As early as 1802, President Thomas Jefferson encouraged Meriwether Lewis to gather notes and materials along his continental trek, apparently with some sense of the need for a record. Jefferson long maintained not only a wide curiosity about the wilderness but also an incipient appreciation for its passing. For thirty years he collected ethnographic materials precisely because he recognized that tribes were dying off without leaving their histories behind.[21] Such awareness and accompanying commitment, rare in the eighteenth century, became characteristic, especially of particular groups of professionals, in the nineteenth. The letters and diaries of survey artists, for example, confirm this development. Even more convincing, the

21 See Paul Russell Cutright, *Lewis and Clark: Pioneering Naturalists* (Urbana: University of Illinois Press, 1969), esp. p. 7, where he quotes from Jefferson's *Notes on the State of Virginia*: " 'It is to be lamented, then, very much to be lamented, that we have suffered so many of the Indian tribes already to extinguish, without our having previously collected and deposited in the records of literature, the general rudiment at least of the languages they spoke.' "

injunctions of art critics toward the end of the century suggest a broad public endorsement of such work.[22]

PAINTERS AS HISTORIANS OF THE WILDERNESS

The work of three major artists whose careers collectively spanned the middle two quarters of the nineteenth century suggests the extent of this concern for wilderness and the extraordinary efforts it produced. John James Audubon, Thomas Cole, and Albert Bierstadt were all immigrants who came or were brought to America for a new and better life; the paintings of each memorialize scenes they had initially wanted to celebrate. Audubon (1785-1851) was the first whose considerable ambitions were strengthened by a sense of imminent threat to the landscape. In 1820, seventeen years after leaving Santo Domingo, he began the vast project of illustrating all of America's birds, and for the next eighteen years he traveled through the North American wilderness, collecting specimens, dashing off sketches, taking voluminous notes, and finishing color plates for his masterwork, *Birds of America* (1827-1838).

The journals Audubon kept of his travels powerfully evoke his growing uneasiness over the incursions settlers were making. The Tennessee warbler and belted kingfisher, the passenger pigeon and yellow-throated vireo represented only a small part of what was threatened. "Nature herself seems perishing," he mourned in the early 1830s,[23] then going on to detail the ravaged landscape, the dwindled herds of buffalo and deer, the disease-ridden Indian tribes. In 1843 he described the Ohio River as it had seemed to him only twenty years earlier, and he concluded:

22 Thomas Nuttall, for example, explained his motives for publishing: "As it may contain some physical remarks connected with the history of the country, and with that of the unfortunate aborigines, who are so rapidly dwindling into oblivion, and whose fate may, in succeeding generations, excite a curiosity and compassion denied them by the present, I have considered myself partly excused in offering a small edition to the scientific part of the community". (Nuttall, *A Journal of Travels into the Arkansas Territory, During the year 1819* . . . [1821], reprinted as vol. 13 of Thwaites, ed., *Early Western Travels*, p. 27). See also Joseph Kastner, *A Species of Eternity* (New York: Alfred A. Knopf, 1977), pp. 254-83; Jessie Poesch, *Titian Ramsey Peale and His Journals of the Wilkes Expedition, 1799-1885* (Philadelphia: American Philosophical Society, 1961), pp. 22-26; S.G.W. Benjamin, *Art in America: A Critical and Historical Sketch* (New York: Harper and Brothers, 1880), p. 88; and Franz Stenzel, *James Madison Alden: Yankee Artist of the Pacific Coast, 1854-1860* (Fort Worth: Amon Carter Museum, 1975), pp. 9-18.

23 Maria R. Audubon, *Audubon and His Journals*, 2 vols. (New York: Charles Scribner's Sons, 1897), 1:407; See also 1:10-11, 406. For good background materials, see Kastner, *A Species of Eternity*, pp. 207-39.

I feel with regret that there are on record no satisfactory accounts of the state of that portion of the country from the time when our people first settled on it. . . . However, it is not too late yet; and I sincerely hope that either or both [Washington Irving and James Fenimore Cooper] will ere long furnish the generations to come with those delightful descriptions which they are so well qualified to give, of the original state of a country that has been so rapidly forced to change her form and attire under the influence of increasing population.[24]

Audubon's cherished hope for an "immortal" picture of "the country as it once existed" found at least some fulfillment in the works of both writers.[25]

Audubon himself set about fixing elements of the landscape in his own immortal picture, and his call to others to join in the task only confirms a personal sense of mission. Professionally ambitious, he nonetheless also felt a less selfish urge to use his skills in capturing pictures of American nature before its transformation. "Audubon attempted to stop time altogether," one scholar has pointed out, "and preserve the static continuity of a soaring bird and a landscape 'before population had greatly advanced.' "[26] That he spent the last decade of his strenuous career preparing *Viviparous Quadrupeds of North America* (1845-1854) testifies to the strength and widening scope of that motivation to stop time. Had he lived longer, Audubon might well have attempted other subjects whose despoliation he had long openly regretted.

Audubon's contemporary fame depended on Americans' new clamoring for paintings with indigenous subjects, a demand most fully satisfied by the Englishman Thomas Cole (1801-1848). Between 1825, when his oils were discovered in a Greenwich Village shop window, and 1848, the year of his death, Cole reigned as America's most popular painter. Buyers of his landscapes demanded accurate transcriptions of specific locales, and, as had Audubon, he learned to take voluminous notes in preparation for his highly detailed compositions. Indeed, Cole would come to feel that his paintings achieved a documentary status. Claiming special privileges for American artists be-

[24] Audubon, *Delineations of American Scenery and Character* (New York: G. A. Baker and Co., 1926), pp. 4-5. See also Robert V. Hine and Edwin R. Bingham, eds., *The American Frontier: Readings and Documents* (Boston: Little, Brown and Co., 1972), pp. 302-4; Alice Ford, *John James Audubon* (Norman: University of Oklahoma Press, 1964), p. 401.
[25] Maria R. Audubon, *Audubon and His Journals*, 1:182-83.
[26] Kolodny, *Lay of the Land*, p. 88.

cause "all nature here is new to art,"[27] he also recognized their collective responsibility to the landscape that was so rapidly passing away. The "meagre utilitarianism" of contemporaries who seemed willing to sacrifice the landscape to the "ravages of the axe" enraged Cole. In an 1835 public address he implored Americans to remember that "we are still in Eden; the wall that shuts us out of the garden is our own ignorance and folly."[28]

As forceful as were his speeches on behalf of preservation, Cole proved far more persuasive as a painter. In some cases, to be sure, his canvases are merely didactic. One, for instance, presents a woodsman senselessly attacking a tree in the midst of a clearing he has already hacked out of the forest.[29] A more profound vision emerges in Cole's celebrated five-panel series, *The Course of Empire* (1836), in which the final two scenes illustrate time's ravaging force as "The Destruction of Empire" and "Desolation."[30] Cole knew from visits to Europe the dangers that Western civilization offered to unprotected landscape. Against his strong sense of historical cycles ever turning to ruinous waste, his native scenes often work as Audubon's color plates had: to hold an image of the fleeting wilderness forever fixed in time. They do not incidentally illustrate the American landscape before mid-century; they were created for that very purpose.[31]

By the mid-1840s, Cole had abandoned efforts to synthesize ideal conceptions with graphic detail. In his last painting, *View of the Falls of Munda* (1847), he completely abandoned a priori formulas to embrace an almost photographic accuracy. "The real and the ideal," one critic has observed, "which had so often conflicted in his art, seem to have separated out like oil and water."[32] A partial reason for this

[27] Cited in Louis L. Noble, *The Course of Empire, Voyage of Life, and Other Pictures of Thomas Cole, N.A.* (New York: Lamport, Blakeman and Law, 1853), p. 202.

[28] Cole, "Lecture on American Scenery, Delivered before the Catskill Lyceum, April 1st, 1841," *Northern Light*, 1 (May 1841), 25-26. See also Cole's poem, "The Lament of the Forest," *Knickerbocker*, 17 (June 1841), 516-19.

[29] See Richard Rudisill, *Mirror Image: The Influence of the Daguerreotype on American Society* (Albuquerque: University of New Mexico Press, 1971), p. 8.

[30] See Louis Legrand Noble, *The Life and Works of Thomas Cole* (1853), ed. Elliot S. Vesell (Cambridge, Mass.: Harvard University Press, 1964), pp. xxi, 129.

[31] See Howard S. Merritt, *Thomas Cole* (Rochester: University of Rochester Memorial Art Gallery, 1969), p. 24. On Cole's "Kaaterskill Falls" (1827) Merritt remarks: "As recorded in the drawing there were, even at this early date, an observation pavilion and guard rails at the head of the falls. Typically, Cole carefully omits these in the painting, thereby emphasizing, or one should say restoring, the unspoiled wilderness of the scene—further underscored by the inclusion of an Indian."

[32] Barbara Novak, *American Painting of the Nineteenth Century: Realism, Idealism, and the American Experience* (New York: Praeger, 1969), p. 79. See also James

2. Thomas Cole, *Landscape: The Wilderness Axeman*, 1825. Oil on canvas. The Minneapolis Institute of Arts.

clarification is suggested in the notes Cole made just prior to his death for an art book taking wilderness as its main theme: "Love of nature more intense and diffused among the moderns than the ancients. One cause of it—the wilderness passing away, and the necessity of saving and perpetuating its features."[33] Whether he would have completed that book had he lived, Cole would certainly have moved landscape painting toward more exacting documentation.

Of course, more detailed landscapes offer in themselves no particular evidence of swelling concern for the wilderness. Cole's successor as America's premier painter, Asher Durand, practiced a far more literal landscape style without ever expressing disquietude over

Thomas Flexner, *That Wilder Image: The Painting of America's Native School from Thomas Cole to Winslow Homer* (1962; rpt. New York: Dover Publications, 1970), pp. 34ff.; Roderick Nash, *Wilderness and the American Mind*, rev. ed. (New Haven: Yale University Press, 1973), p. 97; Arthur A. Ekirch Jr., *Man and Nature in America* (New York: Columbia University Press, 1963), p. 27.

[33] Cited in Noble, *Course of Empire*, p. 398.

the passing of America's forests. Nevertheless, Durand, other Hudson River School practitioners, and American painters generally could not remain unaffected when even art critics elaborated on Cole's pleas. An anonymous reviewer of two Jasper Cropsey landscapes in 1847, for example, ranked the painter with both Cole and Durand because he illustrated the high mission of the American painter. "The axe of civilization is busy with our old forests," the reviewer declared. "Yankee enterprise has little sympathy with the picturesque, and it behooves our artists to rescue from its grasp the little that is left, before it is for ever too late."[34] Artists heeded the plea. Indeed, one art historian has verified this impulse in pre-Civil War America, declaring that "no object is so frequently found in its landscape art as the tree stump."[35] Of course, then as now, artists primarily responded to special aesthetic considerations or more general ones of public remuneration. But some satisfied personal standards and popular taste even as they fulfilled a "high mission."

Albert Bierstadt (1830-1902) does not exemplify this fusion. Capitulating to easy popularity in his grandiloquent landscapes, he and his reputation have suffered the consequences in modern appreciation. During the 1870s and 1880s, however, he epitomized a major strain in national taste and pride by giving form to Americans' vague image of the Far West. Melodramatic in his composition and lighting, unimaginative in his application of colors, Bierstadt can hardly be said to follow either Audubon or the later Cole. Nonetheless, in his finest painting, *The Rocky Mountains* (1863), he offers a paradigm for the intertwined commitments to both landscape and indigenous peoples. The huge canvas presents a grandiose mountain scene that all but compels closer inspection, inspection that reveals a group of Bannock Indians camped on the valley floor. The eye moves, in other words, from an overwhelming alpine vista to the natives below. Without overburdening the analogy, one might note that the initial desire to preserve images of the unaltered land similarly encouraged initial inquiries about the tribes living there.[36]

However seldom Bierstadt's paintings reflect the theses of Audubon or Cole, he identified with their principles on one occasion at least. In 1859, on his first trip to the Rockies, he sent a public letter back

34 Review of Exhibition of National Academy of Design, *Literary World*, May 15, 1847, p. 348.

35 Nicolai Cikovsky Jr., " 'The Ravages of the Axe': The Meaning of the Tree Stump in Nineteenth-Century American Art," *Art Bulletin*, 61 (December 1979), 626.

36 See John C. Ewers, *Artists of the Old West* (Garden City, N.Y.: Doubleday and Co., 1965), p. 183. See also Ellwood Parry, *The Image of the Indian and the Black Man in American Art, 1590-1900* (New York: George Braziller, 1974), pp. 114-16.

3. Albert Bierstadt, *The Rocky Mountains,* 1863. Chromolithograph. Collection of Alfred L. Bush, Princeton, New Jersey.

east, reiterating what others had long proclaimed: "For a figure-painter, there is an abundance of fine subjects. The manners and customs of the Indians are still as they were hundreds of years ago, and now is the time to paint them, for they are rapidly passing away, and soon will be known only in history. I think that the artist ought to tell his portion of their history."[37] Bierstadt later ignored his own injunction, but he could hardly ignore an aspect of the trip that will demand later attention: the presence of a professional photographer. The camera's extraordinary capacity for documentary realism, however little it shaped his own art, provided for countless others a tool to preserve images imminently threatened in the West.[38]

[37] Bierstadt, "Letter from the Rocky Mountains, July 10, 1859," *Crayon,* (September 1859), 287.

[38] Josiah Gregg supposedly made daguerreotype plates on the Santa Fe Trail in 1846. John Mix Stanley had made some three years before on his first trip west, as documented by Russell E. Belous and Robert A. Weinstein in *Will Soule: Indian Photographer at Fort Sill, Oklahoma, 1869-74* (Los Angeles: Ward Ritchie Press, 1969), p. 13. The railroad surveys of the fifties invariably included a photographer, who often focused on Indians and Indian life in the areas visited. Richard and Edward Kern, for example, accompanied John C. Frémont's fourth Southwest expedition; among their plates "are illustrations of designs on fragments of Indian pottery, Indian hieroglyphics, and ground plans of several pueblos, invaluable for the archaeolog[ist]" today, according to Robert Taft in *Artists and Illustrators of*

WRITERS AS HISTORIANS OF THE WILDERNESS

Photography powerfully influenced those ignorant of the craft itself. Not until the last quarter of the century did major innovations in the photographic process make the camera a convenient tool for those interested in documentation. Its language had already crept into general usage, however, and its new perspectives had long since fostered new attitudes among those anxious about the threatened landscape. Hardly three decades after Louis Daguerre and William Henry Fox Talbot perfected the process, Francis Parkman completed a volume of his North American history in which he claimed "to secure the greatest possible accuracy of statement, and to reproduce an image of the past with photographic clearness and truth."[39] For Parkman, as for other historians, the camera provided more than a convenient metaphor. It clarified the very premises of his profession, especially as that profession faced the complex phenomenon of the American West.

the Old West 1850-1900 (New York: Charles Scribner's Sons, 1953), p. 258. S. N. Carvalho's work for Frémont's fifth expedition in 1853 and John Mix Stanley's prints for Isaac Stevens's survey that same year both included a number of studies of Indians and Indian culture, although both men's work has since been lost or destroyed. See also Edward Vischer, Vischer's Pictorial of California: Landscape, Trees and Forest Scenes; Grand Features of California Scenery, Life, Traffic and Customs, 5 series of 12 numbers each (San Francisco: n.p., April 1870), pp. 1-2; Vischer, Sketches of the Washoe Mining Region: Photographs Reduced from Originals (San Francisco: Valentine and Co., 1862), pp. 6 7; John Warner Barber and Henry Howe, All the Western States and Territories . . . (Cincinnati: Howe's Subscription Book Concern, 1868), p. 4; Freeman Tilden, Following the Frontier with F. Jay Haynes: Pioneer Photographer of the Old West (New York: Alfred A. Knopf, 1964), esp. pp. 26, 197, 223, 359ff.; F. Jay Haynes, Indian Types of the North-West (New York: Adolph Wittemann, ca. 1885), p. 3; Mark H. Brown and W. R. Felton, Before Barbed Wire: L. A. Huffman, Photographer on Horseback (1956; rpt. New York: Bramhall House, 1961), pp. 10-12, 19-21; Mark H. Brown and W. R. Felton, The Frontier Years: L. A. Huffman, Photographer of the Plains (New York: Bramhall House, 1955); John S. Hittell, Yosemite: Its Wonders and Its Beauties (San Francisco: H. H. Bancroft and Co., 1868); William Henry Jackson, Descriptive Catalogue of Photographs of North American Indians, U.S. Geological and Geographical Survey of the Territories, Miscellaneous Publication no. 9 (Washington: G.P.O., 1877), pp. iii-v; The Diaries of William Henry Jackson: Frontier Photographer, ed. LeRoy R. Hafen and Ann W. Hafen (Glendale, Calif.: Arthur H. Clark Co., 1959), pp. 275-76, 314; and Victoria Thomas Olson, "Pioneer Conservationist A. P. Hill: 'He Saved the Redwoods,'" American West, 14 (September-October 1977), 32-40.

[39] Francis Parkman, The Jesuits of North America in the Seventeenth Century (1867), vols. 3-4 of the Champlain Edition (Boston: Little, Brown and Co., 1897), 3:vii. Thirteen years later a reviewer of Francis Parkman's collected works invoked the same metaphor: "As we peruse them now, remembering the mighty changes which have been wrought in yesterday's wilderness, we realize that they have a peculiar value of their own. For they are a photographic record of a state of things which has passed away never to return" (Edward G. Mason, "Francis Parkman" Dial, 1 [December 1880], 149).

Parkman (1823-1893) resembles Washington Irving both in his career as historian and in his fascination with America's wilderness. With greater deliberation than Irving and for a longer period, however, he attempted both to explore those wild regions and to document them. In 1841, for example, he hiked into the White Mountains "to see the wilderness where it was as yet uninvaded by the hand of man."[40] Five years later, weak health and a strong desire to observe at firsthand the life of the Plains Sioux led Parkman to make a summer's trek to the West, a trip that confirmed him in his career. Returning to write a personal narrative, *The Oregon Trail* (1849), he followed it with what became a nine-volume study, *France and England in North America* (1892). The first volume in this series, *The Conspiracy of Pontiac* (1851), documents the Anglo-French struggle in colonial America and openly declares both its purpose and Parkman's continuing motive: "The history of that epoch . . . has been, as yet, unwritten, buried in the archives of governments, or among the obscurer records of private adventure. To rescue it from oblivion is the object of the following work. It aims to portray the American forest and the American Indian at the period when both received their final doom."[41] Parkman felt almost compelled to rescue American history from fading memories and crumbling manuscripts, and he even came to view his earlier endeavors in this light. Though he wrote *The Oregon Trail* with no explicitly preservationist purpose, his prefaces to subsequent editions increasingly invest the work with special value. In each he laments the passing of the wilderness, and by 1892 he could conclude: "The Wild West is tamed, and its savage charms have withered. If this book can help to keep their memory alive, it will have done its part."[42]

This concern to preserve America's frontier history may seem incongruous in a sophisticated Boston Brahmin. Insulated by birth, education, and predisposition from the wilderness dramas he described, Parkman nonetheless kept returning to America's past in

[40] *The Journals of Francis Parkman*, ed. Mason Wade, 2 vols. (New York: Harper and Brothers, 1947), 1:31.

[41] *The Conspiracy of Pontiac and the Indian War after the Conquest of Canada* (1851), vols. 16-18 of the Champlain Edition (Boston: Little, Brown and Co., 1898), 16:ix.

[42] *The Oregon Trail: Sketches of Prairie and Rocky-Mountain Life* (1849), ed. E. N. Feltskog (Madison: University of Wisconsin Press, 1969), p. ix. For discussion of Parkman's earlier dismay at the losses incurred through "civilizing" the West (as reflected in *The Oregon Trail*), see esp. Howard Doughty, *Francis Parkman* (New York: Macmillan Co., 1962), pp. 116-17, 151-58. For a more contemporary response admiring Parkman's preservationist achievement, see Mason, "Francis Parkman," p. 150.

order to document the continent as it once had been. Against his rather romantic vision of the American West pressed a strong intimation of loss. Yet, unlike Thomas Cole, who explored this very conjunction in his art, Parkman failed to pursue its darker implications in his historical series. Indeed, his unquestioning belief in material progress prevented him from ever specifically formulating the issue.

A contemporary who failed in a similar fashion was James Fenimore Cooper (1789-1851), though he at least attempted to deal with the implications of progress. Toiling in fictional rather than historical fields, Cooper suffered similar uneasiness about what was being eroded, what plowed under in America's wilderness history. In fact, Parkman's preface to *The Conspiracy of Pontiac* (1851), proclaiming accuracy in his rescued record, may itself have been prompted by Cooper's efforts to reclaim native soil. Following the novelist's death later that year, Parkman wrote a eulogy suggesting such an influence. Though he missed the moral ambiguities at the heart of Cooper's mythic vision, the historian analyzed tellingly in one section:

> Civilization has a destroying as well as a creating power. It is exterminating the buffalo and the Indian, over whose fate too many lamentations, real or affected, have been sounded for us to renew them here. It must, moreover, eventually sweep from before it a class of men, its own precursors and pioneers, so remarkable both in their virtues and their faults, that few will see their extinction without regret. Of these men, Leatherstocking is the representative . . . [and] worthy of permanent remembrance. His life conveys in some sort an epitome of American history, during one of its more busy and decisive periods.[43]

Parkman failed only to grant Cooper the self-conscious intent he argued for his own labors.

Prefaces to the Leatherstocking tales repeatedly proclaim Cooper's fidelity to the wilderness experience. His declaration, for example, that "though the scenes of this book are believed to have once been as nearly accurate as required by the laws which govern fiction, they are so no longer,"[44] is reiterated in three of the four other tales in the series. While New York's eastern woodlands had altered dra-

[43] Parkman, "The Works of James Fenimore Cooper," *North American Review*, 74 (January 1852), 151-52.

[44] Cooper, *The Pathfinder, or The Inland Sea* (New York: W. A. Townsend and Co., 1859), p. viii. All future references will be to this edition of Cooper's works, known as the Author's Revised Edition, illustrated by F.O.C. Darley. See other volumes from this edition, including *The Pioneers*, p. ix; *The Last of the Mohicans*, p. ix; and *The Deerslayer*, p. xiii.

matically between his childhood there and the beginning of his writing career in the 1820s, Cooper hoped to preserve a memory of them through his art, providing historical footnotes that verify otherwise improbable scenes and, in subsequent editions, refuting challenges to portrayed events.[45]

His narrative technique itself manifests a documentary concern that readers from the beginning have identified with the visual arts. His scenes, in the words of one, are "sharp visual images conceived as if they were paintings lacking the dimension of time."[46] Cooper intended that static quality in his novels; those that mythicize the young Leatherstocking, especially, give the impression of stopping time altogether. And this impression holds even in *The Pioneers* (1823) and *The Prairie* (1828), which portray an old and garrulous Natty Bumppo posed against the new pioneer order. Both novels present dislocation in such a way as to make it seem permanent. More profoundly than any of his contemporaries, Cooper felt impelled to flesh out a way of life already relegated to the past.[47]

The commitment to preserving a record of the wilderness that he had known as a child may be seen as an extension of his father's concern for eastern forests. Judge William Cooper settled his family on his vast landholdings in Cooperstown, New York, with the declared intention "to cause the Wilderness to bloom and fructify."[48] But against that promise intruded the fear that America's continental woodlands were inadequate to Americans' usage. In a careful analysis, Judge Cooper defined the specific conditions inevitably leading to a shortage of forested lands. Primary among these was man's thought-

---

[45] See, for example, *The Pioneers*, pp. 255, 257, 468; *The Prairie*, pp. 10, 11, 23, 27, 67, 124; *The Deerslayer*, p. 263.

[46] Henry Nash Smith, introduction to Cooper, *The Prairie: A Tale* (New York: Holt, Rinehart and Winston, 1950), p. ix. See also Honoré de Balzac, "Lettres sur la littérature," *Revue Parisienne*, July 23, 1840, trans. Warren S. Walker, in Walker, ed., *Leatherstocking and the Critics* (Chicago: Scott, Foresman and Co., 1965), p. 2; Blake Nevius, *Cooper's Landscapes: An Essay on the Picturesque Vision* (Berkeley: University of California Press, 1976); H. Daniel Peck, *A World by Itself: The Pastoral Moment in Cooper's Fiction* (New Haven: Yale University Press, 1977), esp. pp. 3-17.

[47] According to William Goetzmann, Cooper makes "time *and* progress stand still." "His great achievement was to render the historical process of change during a period of cultural genesis somehow timeless and permanent while at the same time capturing all of the ambiguities, dislocations, and anomalies of a culture in the throes of a process of acceleration more rapid than any ever seen before" (Goetzmann, "James Fenimore Cooper: *The Prairie*," in Hennig Cohen, ed. *Landmarks of American Writing* [New York: Basic Books, 1969], p. 71).

[48] William Cooper, *A Guide in the Wilderness: or the History of the First Settlements in the Western Counties of New-York with Useful Instructions to Future Settlers* (1810; rpt. New York: George P. Humphrey, 1897), p. 6. Cited in Roderick Nash, *Wilderness and the American Mind*, p. 32.

less waste. Cautioning against such prodigality, he offered informed suggestions for preventing this projected dearth.[49]

Once he began to write professionally, then, young James Fenimore could rely on more than a well-stocked memory of childhood experiences in frontier Cooperstown. The combination of parental opinion, personal temperament, and extensive research led Cooper into a paradox far more extreme than that troubling his father: deeply cherishing undomesticated wilderness, he nonetheless felt deeply pulled by America's westering development. Clearly, the novelist approved the spread of what he thought was the best of western European civilization across the continent. At the same time, he responded powerfully to the claims of an unsettled continent.[50] Cooper's lack of self-awareness about that conflict—hence, his inability to resolve it— prevents his fiction from finally transcending his own profound ambivalences.

Fitfully divided about the issue of civilization versus nature, Cooper nonetheless wanted to do more than preserve an accurate picture of the latter. Even as he celebrated white America's prospects in his essays and letters, in his fiction he gives the impression of wanting to preserve actual wilderness itself—land, Indians, and lone frontiersmen. As did his friend Thomas Cole, he sensed that Americans were selling their patrimony to destruction in the name of progress. Cooper best explores this issue of agrarian progress westward versus undomesticated nature in his Leatherstocking saga, most tellingly in The Pioneers and in The Prairie. The Pioneers, especially, highlights Cooper's imaginative "conflict of allegiances,"[51] perhaps because it is so closely autobiographical, more likely because it inaugurates the series. Artistically less self-conscious than he would be even in his next book, Cooper more readily incorporated contradictory elements into the narrative, defining at its most resonant levels his ambivalence toward America's westering society.[52] The stumps of felled trees sur-

[49] Roderick Nash, *Wilderness and the American Mind*, p. 23. Other public examples of this anticipatory concern include Samuel Akerly, "On the Cultivation of Forest Trees; In a Letter Addressed to Jonathan Thompson," broadside, 1823, American Antiquarian Society, Worcester, Mass.; and D. C. Banks, "To the Citizens of Kentucky," broadside, February 15, 1840, American Antiquarian Society.

[50] For further proof of the strength of Cooper's later feelings in this regard, see John J. McAleer, "Biblical Analogy in the Leatherstocking Tales," *Nineteenth-Century Fiction*, 17 (December 1962), 221-22.

[51] Smith, *Virgin Land*, p. 66.

[52] See D. H. Lawrence, *Studies in Classic American Literature* (1923; rpt. New York: Viking, 1966), pp. 50-51; Edwin Fussell, *Frontier: American Literature and the American West* (Princeton: Princeton University Press, 1965), pp. 56-64; Donald Ringe, *James Fenimore Cooper* (New York: Twayne, 1962), pp. 8off.; Howard Mumford Jones, "Prose and Pictures: James Fenimore Cooper" (1951),

rounding the village of Templeton (to use a deliberately minor example) reappear with surprising frequency, and the very imagery associated with their appearances reflects Cooper's dismay at the necessary process of clearing. In our first view of Templeton, the narrator describes the way stumps "abounded in the open fields, adjacent to the village, and were accompanied occasionally, by the ruin of a pine or a hemlock that had been stripped of its bark, and which waved in melancholy grandeur its naked limbs to the blast, a skeleton of its former glory."[53] A quiet leitmotiv, these stumps reinforce a larger view of advancement as loss, of gain felt more compellingly as sacrifice.

Cooper equates progress with despoliation in each of the novel's major set pieces. Spurred on by civic leaders, the villagers cheerfully exhaust the natural environment, depleting the forests of sugar maples, the lakes of bass, the skies of passenger pigeons. Yet Cooper's distress is not at what Thomas Cole later decried as "meagre utilitarianism." Rather, he indicts the pioneers for their complacent extravagance in turning nature to profit, their thriftless waste in hacking out a community. The outspoken sheriff, Richard Jones, epitomizes this attitude in explaining urban planning to Elizabeth: " 'We must run our streets by the compass, coz, and disregard trees, hills, ponds, stumps, or, in fact, anything but posterity.' "[54]

Cooper best subverts the advocates of such progress through Natty Bumppo, who in *The Pioneers* lives on the outskirts of Templeton. He wins few admirers for his querulous ranting, whether against the villagers' extravagances or the village itself, but the narrative effectively supports his claims. "Civilization" and "progress" appear to Natty to be little more than rubrics justifying wholesale destruction of nature, and though his narrow view does not necessarily bound Cooper's own, the novel nonetheless offers little to counteract the hunter's suspicious conservatism.

A decade after fleeing westward from the sound of Templeton axes, Natty still cannot escape the crash of falling timber. In the first major action of *The Prairie*, he encounters the ironically named Bush family in the act of brutally axing down the only grove of trees in sight. The image sets the tone for the novel, since, as Natty later observes,

---

in Jones, *History and the Contemporary: Essays in Nineteenth-Century Literature* (Madison: University of Wisconsin Press, 1964), p. 76. See also Charvat, *Profession of Authorship in America*, ed. Bruccoli, pp. 68-83; Peck, *A World by Itself*, pp. 61-62, 102-7.

[53] *The Pioneers*, p. 46. See Donald Ringe, *The Pictorial Mode: Space and Time in the Art of Bryant, Irving, and Cooper.* (Lexington: University Press of Kentucky, 1971), pp. 85, 124; Cikovsky, " 'Ravages of the Axe,' " pp. 611-26.

[54] *The Pioneers*, p. 199.

the demise of those trees prefigures his own.[55] Cooper depicts the white "rape of the wilderness" far less equivocally here than elsewhere in the series.[56] For instance, in his initial entrance, Abiram White confirms his defective moral standing when he declares: "The 'arth was made for our comfort; and, for that matter, so ar' its creatur's."[57] Through imagery and characterization, the novel confutes just this assertion. The very immensity of the landscape, the limitless horizon of the prairie, dramatically emphasizes a natural order that all should acknowledge. Cooper's proud Americans fail to do this. Dr. Obed Bat's imposition of a sterile taxonomy on nature is only the humorous obverse of Ishmael Bush's wasteful selfishness; both evince a contemptible arrogance toward the environment.[58]

But against the powerful scene of the axed grove of trees, Cooper places an equally forceful image. In the midst of the vast immensity glimmers the small, lighted circle of family relation as the Bush family camps for the night atop a great rock outcropping. Cooper could not reconcile this conflict between the separate claims of undefiled nature and westward progress. At the heart of his mythic interpretation of America, regret intensifies to tragic loss.[59] For all the value in that small circle of the family on the rock, these Americans represent changes that do not themselves seem inherently desirable. This incipient challenge to Western civilization's premises derives from more complex issues than that of America's vanishing wilderness and will be further examined in Chapter Eight.

For the moment, it is enough to observe that Cooper's disquietude about man's ravaging of nature gave him sufficient reason to document the landscape. Similar distress compelled others to radically different, more concerted forms of preservation that Cooper may never have considered, including the possibility of setting aside actual reserves. His and his father's efforts, however, coincided with the advent of public recommendations for city parks, state preserves, and national forests.

[55] See Joel Porte, *The Romance in America: Studies in Cooper, Poe, Hawthorne, Melville, and James* (Middletown, Conn.: Wesleyan University Press, 1967), pp. 45-46.

[56] See Ringe, *James Fenimore Cooper*, p. 45.

[57] *The Prairie*, p. 25.

[58] See Donald Ringe, "Man and Nature in Cooper's *The Prairie*," *Nineteenth-Century Fiction*, 15 (March 1961), 316-18.

[59] Henry Nash Smith first noted this in his Introduction to *The Prairie*, p. xvi. For other discussions, see Porte, *Romance in America*, p. 52, and Roy Harvey Pearce, *Savagism and Civilization: A Study of the Indian and the American Mind*, rev. ed. (Baltimore: Johns Hopkins University Press, 1965), p. 202.

PRESERVATIONISTS AS HISTORIANS

The commitment to preservation of the land itself grew out of state efforts to set aside scenic wonders and cities' recognition of the benefits of public parks. Supporters of these causes became increasingly involved through the nineteenth century in deciding the future of America's larger wilderness landscape. Frederick Law Olmsted, John Muir, and Henry George, each in his own fashion, aroused Americans to the special claims of their continent. In their separate strategies for preservation, they nicely represent the spectrum of conservationism in the nineteenth century.

The first proposals for public parks, small "blocks of green," came on both sides of the Atlantic during the 1830s. This post-Renaissance idea had initially been conceived for royal, sometimes noble, purposes. Not until the nineteenth century, however, would it be adopted for the common welfare, and nowhere as in America would the pressure grow for city parks as "nature museums." Worldwide romanticism had contributed to an efflorescence of activities associated with the out-of-doors, as well as a growing resistance to the encroachments of the new urban industrialism. The rapid transformation of wilderness to settlement and settlement to crowded city encouraged Americans in particular to feel that urban enclaves should be preserved against the inroads of progress. Similar American patterns would energize indigenous movements for physical culture, landscape architecture, and rural cemeteries. By the 1840s and 1850s, advocates as little known as Thoreau and as popular as landscape architect Andrew Jackson Downing were repeatedly encouraging Americans to set aside generous tracts of city land.[60]

Such proposals united even political rivals. Among the few beliefs shared by William Cullen Bryant, the fiercely Democratic editor of the *New York Evening Post*, and Horace Greeley, editor of the Whiggish *New-York Tribune*, one was that Americans should be proscribed from destroying certain woodlands. More specifically, both men desired a park for New York City. Bryant phrased the need well in an editorial dated July 3, 1844: "As we are now going on, we are making

[60] Thoreau, *The Maine Woods* (1864), ed. Joseph J. Moldenhauer (Princeton: Princeton University Press, 1972), p. 205. See as well *The Journal of Henry David Thoreau*, ed. Bradford Torrey and Francis H. Allen (Boston: Houghton Mifflin Co., 1906), pp. 341, 1529, 1740-41; Andrew Jackson Downing, ed., *The Horticulturist, and Journal of Rural Art and Rural Taste*, 3 (October 1848), 153-57, 4 (July 1849), 9-12, 5 (October 1850), 153-56; and, for a useful survey, Albert Matthews, "The Word Park in the United States," *Publication of the Colonial Society of Massachusetts: Transactions*, 8 (1906), 373-97.

a belt of muddy docks all around the island. We should be glad to see one small part of the shore without them, one place at least where the tides may be allowed to flow pure, and the ancient brim of rocks which border the waters left in its original picturesqueness and beauty."[61] Seven years later, Central Park was conceived, though planned for the center of the city rather than the island's shores. Construction began in 1856, largely at Bryant's initiative.

Frederick Law Olmsted (1822-1903) made his name with the prize-winning design for Central Park. The flattering imitations for which he was commissioned following its 1861 completion—Fairmount Park in Philadelphia, Prospect Park in Brooklyn, South Park in Chicago, Mount Royal Park in Montreal, and park systems in Buffalo and Boston, to name but the largest—attest to the eight-hundred-acre park's resounding success. Olmsted's deft reliance on natural features, as well as his anticipation of future demands, became standards for later park planners. "He had without doubt," according to Lewis Mumford, "one of the best minds that the Brown Decades produced."[62] Driven by an ambition as great as his abilities, Olmsted pursued numerous careers: gentleman farmer, travel writer, editor of *Putnam's Magazine*, co-founder of the *Nation*, and executive secretary of the United States Sanitary Commission. His fame, however, rests on his landscape architecture and his efforts to ensure the preservation of "open spaces."

Olmsted's vision extended well beyond city limits; he recognized that more than urban development needed to be controlled. Government, he believed, had a responsibility to protect all the land for citizens living and unborn. Settlement must be regulated, even proscribed in certain spectacular locations, such as Niagara Falls. The falls, of course, had long attracted visitors, but completion of the Erie Canal in 1825 eased access and attracted a swarm of speculators. The earliest proposals for the site's preservation had been made at the time

61 William Cullen Bryant, "A New Public Park," *New York Evening Post*, July 3, 1844, p. 2; Horace Greeley, *Glances at Europe* (New York: Dewitt and Davenport, 1851), pp. 38-39. See also James Russell Lowell, who made a similar statement in *Crayon*, 55 (1857). Bryant expressed a larger concern with the threat to America's landscape in his poetry, usually stated (as in Cooper) through Indian personas. See his *Poems* (Philadelphia: Carey and Hart), esp. pp. 70-72, 88-91, 94-97, 175-76.

62 Mumford, *The Brown Decades: A Study of the Arts in America, 1865-1895* (1931; rpt. New York: Dover Publications, 1955), p. 93. The discussion of Olmsted relies on three studies: Elizabeth Barlow, *Frederick Law Olmsted's New York* (New York: Praeger, 1972), esp. pp. 5-32; Albert Fein, *Frederick Law Olmsted and the American Environmental Tradition* (New York: George Braziller, 1972); and Laura Wood Roper, *FLO: A Biography of Frederick Law Olmsted* (Baltimore: Johns Hopkins University Press, 1973), esp. pp. 232-87.

Olmsted first visited the falls as an adolescent. The legislation that finally withdrew it from the public domain thirty-odd years later resulted largely from his efforts. It is not merely Olmsted's responsiveness to untransformed landscape, then, that distinguishes him from his contemporaries, but rather his ability to move beyond vague concern to successful political action.

Olmsted helped to shape the most important decade in the history of park preservation. Moving to California in 1863 for reasons of health and career, the landscape architect was soon caught up in the fight for Yosemite Valley and the Mariposa Big Tree Grove. Congress had withdrawn these lands from public sale and granted them to the state of California. Not knowing what to do with them, California established the Yosemite Commission and appointed Olmsted chairman. His 1865 report, according to his biographer, provided "the first systematic exposition of the right and duty of a democracy to take the action that Congress had taken in reserving the Yosemite Valley and the Mariposa Big Tree Grove from private preemption for the enjoyment of all the people."[63] In defending the park premise, Olmsted moved far beyond the commonplace rationale that the out-of-doors ensured "health and vigor." According to him, whole species of indigenous flora had been destroyed back east and supplanted by foreign "weeds"[64]—a calamity he hoped to prevent at Yosemite by creating a "museum of natural science." Despite, or perhaps because of, his conclusion that the state had a "duty of preservation," the report was quietly suppressed. Another quarter of a century would pass before preservationists such as John Muir convinced Congress to adopt Olmsted's recommendations for Yosemite.

Nevertheless, the publicity that he generated inspired others, especially painters, to preservationist efforts. Frederick Edwin Church, one of Thomas Cole's last students, completed numerous drawings of Niagara Falls, and in 1869 he conveyed to Olmsted his hope that the area would be preserved. Fighting together for years against commercial developers, they finally helped to establish an international park in 1885. Thomas Moran's spectacular landscapes of the Yellowstone Canyon likewise energized public support for the first national park in 1872 and garnered him the sobriquet of "the father of the

[63] Roper, FLO, p. 283. See also Starr, Americans and the California Dream, pp. 182-83.

[64] Frederick Law Olmsted, "The Yosemite Valley and the Mariposa Big Trees: A Preliminary Report" (1865), with an introductory note by Laura Wood Roper, Landscape Architecture, 43 (October 1952), 22. For a more general, but valuable, discussion of the background to popular conceptions of the idea of a "wild park," see Roderick Nash, "The American Invention of National Parks," American Quarterly, 22 (Fall 1970), 726-35.

4. Thomas Moran, *Giant Geyser*, 1872. Watercolor. Private collection, New York City.

park system."[65] Similarly, in the 1890s, photographer A. P. Hill used his art to popularize the California redwoods and thereby prevent their destruction. In each case, however, actual preservation depended on those who shared Olmsted's administrative skills.

This protective attitude toward spectacular sites emerged slowly but steadily through the century, forming a major strand in the development of the land conservation movement in America. The movement's vigorous growth can be attributed in part to America's unique possession of a public domain; all land not privately owned remained the common property of the American people. As early as 1815, Thomas Jefferson had refused to sell Virginia's Natural Bridge because he viewed it as a "public trust." Later efforts on behalf of national parklands grew out of similar concern, though almost always for "natural wonders," never for undistinguished virgin forests or wildlife breeding areas. After all, America seemed to have limitless wilderness regions at its disposal. Although more than two million acres were set aside in 1872 to establish Yellowstone National Park, few who supported this bill felt concerned about the wilderness as such. As one historian of the public domain observed in 1880: "Natural wonders and venerable or interesting relics of architectural value or domestic use on the public domain should be preserved. The Shoshone Falls, on Snake River, Idaho . . . [and] many of the old Indian and Mexican ruins . . . should be reserved, along with other remains of former civilizations. The big trees of California . . . should also be reserved."[66] Only afterwards did people realize that they had saved unspoiled forests and waterways along with historical curiosities, threatened species of wild game along with natural wonders.[67]

[65] See Ronald L. Way, *Ontario's Niagara Parks: A History* (Niagara: Niagara Parks Commission, 1946), pp. 15-18. Albert Fein, in *Frederick Law Olmsted*, pp. 42ff., further describes this history, while Kermit Vanderbilt has documented the substantial efforts of Charles Eliot Norton in preserving a park at Niagara Falls in *Charles Eliot Norton: Apostle of Culture in a Democracy* (Cambridge, Mass.: Harvard University Press, 1959), pp. 188-90. Norton was, moreover, close friends with his cousin, Francis Parkman, as confirmed by Howard Doughty in *Francis Parkman*, pp. 145-46. See also Thurman Wilkins, *Thomas Moran: Artist of the Mountains* (Norman: University of Oklahoma Press, 1966), pp. 4-6, 33, 70.

[66] Thomas Donaldson, *The Public Domain: Its History, with Statistics*, 3d ed. (Washington: G.O.P., 1884), p. 1294. Jefferson expressed his views to William Caruthers, March 15, 1815; cited in Roper, *FLO*, p. 285. For a contrasting view of the history of forest preservation, see Ralph H. Brown, *Historical Geography of the United States* (New York: Harcourt, Brace and World, 1948), esp. pp. 107-8.

[67] See Ferdinand Vandeveer Hayden, *The Great West: Its Attractions and Resources* (Philadelphia: Franklin Publishing Co., 1880), p. 36; Hiram Martin Chittenden, *The Yellowstone National Park* (1895), ed. Richard A. Bartlett (Norman: University of Oklahoma Press, 1964), esp. pp. 86ff.; Richard A. Bartlett, *Nature's Yellowstone* (Albuquerque: University of New Mexico Press, 1974), esp. pp. 194-97.

The movement to preserve intact less spectacular acreage did not develop until after the Civil War. DeWitt Clinton in the 1820s and Washington Irving in the 1830s had separately proposed that large tracts of otherwise unexceptional wilderness be maintained in their pristine state, but these early suggestions lacked popular support.[68] Not until Americans anticipated the closing of the frontier—not until the devastation of the land had altered from threatening portent to confirmed pattern—did they sympathize not merely with preservation but with conservation.[69]

The single individual most instrumental in altering public attitudes was John Muir (1838-1914), who arrived in Yosemite three years after Olmsted's ill-fated 1865 report on California lands. During the next forty years, he became America's premier naturalist, the first to popularize the western wilds, including Alaska, and to celebrate their undomesticated virtues in widely read essays. He also ensured that legislation on behalf of conservation never suffered from public ignorance, and he deserves special credit for the Yosemite Act, passed by Congress in 1890. Olmsted's earlier pressure to withdraw state lands made possible Muir's successful efforts to establish fifteen hundred square miles of national parkland.[70] More than in particular

[68] John F. Reiger, *American Sportsmen and the Origins of Conservation* (New York: Winchester Press, 1975), p. 86; Irving, *Captain Bonneville*, ed. Todd, p. 372. See also Akerly, "Cultivation of Forest Trees"; Lt. Francis Hall, *Travels in Canada, and the United-States in 1816 and 1817*, 2d ed. (London: Longman, Hurst, Rees, Orme and Brown, 1819), pp. 35-36; Andrew S. Fuller, *The Forest Tree Culturist: A Treatise on the Cultivation of American Forest Trees* (New York: George E. and F. W. Woodwald, 1866), pp. iv, 5-6; Roderick Nash, *Wilderness and the American Mind*, esp. p. 98.

[69] See Charles William Eliot, *Charles Eliot: Landscape Architect* (Boston: Houghton Mifflin and Co., 1902), esp. 304-49; John Gifford, ed., *The New Jersey Forester: A Bi-Monthly Pamphlet Devoted to the Development of Our Forests*, 1 (January 1895), 1; "Forests," *Hours at Home*, 3 (September 1866), 398-402; Isabella James, "American Forests," *Lippincott's Magazine*, 1 (June 1868), 598-602; Franklin B. Hough, "On the Duty of Governments in the Preservation of Forests," *Proceedings of the American Association for the Advancement of Science*, 22, pt. 2 (1873), 1-10; Felix L. Oswald, "The Preservation of Forests," *North American Review*, 128 (1879), 46; Charles Howard Shinn, *Mining Camps: A Study in American Frontier Government* (1885; rpt. New York: Alfred A. Knopf, 1948), p. xvi; Henry George, *Our Land and Land Policy* (1871; rpt. New York: Doubleday Page and Co., 1904); Starr, *Americans and the California Dream*, p. 175; Stewart L. Udall, *The Quiet Crisis* (New York: Avon, 1963), pp. 69-74; Roderick Nash, *Wilderness and the American Mind*; Hans Huth, "Yosemite: The Story of an Idea," *Sierra Club Bulletin*, 33 (March 1948), 47ff. See also Huth, *Nature and the American: Three Centuries of Changing Attitudes* (Berkeley: University of California Press, 1957); H. Duane Hampton, *How the U.S. Cavalry Saved Our National Parks* (Bloomington: Indiana University Press, 1971), esp. pp. 5-19; Ekirch, *Man and Nature in America*, esp. pp. 29-30; Alfred Runte, *National Parks: The American Experience* (Lincoln: University of Nebraska Press, 1979), esp. pp. 1-9, 38-81.

[70] Roderick Nash, *Wilderness and the American Mind*, pp. 131-32.

legislative coups, Muir's achievement lies in having educated Americans to the intrinsic value of wild places. He applied transcendentalist principles to the public domain so successfully that an aging Emerson came to see at first hand the region that Muir celebrated.

Whereas Emerson's insights had given inspiration to Muir's preservation goals, Henry George's ideas helped to direct his conservation ethos. The federal government's prodigal history of land cession had troubled George (1839-1897). Three years after Muir arrived at Yosemite, the San Francisco-based journalist concluded his preliminary study of *Our Land and Land Policy* (1871). "A generation hence," he declared, "our children will look with astonishment at the recklessness with which the public domain has been squandered. It will seem to them that we must have been mad."[71] Although George failed to offer specific remedies for this squandering, the expanded version of his study, *Progress and Poverty* (1879), awakened Americans to the unequal disposition of their continent as no one might have predicted. The rather simple economic solution he offered was never adopted; nonetheless, George became nineteenth-century America's most popular nonfiction author by engaging Americans' emotions. His damning history of land waste inspired thousands—John Muir most importantly[72]—who then were able to formulate and carry through practical legislation. The question George asked in 1871 crackled with too much rhetorical charge to be ignored: "Why should we seek so diligently to get rid of this public domain as if for the mere pleasure of getting rid of it? What have the buffaloes done to us that we should sacrifice the heritage of our children to see the last of them extirpated before we die?"[73] In the next three decades, Americans would find themselves similarly troubled by the disappearance not only of wild lands but of wildlife as well.

GAME PROTECTION AND THE LAND

The conservation movement brought together trappers and transcendentalists, animal lovers and hunters. Indeed, as important as were "pure" conservationists such as Muir and Olmsted, their projects

[71] George, *Our Land and Land Policy*, p. 11, also p. 91.
[72] Linnie Marsh Wolfe, *Son of the Wilderness: The Life of John Muir* (New York: Alfred A. Knopf, 1945), p. 182; see pp. 184, 227-28, 245-46, 251 for supporting documentation of this passage. See also John Muir, *Our National Parks* (New York: Houghton Mifflin Co., 1901), pp. 337, 364; Douglas H. Strong, "The Sierra Club—A History. Part 1: Origins and Outings," *Sierra*, October 1977, pp. 10-14; Starr, *Americans and the California Dream*, pp. 183-91.
[73] George, *Our Land and Land Policy*, p. 91.

might well have failed in Congress without the support of the thousands of sports hunters who shared their goals, though they were often seen as adversaries.[74] Irving and Cooper again offer apt examples. Irving's tour of the prairies had made him aware of the threatened extinction of buffalo and beaver, perhaps all fur-bearing animals, and in his subsequent western books he prayed that "the avidity of the hunter [might] be restrained within proper limitations."[75] Indeed, he even proposed the establishment of a permanent wilderness preserve.[76] Similarly, Cooper put into the mouth of his expert hunter, Natty Bumppo, his own fears about the slaughter of passenger pigeons and made a narrative case for restrictive hunting laws.[77]

By the end of the century, sportsmen and animal lovers alike would be concerned for many species, above all, for the buffalo. Long before Henry George deplored their disappearance, John James Audubon, himself a skilled marksman, had noted their precipitous decline. "What a terrible destruction of life as it were for nothing," he sadly mused in 1843. "Daily we see so many that we hardly notice them more than the cattle in our pastures about our homes. But this cannot last; even now there is a perceptible difference in the size of the herds, and before many years the Buffalo, like the Great Auk, will have disappeared."[78] From the early 1820s, when buffalo roamed in enormous herds even east of the Mississippi, until the mid-1880s, when they were reduced to a scraggly few, hunters and travelers concurred on their steady demise.[79] The *even nows* and *before longs* abound

---

[74] This is John Reiger's main thesis in *American Sportsmen and the Origins of Conservation.* See also Starr, *Americans and the California Dream,* p. 176. For two convincing examples of conservationist hunters, see William Elliott, *Carolina Sports by Land and Water* (1867?; rpt. Columbia, S.C.: State Co., 1918), pp. 252-60, and Samual H. Hammond, *Wild Northern Scenes; or Sporting Adventures with the Rifle and the Rod* (New York: Derby and Jackson, 1857), p. 83.

[75] Irving, *Captain Bonneville,* ed. Todd, p. 372; Irving, *Astoria,* pp. 516-17.

[76] Irving, *Captain Bonneville,* ed. Todd, p. 372.

[77] Cooper, *The Pioneers,* pp. 270-74.

[78] Cited in Francis Hobart Herrick, *Audubon the Naturalist: A History of His Life and Time,* 2d ed., 2 vols. (New York: D. Appleton-Century Co., 1938), 2:255-56.

[79] See Edwin James, *Account of an Expedition from Pittsburgh to the Rocky Mountains,* 2 vols. (1822-23; rpt. Ann Arbor: University Microfilms, 1966), p. 472; William A. Bell, *New Tracks in North America: A Journal of Travel and Adventure Whilst Engaged in the Survey for a Southern Railroad to the Pacific Ocean During 1867-8* (Albuquerque: Horn and Wallace, 1965), p. xx; Col. Richard Irving Dodge, *The Plains of the Great West and Their Inhabitants* (New York: G. P. Putnam's Sons, 1877), pp. 131-32; George Bird Grinnell, *The Passing of the Great West: Selected Papers of George Bird Grinnell,* ed. John F. Reiger (New York: Winchester Press, 1972), pp. 62, 65, 118-19; Pierre Jean de Smet, S.J., *Western Missions and Missionaries: A Series of Letters* (1859) (2d ed. 1863; rpt. Shannon: Irish University Press, 1972), pp. 5, 55; Messiter, *Sport and Adventures,* p. v; Col.

in their narratives, as if many observers realized that the scenes they were describing rarely equaled those seen by the earlier travelers whose accounts had inspired their own westward journeys. "Taming" the land seemed to require exterminating the species.

By the 1880s, the federal government finally grew alarmed at the dire prospects for the buffalo. Along with the bald eagle and the wild turkey, the buffalo had always seemed to symbolize the spirit of America itself. Yet hunting proceeded ruthlessly, and even the attempt to supplement stuffed models in the national collection seemed an eleventh-hour effort. Spencer F. Baird, secretary of the Smithsonian Institution (who had been nominated for the job, appropriately, by Audubon), decided in the mid-1880s to inaugurate a search for a representative bison before the species' extinction:

> The work of exterminating the American bison had made most alarming progress, and also . . . the representatives of this species then in the National Museum were far from being what they should be. . . . Realizing the imperative need of securing at once and at all hazards a complete and unexceptional series of fresh skins for mounting, before it should become too late, the Secretary directed the chief taxidermist, Mr. Hornaday, to take immediate steps toward the accomplishment of that end.[80]

William Hornaday's subsequent report severely criticized the national attitudes that had led to the crisis. He hoped a lesson had been learned that would benefit other large indigenous game. In phrasing similar to Henry George's, he declared, "A continuation of the record we have lately made as wholesale butchers will justify posterity in dating us back with the mound-builders and cave-dwellers, when man's only function was to slay and eat."[81] Hornaday at last won protection for the few buffalo herds that remained.

The shaggy buffalo head came to represent the issue of game preservation at about the time that other wildlife species acquired

---

Randolph Barnes Marcy, *Thirty Years of Army Life on the Border* (New York: Harper and Brothers, 1866), pp. 334ff.; George Frederick Ruxton, *Ruxton of the Rockies*, ed. LeRoy R. Hafen (Norman: University of Oklahoma Press, 1950), pp. 249, 252; Theodore B. Comstock, cited in Reiger, *American Sportsmen*, p. 99. See also Frank Luther Mott, *A History of American Magazines, 1865-1885*, 3 (Cambridge, Mass.: Harvard University Press, 1938), pp. 60-61; Robertson, "An Army Hunter's Notes," p. 305.

[80] Spencer F. Baird, "Letter from the Secretary of the Smithsonian Institution," in *Annual Report of the Board of Regents of the Smithsonian Institution for the Year Ending June 30, 1887* (Washington: G.P.O., 1889), pp. 5-6.

[81] Hornaday, *The Extermination of the American Bison* (Washington: G.P.O., 1889), p. 464.

constituencies working on their behalf. After the Civil War, books and essays increasingly helped to inform national discussion on the subject, detailing threats to wild cattle, elk, deer, antelope, mountain sheep, and even wolves.[82] An article from 1870 is representative in its concluding hope: "May you and I, my reader, live to see the day when the game-laws of our land, now inefficient and worthless, shall be redeemed; when the wholesale, cruel, indiscriminate, and unmanly slaughter which is now carried on shall be abolished."[83] The 1860s had already witnessed the first organized concern for declining wildlife in the formation of the Audubon Society and the American Ornithological Union, meant to protect bird species threatened by millinery fashion's insatiable demand for feathers.[84] Sportsmen's associations such as the Boone and Crockett Club and the Rocky Mountain Sportsmen's Association would soon organize outdoorsmen to call for further protective government legislation and for more energetic enforcement of existing laws.[85] By the end of a century often characterized as driven by brute manifest destiny, one popular author found it possible seriously to claim: "Animals are creatures with wants and feelings differing in degree only from our own."[86]

The patrician George Bird Grinnell (1849-1938) may seem an unlikely choice as the figure most representative of these and other aspects of wilderness conservation. Nevertheless, in addition to helping to found nearly all of the organizations mentioned above, he publicly, tirelessly, and self-effacingly encouraged far-sighted national

[82] See Robertson, "An Army Hunter's Notes," p. 308; Frederick Schwatka, "An Elk-Hunt on the Plains," *Century Magazine*, 35 (January 1888), 447; Frederick Gerstaecker, *Wild Sports in the Far West* (Boston: Crosby, Nichols and Co., 1859), p. v; De Smet, *Western Missions*, p. 5; *Ruxton of the Rockies*, ed. Hafen, pp. 255-57; George P. Belden, *Belden, The White Chief; or Twelve Years Among the Wild Indians of the Plains*, ed. Gen. James S. Brisbin (1870; rpt. Cincinnati: E. W. Starr and Co., 1875), p. 90; *The Journals of Captain Nathaniel J. Wyeth* (Fairfield, Wash.: Ye Galleon Press, 1969), p. 131.

[83] W. Waddle Jr., "The Game Water-Fowl of America," *Harper's New Monthly Magazine*, 40 (February 1870), 437.

[84] See Frank M. Chapman, *Autobiography of a Bird-Lover* (New York: D. Appleton-Century Co., 1933), esp. pp. 37-38, 180-82; Reiger, *American Sportsmen*, esp. pp. 65ff. See also *The Letters of Theodore Roosevelt*, ed. Elting E. Morison, 8 vols. (Cambridge, Mass.: Harvard University Press, 1951), 1:948, 1292, 1421-22.

[85] See Reiger, *American Sportsmen*. See also *American Big-Game Hunting: The Book of the Boone and Crockett Club*, ed. Theodore Roosevelt and George Bird Grinnell (New York: Forest and Stream Publishing Co., 1893), pp. 9-10, 240-70, 326-33; *American Big Game Hunting in Its Haunts*, ed. George Bird Grinnell (New York: Forest and Stream Publishing Co., 1904), p. 7; Earl Pomeroy, *In Search of the Golden West: The Tourist in Western America* (New York: Alfred A. Knopf, 1957), pp. 93-94.

[86] Ernest Seton-Thompson, *Wild Animals I Have Known* (New York: Charles Scribner's Sons, 1898), p. 12.

policies toward birds, buffalo, and large game, as well as toward forests and wilderness areas. Grinnell could lay claim to a number of conservation firsts, including the very use of the word *conservation* in its modern ecological sense.[87] As a young scientist accompanying the famous Ludlow expedition to Yellowstone in 1875, he wrote a letter included in the official report, a plea for federal restrictions on hide hunters.[88] The initial issue of *Forest and Stream* (1873), the publication he had helped to found and would edit through the last quarter of the century, proclaimed battle on all those willing to see American forests diminished. The magazine provided a continuing forum for writers who favored restricting development of natural resources. In the early 1880s, Grinnell vigorously endorsed the "Save the Adirondacks" campaign, which resulted in 715,000 acres being set aside as state forests. His editorials on game extinction in Yellowstone during the same period, and his later defense of the national park system, aroused sportsmen against the depredations of industry, fashion, land speculation, and a thoughtlessly westering mentality. Grinnell became the leader of America's conservation movement just when it was gaining an identifiable constituency.[89]

Of course, concern for the threatened landscape was not a matter for sportsmen alone. Increasing leisure time and disposable income in the post-Civil War period offered greater numbers of men and women the opportunity to hunt and fish, which in turn swelled the constituency supporting conservation at a national level. In addition, these economic forces spawned the middle-class western tourist.[90] Earlier in the century, travel had at best meant discomfort and delay; at worst, it involved genuine danger. Besides, it required substantial means, and only the adventurous and restless felt the effort worth the expense. With the completion of the transcontinental railway in 1869, cross-country travel became steadily safer, more reliable and comfortable, and increasingly attractive to Americans of moderate means. Among those who embarked on western excursions, some returned in alarm at what they had witnessed. The buffalo they had come to marvel at had been thoughtlessly sacrificed to the very railroad crews that made their trips possible. Wonder gave way to regret as they glimpsed uniquely American scenes that their children would never know.

[87] Reiger, *American Sportsmen*, p. 84. Reiger's is the finest treatment of Grinnell's efforts on behalf of conservation.

[88] Grinnell, *Passing of the Great West*, ed. Reiger, pp. 118-19.

[89] See Pomeroy, *In Search of the Golden West*, pp. 93-94.

[90] See ibid. for background to this section.

CONSERVATION

Roderick Nash has sharply observed those factors unique to America that contributed to national conservationist activity in the nineteenth century: a public domain; tracts of wilderness still untenanted; settlement patterns; and the national affluence that made preservation of natural resources conceivable at all. In Nash's wry phrasing: "Ironically, our success in exploiting the environment increased the likelihood of its protection."[91] Out of the nineteenth century's particular pairing of opportunities and apprehensions, Americans "invented" a national park and forest reserve system. Conservation, at least by the last two decades of the nineteenth century, gained headlines in newspapers, supporters in legislatures, and students in new university schools of forestry. The examples of German forestry measures and royal hunting preserves in England fundamentally influenced American thinking, to be sure.[92] But even the conservation ideas propounded in Europe had been reciprocally shaped by the thinking of Americans, in particular by George Perkins Marsh (1801-1882).

Marsh's varied career as lawyer, businessman, linguist, politician, and diplomat offers little clue to the seminal importance of his ideas on conservation. In the 1840s, as a one-term congressman from Vermont, he had lobbied vigorously for a national museum to preserve artifacts of natural and human history. Joining forces with John Quincy Adams, he persuaded his colleagues to use the bequest of the English scientist James Smithson to establish such an institution.[93] Through this and like efforts, Marsh gained a reputation as the defender of a variety of endangered objects, from human artifacts to state forests and woodlands. In an 1847 speech to a Vermont agricultural society, he condemned devastation of the landscape and called for a prohibition on agricultural clearing in order that future generations might enjoy American wilderness.[94] Seventeen years later, Marsh extended these ideas in a profound study of conservation that ranks among the seminal works of the nineteenth century. Appearing long before the word *ecology* even existed, *Man and Nature* (1864) assiduously defines that science, much as Grinnell had first helped

[91] Roderick Nash, "American Invention of National Parks," pp. 726-34.

[92] See Clarence J. Glacken, "Changing Ideas of the Habitable World," in William L. Thomas, ed., *Man's Role in Changing the Face of the Earth* (Chicago: University of Chicago Press, 1956), p. 74.

[93] David Lowenthal, *George Perkins Marsh: Versatile Vermonter* (New York: Columbia University Press, 1958), pp. 82ff.

[94] Marsh, *Address Delivered Before the Agricultural Society of Rutland County, Sept. 30, 1847* (Rutland, Vt.: n.p., 1848), esp. pp. 17-19.

to develop conservation into firm legislative policies. The book became, in Lewis Mumford's words, "the fountain-head of the conservation movement."[95]

Marsh opens with an indictment of characteristic western European thoughtlessness about the natural environment: "Man has too long forgotten that the earth was given to him for usufruct alone, not for consumption, still less for profligate waste."[96] Quickly moving beyond moral outrage, he demonstrates in chapter-by-chapter analysis the tremendous economic waste exacted by the carnage of buffalo, beaver, cattle, walrus, and whales. That whole species neared extinction seemed condemnation enough. Even worse, in his judgment, was the threatened imbalance of entire ecological systems. Deforestation, for instance, results first in blighted landscapes, then in drought, flooding, mud slides, and general soil exhaustion. Its effects were already apparent: "The earth is fast becoming an unfit home for its noblest inhabitant, and another era of equal human crime and human improvidence . . . would reduce it to such a condition of impoverished productiveness, of shattered surface, of climatic excess, as to threaten the deprivation, barbarism, and perhaps even extinction of the species."[97] Wantonly to kill animals or destroy trees meant simply to threaten one's own welfare.

To Marsh, the solution seemed obvious, at least politically: each state should preserve the woodland it presently possessed. True material progress, as contrasted with hasty national expansion, could be achieved only through social foresight. "Careful control and intelligent planning" might help to heal the wounds already inflicted.[98] Marsh's conclusion recalls Thomas Cole's earlier plea: "It is . . . a question of vast importance, how far it is practicable to restore the garden we have wasted."[99]

Man and Nature drew a highly favorable response both in war-torn America and abroad, selling out its first edition within months. Subsequent editions and translations brought Marsh firm disciples, including Muir and Olmsted, who developed his proposals into practical legislation. According to Marsh's biographer:

Together with the enthusiasm for tree-planting, which swept the country in the Arbor Day movement, *Man and Nature* inaugu-

---

[95] Mumford, *Brown Decades*, p. 78.

[96] Marsh, *Man and Nature* (1864), ed. David Lowenthal (Cambridge, Mass.: Harvard University Press, 1965), p. 36.

[97] Ibid., p. 43. [98] Ibid., p. 272.

[99] Ibid., p. 353. See as well Marsh, "The Study of Nature," *Christian Examiner*, 5th ser., 68 (January 1860), esp. p. 33.

rated a revolutionary reversal of American attitudes toward resources. It stimulated the American Association for the Advancement of Science to submit a memorial on forests to Congress in 1873; the outcome was a national forestry commission, the establishment of forest reserves and the national forest system in 1891, then watershed protection, eventually a governmental program for the conservation of all natural resources. A quarter of a century after Marsh's death, *Man and Nature* was still the only work in its field.[100]

However, with the exception of Carl Schurz, Secretary of the Interior Department under President Hayes, federal policy remained indifferent to conservation in the decades following the Civil War. Lower-ranking government officials, including John Wesley Powell and W. J. McGee, read Marsh, but it was not until the late 1880s that they would finally effect new federal policies on land usage and development.[101] Counseled by his good friend Gifford Pinchot, President

[100] Lowenthal, *George Perkins Marsh*, p. 268. The methods of Marsh's disciples are discussed by Lowenthal on pp. 246ff. For only two examples, see N. H. Egleston, "What We Owe to the Trees," *Harper's New Monthly Magazine*, 64 (April 1882), 675-82; G. W. Powell, "American Forests," ibid., 59 (August 1879), 371-74.

[101] See Claude Moore Fuess, *Carl Schurz: Reformer (1829-1906)* (New York: Dodd, Mead and Co., 1932), pp. 267-68; Wallace Stegner, *Beyond the Hundredth Meridian: John Wesley Powell and the Second Opening of the West* (Boston: Houghton Mifflin Co., 1954), pp. 6, 210ff.; John Upton Terrell, *The Man Who Rediscovered America: A Biography of John Wesley Powell* (New York: Weybright and Talley, 1969), pp. 1-8; Henry Nash Smith, "Clarence King, John Wesley Powell, and the Establishment of the United States Geological Survey," *Mississippi Valley Historical Review*, 34 (June 1947), 37-58; William Goetzmann, *Exploration and Empire: The Explorer and the Scientist in the Winning of the American West* (New York: Alfred A. Knopf, 1966), esp. pp. 530-31; W. J. McGee, "The Conservation of Natural Resources," *Proceedings of the Mississippi Valley Historical Association*, 3 (1909-10), 361-79; Bernhard Eduard Fernow, *Economics of Forestry: A Reference Book for Students of Political Economy and Professional and Lay Students of Forestry* (New York: Thomas Y. Crowell, 1902), esp. pp. 1-10, 369ff.; Fernow, *Report upon the Forestry Investigations of the United States Department of Agriculture, 1877-1898* (Washington: G.P.O., 1899), pp. 3-6. For good general surveys of the development of conservationist sentiments toward the end of the nineteenth century, see: Ekirch, *Man and Nature in America*, esp. pp. 70-120; Hampton, *How the U.S. Cavalry Saved Our National Parks*, esp. pp. 18ff.; Russell Lord, *The Care of the Earth: A History of Husbandry* (New York: Thomas Nelson and Sons, 1962), pp. 225-47; Maxine E. McCloskey and James P. Gilligan, eds., *Wilderness and the Quality of Life* (New York: Sierra Club, 1969), pp. vii, 66-73; Roderick Nash, *Wilderness and the American Mind*, pp. 96-160; Nash, ed., *The American Environment: Readings in the History of Conservation* (Reading, Mass.: Addison-Wesley, 1968), pp. 24-71; Russel B. Nye, *This Almost Chosen People: Essays in the History of American Ideas* (East Lansing: Michigan State University Press, 1966), pp. 256-304; Robert Shankland, *Steve Mather of the National Parks* (New York: Alfred A. Knopf, 1951), pp. 4, 48ff.; Donald C. Swain, *Wilderness Defender: Horace M. Albright and Conservation* (Chicago: University of Chicago

Theodore Roosevelt, looking back on a long history of developing apprehensions as well as more recent efforts responsibly to ease them, succeeded in making conservation a major component of his domestic policy. Together, the President and his chief of the forestry division of the Department of Agriculture withdrew tens and hundreds of thousands of acres from the public domain; encouraged game legislation, as well as stricter enforcement of existing laws; and they provided government grants for universities to establish forestry departments.[102] In a variety of fashions, the public encouraged its legislators, and was encouraged by them, to save what remained of the once unspoiled continent.

CONCLUSION

The widespread public commitment to conservation reflects only one aspect of concern for the wilderness—important historically, to be sure, but less a development in the concept of "wilderness" than in that of preservation. By the time Americans appreciated the natural landscape enough to want to save actual forests and wildlife, the need for mere records had subsided. Only a few diehards any longer rushed west with pencils in hand to transcribe the landscape. That "wilderness," Americans had come to recognize, deserved preservation in fact, not on paper.

Apprehension about the landscape radiated out along the fissures of Americans' awareness, and—whatever the hopes for America's prospects—this feeling encouraged efforts both to record it and to save it. Wilderness, after all, remains a vaguely idyllic sanctuary only so long as one remains in the East. Come west, and immediately its soft outlines firm. The rubrics of "wilderness" and "frontier" break down not only into slaughtered flocks of passenger pigeons and herds of buffalo, devastated forests, and mine-ravaged mountain valleys, but they also bring to mind other images and activities, including fur trapping, prospecting, pioneer farming, and cow-punching. Material

Press, 1970), esp. pp. 46ff.; Runte, *National Parks*; Andrew Denny Rodgers III, *Bernhard Eduard Fernow: The Story of North American Forestry* (Princeton: Princeton University Press, 1951). For a corrective to some of the overstatements of these books, see Sherry H. Olson, *The Depletion Myth: A History of Railroad Use of Timber* (Cambridge, Mass.: Harvard University Press, 1971), esp. pp. 31-40, 75ff., 178-92. Also see Udall, *Quiet Crisis*, pp. 81-170.

102 William H. Harbaugh, *The Life and Times of Theodore Roosevelt*, rev. ed. (New York: Oxford University Press, 1963), pp. 304ff.; Harold T. Pinkett, *Gifford Pinchot: Private and Public Forester* (Urbana: University of Illinois Press, 1970), esp. pp. 44-81; M. Nelson McGeary, *Gifford Pinchot: Forester-Politician* (Princeton: Princeton University Press, 1960).

progress threatened these vocations just as predictably as it did the land, and with an intrinsic irony: human success at these activities posed a threat to the land and thereby, finally, to the very way of life that had made success possible. Far-sighted individuals realized this danger and set about to ensure that frontier life would not pass unrecorded, that successive generations would know it as something more than embellished myth. If their histories took an affectionate, sometimes uncritical perspective, it was because they recognized how imperiled the white frontier was.

CHAPTER THREE

PRESERVING
FRONTIER HISTORY

[T]o record the events connected with the early history of the country, to note characteristics of its early inhabitants, to delineate the privations and hardships experienced by its pioneers . . . is a useful and laudable undertaking. . . . [It] will soon be the only record left of a class of people fast fading from the view of those who now occupy the stage of public life.

—*Henry S. Baird*
"Recollections of the Early History
of Northern Wisconsin" (1859)

All these subjects of my description—men, conditions of life, races of aboriginal inhabitants, and adventurous hunters and pioneers—are passing away. . . . It can not be entirely in vain that any one contributes that which he knows from personal experience, however little, to aid in preserving the memory of the people and the customs of the West in the middle of the nineteenth century.

Col. Randolph Barns Marcy
Thirty Years of Army Life on the Border
(1866)

$\mathcal{J}$o Hector St. John de Crèvecoeur fully shared his contemporaries' belief in westward progress. His *Journey in Northern Pennsylvania and the State of New York* (1801)—that lively journal-dialogue of frontier peregrinations made more than thirty years earlier—rarely strays from well-beaten paths through the intellectual wilderness. At one point, however, Crèvecoeur remarks on the whirlwind transformation of pioneer communities and unexpectedly suggests preserving their scattered ruins, the "traces of the passing of generations that preceded us." He adds: "instead of hastening the ruin of this debris, one should consider its destruction a sacrilege; its conservation a religious act."[1]

At the turn of the century, Crèvecoeur's adjuration stands alone, unsupported by him and ignored by others. His contemporaries no more considered preserving log cabins than woodlands; nor did they deem worthwhile a record of those who had built the cabins and developed the land. Yet during the nineteenth century, as many came to value a threatened wilderness, concern also grew for the pioneers who were being similarly displaced. By mid-century, Francis Parkman could assume that public consensus had shifted. In his eulogy of James Fenimore Cooper he claimed that Cooper's fame would endure for more than artistic reasons. The novelist had ensured the "permanent remembrance" of a "class of men" suddenly swept from history.[2]

Although Parkman referred to only one frontier type, the hunter-trapper represented by Leatherstocking, material progress had also swept aside a distressing number of other characteristically American classes of men and women. The shift from early frontier settlements to burgeoning agricultural and industrial centers transformed Americans even as they transformed the landscape.[3] Nor were the evolving characteristics of American life the result merely of accumulating assumptions; also critical was a casting off of old ways. Americans became their most distinctive selves through the activities and vocations that sprang up, blossomed, and died off like rare prairie wildflowers,

[1] Crèvecoeur, *Journey into Northern Pennsylvania and the State of New York* (1801), trans. Clarissa Spencer Bostelmann, 3 vols. in 1 (Ann Arbor: University of Michigan Press, 1964), p. 102.

[2] Francis Parkman, "The Works of James Fenimore Cooper," *North American Review*, 74 (January 1852), 151. Parkman himself had performed a similar service in his portrait of the mountain man and guide Henri Chatillon (1816-1875), in *The Oregon Trail* (1849).

[3] Frederick Jackson Turner first formulated this, his frontier theory, in his essay, "The Significance of the Frontier in American History" (1893).

never to bloom again. Trappers, keelboatmen, and placer miners; pony express riders and cowboys; army scouts, stagecoach hands, and booster newspapermen—among a myriad of other types, these burst onto the western scene as quickly as buffalo disappeared from it, and then vanished themselves before the next, scarcely more stable arrivals. Frequently, apocryphal anecdotes of their exploits alone survived. Or, as one self-styled "gold miner, trader, merchant, rancher and politician" mused at the turn of the century, "It would be impossible to make persons not present on the Montana cattle ranges realize the rapid change that took place on those ranges in two years. In 1880 the country was practically uninhabited. One could travel for miles without seeing so much as a trapper's bivouac. Thousands of buffalo darkened the rolling plains. . . . In the fall of 1883 there was not one buffalo remaining. . . . In 1880 no one had heard tell of a cowboy . . . but in the fall of 1883 there were six hundred thousand head of cattle on the range."[4]

The land had always demanded as much in energy and adaptability, imagination and sheer brute force as it promised in opportunity. But by the 1880s, Americans' power to alter the land, and thereby to be altered themselves, had risen exponentially. They rarely argued against that power or its promise, of course, however buffeted they felt by gusts of progress. Jobs went out of date like fashions, almost annually, and boom and ghost towns only underscored the difficulty of prophesying what or where development would occur. The enthusiastic pioneer quoted above marveled at the transformation of an entire region, the miraculous advent of a whole way of life. Others, though equally impressed by the pace of change, could only regret the lost ways. Out West in 1894 to collect material for stories that would eventually mythicize the cowboy, Owen Wister wrote to his patrician Philadelphian mother, "The frontier has yielded to a merely commonplace society. . . . The survivors of Tombstone sit there and dwell on how things used to be. In 1882 there were from six to eight thousand people; there are now six hundred, and all over the adjacent hills stand silent silver mines—the machinery rusty, falling to pieces, and a good deal of it burned."[5]

Such matter-of-fact observations on the rapidity of change and its human toll were commonplace long before the end of the century.

[4] *Forty Years on the Frontier as seen in the Journals and Reminiscences of Granville Stuart, Gold-Miner, Trader, Merchant, Rancher and Politician*, ed. Paul C. Phillips, 2 vols. (1925; rpt. Glendale, Calif.: Arthur H. Clark Co., 1957), 2:187-88.

[5] *Owen Wister Out West: His Journals and Letters*, ed. Fanny Kemble Wister (Chicago: University of Chicago Press, 1958), p. 210.

To be sure, frontier conditions had been altering ever since the settlement of Jamestown and the Massachusetts Bay Colony. Yet reflections on those altering conditions only begin to appear around 1820, as already noted. The land needed to be stamped "American" by wars in 1776 and 1812 before its citizens came to recognize that their national heritage was the vanishing landscape.

Individuals felt impelled to preserve records of passing white history only as that history also began to seem uniquely and nationally American. As the society grew self-conscious about its claim to a special identity, a more demanding audience, its nationalist appetite whetted, consumed all kinds of histories, biographies, and genre paintings and illustrations. In the words of one energetic publisher of American works, "the tendency of the present age has been justly and philosophically designated historick."[6] Americans wanted to find out all about themselves. They also wanted to ensure that the contemporary selves they did know would be preserved—written about, painted, or photographed—before passing from the western scene. This is hardly surprising. Indeed, it is less remarkable that the trapper's rapid advent and decline should have prompted anxious attempts at documentation than that the buffalo's far slower demise, as we have seen, encouraged similar endeavors.

The reasons for these attempts are as diverse as their subjects. Even more than those who first documented the landscape, recorders of frontier life strove to present exotic instances of the American experience to jaded easterners. Rocky Mountain fur trader Hugh Glass, for example, inspired countless writers with his incredible story of survival in the 1820s. Left for dead by his companions after having been horribly mauled by a grizzly bear, Glass crawled more than a hundred miles, feeding on berries and buffalo carcasses, before reaching aid. Setting out after his former companions, he joined a party that was soon attacked by Indians. Glass alone escaped with his life. After further trials and failures, he finally caught up with his companions, confronted them, and recovered his rifle. Glass's exploits are the stuff of legend. Yet, however unreliable such accounts, whatever the impulse to record them, Americans recognized a transience to these and less extraordinary frontier experiences.

Mountain men and frontiersmen themselves sometimes wrote with

---

6 Cited in Eric F. Goldman, "The Historians," in Robert E. Spiller et al., eds., *Literary History of the United States: History*, 3d ed. rev. (New York: Macmillan Co., 1963), pp. 526-27. See for a good general survey, George H. Callcott, *History in the United States, 1800-1860: Its Practice and Purpose* (Baltimore: Johns Hopkins University Press, 1970), esp. pp. 25-53, 83-173.

the clear intention of setting the record straight. They wanted to humanize the mythical pose into which writers like Cooper had cast them and to correct Americans' distorted view of their history and perhaps of their illiteracy.[7] Those lacking firsthand experience sought out old hunters and trappers or collected extensive records in order to depict what the popular novelist Timothy Flint characterized in 1831 as "a race passing unrecorded from history."[8]

Whether buckskin-fringed scout or gregarious flatboatman, hunter or trapper, the frontiersman represents only one colorful aspect of American life in the West. Likewise, those who labored to preserve records of him represent only part of a more considerable movement. Long-suffering "black-robes" and frontier camp revivalists; battles between "blue coats" and recalcitrant tribes; county wars between ranchers and farmers—all were recognizably passing from experience and were salvaged for history by anxious observers.[9] Old frontier ways acquired a retrospective allure they may only rarely have held for those who learned them of necessity. The allure was especially strong in a nation progressively more self-conscious about what it was sacrificing to the charms of progress. More important, these fleeting

[7] For instance, see Howard Louis Conrad, *"Uncle Dick" Wootton, the Pioneer Frontiersman of the Rocky Mountain Region* (Chicago: W. E. Dribble and Co., 1890), preface (unpaginated); William Thomas Hamilton, *My Sixty Years on the Plains: Trapping, Trading, and Indian Fighting* (1905; rpt. Norman: University of Oklahoma Press, 1960), p. 3; George Frederick Ruxton, *Life in the Far West*, ed. LeRoy R. Hafen (Norman: University of Oklahoma Press, 1951), esp. pp. xiii, 112.

[8] Timothy Flint, ed., *The Personal Narrative of James O. Pattie of Kentucky* (1831), reprinted in vol. 18 of Reuben Gold Thwaites, ed., *Early Western Travels: 1748-1846*, 32 vols. (Cleveland: Arthur H. Clarke Co., 1904-07), p. 27. See also Col. Randolph Barnes Marcy, *Thirty Years of Army Life on the Border* (New York: Harper and Brothers, 1866), pp. 356, 397; David H. Coyner, *The Lost Trappers: A Collection of Interesting Scenes and Events in the Rocky Mountains* (Cincinnati: J. A. and U. P. James, 1847), p. 240; Samual Asahel Clarke, *Pioneer Days of Oregon History*, 2 vols. (Portland, J. K. Gill Co., 1905), 1:84; Mrs. Anna Brownell Jameson, *Winter Studies and Summer Rambles in Canada*, 2 vols. (New York: Wiley and Putnam, 1839), 2:205; Mrs. Frances Fuller Victor, *The River of the West: Life and Adventure in the Rocky Mountains and Oregon* (Hartford, Conn.: R. W. Bliss and Co., 1869), pp. iv-vi; John Crittenden Duval, *Early Times in Texas* (Austin: H.P.N. Gammel and Co., 1892), preface (unpaginated).

[9] Rev. Asa Mahan, *Autobiography: Intellectual, Moral and Spiritual* (London: T. Woolmer, 1882), p. 215; Rev. Stephen R. Beggs, *Pages from the Early History of the West and North-West* (Cincinnati: Methodist Book Concern, 1868), introduction by T. M. Eddy (unpaginated); Mrs. Margaret I. Carrington, *Absaraka, Home of the Crows* (1868), ed. Milo Milton Quaife (Chicago: R. R. Donnelley and Sons, 1950), pp. 63-64; Gen. Randolph B. Marcy, *Border Reminiscences* (New York: Harper and Brothers, 1872), pp. v-vi, 358; James W. Steele, *Frontier Army Sketches* (Chicago: Jansen, McClurg and Co., 1883), pp. 3-4; John Bauman, "On a Western Ranche," *Fortnightly Review*, new ser., 41 (1887), 516, 535; Emerson Hough, *The Story of the Cowboy* (New York: D. Appleton and Co., 1897), pp. v-vi.

forms of life were not to be abandoned in this the most forward-looking of countries and ages without energetic efforts to preserve their images.

GENRE PAINTING AND PHOTOGRAPHY

The impulse to preserve the western experience took its clearest form in the commitment to pictorial representation, a commitment partly registered in the sizable number of painters and illustrators attracted to the frontier. Motives once again resist easy recovery. Moreover, eastern enthusiasm for frontier scenes made most pictorial efforts at best a compound of commercial and historical hopes. Currier and Ives, for instance, identified a strong public desire for sentimental prints of American life and scenery and from mid-century on tapped it with unprecedented success. They produced numerous images of threatened rural and pioneer life as well, though neither publisher ever intimated historical preservation as his motive.[10] Perhaps they did not need to do so. National pride mixed with curiosity to keep genre art popular enough for publishers to look only to profits. On a deeper, psychological level, paintings of passing ways helped to calm forebodings by giving a face to the process of change itself. Pictures of "Home, Sweet Frontier Home" warmed pioneer parlors not just by defining the distance that proud owners had come; they also recalled conditions too easily fading in memory.

Thomas Cole had clarified the aims of the Hudson River School when he pleaded with his countrymen to revere their native scenes. Similarly, America's leading genre artist, George Caleb Bingham (1811-1879)—the only major painter raised on the frontier—identified widely held aspirations in one of his rare comments about art. Referring to the claim that his and his colleagues' paintings would have on future attention, Bingham observed, "The humorous productions of [William Sydney] Mount and others as seen in the 'Bargaining for a horse,' 'The Jolly Flatboatmen' and 'County Election,' assure us that our social and political characteristics as daily and annually exhibited will not be lost in the lapse of time for want of an Art record rendering them full justice."[11] Indeed, one must today consult the work of these painters in order to see what the West looked like in its early settle-

10 Yet see A. K. Baragwanath's introduction to *Currier and Ives: Chronicles of America*, ed. John Lowell Pratt (Maplewood, N.J.: Hammond Inc., 1968), p. 13.
11 Letter written June 19, 1871, cited in Albert Christ-Janer, *George Caleb Bingham of Missouri: The Story of an Artist* (New York: Dodd, Mead and Co., 1940), pp. 109-10.

ment period.¹² The paintings that Bingham completed in the decade after 1845 form an authentic chronicle of the life that Mark Twain would later nostalgically recall. Bingham's canvases of trappers and riverboatmen, of squatters and county politicians self-consciously preserve a way of life never to be restored.¹³

In the late 1830s, at the very time that Bingham first devoted himself to "historic painting," the invention of the daguerreotype encouraged those less patient or well trained to render scenes more simply and objectively.¹⁴ Improvements in the photographic process throughout the century induced practitioners to risk westward travel in order to capture images of what they had hitherto only heard and read about. Celebrated for his stunning photographic record of the Civil War, Alexander Gardner traveled to Kansas in 1867 to preserve images of frontier life.¹⁵ Indeed, the Civil War released dozens of trained battlefield photographers who turned west after Appomattox. Others soon followed. Solomon D. Butcher spent the last quarter of the century compiling a superb chronicle of midwestern homesteading. Starting early in the eighties, George Edward Anderson spent the next forty-odd years shooting thousands of photographs of rural industry, civic activities, and community celebrations in Mormon Utah. Erwin E. Smith devoted himself in the early 1900s to photographing cowboy life on the Texas range. These and others, amateur and professional alike, received little pay for their countless uncommissioned photographs of local life in the West. Few confessed their motives

¹² Henry Worrall, for only one example, pursued a career like Bingham's as a pictorial recorder of western community life, though in the post-Civil War period. See Robert Taft, *Artists and Illustrators of the Old West, 1850-1900* (New York: Charles Scribner's Sons, 1953), pp. 117-28.

¹³ For background on Bingham, see Christ-Janer, *George Caleb Bingham*; E. Maurice Bloch, *George Caleb Bingham: The Evolution of an Artist* (Berkeley: University of California Press, 1967); Larry Curry, *The American West: Painters from Catlin to Russell* (New York: Viking, 1972), pp. 21-22. Contemporaries appreciated Bingham's efforts for similar reasons; see, for example, a statement from an 1847 issue of the *Missouri Republican*: "Mr. Bingham has struck out for himself an entire new field of historic painting, if we may so term it. He has taken our Western rivers, our boats and boatmen, and the banks of the streams for his subjects" (cited in Barbara Novak, *American Painting of the Nineteenth Century: Realism, Idealism, and the American Experience* [New York: Praeger, 1969], pp. 152-53).

¹⁴ The advent of the camera accompanied a renewed concern for detailed accuracy, as described in the preceding chapter. Nor was this a particularly American phenomenon, as many have noted. Susan Sontag, in *On Photography* (New York: Farrar, Straus and Giroux, 1977), has provided a provocative examination of many of the issues to be discussed here and later; see especially pp. 56-62, 65-70.

¹⁵ See Russell E. Belous and Robert A Weinstein, *Will Soule: Indian Photographer at Fort Sill, Oklahoma, 1869-74* (Los Angeles: Ward Ritchie Press, 1969), p. 15.

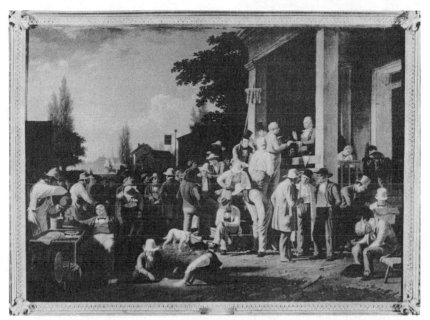

5. George Caleb Bingham, *The County Election (2)*, 1852. Oil on canvas. Collection of The Boatmen's National Bank of St. Louis.

6. Solomon D. Butcher, "Log Cabin of E. S. Finch in Early Days. Built in 1875." From the photograph reproduced in *S. D. Butcher's Pioneer History of Custer County* (Broken Bow, Nebr., 1901).

in writing, whatever their accomplishments.[16] Yet their work, bankruptcies, and broken homes tacitly attest to costly, arduous commitments.

FRONTIER AND PIONEER HISTORIES

An exhaustive record of frontier life could not be compiled through pictures alone. Nor were frontier activities the only subjects of those concerned with rescuing documents. Far less dramatic aspects of western life also cried out to be preserved, and most Americans who responded did so in writing, either from firsthand experience or from others' collected histories. As one amateur historian before mid-century observed about his efforts:

> There having been no historical account published of the first settlement of the Ohio Company at Marietta . . . and the materials on which it was to be founded becoming annually more and more scarce, from the death of the early inhabitants, the author, in the year 1841, was led to commence this difficult, but, to him, pleasant labor. . . . One mode of collecting materials for the history, was to employ some of the few that remained of the first settlers to write down their recollections . . . and by collating these several sketches, the truth could be very nearly ascertained. The larger portion of these men are now dead, and many of the events would have perished with them, had they not been preserved in this manner.[17]

Extraordinary as this man's devotion to the task may seem, such statements of intention might be multiplied almost indefinitely. Even the dull prose is representative, intimating the slogging, unimaginative presentation of so many of these accounts. Too often they merely recite events unique in name and date alone. And in so doing, they defeat their stated purpose by reducing uncommon past experiences to commonplaces.

[16] *Frontier America: The Far West* (Boston: Museum of Fine Arts, 1975), introduction by Jonathan L. Fairbanks, p. 130; J. Evetts Haley, *Life on the Texas Range*, with photographs by Erwin E. Smith (Austin: University of Texas Press, 1952), esp. pp. 15, 18, 23, 29; Rell G. Francis, "Views of Mormon Country: The Life and Photographs of George Edward Anderson," *American West*, 15 (November-December 1978), 14-29. For exceptions to the rule of implicit commitment, see Ferdinand Vandeveer Hayden, *Sun Pictures of Rocky Mountain Scenery* (New York: Julius Bien, 1870), p. 33; *Centenniel State, 1776-1882: A Memorial Offering of the Business Men and Pioneers of Denver, Colorado* (Denver: Rebanks, Wilson and Co., 1882).

[17] S. P. Hildreth, *Pioneer History: Being an Account of the First Examinations of the Ohio Valley and the Early Settlement of the Northwest Territory* (Cincinnati: H. W. Derby and Co., 1848), pp. v-vi.

Yet intention should not be faulted for poor execution. However cliché-ridden and repetitive, these works claim our attention because of their expressed hopes: "Facts and circumstances, which may now be attested to by the living, in a few years, could only be reported upon the faith of tradition."[18] Like the refrain of a backwoods ballad, the plea for old-timers to recollect their experiences recurs. A quick review of such accounts illustrates the limited variety of these pleas, all sung in the same key: "almost too late"; "soon be the only record"; "now was the time"; "might have been lost"; "must now be very quickly done, if done at all"; "an almost-dead past"; "to rescue and preserve some of the doings of the common people."[19] Life in the West was changing as quickly as the landscape, and similar phrasings echo across the continent and the nineteenth century. Kentucky in the 1820s, Ohio and the old Northwest Territory in the 1840s, California in the 1860s—each locale felt similar concern at the time when pioneers settling there began progressively to abandon frontier modes and manners.[20]

Of course, more than a touch of nostalgia fed this impulse, distorting accounts that were in many cases hastily prepared. But the impulse could also encourage accuracy,[21] to the extent that some felt un-

[18] Humphrey Marshall, *The History of Kentucky* (Frankfort: n.p., 1824), introduction (unpaginated).

[19] Respectively, the quotations are from: Charles McKnight, *Our Western Border . . . One Hundred Years Ago* (Philadelphia: J. C. McCurdy and Co., 1875), p. xi; Henry S. Baird, "Recollections of the Early History of Northern Wisconsin," *Collections of the State Historical Society of Wisconsin*, 4 (1859), 197; Alice Polk Hill, *Tales of the Colorado Pioneers* (Denver: Pierson and Gardiner, 1884), preface (unpaginated); Clarke, *Pioneer Days of Oregon History*, 1:iii; Arthur A. Denny, *Pioneer Days on Puget Sound* (1888; rpt. Seattle: Alice Harriman Co., 1908), p. 22; Frances Chamberlain Holley, *Once Their Homes; or, Our Legacy from the Dahkotahs* (Chicago: Donohue and Henneberry, 1890), p. v, also p. 18; John Carr, *Pioneer Days in California* (Eureka, Calif.: Times Publishing Co., 1891), p. 24. See also Charles Loring Brace, *The New West: or, California in 1867-1868* (New York: G. P. Putnam and Son, 1869), pp. iii-iv, 371-73; J.D.B. Stillman, *Seeking the Golden Fleece; A Record of Pioneer Life in California* (San Francisco: A. Roman and Co., 1877), p. 5.

[20] Kevin Starr, in *Americans and the California Dream, 1850-1915* (New York: Oxford University Press, 1973), pp. 110ff., claims that "From the start, Californians cherished their history." The rest of his chap. 4 documents both individual and institutional efforts in this state at mid-century and after. See also Thomas D. Clark, *Frontier America: The Story of the Westward Movement*, 2d ed. (New York: Charles Scribner's Sons, 1969), pp. 22-23; Callcott, *History in the United States*, pp. 67-82.

[21] See, for example, *The American Pioneer: A Monthly Periodical, Devoted to the Objects of the Logan Historical Society; or, To Collecting and Publishing Sketches to the Early Settlement and Successive Improvement of the Country* (Cincinnati), ed. John S. Williams, 1 (January 1842), 3; Ferdinand F. Crèvecoeur, *Old Settlers' Tales . . .* (Onaga, Kan.: n.p., 1902), pp. 3-4; Bela Hubbard, *Memorials of a Half-Century* (New York: G. P. Putnam's Sons, 1887), p. iii; Henry H. Hurlbut, *Chicago Antiquities* (Chicago: n.p., 1881), p. 4; Albert D. Richardson, *Beyond the Mississippi: From the*

equal to the task, ruefully self-conscious about their lack of talent or knowledge.[22] Others awoke to the value of old diaries and letters that preserved what they only much later realized was ephemeral. Still others began to rummage through collections for the public's sake—in the words of one, "simply to rescue from the hopeless oblivion to which they would soon be consigned, a few facts, concerning the people and their doings of those early times, that ought to be preserved, if ever a full and correct history is written."[23] Family pride only partly explains the willingness of relatives of pioneers to meet the expense of printing old reminiscences and family histories, pedestrian accounts and banal correspondence.[24] The larger purpose threading together all of these publishing ventures was a strong preservationist motive.[25]

Great River to the Great Ocean . . . 1857-1867 (Hartford: American Publishing Co., 1867), p. i; J. Fletcher Williams, "A History of the City of St. Paul and of the County of Ramsey, Minnesota," *Collections of the Minnesota Historical Society*, 4 (1876), 3; I. Winslow Ayer, *Life in the Wilds of America, and Wonders of the West in and beyond the Bounds of Civilization* (Grand Rapids, Mich.: Central Publishing Co., 1880), pp. 7-8, 15.

22 See Mrs. John H. [Juliette Augusta] Kinzie, *Wau-Bun, The "Early Day" in the North-West* (New York: Derby and Jackson, 1856), pp. vi-vii; Peter H. Burnett, *Recollections and Opinions of an Old Pioneer* (New York: D. Appleton and Co., 1880), pp. vi-vii; Annie D. Tallent, *The Black Hills; or, The Last Hunting Ground of the Dakotahs* (St. Louis: Nixon-Jones, 1899), pp. v-vii; Francis Parkman, *The Oregon Trail: Sketches of Prairie and Rocky-Mountain Life* (1849), ed. E. N. Feltskog (Madison: University of Wisconsin Press, 1969), pp. viii-ix.

23 Rev. George R. Carroll, *Pioneer Life In and Around Cedar Rapids, Iowa from 1839 to 1849* (Cedar Rapids: n.p., 1895), preface (unpaginated). See also Horatio Hale, *An International Idiom: A Manual of the Oregon Trade Language or "Chinook Jargon"* (London: Whittaker and Co., 1890), pp. 19-20; Alexander Ross, *Adventures of the First Settlers on the Oregon or Columbia River . . .* (1849), reprinted as vol. 7 of Thwaites, ed., *Early Western Travels*, p. 22.

24 Preface to J. W. Spencer, *Reminiscences of Pioneer Life in the Mississippi Valley* (1872), reprinted in Milo Milton Quaife, ed., *The Early Days of Rock Island and Davenport* (Chicago: R. R. Donnelley and Sons, 1942), p. iii. See also Daniel Drake, *Pioneer Life in Kentucky: A Series of Reminiscential Letters from Daniel Drake, M.D., of Cincinnati, to His Children*, ed. Charles Drake (Cincinnati: Robert Clarke and Co., 1870), pp. v-vi; Gabriel Franchère, *Narrative of a Voyage to the Northwest Coast of America in the Years 1811, 1812, 1813, and 1814; or, The First American Settlement on the Pacific* (1820), trans. and ed. J. V. Huntington (1854), reprinted in vol. 6 of Thwaites, ed., *Early Western Travels*, p. 175; Edmund De Schweinitz, *The Life and Times of David Zeisberger: The Western Pioneer and Apostle of the Indians* (Philadelphia: J. B. Lippincott and Co., 1870), pp. 161-62.

25 See, for example, Hermann E. Ludewig, *The Literature of American Local History: A Bibliographical Essay* (New York: R. Craighead, 1846). For a general background to travel literature as well as to local histories during this period, see John Francis McDermott, ed., *Research Opportunities in American Cultural History* (Lexington: University Press of Kentucky, 1961), esp. Thomas Clark, "Travel Literature," pp. 46-65, and Richard M. Dorson, "Folklore and Cultural History," pp. 102-23.

Antiquarians, Historians, and Societies

Preservationist sentiment did not grow uniformly throughout the century, though it is possible to see offhand comments giving way to determined efforts, isolated gestures to committed careers. In some cases, determination and commitment emerged already fully formed. For example, Jared Sparks, later Harvard's and America's first professor of history, undertook the first archival tour of the country in 1826. Examining as many colonial and Revolutionary materials as he could uncover along the eastern seaboard, he returned to his Cambridge study to establish "an editorial assembly-line" where those and other original accounts, purchased and borrowed, could be duplicated.[26]

Though most recorders had neither the time nor the funds for such selfless dedication, some at least shared Sparks's initiative. John Leeds Bozman in Maryland in the 1830s, Reverend William B. Sprague in New York in the 1840s, and Hubert Howe Bancroft in California in the 1850s assiduously sought out pioneers, tracked down books, pamphlets and manuscripts, and ferreted out a wide assortment of other half forgotten and disintegrating materials.[27]

Among these remarkable individuals, Lyman Draper (1815-1891) towers over his contemporaries in his devotion to the task of historical preservation. As a student in Ohio in the mid-1830s, Draper had found himself absorbed by the lives and deeds of local pioneers, and he began to write to them. It occurred to him that "very much precious historical incident must still be treasured up in the memory of aged Western Pioneers, which would perish with them if not quickly rescued."[28] His mission in life soon took form: to search out those individuals, their relatives and descendants; to pry into memories already hazy; to ransack attics and packing barrels for letters and documents; to buy what he could and transcribe what he could not.

Blessed with a charm that made his enthusiasm contagious, Draper convinced Mobile businessman Peter Remsen to become his patron.

[26] Lyman H. Butterfield, "Draper's Predecessors and Contemporaries," in Donald R. McNeil, ed., *The American Collector* (Madison: State Historical Society of Wisconsin, 1955), p. 16; see also p. 7.

[27] See John Leeds Bozman, *The History of Maryland*, 2 vols. (Baltimore: James Lucas and E. K. Deaver, 1837); Hubert Howe Bancroft, *The Early American Chroniclers* (San Francisco: A. L. Bancroft and Co., 1883); "California Historical Society, 1852-1922," *California Historical Society Quarterly*, 1 (July 1922), 10; Butterfield, "Draper's Predecessors and Contemporaries," pp. 11-15.

[28] Draper to Mrs. Lucy S. Green, October 28, 1849. Cited in William B. Hesseltine, *Pioneer's Mission: The Story of Lyman Copeland Draper* (Madison: State Historical Society of Wisconsin, 1954), p. 27. This paragraph relies on Hesseltine's account.

This arrangement freed him to roam the Allegheny region in the 1840s, "delving and rummaging,"[29] interviewing and corresponding, and always collecting. Local antiquarians willingly helped. Following Remsen's death in late 1851, historical societies eagerly offered to house Draper's well-known collection, but the historian needed a new source of funding in order to continue his mission. Moving to Madison, Wisconsin, a year later, he won the appointment of secretary to the State Historical Society in 1854, a post he held for the next thirty years.

Draper's career embodies the strain of apprehension felt by so many of his contemporaries at less committed, less professional levels. As were Reubon T. Durret, William M. Darlington, and Philip Ashton Rollins later in the century, he was an impressive collector of invaluable materials "against accident and the mouldering of time."[30] But he moved beyond even them in encouraging the establishment of antiquarian and historical societies in order to ensure that second-generation settlers, given to discarding reminders of old frontier ways, did not thereby altogether frustrate the possibility of a record.

European countries had long provided models for similar organizations in the form of research libraries and private archives. London's Society of Antiquarians, for instance, had been established in 1572. The evidence suggests, however, that America's historical societies emerged largely uninfluenced by foreign models.[31] First seriously supported in the years following national independence, they proliferated during the antebellum period. During that three-quarters of a century, moreover, the tone with which these sober societies asserted themselves underwent a significant change, reflecting the increasing urgency with which Americans established them. In 1791 Bostonians founded the first such American group, the Massachusetts Historical Society, with calmly measured words: "the professed design of [the society] is, to collect, preserve and communicate materials for a complete history of this country, and accounts of all valuable efforts of human ingenuity and industry, from the beginning of its settle-

29 The phrase is Hesseltine's, in ibid., p. 47. See also *Dr. J.G.M. Ramsey: Autobiography and Letters*, ed. William B. Hesseltine (Nashville: Tennessee Historical Commission, 1954).

30 The phrase is John Leeds Bozman's, in *The History of Maryland*, 1:v; see also pp. viii-ix.

31 Leslie W. Dunlap, *American Historical Societies, 1790-1860* (Madison: privately printed, 1944), pp. 7-19; Henry Nash Smith, "The Widening of Horizons," in Spiller et al., eds., *Literary History of the United States*, pp. 644-46; Arthur Palmer Hudson, "Folklore," in ibid., pp. 717ff.; Jay Martin, *Harvests of Change: American Literature, 1865-1914* (Englewood Cliffs, N.J.: Prentice-Hall, 1967), p. 83n. For a comparative view, see Richard M. Dorson, "Folklore and Cultural History," esp. pp. 104-8.

ment."[32] The resolution inaugurating the Indiana Historical Society in 1830 struck a more forceful, more anxious note: "This meeting is fully impressed with the importance and necessity of collecting and preserving the materials for a comprehensive and accurate history of our country, natural, civil and political, [which] in the absence of well directed efforts to preserve them are rapidly passing into oblivion. . . ."[33] In the 1860s and 1870s, newly admitted western states formed similar organizations in an ever more self-conscious race against time and progress.[34]

The professionalization of antiquarian efforts, combined with the establishment of sixty-five major state and private historical societies by 1860, attests to unusual enthusiasm in a young society. These and similar efforts reached a fever pitch in the immediate post-Civil War years, and the founding of the American Folklore Society in 1888 consolidated hitherto fragmented efforts into a national organization. Ancestral societies such as the Sons of the American Revolution (1889) and the Colonial Dames of America (1890) gave form to this same spirit, which also prompted those further west to establish the Society of California Pioneers (1850) and the Daughters of the Republic of Texas (1891). Perhaps this historical interest was intensified psychologically by a war that destroyed a beloved southern subculture. Or perhaps less precise reasons contributed: a new ease of transcontinental travel, which stepped up the process of change, or an accelerating industrialization and urbanization, which fostered increasing social discontent. More important, after a half century of dizzying national growth, coupled with a new self-consciousness about what "modernization" had displaced, efforts to preserve records of earlier patterns no longer appeared quixotic. On the contrary, respected postbellum figures acquired additional prestige through their efforts to preserve features of pioneer life.

FIVE REPRESENTATIVE FIGURES

Four men who powerfully shaped post-Civil War popular opinion— George Bird Grinnell, Theodore Roosevelt, Frederick Remington,

---

[32] "Circular Letter of the Historical Society," *Proceedings of the Massachusetts Historical Society*, 1 (1791-1835), 1. See also Roy Harvey Pearce, *Savagism and Civilization: A Study of the Indian and the American Mind*, rev. ed. (Baltimore: Johns Hopkins University Press, 1965), 112-14; "Petition to the Massachusetts Legislature" (October 1812), *American Antiquarian Society Collections*, 1 (1820), 17-18.

[33] "Minutes of the Indiana Historical Society for December 11, 1830," *Indiana Historical Society Publications: Proceedings of the Indiana Historical Society, 1830-1836*, 1 (1897), 9.

[34] For one example among many, see the "General Circular Issued by the State Librarian," *Pioneer Collections: Report of the Pioneer Society of the State of Michigan*, 1 (1877), 3-4.

and Owen Wister—all grew up in eastern, patrician families. As young men, they attended either Harvard or Yale; in their early twenties, each traveled to Montana or the Dakotas. Enamored of western life, Remington and Roosevelt even bought sizable ranches. Common backgrounds, interests, and experiences encouraged friendships and influences among them and make them an unusually representative group. Once again, their individual popularity hinged upon a growing public interest in efforts on behalf of wilderness preservation and frontier history; but that interest took shape in turn from their own accomplishments.

Easily the most popular of the four, Roosevelt (1858-1919) is usually remembered for his bold conservation policy while president. Nearly two decades before being elected president, he wrote a series of essays from his North Dakota ranch in which his enthusiasm for western ranch life was tempered by a wry regret for its imminent demise. It is, he observed, "a phase of American life as fascinating as it is evanescent, and one well deserving an historian."[35] After he returned east to politics and Sagamore Hill, Roosevelt continued to turn out essays lamenting the rude transformation of western landscape and life. Published in popular periodicals such as *Century Magazine*, his accounts of "Frontier Types" and "Ranch Life in the Far West in the Cattle Country" celebrated the occupations still to be found on the frontier: trapper, cowpuncher, horse thief, buckskin maker, highwayman, hunter.[36] He read widely in the literature, corresponded frequently with fellow western artists and historians, and continued throughout his career to press for the West's accurate documentation. Whether or not his direct experiences made him a conservationist later, Roosevelt certainly lent a presidential "seal of approval" to writing about western life.

One of Roosevelt's correspondents was Frederic Remington (1861-1909), who was commissioned by *Century Magazine* to illustrate some of the politician's early genre essays. The young artist grew to admire the writer whose prose so brightly complemented his own style. According to his later recollection, Remington conceived his artistic purpose at nineteen while sitting around a Montana campfire. An old wagon freighter concluded a reminiscence by bemoaning that "now

---

[35] Roosevelt, *Hunting Trips of A Ranchman / Hunting Trips on the Prairie and in the Mountains* (1885; rpt. New York: G. P. Putnam's Sons, 1905), p. 35; see also pp. 24-25, 55, 261, 269-70.

[36] Roosevelt, "Frontier Types," *Century Magazine*, 36 (October 1888), 832-43; "Ranch Life in the Far West," ibid., 35 (February 1888), 495-510. See also "The Ranchman's Rifle on Crag and Prairie," ibid., 36 (June 1888), 200-212; "Sheriff's Work on A Ranch," ibid., 36 (May 1888), 39-51.

7. Frederic Remington, *A Fur Train from the Far North*, 1888. Wood engraving from *Harper's Weekly*, August 25, 1888.

there is no more West." "The old man had closed my very entrancing book almost at the first chapter. I knew the railroad was coming. . . . I knew the wild riders and the vacant land were about to vanish forever—and the more I considered the subject, the bigger the *forever* loomed. Without knowing exactly how to do it, I began to try to record some facts around me, and the more I looked the more the panorama unfolded."[37] This passage, written through nearly a quarter century of affectionate hindsight, helps to explain Remington's stylistic precision, from his first published pictures half a year later, in 1882, through much of the career to follow. By the end of the eighties, both subject matter and treatment allowed him to command hefty commissions from America's best-selling periodicals, including *Harper's Weekly*, *Century Magazine*, and *Outing Magazine*.

[37] Cited in Harold McCracken, *Frederic Remington: Artist of the Old West* (Philadelphia: J. B. Lippincott Co., 1947), pp. 34, 36. See also G. Edward White, *The Eastern Establishment and the Western Experience: The West of Frederic Remington, Theodore Roosevelt, and Owen Wister* (New Haven: Yale University Press, 1968), p. 121.

As did Grinnell and Roosevelt, Remington spent much of the 1880s wandering through the West. Success allowed him to travel extensively, but it also constrained him to popular forms. His illustrations, paintings, and sculptures too often border on the sentimental, barely redeemed by their accurate detail, the result of his concern to document what was already past or passing. Even his rather maudlin essays on aspects of western life rarely fail to point to their subject's evanescence. His popular western stories, collected in *Pony Tracks* (1895) and *Crooked Trails* (1898), incorporate this strain of ephemerality in their very structures. In one, for example, two boys meet an "old-time Texas Ranger" and begin "the approaches by which we hoped to loosen the history of a wild past from one of the very few tongues which can still wag on the days when the Texans, the Comanches, and the Mexicans chased one another over the plains of Texas."[38] Other examples imitate this narrative premise of rescuing valuable western lore in the nick of time.

Owen Wister (1860-1938) also looked back from the peak of his success to recall his reasons for writing about the West:

> And so one Autumn evening of 1891, fresh from Wyoming and its wild glories, I sat in the club dining with a man as enamored of the West as I was. . . . From oysters to coffee we compared experiences. Why wasn't some Kipling saving the sage-brush for American literature, before the sage-brush and all that it signified went the way of the California forty-niner, went the way of the Mississippi steamboat, went the way of everything? Roosevelt had seen the sage-brush, true, had felt its poetry; and also Remington, who illustrated his articles so well. But what was fiction doing, fiction, the only thing that has always outlived facts?[39]

Wister had asked himself that question some time earlier and attempted to fill the need. In fact, his trip during that summer of 1891 had been planned in order to study the people of Wyoming, their activities and habits. Wister strove tirelessly to ensure fictional authenticity in a conscious race against time.[40] He too lamented the rapidly changing character of western life, growing at once bitter about civilized progress and mythic in his characterization of the men

---

38 Remington, "How the Law Got into Chaparral," in *Crooked Trails* (1898; rpt. Freeport, N.Y.: Books for Libraries Press, 1969), pp. 1-2, also p. 63.

39 *Owen Wister Out West*, ed. F. K. Wister, pp. 11-12. See also p. 35 for a journal entry dated July 16, 1885, which partly verifies this later recollection.

40 Ben Merchant Vorpahl, ed., *My Dear Wister: The Frederic Remington-Owen Wister Letters* (Palo Alto, Calif.: American West Publishing Co., 1972), p. 28. On Wister's commitment, one should look particularly at *Owen Wister Out West*, ed. F. K. Wister, pp. 123-24, 209-10, for appropriate references in his letters to his mother during the nineties.

and order it replaced. His short stories in the 1890s led finally to *The Virginian* (1902), which not only established the general outlines for subsequent western fiction but also recovered an encyclopedic array of colloquial expressions. By this time, as his preface notes, the Far West had been "tamed."[41]

As we have already seen, George Bird Grinnell, the fourth and eldest member of this group, educated his friends and his generation to the need for forest and wildlife legislation. His career began as a graduate student of the Yale paleontologist O. C. Marsh, on one of whose collecting expeditions he had already traveled west in 1870. That early experience sparked his interest in the West, and during the next forty-odd years, he devoted himself to all forms of preservation—records and objects, wilderness and wild game—as well as to ethnology and frontier history.[42] Late in his life, in a preface to a series of sketches entitled *Beyond the Old Frontier* (1913), Grinnell expressed encouragement about the growing efforts to preserve what remained of western materials:

> Not many years ago a change began to take place in the viewpoint of many Americans. Far-sighted men and women came to feel that the history made by their fathers and mothers was worth preserving, and they began to write and talk about this. What they said fell on sympathetic ears, and interest was easily aroused, so that before long, in many of the Western States historical societies were established, and earnest men gave time and effort to the work of inducing the early settlers to set down their recollections—to describe the events in which they had taken part. Later came the marking of historic spots and trails by monuments.[43]

Roosevelt, Remington, and Wister had won considerable acclaim by the closing decade of the nineteenth century. Contemporary reviewers fully recognized the historical and sociological value of their western records.[44] Yet, even as these critics wrote, the Wild West was

[41] Wister, *The Virginian: A Horseman of the Plains* (1902; rpt. New York: Macmillan Co., 1903), p. viii.

[42] John Reiger suggests that Grinnell's very background encouraged this commitment: "He possessed the aristocrat's dislike for change, a characteristic that compelled him to record his experiences in an effort to preserve—at least on paper—the life they represented" (in Grinnell, *The Passing of the Great West: Selected Papers of George Bird Grinnell*, ed. Reiger [New York: Winchester Press, 1972], p. 2, also pp. 100-104).

[43] Grinnell, *Beyond the Old Frontier: Adventures of Indian-Fighters, Hunters, and Fur Traders* (New York: Charles Scribner's Sons, 1913), p. vii.

[44] See the review of Roosevelt, *The Wilderness Hunter*, in *Atlantic Monthly*, 75 (June 1895), 829-30. For a similar statement, see "Roosevelt's Ranch Life," review of Roosevelt, *Ranch Life and the Hunting Trail*, in *Overland Monthly*, 2d ser., 28 (November 1896), 604.

no longer there for artists to see, much less to preserve through the "sharp realism" admired by their contemporaries.[45] By the close of the century, that landscape could be mapped only in memory or imagination. Artists like Remington and Wister, for all their preservationist intentions, found themselves drawn rather to outsized, mythic renderings. Their willing acceptance of such a style, and the public's enthusiasm for it, suggests a larger issue worth examining later: the growing aversion to eastern, industrial society.

Here, attention should shift for a moment away from these gifted easterners inclined toward nostalgic wistfulness. Perhaps favored backgrounds or national influence and popularity encouraged them to express historiographic motives rarely voiced, though felt, by others. Remington's foremost rival, Charles Marion Russell (1864-1926), for instance, lacked the Yale education and small income that eased Remington's excursions. In 1880, at the age of sixteen, Russell ran away from his St. Louis home to live among the cowboys and Indians of Montana, where he longed to teach himself the skills required to sketch their life. If Russell suffered from the common tendency to sentimentalize the Old West, despite his long apprenticeship in hardship, he nevertheless broke important stereotypes, unlike Remington and artists inferior to them both. For example, he rarely depicted white frontiersmen in conflict with one another or with native tribes. Instead, his vignettes attempt to isolate frontier modes of life, illustrating codes, patterns, and activities from a neutral perspective. The one theme common to his paintings, one spiritually binding all Indians to all frontiersmen, is the threat of mechanical progress. His very titles indicate Russell's resistance: *When Guns Were Their Passports; When Meat Was Plentiful; Before the White Man Came.* Like Wister and Remington, he rued the loss of a frontier world by confirming it in the past tense and then elevating it to the stature of myth. Whether or not he ever articulated the impulse, his paintings express a lifelong commitment to documenting not only those pioneer experiences that were so obviously passing but also those that loomed heroic in memory against the banal exigencies of the present.[46]

[45] "Mr. Remington as Artist and Author," review of Remington, *Crooked Trails*, in *Dial*, 25 (October 16, 1898), 265. See also Julian Ralph, "Frederic Remington," *Harper's Weekly*, 39 (July 20, 1895), 688.

[46] For background on Russell, see: Charles M. Russell, *Good Medicine: Memories of the Real West* (New York: Garden City Publishing Co., 1929); Harold McCracken, *The Charles M. Russell Book: The Life and Work of the Cowboy Artist* (Garden City, N.Y.: Doubleday and Co., 1957); Ramon F. Adams and Homer E. Britzman, *Charles M. Russell: The Cowboy Artist* (Pasadena: Trail's End Publishing Co., 1948); J. Frank

FICTIONAL PRESERVES

The urge to preserve records of life on the frontier was expressed in two characteristic voices, which are easily identifiable late in the century, but can also be discerned in earlier statements. The louder one spoke out for historical documents, and everyone from genre painters and local antiquarians to professional historians and their societies joined in. The second voice, somewhat fainter, expressed a more diffuse commitment to preservation in fictional forms. As Owen Wister demanded after a summer of collecting "local colour," "what was fiction doing, fiction, the only thing that has always outlived facts?"[47] Of course, Americans had always wanted to forge a literature of their own from indigenous materials. That desire bears little relationship to the self-conscious documenting of characteristic, threatened modes of life, however. Cooper, for instance, created one of America's most powerful myths in the figure of Leatherstocking. But his acceptance of the formal conventions of the English novel of manners and the historical romance suggests that he was less concerned at first with establishing a uniquely American fictional world than with recording his experiences.

Other novelists in the 1820s and 1830s shared this commitment, though they only declared it openly in their essays and nonfiction studies. Timothy Flint's *Recollections of the Last Ten Years* (1826), Robert Montgomery Bird's *Peter Pilgrim; or, A Rambler's Recollections* (1838), and Mrs. Caroline Kirkland's *A New Home—Who'll Follow?* (1839) represent, as do the later paintings of Bingham, Remington, and Russell, a considerable investment in documenting frontier experience for its own value. Mrs. Kirkland, for instance, had found life in an early Michigan settlement altogether unlike what she had expected from reading Châteaubriand's sentimental *Atala*. Her trials as a frontier housewife provoked her to a brisk account of pretentious rustic belles and old-maid gossips, crass woodsmen and flamboyant embezzlers, unfailingly generous neighbors and crude frontier holidays. Like Bird and Flint, she aspired to a degree of accuracy about which she seems unduly defensive when she forthrightly offers her book as a "veritable history; an unimpeachable transcript of reality."[48]

Dobie, *The Conservatism of Charles M. Russell* (El Paso: C. R. Smith, 1950); Frank Bird Linderman, *Recollections of Charley Russell*, ed. H. G. Merriam (Norman: University of Oklahoma Press, 1963), esp. pp. 52ff.

[47] *Owen Wister Out West*, ed. F. K. Wister, pp. 11-12.

[48] Caroline Matilda Kirkland, *A New Home—Who'll Follow? or, Glimpses of Western Life* (1839), ed. William S. Osborne (New Haven: College and University Press,

Each of the three popular authors vigorously proclaimed their documentarian intentions, which suggests that in later fictionalizing these settings and subjects, their motives changed little.[49]

Likewise, the attempt accurately to portray frontier life through fiction made a well-worn device, that of a narrator discovering a pioneer's long-forgotten manuscript, a frequently used framework during this period. The first American novel about whaling provides a curious instance. Joseph Hart's *Miriam Coffin* (1834) is now justly ignored by all but literary scholars, whose interest derives solely from Melville's having incorporated sections of it into *Moby-Dick*. Yet its contrived rationale reflects another aspect of the growing concern for frontier histories.[50] In an extended introduction, Hart denies having written the ensuing narrative of eighteenth-century Nantucket. Instead, he claims to have sailed to the island in order to prepare a study of whaling. There he searched out an old pioneer "possessing a remarkably retentive memory,—particularly in what related to the early history of the island." Garrulously answering Hart's queries, the man at last ends the interview by offering his visitor a bulky manuscript, which, he assures Hart, will explain all. It satisfies as well Hart's reiterated desire to preserve such moldering accounts by publishing them.[51]

Such artifices and motifs were by no means restricted to a special brand of pioneer fiction. Following the Civil War, regionalism and the local-color movement rose to prominence, taking over the task of preservation hitherto shouldered by professional and amateur historians. Writers turned to the delineation of local folkways and dialects in order to perpetuate in literature the patterns rapidly being abandoned or disrupted. Their efforts, like those of the artists discussed above, often ease into nostalgia or sacrifice accuracy for an ideal. Yet they were motivated by the same concern we have seen elsewhere, as Carlos Baker notes: "At a crucial period in American history, when

---

1965), p. iii. See also William S. Osborne, *Caroline M. Kirkland* (New York: Twayne Publishers, 1972), esp. pp. 7-10, 36-37.

[49] Timothy Flint, *Recollections of the Last Ten Years Passed in Occasional Residences and Journeyings in the Valley of the Mississippi* . . . (Boston: Cummings, Hilliard, and Co., 1826), pp. 188-89, also pp. 27-28, 53, 203, 389-90; Robert Montgomery Bird, *Peter Pilgrim; or, A Rambler's Recollections* 2 vols. (Philadelphia: Lea and Blanchard, 1838), 1:23; Kirkland, *A New Home*, p. 7.

[50] See Benjamin Keen, *The Aztec Image in Western Thought* (New Brunswick: Rutgers University Press, 1971), pp. 373-74; Louise K. Barnett, *The Ignoble Savage: American Literary Racism, 1790-1890*, Contributions in American Studies, no. 18 (Westport, Conn.: Greenwood Press, 1975), pp. 39-40.

[51] Col. Joseph C. Hart, *Miriam Coffin, or The Whale Fishermen: A Tale* (1834), new ed., 2 vols. in one (San Francisco: H. R. Coleman, 1872), p. xvii; see the whole introduction, pp. ix-xxviii.

old faces, manners, customs, recipes, styles, attitudes, and prejudices were undergoing rapid change or total extirpation, they seized and perpetuated, through the medium of fictional character, the cultural landscape: the native idiom, the still unravished rural peace, the feel and flavor of things as they were, and would never be again."[52]

The local-color and regionalist movements were fueled by paradoxically opposed impulses: on the one hand, writers attempted to idealize the quickly passing; on the other, they wanted to correct idealistically accurate depictions. The efforts of authors who glorified the agrarian past, such as Thomas Nelson Page of Virginia and Sarah Orne Jewett of Maine, and those of western regionalists such as Edgar Watson Howe and Hamlin Garland, whose grim portraits of pioneer life challenge such conceptions, reflect motives essentially aesthetic or sociological rather than historiographic.[53] In any case, local color and regionalism grew more readily in the Northeast and the South than in the West, partly because the West changed almost too rapidly to accommodate serious fiction.[54] There were exceptions, of course. Edward Eggleston wrote *A Hoosier Schoolmaster* (1871), as he said, to subvert James Fenimore Cooper's "unreal world" and to capture in realistic fiction the "manners, customs, thoughts and feelings" of "life in the back-country districts of the Western States."[55] For the most part, however, writers were inadequate to the region—understandably so, given the frenetic rate at which the unstoried frontier gave way to full-scale agrarian and industrial development. The pace of change helps to explain why those who began their careers by writing realistic western fiction often found that they could do justice to the region only by writing histories.[56]

52 Carlos Baker, "Delineation of Life and Character," in Spiller et al., eds., *Literary History of the United States*, p. 861, also pp. 847-48, 856.

53 See Warner Berthoff, *The Ferment of Realism: American Literature, 1884-1919* (New York: Free Press, 1965), pp. 90-100; Martin, *Harvests of Change*, pp. 86-88, 111-59. For a contrasting instance, see Hamlin Garland, *Crumbling Idols: Twelve Essays on Art Dealing Chiefly with Literature Painting and the Drama* (1894), ed. Jane Johnson (Cambridge, Mass.: Harvard University Press, 1960), pp. 59-60, 62, 65.

54 See Baker, "Delineation of Life and Character," pp. 844, 848; Berthoff, *Ferment of Realism*, pp. 90-91.

55 Edward Eggleston, *The Hoosier Schoolmaster* (1871; rpt. New York: Orange Judd Co., 1890), pp. 5-6. See also Ernest E. Leisy, *The American Historical Novel* (Norman: University of Oklahoma Press, 1950), pp. 125ff.; [Augustus Baldwin Longstreet], *Georgia Scenes, Characters, Incidents, &c. in the First Half Century of the Republic*, 2d ed. (New York: Harper and Brothers, 1860), p. iii.

56 Joseph Kirkland, for example, a generation after his mother, Caroline, documented the building of *A New Home*, turned for just this reason from writing novels about small-town life in the Middle West to compiling chronicles and local histories.

PHYSICAL PRESERVATION

The popularity of the local-color movement reflects a national disposition to hold on to ways of life obviously in decline. True, that mood did not confine itself to national borders or continental limits. Thomas Hardy proved a more thorough and better "chronicler of decay" than Edward Eggleston; European artists also seized on their own threatened local lore. In America, however, partly because so much more in addition to historical lore was vanishing, the regionalist movement drew more widespread support. Perhaps it contributed in turn to more literal kinds of preservation than envisioned by those who wrote fiction or those who collected histories. The preceding chapter suggested that no clear connection can be made between those who recorded wilderness landscapes and those who struggled in political arenas for their preservation. To link recorders of pioneer history, local-color artists, and the relatively few who worked to preserve actual artifacts would prove even more difficult.

Most nineteenth-century Americans remained unaware of any need for physical preservation. George Washington's neglected home began to be rescued by the newly formed Mount Vernon Ladies' Association only in 1858 and was not secured until the 1870s.[57] The homes of other political notables, much less anonymous log cabins or adobe houses, hardly seemed worth the trouble or expense of preservation.

Toward the end of the century, the Spanish missions of southern California almost alone escaped decay due to apathy. Monuments to a distinctly non-Anglo Saxon past, they had been allowed to suffer years of crumbling disrepair, until two concerned Los Angeles civic leaders, George Wharton James and Charles F. Lummis, encouraged their restoration in the 1880s. Their friend, the photographer Adam Clark Vroman, felt anxious enough about the missions' dilapidated state to spend the decade after 1895 photographing an exhaustive record of them. Delivering lectures throughout the state, these three men gathered support for the Association for the Preservation of the Missions, organized in 1888. The language James used, curiously, bears comparison with that of contemporary conservationists speaking about forests and wild game: "Buildings that come down to us out of the past, if ever worth anything, are worth preserving,—keeping, just as they are, as a valuable heirloom *that is not ours* except to look at, use, and pass on to our posterity. Our science is daily broadening. . . . Therefore we have awakened senses as to our duty to

[57] Gerald W. Johnson, *Mount Vernon: The Story of a Shrine* (New York: Random House, 1953), pp. 21-24, 42-43.

8. Adam Clark Vroman, "San Luis Rey Mission, Entrance to the Inner Court," 1897. Photograph. The Natural History Museum of Los Angeles County.

the historic remains of the past and the rights and claims of those who will come after us to them."[58] By 1900, shrewdly opportunistic Randolph Hearst sensed the popular enthusiasm for saving the missions and threw the influence of his *San Francisco Examiner* behind the movement.[59]

In the same way that conservationists came to defend all wilderness, not merely spectacular enclaves, all worthy historic buildings, not just

[58] George Wharton James, *In and Out of the Old Missions of California: An Historical and Pictorial Account of the Franciscan Missions* (Boston: Little, Brown and Co., 1905), p. 383. See also James, *Old Missions and Mission Indians of California* (Los Angeles: B. R. Baumgardt and Co., 1895), esp. pp. 29, 52, 121; Ruth I. Mahood, *Photographer of the Southwest: Adam Clark Vroman, 1856-1916* (New York: Bonanza Books, 1961), pp. 23-24; Dudley C. Gordon, *Charles F. Lummis: Crusader in Corduroy* (Los Angeles: Cultural Assets Press, 1972), esp. pp. 90-91; Charles Howard Shinn, "San Fernando Mission by Moonlight," *Land of Sunshine*, 2 (April 1895), 80.

For a contrasting example, see the antiquarian photography of Philadelphia's older buildings completed by Frederick Richards, ca. 1859, in *Philadelphia: Three Centuries of American Art*, Catalogue of Bicentennial Exhibit (Philadelphia Museum of Art, 1976), p. 31.

[59] James, *In and Out of the Old Missions*, pp. 387-88.

the Spanish missions, came to be seen as deserving preservation. The Landmarks Club, incorporated in 1896 to safeguard and reclaim any "historic monuments, relics, or landmarks" in southern California,[60] drew support from members of the Sierra Club and other wilderness conservation groups. Elsewhere across the nation similar concern had led to the organization of the Association for the Preservation of Virginia Antiquities (1889) and the American Scenic and Historic Preservation Society (1895). These would be followed by numerous preservation organizations at the turn of the century. Unlike the conservation movement, however, the relatively few citizens committed to landmark preservation maintained a primarily local solidarity.

Conclusion

Frederick Jackson Turner first formulated how the risks and rewards of an ever-retreating western frontier had uniquely shaped America's national character. To understand that character requires an understanding of the pioneer experiences that molded it. In large part, as Turner also noted, the passing of the frontier confirmed the passing of America's most challenging guarantee of political, social, and moral growth. Perhaps substituting "settler" for Emerson's "savage" best identifies the irony here: "In history the great moment is when the [settler] is just ceasing to be a [settler]. . . . Everything good in nature and the world is in that moment."[61] The ideal American society, in other words, needs continuous regeneration through contact with nature, but nature everywhere recedes before that society. That this ideal could only be approached in the process of passing, that is, in the pioneer experience, clarifies an irresolvable contradiction at the heart of America's self-conception. Few of those touched by this social paradox in the nineteenth century could appreciate it. We can better understand their attachment to frontier life, cherished less in the present than in the past tense, sometimes in the form of sentimental tales, sometimes in attempted histories, but increasingly as irrecoverable experience.

In the broadest sense, nineteenth-century Americans wanted to freeze all aspects of the wilderness experience. Vanishing forests, polluted streams, and eroded prairies; decimated flocks, dwindling herds, and disappearing evidence of pioneer exploits—each reminder elicited sympathetic attempts to preserve what was left for posterity, either

---

60 Ibid., p. 384.
61 Ralph Waldo Emerson, "Power," in *The Complete Writings of Ralph Waldo Emerson*, 2 vols. (New York: William H. Wise, 1929), 1:541.

through accurate records or by physical conservation. Missing from that list, however, is a far more striking embodiment of North America's wilderness: the Indian, human representative of all that the continent had symbolized prior to white settlement. Assuredly, he was not absent from the nineteenth-century consciousness of passing wilderness. But white understanding of native ways—much less white concern for their passing—remained complex and contradictory. Before examining the varied responses to the Indian and his place in the wilderness, we might first turn to a man who committed his life to preserving both images and records of vanishing native tribes. In so doing, we shall find in the paradigm of George Catlin's career all the issues traced so far.

CHAPTER FOUR

GEORGE CATLIN'S MISSION

Those tribes, sir, that have preceded
us, to whose lands we have succeeded, and
who have no written memorials of their
laws, their habits, and their manners, are
all passing away to the world of forgetfulness. Their likeness, manners, and
customs are portrayed with more accuracy
and truth in this collection by Catlin than
in all the other drawings and representations on the face of the earth. Somebody
in this country ought to possess this collection. . . .

. . . I go for this as an American subject—as a thing belonging to us—to our
history—to the history of a race whose
lands we till, whose obscure graves and
bones we tread every day. I look upon it
as a thing more appropriate for us than
the ascertaining of the South Pole, or anything that can be discovered in the Dead
Sea, or the River Jordan.

Daniel Webster
Senate speech (1849)

F EW NINETEENTH-CENTURY AMERICANS committed themselves as completely to America's vanishing wilderness as did George Catlin (1796-1872). Others, witness to troubling changes, went to extraordinary pains to compile accurate records. But they did so only as the western experience touched some part of their careers, and even then only as isolated gestures against the inevitable. The conventional demands of work and family prevented greater sacrifice. Indeed, Catlin's devotion to such a professional life led some to regard him as merely eccentric, a judgment he himself encouraged. In *Shut Your Mouth and Save Your Life* (1860), for instance, he attempted to prove that whites are less healthy than Indians because they snore.[1] Happily, such aberrant theories had little effect on the popularity Catlin won for his lifelong efforts. That broad popularity, moreover, helps to define the age's aspirations.

Most recent historians have not appreciated this context, coupling praise for Catlin's paintings with strained arguments for his supposedly unique vision.[2] Yet Catlin differed from his fellow Americans less in the substance of his beliefs than in the quality of his devotion. His commitments to preservation—whether of forests or game, Indian ethnography or painting—remain unusual only in having characterized one man's life. The uniqueness of his career resulted from his having recognized the vital interrelation between the destruction of indigenous cultures and a vanishing landscape. He rarely viewed tribes in isolation from their surroundings or apart from the effects of white Americans on the land and its wildlife. As early as the summer of 1832, while on his first painting expedition to the West, he lamented the decline of wild game in the upper Missouri country.[3] Using sketchbooks and canvases to preserve an accurate image of the remaining buffalo herds, he at the same time created the very conventions of buffalo painting that other painters would adopt.[4]

1 Catlin, *Shut Your Mouth and Save Your Life* (1860; rpt. London: Trübner and Co., 1876).

2 See, for instance, James Thomas Flexner, *That Wilder Image: The Painting of America's Native School from Thomas Cole to Winslow Homer* (1962; rpt. New York: Dover Publications, 1970), esp. pp. 69-71; Bernard DeVoto, *Across the Wide Missouri* (Boston: Houghton Mifflin Co., 1947), pp. 394-95; Harold McCracken, *George Catlin and the Old Frontier* (New York: Bonanza Books 1959), p. 16. For a more tempered assessment, see Larry Curry, *The American West: Painters from Catlin to Russell* (New York: Viking, 1972), p. 19.

3 George Catlin, *Letters and Notes on the Manners, Customs, and Conditions of the North American Indians* (1844), reprinted with an introduction by Marjorie Halpin, 2 vols. (New York: Dover Publications, 1973), 1:256.

4 See DeVoto, *Across the Wide Missouri*, p. 395; Flexner, *That Wilder Image*, p. 74.

9. George Catlin, *Buffalo Bulls Fighting in Running Season, Upper Missouri,*
1830-1839. Oil on canvas. The National Collection of Fine Arts, Smithsonian
Institution; gift of Mrs. Sarah Harrison.

But Catlin did more than rescue the buffalo's image for posterity.
He formulated a reasonable alternative to its extinction, which he
viewed as connected with the decline of native cultures and, more
broadly, with the transformation of the land itself. In 1833 he publicly suggested a stunningly original undertaking: a national park
system.

And what a splendid contemplation too, when one (who has
travelled these realms, and can duly appreciate them) imagines
them as they *might* in future be seen (by some great protecting
policy of government) preserved in their pristine beauty and
wildness, in a *magnificent park*, where the world could see for
ages to come, the native Indian in his classic attire. . . . A *nation's
Park*, containing man and beast, in all the wild and freshness of
their nature's beauty!
I would ask no other monument to my memory, nor any other

enrollment of my name amongst the famous dead, than the reputation of having been the founder of such an institution.[5]

Olmsted's, Bryant's and Greeley's plans for city parks each were radical anticipations of public concern for preservation. Catlin's earlier conception attests to a greater awareness of the problems of western expansion and a more incisive perception of the necessary solution. He urged the government to withdraw most of the high plains country; a preserve any smaller, he knew, would have the same effect on native life as none at all.

The very originality of his suggestion meant that few took it seriously. Those sympathetic to proposals for a national park system would not gain power for nearly forty years. Yet Catlin's accomplishments in the 1830s and his widespread self-publicizing in the 1840s shaped a change in public attitudes toward the West. Of course, he achieved his greatest fame as a painter of Indians, a preeminence confirmed not only by his general popularity and the interest he stimulated among ethnologists but also by his dominant effect on almost every other artist similarly engaged.[6] At a minimum, his paintings provided credible source material for the less adventurous. But he also inspired others to follow him to Indian country.

BORN IN 1796, George Catlin grew up in the wilderness area separating Pennsylvania and New York that was so affectionately described by Crèvecoeur some two decades earlier. Like other frontier children, he spent much of his youth fantasizing about "wild Indians," listening to tales of older settlers, and searching out abandoned campsites. Catlin may have found these occasions particularly vivid: his own mother and grandmother had been briefly captured by Miami Indians in the celebrated Wyoming Valley massacre of 1778, and his mother's playmate had been permanently adopted by the tribe. Interest in such history spurred an adolescent delight in sketching his frontier environs that was sustained through a short stint as a lawyer. In 1823 Catlin finally abandoned the law to take his growing portfolio of portrait miniatures to Philadelphia, where within months he attracted professional attention and lucrative commissions. By 1826, he enjoyed a reputation that extended throughout the East.[7]

5 Catlin, *Letters and Notes*, 1:261-62.

6 See Flexner, *That Wilder Image*, p. 79; John C. Ewers, *Artists of the Old West* (Garden City, N.Y.: Doubleday and Co., 1965), p. 94.

7 Marjorie Catlin Roehm, ed., *The Letters of George Catlin and His Family: A Chronicle of the American West* (Berkeley: University of California Press, 1966), p. 29; Royal Hassrick, *George Catlin Book of American Indians* (New York: Watson-

Catlin discovered his life's mission during his first year in Philadelphia. As he later recalled, he had been "continually reaching for some branch or enterprise of the art, on which to devote a whole life-time of enthusiasm,"[8] when in 1824 a native delegation from the "Far West" passed through Philadelphia. The young painter was indelibly impressed. "The history and customs of such a people, preserved by pictorial illustrations," he later declared, "are themes worthy the life-time of one man, and nothing short of the loss of my life, shall prevent me from visiting their country, and of becoming their historian."[9]

During the rest of the 1820s, Catlin drew more portraits, broached his idea to possible patrons, and in general set about acquiring financial support for his proposed expeditions. A sympathetic New York City publisher, Colonel William F. Stone, finally made it possible for the painter to turn west.[10] In the spring of 1832, as the ice was breaking on the river, he boarded the steamboat *Yellowstone* for its historic first journey up the Missouri. Catlin knew what he wanted, as he made clear in a letter to Colonel Stone. One long passage is worth quoting in full:

> I have, for many years past, contemplated the noble races of red men who are now spread over these trackless forests and boundless prairies, melting away at the approach of civilization. Their rights invaded, their morals corrupted, their lands wrested from them, their customs changed, and therefore lost to the world; and they at last sunk into the earth, and the ploughshare turning the sod over their graves, and I have flown to their rescue—not of their lives or of their race (for they are "*doomed*" and must perish), but to the rescue of their looks and their modes, at which the acquisitive world may hurl their poison and every besom of destruction, and trample them down and crush them to death; yet, phoenix-like, they may rise from the "stain on a painter's palette," and live again upon canvass, and stand forth for centuries yet to come, the living monuments of a noble race. For this purpose, I have designed to visit every tribe of Indians on the Continent, if my life should be spared; for the purpose of procuring portraits of distinguished Indians, of both sexes in each tribe, painted in their

Guptill, 1977), p. 20; Catlin, *Letters and Notes*, 1:vii-viii; William Goetzmann, *Exploration and Empire: The Explorer and the Scientist in the Winning of the American West* (New York: Alfred A. Knopf, 1966), pp. 184-91.

8 Catlin, *Letters and Notes*, 1:2.

9 Ibid.

10 Hassrick, *Catlin Book*, pp. 20, 25; George Catlin, *Letters and Notes on the North American Indians*, ed. and abr. Michael MacDonald Mooney (New York: Clarkson N. Potter, 1975), pp. 14-19; Roehm, ed., *Catlin Family Letters*, pp. 47-49.

native costume; accompanied with pictures of their villages, domestic habits, games, mysteries, religious ceremonies, etc. with anecdotes, traditions, and history of their respective nations.[11]

Catlin's theme is clear; the need to race against time, to paint as many tribes as possible before they alter forever, recurs in his writings often enough to form a personal manifesto.

The *Yellowstone*'s three-month, two-thousand-mile voyage upriver inaugurated Catlin's true western career and also modified his notions of what that career would entail. To refresh his memory for later studies, for instance, he scribbled notes on the tribes he observed, reminders that soon grew into an extensive encyclopedia finally published as his *Letters and Notes*. Moreover, the focus of his painting shifted from an initial concentration on portraits to a fascination with exuberant scenes of tribal life, including dances, ceremonies, architecture, buffalo hunts, artwork, and domestic activities. Even his style evolved. Catlin's furious pace, dictated by his desire to record as much as possible, often meant a sacrifice of conventional artistic standards of composition, perspective, and even color in the numerous sketches he completed. Yet he converted liabilities into assets, moving beyond a forgivable crudeness to achieve masterful studies. Entranced by the Assiniboin, Blackfoot, Crow, and Cree Indians at Fort Union, Montana, he spent a full month sketching scenes that he would later only rarely excel.[12]

During his return trip by canoe that summer, Catlin visited the two remaining Mandan villages located north of present-day Bismarck, North Dakota. At once he sensed the importance of this beleaguered tribe, which remained one of the most complex of Plains Indian cultures: "so forcibly have I been struck with the peculiar ease and elegance of these people, together with . . . their peculiar and unaccountable customs, that I am fully convinced that they have sprung from some other origin than that of the other North American tribes, or that they are an amalgam of natives with some civilized race."[13] Catlin soaked up information, "trusting that by further intimacy and familiarity with these people I may yet arrive at more satisfactory and important results."[14] In only a fortnight he gained an extraordinary intimacy. Permitted to attend rituals rarely witnessed by

11 Catlin, *Letters and Notes*, intro. by Halpin, 1:16.

12 Roehm, ed., *Catlin Family Letters*, pp. 57, 64-65; Thomas Donaldson, *The George Catlin Indian Gallery in the United States National Museum*, author's ed. (Washington: G.P.O., 1887), pp. 369, 438; Hassrick, *Catlin Book*, pp. 21-25.

13 Catlin, *Letters and Notes*, 1:93.

14 Ibid., 1:177.

whites, Catlin completed a series of invaluable canvases, the most cele-brated of which illustrate the Mandans' renowned four-day torture ceremony. His description of the O-kee-pa ceremony, in which initiates were suspended by splints in their flesh, challenges credulity even today, especially since his was one of the few records made. When Audubon visited the Mandans in 1843—six years after a smallpox epidemic decimated the tribe—he could only lament: "Ah! Mr. Catlin, I am now sorry to see and to read your accounts of the Indians *you* saw—how very different they must have been from any that I have seen!"[15] Audubon's description of thieving Mandans scavenging among putrid, drowned buffaloes and crowding into hovels during winter storms forms a cruel juxtaposition to Catlin's account.

Catlin devoted the year 1833 to completing his rough sketches and painting large oil canvases. He returned to Indian territory the fol-lowing year, this time to the southern plains of the little-known Comanches and Kiowas, which had also become the home of the displaced Osage, Choctaws, and Cherokees. Continuing to make some-times dangerous, always exhausting, tours in search of other tribes, by late 1836 he had nearly completed his "Indian Gallery": 422 paint-ings and thousands of sketches made among at least forty-eight tribes.

Starting with his first trip to St. Louis in 1830, the financial costs of his seven-year venture were substantial. In turning to the public, Catlin hoped at once to recoup his losses and to gain a permanent museum for his collection. It was time to inspire others. Catlin opened the first major exhibit of his Indian Gallery in New York City in 1837, successfully moving it later to Washington, Philadelphia, and Bos-ton.[16] Hundreds came to see the enormous collection of costumes and artifacts, as well as paintings, and to purchase Catlin's thirty-six-page catalogue. For the first time, easterners were treated to a large western exhibit—a precursor of the shows that Buffalo Bill Cody would make commercially popular half a century later. If Catlin's innate show-manship helped to draw enthusiastic crowds, however, his poor busi-ness sense ensured that costs soon exceeded admission fees. Financial pressures finally became · intolerable after the federal government narrowly refused to purchase his collection in 1839.

15 Cited in Maria R. Audubon, *Audubon and His Journals*, 2 vols. (New York: Charles Scribner's Sons, 1897), 1:497, 2:10-11. See also Alice Ford, *John James Audu-bon* (Norman: University of Oklahoma Press, 1964), p. 398; Robert Buchanan, *Life and Adventures of Audubon the Naturalist* (1868; rpt. New York: E. P. Dutton and Co., 1913), p. 321.

16 See DeVoto, *Across the Wide Missouri*, p. 391; Roehm, ed., *Catlin Family Let-ters*, pp. 119-22.

10. George Catlin, *The Cutting Scene, Mandan O-kee-pa Ceremony*, 1832. Oil on canvas. The Harmsen Collection, Denver.

Hoping to win a reputation abroad that would convince a future Congress to reverse this decision, Catlin sailed for Liverpool that fall with eight tons of freight, including paintings, Indian artifacts, and two live grizzly bears.[17] As Bernard DeVoto describes Catlin's European tour: "There were more than six hundred paintings and Catlin went on adding to them through the years. (He also made many copies, some of which hang in English town and country houses today.) A visitor who remained unsatiated after looking at six hundred canvases could go on to two dozen dummies dressed in genuine Indian costumes and a sizable museum of medicine bundles, shields, amulets, baskets, robes, travois, moccasins, weapons, pipes, and other artifacts. There were learned, dramatic lectures by the proprietor and *tableaux vivants* posed by local supernumeraries in Indian dress."[18] His reception in London and Paris augured well. Royalty feted him; artists as

[17] DeVoto, *Across the Wide Missouri*, pp. 391-92.
[18] Ibid.

diverse as Charles Dickens, Charles Baudelaire, Eugène Delacroix, and George Sand showered accolades upon him.

At this peak of interest, Catlin decided to bring out his *Letters and Notes*, hoping thereby to encourage a solid financial commitment from his countrymen. Many, it might go without saying, were simply impressed by Catlin's exotic subjects; they thronged to his shows or purchased his book because it was the fashionable thing to do.[19] But others genuinely appreciated Catlin's achievement in terms he himself might have formulated. "Had he been like other mortals," one anonymous American reviewer observed, "he would probably have lived a quiet and decent citizen of his native State; and the tribes of the more remote western territories might perhaps for ever have remained unvisited by any one capable of thus portraying to the world their habits and features. It is a well known fact that the interesting tribe of Mandans . . . exist now only on his canvass and in his pages. Since the visit of Mr. Catlin they have been swept by disease from the face of the earth, and little else than a few ruined huts now remains to tell that a people once existed there. So may it perhaps be with many others of the nations among whom he dwelt. . . ."[20] Americans and Europeans alike realized that Catlin's work justified his fame. American artists living in Paris, in the late 1840s, including John Vanderlyn, William Morris Hunt, John Frederick Kensett, and William B. Chambers, supported his efforts and urgently petitioned Congress to purchase the collection "as a nucleus for a national museum, where American artists may freely study that bold race who once held possession of our country, and who are so fast disappearing before the tide of civilization."[21] Senators Henry Clay and William Henry Seward attempted to rally fellow legislators to Catlin's cause. Daniel Webster's Senate plea that "this race is going into forgetfulness" and that America "ought to possess this collection"[22] nearly clinched the vote, despite Catlin's steep offering price. By a narrow margin of four votes, however, Congress again decided against the purchase. Three years later, in 1852, that decision was confirmed when a similar bill was tabled, this time by a single vote.

[19] Hugh Honour, *The New Golden Land: European Images of America from the Discoveries to the Present Time* (New York: Pantheon Books, 1975), pp. 236-37; Roehm, ed., *Catlin Family Letters*, pp. 170, 176, 305-7, 309-12.

[20] Review of "Catlin's North American Indians," *United States Magazine, and Democratic Review*, new ser., 11 (July 1842), 45.

[21] Donaldson, *Catlin Indian Gallery*, p. 747.

[22] Ibid., p. 770. See also Lloyd Haberly, *Pursuit of the Horizon: A Life of George Catlin, Painter and Recorder of the American Indian* (New York: Macmillan Co., 1948), pp. 110, 114; Catlin, *Letters and Notes*, ed. Mooney, pp. 66-67; Flexner, *That Wilder Image*, p. 80.

Catlin, now heavily overextended, suffered a short incarceration in Britain's debtors' prison before a sympathetic creditor, a rich American boilermaker, bought the collection and shipped it to his Philadelphia warehouse. (Little could the disappointed Catlin guess that his paintings would thereby be saved from the devastating Smithsonian Institution fire of 1865.) At fifty-six he felt beaten: his family had been destroyed through disease and debt; his life's work lay bundled in a warehouse; his health was ruined.[23]

Nevertheless, Catlin abandoned neither his conception of a public gallery nor his commitment to record threatened tribes. In 1852 he left Europe for South America, once again to paint Indians in their native habitats. At the same time, he patiently recreated from sketches and memory much of his original collection. His style further evolved, as did the mood he expressed through his art. In uncolored pencil sketches he presented South American Indians as accurately as ever. Yet they "stare with level-fronting eyes at some tragic vision that is to each his own but which they all share," one art historian has noted. "These exotic-faced dreams composed separately together personify a stoic nobility that transcends the world's troubles. But Catlin's renditions of ceremonies and hunts, where the world has interposed, where people are conscious of each other and acting in concert, express a bitterness, a revulsion, and all-embracing cruelty he had never felt when in actuality among the tribes."[24] Reflecting in part his own feelings, these later studies also evince the diminished prospects available to American tribes in the second half of the nineteenth century.

Though embittered, Catlin never lost his sense of mission. Only a few years before he died in 1872, he wrote a long manuscript to accompany his new collection, prefaced by a statement of purpose that differs hardly at all from the one he had written on the *Yellowstone* more than thirty-five years earlier:

> Nations of people yet unborn, and even many of those of the present generation, will look through the pages of this work with feelings of surprise and profound regret that a numerous Race of human beings, with the looks and customs herein described, existing over most parts of the American Continent in the middle of the nineteenth century, should have passed away before the destructive wave of civilization, leaving few, if any, monuments behind them. . . .
>
> Deeply impressed with the irresistible fate awaiting these poor people . . . I conceived the plan of visiting their various countries

---

[23] Catlin, *Letters and Notes*, 1:xii.   [24] Flexner, *That Wilder Image*, p. 81.

with my canvass and brushes, and note book, gathering and rescuing from oblivion everything I could of their looks and customs,
for the instruction of future ages. . . . I resolved, if my life should
be spared, to make a pictorial history of those vanishing Races.[25]

Catlin cherished an unassailable belief in the value of his labors.
Never reconciled to America's failure to purchase his original Indian
Gallery, he wondered even on his deathbed about its fate.[26] Seven
years later, in 1879, the owner made a gift of it to the nation.

To Americans then as now, Catlin's career epitomized intelligent
concern for the vanishing wilderness and particularly for the Indian.
Numerous countrymen shared his anxiety; others supported his efforts. Yet, if his intentions were rarely questioned, his actual skills
provoked doubts. Just as Herman Melville's descriptions of Polynesian
cannibals met with disbelief, so did Catlin's Mandans and their
"strange and peculiar" rituals.[27] Particularly damaging was the bitter
war of letters in which Henry Rowe Schoolcraft engaged him. The respected ethnologist arrogantly questioned every aspect of Catlin's
Mandan report well after the few other reliable witnesses to the
O-kee-pa ceremony had substantiated Catlin.

Bernard DeVoto well sums up Catlin's faults and achievements: "It
is true that he was an enthusiast and even a monomaniac, that he
misunderstood much of what he saw, as anyone in his place must have
done, that he held some wildly untenable theories, that he never lost
his Rousseauian prepossessions about savages in a state of nature,
that he made many mistakes, and even that he falsified or invented
some details. Nevertheless, he is in the main reliable and both his
books and paintings have been immensely important to American
ethnology ever since 1837."[28] Insofar as one may claim, as DeVoto
does, that American ethnology began with Catlin, it is because Catlin
for the most part succeeded in painting what he saw, rather than what

[25] Preface to Catlin, "The North Americans in the Middle of the Nineteenth Century: A Numerous and Noble Race of Human Beings fast passing to oblivion and
leaving no monuments of their own behind them," bound ms., Huntington Library,
San Marino.

[26] Roehm, ed., Catlin Family Letters, p. 411.

[27] Catlin, Letters and Notes, 1:55. See Donaldson, Catlin Indian Gallery, pp. 376-
83; Roehm, ed., Catlin Family Letters, pp. 344-45. John C. Ewers has best described
the reception and continuing importance of Catlin's descriptions in his introduction
to George Catlin, O-kee-pa: A Religious Ceremony and Other Customs of the Mandans, ed. John C. Ewers (New Haven: Yale University Press, 1967), pp. 1-33.

[28] DeVoto, Across the Wide Missouri, p. 392. See, for only one example of con-
temporary disbelief by knowledgeable observers among tribes Catlin had visited,
Edwin Thompson Denig, Five Indian Tribes of the Upper Missouri, ed. John C.
Ewers (Norman: University of Oklahoma Press, 1961), pp. xxx-xxxi.

11. George Catlin, *Bull Dance, Part of Mandan Okipa Ceremony*, ca. 1838. Oil on canvas. The National Collection of Fine Arts, Smithsonian Institution; gift of Mrs. Sarah Harrison.

he said he saw. For in his writings he sentimentalized Indians as noble savages, a conception differing little from the alleged childlike quality that Schoolcraft condemned. Catlin too believed that "the Indian's mind is a beautiful blank, on which anything might be written, if the right mode were taken to do it."[29] Neither man could appreciate the cultural integrity their very descriptions revealed.

In important ways, Catlin fell victim to his sense of mission. The same considerations impelling him to document individuals and tribal activities also define flaws in his work. He was obsessed by the fact that Indians were, as he noted, "on the wane," which explains his repeated urging "that the traveller who would see these people in their native simplicity and beauty, must needs be hastily on his way to the prairies and Rocky Mountains, or he will see them only as they

[29] Catlin, *Letters and Notes*, 2:245. See also Catlin, *Life Among the Indians* (London: Gall and Inglis, [187?]), pp. 18-20.

are now seen on the frontiers, as a basket of *dead game*,—harassed, chased, bleeding and dead."[30] In one sense, however, such adjurations exacted the consequence against which they warned. Inspired imitators would demoralize western tribes by their very enthusiasm, their eagerness to confirm and picture sacred rites. In another sense, Catlin's imperative haste suggests why ethnologists have sometimes found his portraits and genre scenes inadequately detailed. They compare poorly, for example, with those painted by his Swiss contemporary, Karl Bodmer. As established critics of the time observed, Catlin seemed an "intrepid traveler" but a "mediocre painter."[31]

Catlin cherished little affection for conventional artistic standards, having realized that the older methods were inadequate to the mammoth task he had set himself and to the unforgiving demands of time. The challenges posed by frontier conditions led him to employ short-cuts in field sketches—using pigments in their unmixed form, or painting in thin, quick-drying layers—that could be compensated for later in his studio. Probably his most trying problem resulted from Indians' common reluctance to having their portraits painted. Well into the twentieth century they warily resisted those who came to "steal" their likenesses, fearing the consequences of this unknown ritual: that they would never again sleep, since their painted eyes remained open; that profile portraits might destroy the unrendered side of their faces; or, even worse, that their souls would escape into the paintings. Though Catlin learned to persuade his models otherwise, assurances rarely stood warrant for long, and finishing a portrait expeditiously offered the sole guarantee of finishing one at all. Luckily, as one wag put it, Catlin had the fastest brush in the West.[32] He sometimes sketched half a dozen portraits in a single day, and during his 1832 canoe trip down the Missouri River, he completed one hundred oils. Of course, this meant that he sometimes sacrificed or simplified detail, compounding his problems of landscape perspective and figural proportions. Yet, with few exceptions, Catlin painted "with passionate accuracy."[33] The certificates of authenticity that he obtained from reliable officials are still attached to some paintings. More important, he gained a fresh realism that even the trained

[30] Catlin, *Letters and Notes*, 1:10.

[31] Honour, *The New Golden Land*, p. 237; Hassrick, *Catlin Book*, p. 29; Catlin, *Letters and Notes*, ed. Mooney, p. 81; Catlin, *Letters and Notes*, intro. by Halpin, l:xiv; DeVoto, *Across the Wide Missouri*, p. 405; Flexner, *That Wilder Image*, pp. 75-76. For information on Bodmer, see Chapter Five, p. 127.

[32] Cited by Hassrick, *Catlin Book*, p. 29.

[33] Flexner, *That Wilder Image*, p. 72. See also pp. 73-74; Catlin, *Letters and Notes*, ed. Mooney, editor's introduction; DeVoto, *Across the Wide Missouri*, p. 394.

draftsman Bodmer failed to achieve. To say, as did one admirer, that "Bodmer was painting real paintings, Catlin real Indians,"[34] defines the special strength of Catlin's vision. Another critic has more revealingly characterized his Indians "as neither the bloodthirsty enemies nor the pathetic victims of the march of progress."[35] Catlin portrayed his subjects as individual human beings.

At the age of seventy-five, reflecting on his career, Catlin hoped that future generations would "find enough of historical interest excited by faithful resemblance to the physiognomy and customs of these people to compensate for what may be deficient in them as works of art."[36] Before the camera made a different kind of exact documentation possible, he completed paintings that can be trusted to present scenes as he saw them. Before westward expansion in the 1840s forever altered Plains Indian life, he captured nearly the final impression of those cultures as they had continued for generations. In words he repeated frequently, "I was luckily born in time to see these people in their native dignity, and beauty, and independence."[37]

Catlin was the first to teach his countrymen to observe their western landscape and to examine the people who lived there. The viewing public, which had contented itself with the sentimental "Lo, The Poor Indian" or the savage "Death of Jane McCrea," began to appreciate the inadequacies of such uninformed fantasies and to demand more from its artists.[38] Catlin covered more territory in the 1840s and depicted more different tribes in greater detail than did any other painter who followed.[39] But he was certainly not alone. Many of those who took their lead from him and went on to surpass him in the quality of their records will be discussed in Chapter Five. The achievements of those spurred to more exacting ethnographic efforts by his written descriptions of native behavior will be examined in Chapter Six. Yet few shared commitments to the range of interests that both these forms of preserved record exemplify.

For all Catlin's extraordinary popularity, his long moment in the sun·ended rather abruptly. Nor was he ever to emerge from under the cloud of debt that ruined him in 1852. His concern for dwindling

[34] Quoted in Catlin, *Letters and Notes*, ed. Mooney, p. 81. See also DeVoto, *Across the Wide Missouri*, p. 395.

[35] Honour, *The New Golden Land*, p. 236.

[36] Catlin, *Letters and Notes*, ed. Mooney, p. 82. See also Flexner, *That Wilder Image*, pp. 74-75, 81-82.

[37] Cited in Donaldson, *Catlin Indian Gallery*, p. 745.

[38] Ellwood Parry, *The Image of the Indian and the Black Man in American Art, 1590-1900* (New York: George Braziller, 1974), p. 83.

[39] DeVoto, *Across the Wide Missouri*, p. 393.

tribes, despite the many individuals thus spurred to similar efforts, seemed excessive, even perverse, to others who thought him a "flaming enthusiast."[40] His strong claims and speculations, sometimes bordering on the ridiculous—for example, that the Mandans were related to migrating Welsh tribes and that all Indians displayed uniformly temperate, generous spirits[41]—seemed proof of a lack of perspective, placing even his firsthand reports under suspicion. By the time he published his theory of Indian health in 1860, he had long since fallen into obscurity.

A fierce irony to Catlin's career is that his hopes for his collection approached fulfillment shortly after he died. In 1879 the secretary of the Smithsonian Institution and a few others finally persuaded the boilermaker's generous widow to give the Indian Gallery—by then badly water damaged—to the nation.[42] Less than a decade later, a dedicated government employee, Thomas Donaldson, ferreted out as much information about Catlin as possible in compiling a thick government publication, *The George Catlin Indian Gallery in the United States Museum* (1887). The work is uncritical and sometimes inaccurate. Nonetheless, Donaldson felt that the sixty-odd years since Catlin saw his first Indian delegation had wrought changes that only confirmed his lifelong mission: "The plains are silent; neither structure nor monument tells their past glory. . . . The painter's art, the museum, and the art preservative alone tell the story."[43] Catlin himself stated the issue more exactly, and for once less rhetorically, when in 1868 he recalled the efforts that had shaped his unique career: "I have said that I was lucky enough to have been born at the right time to have seen these people (Indians) in their nature, dignity, and elegance; and thanks to Him in whose hands the destinies of all men are, that my life has been spared to visit most of the tribes in every latitude of the American continent, and my hands enabled to delineate their personal looks and their modes, to be seen and to be criticized after this people and myself shall have passed away."[44]

[40] Ibid., p. 404.

[41] Catlin, *Letters and Notes,* 1:8-10, 23, 61, 205-7, 2:277; Catlin, *Life Among the Indians,* pp. 18-19. Also see Donaldson, *Catlin Indian Gallery,* pp. 463-66.

[42] Catlin, *Letters and Notes,* ed. Mooney, p. 79; Hassrick, *Catlin Book,* p. 33; McCracken, *Catlin and the Old Frontier,* pp. 207-8.

[43] Donaldson, *Catlin Indian Gallery,* p. 742. See DeVoto, *Across the Wide Missouri,* p. 393, for a critique of this effort.

[44] Cited by Donaldson, *Catlin Indian Gallery,* p. 745. Yet even at this time, Catlin worked to see his record permanently installed, as suggested by his 1872 proposal for a monument to the Indian to be erected in Central Park: a sheet-iron replica of

Catlin's fears for the vanishing Indian were hardly unique. But he attempted sooner, more completely, and more publicly than most to rescue an invaluable history. And with no predecessors of any influence, he produced a comprehensive image that continues to inform our understanding of the West.

a Crow wigwam, seventy-five feet high, inside of which was to be contained his paintings and artifacts. See *Frank Leslie's Illustrated Newspaper* (New York), March 2, 1872, pp. 385, 391, cited by Richard A. Bartlett, *The New Country: A Social History of the American Frontier, 1776-1890* (New York: Oxford University Press, 1974), p. 19.

CHAPTER FIVE

INDIANS AND
IMAGE CATCHERS

I began my work among them twenty-two years ago, and have seen many changes. Entire tribes have been destroyed by disease, and others have been scattered by encroaching civilization. The Indian, as an Indian, is rapidly disappearing. He is adopting the white man's ways and losing his tribal characteristics. He is gradually giving up his deeply significant nature-lore, his religions and his ceremonies, and it will not be long before his tribal communities, ancestral manners and customs will have passed from his life.

Realizing these conditions, I have devoted many years to the making of an ethnographic record of the Indians, photographing their life, manners and habitat, and thus preserving for future generations a picture-history which will show what these most interesting early Americans were like, before they were disturbed by the influences of the white man.

—*Frederick Monsen*
"Picturing Indians with the Camera"
(1910)

Few major american writers in the first half of the nineteenth century seemed less interested in Indian tribes than Nathaniel Hawthorne. His literary career traces a series of moral and symbolic fictions; efforts at authentication led him more often to the seventeenth century than to the nineteenth, to New England than to the West. At the age of thirty-one, however, with his career still before him, Hawthorne recognized with some sadness a direction that his writing would not take: "It has often been a matter of regret to me, that I was shut out from the most peculiar field of American fiction, by an inability to see any romance, or poetry, or grandeur, or beauty in the Indian character, at least, till such traits were pointed out by others. I do abhor an Indian story. Yet no writer can be more secure of a permanent place in our literature, than the biographer of the Indian chiefs. His subject, as referring to tribes which have mostly vanished from the earth, gives him a right to be placed on a classic shelf, apart from the merits which will sustain him there."[1] This curious mix of sentiments reveals the pervasive grip that the idea of the Indian had on nineteenth-century American thought. Catlin, traveling among Plains Indians even as Hawthorne penned these words in his Salem study, was neither alone nor first in wanting to document tribes that would soon, according to Hawthorne, "have mostly vanished from the earth."

Portraits and biographies of various tribal dignitaries had spiced America's artistic and literary diet for centuries. Even Catlin's patron, Colonel William L. Stone, contributed to that tradition in the 1830s by writing commendable biographies of Joseph Brant and Red-Jacket.[2] Following prescribed convention, Stone presented his Indian chiefs as models of the unacculturated, not as exemplary products of alternative cultures. Their claim on white attention depended on the white virtues they displayed in red-face, traits that supposedly explained their tribal preeminence. Up to 1800, most white Americans conceived of Indians in Crèvecoeur's terms, as merely uncivilized, having neither cultural constraints nor intellectual capacities. Oblivious to sometimes radical tribal differences, they authored biographies and painted portraits that reveal far more of themselves than of their

[1] Nathaniel Hawthorne, "Our Evening Party Among the Mountains," in *Mosses from an Old Manse* (1835; rpt. Ohio State University Press, 1974), p. 428.

[2] William L. Stone, *Life of Joseph Brant—Thayendanegea, Including the Indian Wars of the American Revolution*, 2 vols. (New York: George Dearborn and Co., 1838), and *The Life and Times of Red-Jacket, or Sa-Go-Ye-Wat-Ha; Being the Sequel to the History of the Six Nations* (New York: Wiley and Putnam, 1841).

subjects. Predictably, early portraits of the savage seem bland and interchangeable;[3] biographies reflect distinctly European assumptions about individual motivation and historical causality. Colorful exaggerations and inaccuracies abound in descriptions of tribal life and accounts of historical events. Conventional assumptions about Indian "savagery" so thoroughly shaped artists' responses that objective representation was almost impossible.[4]

"In America," Perry Miller once claimed, "the artist has a calling above and beyond an accurate reporting of scenery: he must work fast . . . to strive to fix the fleeting moment of primitive grandeur."[5] Yet, although white men and red had lived together for nearly three centuries, the need to preserve an accurate record of the Indians' "primitive grandeur" was not widely felt until the early nineteenth century. Of course, Europeans and Americans from Columbus on had been intensely curious about native life. But the westward advance of settlement brought to the raw new federal city on the Potomac Indian delegations hoping to influence national policy toward their tribes. Now these compellingly real reminders of the exotic West jostled elbows with the men and women trying to establish an "American" culture.[6]

Coincidentally, older conventions of idealization in American painting gave way to a singular devotion to pictorial accuracy. As Barbara Novak has observed, art increasingly concentrated on "the stopped moment, the frozen continuum, the fixation of becoming to being."[7] The transcendentalists' delight in the ultimate significance of the immediate and particular constituted one aspect of this development. The Hudson River School paintings reflect another, as do those of local genre artists. This increasing attentiveness to painterly detail, requiring "greater accuracy, or objectivity, or truth to nature by allowing each subject to begin to speak for itself, instead of imposing

[3] For remarkable exceptions to this general rule, however, see William J. Buck, "Lappawinzo and Tishcohan, Chiefs of the Lenni Lenape," *Pennsylvania Magazine of History and Biography*, 7 (1883), 215-318; Luke Vincent Lockwood, "The St. Memin Indian Portraits," *New-York Historical Society Quarterly Bulletin*, 12 (April 1928), 3-26; Ellwood Parry, *The Image of the Indian and the Black Man in American Art, 1590-1900* (New York: George Braziller, 1974), pp. 24, 64-65.

[4] Parry, *Image of the Indian*, pp. 53-64; Roy Harvey Pearce, *Savagism and Civilization: A Study of the Indian and the American Mind*, rev. ed. (Baltimore: Johns Hopkins University Press, 1965).

[5] Perry Miller, "The Romantic Dilemma in American Nationalism and the Concept of Nationalism," *Harvard Theological Review*, 48 (October 1955), p. 240.

[6] Parry, *Image of the Indian*, pp. 68ff.

[7] Barbara Novak, *American Painting of the Nineteenth Century: Realism, Idealism, and the American Experience* (New York: Praeger, 1969), p. 121. See also Parry, *Image of the Indian*, p. 82.

artificial or extrinsic interpretations,"[8] grew from a variety of causes. At least one of the reasons, however, as we have already seen in the discussions of Thomas Cole and George Caleb Bingham, was a sense of their subjects' ephemerality, a recognition that Indian delegations were traveling east precisely to negotiate terms by which their present lives might be preserved.

Thus, both style and interest converged when artists for the first time recognized Indian cultures as at once fragile and irrevocably disappearing. In addition, the romantic movement swept much of western Europe into an excessive regard for the effects of time's passing. "The nostalgia and pity aroused by the dying race," one historian notes, "produced the best romantic sentiments and gave that sense of fleeting time beloved of romantic sensibilities."[9] Another has claimed that with "economic mastery of nature and the physical world" arises the urge to render it with artistic exactness.[10] Whatever its origins, a widely shared impulse developed among American painters and, later, photographers to fix the various images of the Indian. By the 1890s, when the extinction or acculturation of nearly every North American tribe had been effected, pictorial artists had recorded much of what had been. Self-consciously, they completed an ex-

[8] Parry, *Image of the Indians*, p. 82. See also Warner Berthoff, *The Example of Melville* (1962; rpt. New York: W. W. Norton, 1972), pp. 81-82.

[9] Robert F. Berkhofer Jr., *The White Man's Indian: Images of the American Indian from Columbus to the Present* (New York: Alfred A. Knopf, 1978), p. 88. See also A. Irving Hallowell, "The Backwash of the Frontier: The Impact of the Indian on American Culture," in Walker D. Wyman and Clifton B. Kroeber, eds., *The Frontier in Perspective* (Madison: University of Wisconsin Press, 1957), pp. 232-33. Brian William Dippie, in "The Vanishing American: Popular Attitudes and American Indian Policy in the Nineteenth Century" (Ph.D. diss., University of Texas, Austin, 1970), claims that "the Vanishing Indian" was mere tradition and did not reflect actual conditions. Yet he also admits, "In one way or another it colored all thought on the Indian throughout the nineteenth century" (v). See also ibid., pp. 1, 7, 27.

[10] Berthoff, *Example of Melville*, p. 64. See also Hallowell, "Backwash of the Frontier," p. 248; Richard Rudisill, *Mirror Image: The Influence of the Daguerreotype on American Society* (Albuquerque: University of New Mexico Press, 1971), pp. 9-28; Dorothy Harmsen, *Harmsen's Western Americana: A Collection of One Hundred Western Paintings with Biographical Profiles of the Artists* (Flagstaff: Northland Press, 1971), p. 2; Frank Weitenkampf, "Early Pictures of North American Indians: A Question of Ethnology," *Bulletin of the New York Public Library*, 53 (December 1949), 596-598; John C. Ewers, *Artists of the Old West* (Garden City, N.Y.: Doubleday and Co., 1965), pp. 7-8; Ewers, "Fact and Fiction in the Documentary Art of the American West," in John Francis McDermott, ed., *The Frontier Reexamined* (Urbana: University of Illinois Press, 1967), pp. 79ff.; Jonathan L. Fairbanks, introduction to *Frontier America: The Far West* (Boston: Museum of Fine Arts, 1975), pp. 15-16; James Thomas Flexner, *That Wilder Image: The Painting of America's Native School from Thomas Cole to Winslow Homer* (1962; rpt. New York: Dover Publications, 1970), p. 66.

tensive gallery of pencil sketches, watercolors, and oil paintings, daguerreotypes and photographs documenting the lives of native Americans in their cultural richness.

Even among people as committed as these, however, few found it possible to abandon stereotypes. From Catlin across the century to Edward Curtis, artists allowed earnest sympathy to blind them to the complexities of Indian cultures. Yet, as Catlin's work demonstrates, their reasonably objective illustrations mostly escape the distorting influence of their otherwise facile ideas. In aspiring to exact documentation, moreover, the very fact of close observation brought some to a more profound understanding of native life. Later in the century, this greater understanding encouraged a shift away from simple notions of cultural absolutism. Heroic portraits of characteristic types or of celebrated chieftains in the 1820s gradually gave way to more precise illustrations of otherwise unremarkable figures and of everyday domestic life.

By the late 1830s, as Hawthorne's regretful claim and the popularity of Catlin's exhibit suggest, many Americans accepted the value of preserving accounts and illustrations of ephemeral tribal life.[11] Even within the elite literary circle defined by Hawthorne and his friends, the scholarly, cosmopolitan Margaret Fuller came to appreciate these issues. Before making a trip to Chicago in the early 1840s, she "read all the books I could find about the new region," including Catlin's and Irving's, and in turn wrote perceptively of life in northern Illinois and Wisconsin.[12] Repeatedly, deploring the depredations whites had made on the wilderness, she empathized with the original occupants of the land: "I have no hope of liberalizing the missionary, of humanizing the sharks of trade, of infusing the conscientious drop into the flinty bosom of policy, of saving the Indian from immediate degradation and speedy death. . . . Yet ere they depart I wish there might be some masterly attempt to reproduce in art or literature what is proper to them. . . . We hope some other mind may be bent upon it, ere too late."[13] Her high regard for Catlin led her to hope that others would complete the record he had begun.

Fuller looked to more than individual effort, however. That the federal government should support such endeavors was an idea possibly suggested to her by Catlin's book. "We hope there will be a na-

[11] See, for example, Jessie Poesch, *Titian Ramsey Peale and His Journals of the Wilkes Expedition, 1799-1885* (Philadelphia: American Philosophical Society, 1961), p. 24.

[12] Margaret Fuller, *Summer on the Lakes* (1843), in *The Writings of Margaret Fuller*, ed. Mason Wade (New York: Viking, 1941), pp. 24-25.

[13] Ibid., p. 88.

tional institute containing all the remains of the Indians, all that has been preserved by official intercourse at Washington, Catlin's collection, and a picture-gallery as complete as can be made, with a collection of skulls from all parts of the country. To this should be joined the scanty library that exists on the subject."[14] Three years later, responding to a campaign begun long before Fuller's advocacy, Congress established this "national institute," the Smithsonian. Somewhat ironically, given the federal government's expansionist policies, Fuller's predecessors included government bureaucrats using federal funds first to achieve, then to popularize, a full record of American Indian life.

THOMAS McKENNEY'S INDIAN ARCHIVES

During the first third of the nineteenth century, the single most influential official concerned with the destinies of America's Indian tribes was Colonel Thomas L. McKenney (1785-1859). Serving under four presidents, from James Madison to Andrew Jackson, he persuaded the government to invite delegates from Indian tribes to Washington for treaty negotiations, and he acquired a reputation as a fierce champion of their human rights, first as Superintendent of the Indian Trade Bureau and then as chief of the Bureau of Indian Affairs. His sympathy for the native plight hardly altered immediate government policy, however. Jackson's administration, bent on permanently removing the Indian population out of the white man's way, had no place for McKenney and finally forced him from office.[15]

To be sure, McKenney like many other well-intentioned officials up to the present, wanted to save the native population by assimilating it into white American culture. But although he deliberately encouraged the dismantling of tribal cultures for what he took to be their own good, he valued their manifold accomplishments nonetheless. Of greater consequence than his pleas to the federal government on behalf of Indian rights was what he liked to call his "Archives," a

[14] Ibid., p. 91.
[15] For background material on McKenney, see Herman J. Viola, *Thomas L. McKenney, Architect of America's Early Indian Policy: 1816-1830* (Chicago: Swallow Press, 1974), esp. pp. 143-44, 185ff.; Thomas L. McKenney, *Memoirs, Official and Personal; With Sketches of Travels among the Northern and Southern Indians*, 2d ed., 2 vols. (New York: Paine and Burgess, 1846); Michael Rogin, "Indian Extinction, American Regeneration," *Journal of Ethnic Studies*, 2 (Spring 1974), 96-97; James D. Horan, *The McKenney-Hall Portrait Gallery of American Indians* (New York: Crown, 1972), pp. 21-111; Bernard W. Sheehan, *Seeds of Extinction: Jeffersonian Philanthropy and the American Indian* (New York: W. W. Norton, 1973), pp. 121ff.

collection of items "relating to our aborigines preserved there for the inspection of the curious and for the information of future generations and long after the Indians will have been no more."[16] While on far-ranging travels along the western and southern frontiers, he gathered countless artifacts, as well as a series of anecdotes, narratives, and myths. At an early stage, McKenney realized the unique power of his position as Superintendent of the Indian Trade Bureau, and by 1817 he was sending general requests to anyone who might be of help. Missionaries, Indian agents, frontiersmen, factors, and government representatives soon forwarded journals, tribal vocabularies, descriptions of Indian medicinal lore, and much other information. "Apparently it became known on the frontier," one scholar has observed, "that McKenney was collecting anything to do with Indian culture; there was always a letter from an old frontiersman offering a 'manuscript' or a 'journal' of Indian captivity or a missionary with 'a scholarly work on the tribes.' "[17] In McKenney's words, he set this project in motion "with the view of preserving in the archives of the Government whatever of the aboriginal man can be rescued from the destruction which awaits his race."[18]

McKenney was already dreaming of an Indian archive when he took office in 1816. The idea of a portrait gallery occurred to him in the winter of 1821-1822, when a large delegation of midwestern natives arrived in Washington. Caught up in the town's enthusiasm, he commissioned from the reputable portraitist Charles Bird King twenty-five paintings of chiefs and warriors in that delegation. King, though he continued to paint Indian visitors in his Washington studio for twenty more years, never shared the younger Catlin's extraordinary excitement for this work. McKenney, however, came much closer to that feeling and worked indefatigably to persuade his immediate superiors of the value of such records. John C. Calhoun, Secretary of War at the time, was already convinced that native tribes

---

[16] Cited in Horan, *McKenney-Hall Portrait Gallery*, p. 23; see also p. 51.
[17] Ibid., p. 62.
[18] Cited in ibid., p. 61. Herman J. Viola, in *Thomas L. McKenney*, p. 244, quotes from the circular that McKenney sent to all superintendents, agents, and missionaries on August 22, 1825: " 'It is for us of the present generation, if possible, to put it in the power of history to say something more of these wonderful people, than that "they once lived." ' Although all Indian languages were important to the study, McKenney asked that particular attention be given to 'any such isolated being known to you as the "last man" of his Tribe—to get from him the words called for. Such a man may be looked upon as the connecting link between time and eternity, as to all that regards his people; and which, if it be lost, all that relates to his Tribe is gone forever! When a preservation of it might lead to the most enlightening and gratifying results.' "

were "about to become extinct,"[19] and in 1824 he formalized and extended King's commission. The unflagging McKenney then encouraged Calhoun to employ another painter as well. From that point on, King made portraits of chiefs visiting the nation's capital, while the self-taught artist James Otto Lewis worked out of St. Louis, painting treaty negotiations on the spot.[20]

Calhoun's successor as Secretary of War, James Barbour, shared his predecessor's regretful conviction and gladly extended the official arrangements.[21] However, a belt-tightening Congress compelled McKenney to account for nearly every penny expended by his office. In an 1828 letter to the public, the bureau chief defended his policy in familiar terms: he and his colleagues were preserving a record of an aspect of American life that was too rapidly disappearing.[22] His motives failed to move Indian-despising congressmen, who charged the beleaguered chief with having wasted $3,190, as one sneered, "for the pictures of those wretches."[23] Following McKenney's dismissal in 1830, such expenditures ceased.

By the spring of 1832, as George Catlin set out on his seven-year research mission, McKenney had already pressed well ahead on an elephant folio of color lithographs of Indian portraits. Judge James Hall, a popular western novelist and man of letters, had agreed to write an accompanying text for McKenney's materials. Though a financially ruinous project, the three-volume *History of the Indian Tribes of North America* (1836-1844) proved far more fortunate than Hall could have guessed or McKenney would ever know: the devastating 1865 fire in the Smithsonian Institution destroyed McKenney's entire archives, with the exception of only thirty of the hundreds of original portraits by King and Lewis.[24]

Of the four men involved in this project, Judge Hall seems the least likely to have concerned himself with Indians. Nevertheless, his narrow race prejudice did not prevent him from coming to recognize

---

[19] Cited in Flexner, *That Wilder Image*, p. 78.

[20] See Herman J. Viola, *The Indian Legacy of Charles Bird King* (Washington: Smithsonian Institution Press, 1976), for discussion of King's career.

[21] See Thomas L. McKenney and James Hall, *The Indian Tribes of North America, with Biographical Sketches and Anecdotes of the Principal Chiefs* (1836-44), new ed. Frederick Webb Hodge, 3 vols. (Edinburgh: John Grant, 1933-34), 1:xxxiii.

[22] Ibid., 1:xxxiv. See also Flexner, *That Wilder Image*, p. 78.

[23] Horan, *McKenney-Hall Portrait Gallery*, p. 91; Viola, *Thomas L. McKenney*, pp. 248-50.

[24] See Bernard DeVoto, *Across the Wide Missouri* (Boston: Houghton Mifflin Co., 1947), p. 399.

12. Charles Bird King, *No-Way-Ke-Sug-Ga, Oto Tribe,* 1837. Lithograph colored with watercolor. Author's collection.

the need for a comprehensive record.[25] Similar motives seem to have compelled the two painters. Certainly Lewis felt this way, as he made clear in the introduction to his *North American Aboriginal Port-Folio* (1835-1836).[26] Although King left no written record of his reasons for undertaking the 143 portraits he completed in the course of twenty years, a great deal is suggested by his willingness to paint nearly thirty portraits of native dignitaries—some without remuneration—during the years following McKenney's dismissal.[27]

Aside from its quality and exhaustiveness, McKenney's project continues to deserve praise, along with Catlin's, as one of the few private attempts to publish western scenes. Lewis and King completed the first paintings we have of the Plains Indians, and the *History of the Indian Tribes* remains "a monument of American culture, solely because of the portraits."[28] More to the point, the four men wanted to ensure a pictorial record of vanishing native life. McKenney in particular committed himself no less energetically than Catlin and over a similarly long career, and like Catlin too, he saw that extraordinary commitment completely drain his funds. An 1830 guide to Washington best describes the monument to his pennilessness. Directing visitors to the "Indian Archives" on the second floor of the War Department building, it concludes: "But for this gallery, our posterity would ask in vain—'*what sort of a looking being was the red man of this country?*' In vain would the inquirers be told to *read* descriptions of him—these never could satisfy. He must be *seen* to be known. Here then is a gift to posterity."[29]

SURVEY PAINTERS AND THE EASTMANS IN THE 1840S

Prior to the 1850s, the prohibitive expense of lithographed or steel-engraved prints meant that publishers only rarely considered the venture; crude wood-block sketches served well enough. The federal government alone could consistently afford to send artists west and to illustrate subsequent reports with fine-lined prints.[30] The character-

25 James Hall, *Sketches of History, Life, and Manners in the West*, 2 vols. (Philadelphia: Harrison Hall, 1835), p. 27.

26 James Otto Lewis, *The North American Aboriginal Port-Folio* (1835-36; rpt. New York: J. P. Callender, 1838), p. 2. See also DeVoto, *Across the Wide Missouri*, pp. 399-400, for background information.

27 Viola, *Charles Bird King*, p. 88.

28 DeVoto, *Across the Wide Missouri*, p. 399.

29 Cited in Viola, *Thomas L. McKenney*, p. 231. For another tribute, see Minnie Myrtle, *The Iroquois; or, The Bright Side of Indian Character* (New York: D. Appleton and Co., 1855), pp. 14-15.

30 DeVoto, *Across the Wide Missouri*, p. 398.

istic art of the West before mid-century, then, resulted not from costly individual efforts but from railroad surveys and army exploratory expeditions.

Men like Samuel Seymour, Titian Ramsey Peale, and Samuel Carvalho, Gustavus Sohon, George Gibbs, and Edward and Richard Kern accompanied the various government expeditions of the second quarter of the century, giving Americans their earliest accurate images of the newly explored West and its inhabitants.[31] Characteristically, they left few written accounts; many surely sought their positions in hopes of excitement and exotic scenes and the promise of security offered by regular salary and relatively comfortable travel. Yet how can one account for the frequent attempts by these artists and draftsmen to achieve a far more exhaustive illustration of tribal life than required? The accounts left by a handful of survey artists from the 1840s and 1850s, including those of Balduin Möllhausen, Carl Wimar, Albert Bierstadt, and especially John Mix Stanley, reveal their self-conscious urge to complete such illustrations before whites had irrevocably altered native life.[32] Far from applying their skills indiscriminately,

[31] John Francis McDermott, "Samuel Seymour: Pioneer Artist of the Plains and the Rockies," in *Annual Report of the Board of Regents of the Smithsonian Institution, 1950* (Washington: G.P.O., 1951), pp. 498-501; Poesch, *Titan Ramsey Peale*, esp. pp. 22-24; Joan Sturhahn, *Carvalho: Artist—Photographer—Adventurer —Patriot: Portrait of a Forgotten American* (Merrick, N.Y.: Richwood Publishing Co., 1976), esp. pp. 70, 85-88, 105-6, 115; John C. Ewers, "Gustavus Sohon's Portraits of Flathead and Pend D'Oreille Indians, 1854," *Smithsonian Miscellaneous Collections*, 110 (Washington: G.P.O., 1948), 5-6; George Gibbs, *Indian Tribes of Washington Territory: Pacific Northwest Letters of George Gibbs* (1854; rpt. Fairfield, Wash.: Ye Galleon Press, 1967); David I. Bushnell Jr., "Drawings by George Gibbs in the Far Northwest, 1849-1851," *Smithsonian Miscellaneous Collections*, 97 (Washington: G.P.O., 1938), 1-28; Lt. James H. Simpson, *Journal of a Military Reconnaissance from Santa Fé, New Mexico to the Navajo Country* (Philadelphia: Lippincott, Grambo and Co., 1852); Robert V. Hine, *Edward Kern and American Expansion* (New Haven: Yale University Press, 1962); *The Published Pictures, Portraits and Maps Collectively Depicting the Indians, Scenery and Topography of the Far West, Drawn by Edward Kern and Richard Kern, 1846-1851*, Fort Sutter Papers, vol. 39, Huntington Library, San Marino; Ewers, "Fact and Fiction," pp. 79-89; H. Chadwick Hunter, "The American Indian in Painting," *Art and Archaeology*, 8 (April 1919), 80-96; Fairbanks, introduction to *Frontier America*, pp. 15-23; William H. Truettner, "Natural History and the Natural Man: Art and Science in the West," in *Frontier America*, pp. 40-42.

[32] Balduin Möllhausen, *Diary of a Journey from the Mississippi to the Coasts of the Pacific*, trans. Mrs. Percy Sinnett, 2 vols. (London: Longman, Brown, Green, Longmans, and Roberts, 1858), esp. 1:xii-xiii; Preston Albert Barba, *Balduin Möllhausen: The German Cooper* (Philadelphia: University of Pennsylvania Press, 1914), pp. 46-52, 135-36; Perry T. Rathbone, *Charles Wimar, 1828-1862: Painter of the Indian Frontier* (St. Louis: City Art Museum, 1946), pp. 5, 15-17; William Romaine Hodges, *Carl Wimar: A Biography* (Galveston: Charles Reymershoffer, 1908), esp. epigraph; Gordon Hendricks, *Albert Bierstadt: Painter of the American West* (New York:

these men pursued positions with western surveys expressly to paint Indian tribes as they still remained.[33]

From the 1820s on, the army's developing system of forts in Indian country provided military personnel a unique opportunity to fill sketchbooks with illustrations of Indian life. Lieutenant Seth Eastman (1809-1875), a West Point graduate trained in art, was first assigned to Fort Snelling, Minnesota, in the spring of 1830. Almost immediately, he conceived the idea of producing an Indian gallery, and on his own time he started drawing nearby tribes.[34] His project was interrupted early in 1833 for tours of duty at West Point and in Florida. Only in 1841 was he able to rejoin the regiment at Fort Snelling. During the next seven years he learned a number of Dakota languages fluently and devoted his free hours to unobtrusively sketching Chippewa and Sioux domestic scenes and ceremonies. So careful a student could hardly fail to notice the new patterns altering tribal life. For this reason, perhaps, his sketching was "not a mere occupation"; according to his wife, "it became a passion with him."[35]

By 1846 Eastman had completed more than four hundred oils and watercolors. A visitor to the fort that summer who wandered into Eastman's crowded little studio, described his amazement at the stunning canvases "comprising every variety of scenes, from the grand Medicine Dance to the singular and affecting Indian Grave. When

Harry N. Abrams, 1974), pp. 63, 69-70, 94; Hendricks, "The First Three Western Journeys of Albert Bierstadt," *Art Bulletin*, 46 (September 1964), 337-39; John Mix Stanley, "Portraits of North American Indians with Sketches of Scenery, Etc.," *Smithsonian Miscellaneous Collections*, 2 (1862), 1-76; Nellie B. Pipes, "John Mix Stanley, Indian Painter," *Oregon Historical Quarterly*, 33 (September 1932), 253, 256; W. Vernon Kinietz, *John Mix Stanley and His Indian Paintings* (Ann Arbor: University of Michigan Press, 1942); Robert Taft, *Artists and Illustrators of the Old West 1850-1900* (New York: Charles Scribner's Sons, 1953), pp. 27, 35, 258-59, 8, 18.

33 John Mix Stanley, whose career included the most extensive experiences of any major western artist, joined a number of expeditions in the 1840s for just this reason. In 1852 he loaned his marvelous collection to the Smithsonian Institution, declaring in his preface to the catalogue of 152 paintings: "Even these brief sketches, it is hoped, will not fail to interest those who look at their portraits, and excite some desire that the memory, at least, of these tribes may not become extinct" ("Portraits of North American Indians," preface). Unforunately, his paintings were lost in the great Smithsonian fire, and he left no other testament to his motives. See also DeVoto, *Across the Wide Missouri*, pp. 398-99, 450-51; Harold McCracken, *Portrait of the Old West, With a Biographical Check List of Western Artists* (New York: McGraw-Hill, 1952), pp. 97-98; Larry Curry, *The American West: Painters from Catlin to Russell* (New York: Viking, 1972), p. 23.

34 John Francis McDermott, *Seth Eastman: Pictorial Historian of the Indian* (Norman: University of Oklahoma Press, 1961), p. 3.

35 Mary Eastman to Benjamin Pringle, March 14, 1856, cited in McDermott, *Seth Eastman*, p. 39. See also ibid., pp. 4-5, 36-37, 52, 91-92, 102-110; David I. Bushnell Jr., "Seth Eastman: The Master Painter of the North American Indian," *Smithsonian Miscellaneous Collections*, 87 (April 11, 1932).

13. Seth Eastman, *Indians Playing Draught*, 1848. Oil on canvas. Private collection. Photograph courtesy of M. Knoedler & Co., Inc., New York.

the extent and character of this Indian Gallery are considered, it must be acknowledged the most valuable in the country, not even excepting that of George Catlin."[36] Eastman had steadily refused to part with any paintings, even rejecting handsome professional offers

[36] Charles Lanman, *A Summer in the Wilderness*, p. 59, cited in John Francis McDermott, *Seth Eastman's Mississippi: A Lost Portfolio Recovered* (Urbana: University of Illinois Press, 1973), p. 6.

in order to continue among the tribes he knew so well.[37] In the three years after 1848, however, he sold twenty-odd paintings to the Western Art Union in Cincinnati and the American Art Union in New York, where they were immediately exhibited—striking evidence of his almost instant popularity.

During this same period, Congress authorized the Office of Indian Affairs to publish an exhaustive volume on American Indian tribes. Legislative sympathies had altered dramatically in the dozen years since McKenney's project had been terminated. Henry Rowe Schoolcraft, considered the most distinguished ethnologist in America, agreed to collect material and write the text. George Catlin, the most celebrated among contemporary painters of the Indian, haughtily refused to supply illustrations to a government that had refused to purchase his collection. On the other hand, Schoolcraft's second choice actively solicited the position. In 1849 Eastman was transferred to Washington, where for the next six years he prepared three hundred plates for Schoolcraft's celebrated *Indian Tribes of the United States* (1851-1857).[38]

Eastman's achievement warrants consideration for a number of reasons. As a trained watercolorist, he anticipated by more than a quarter century the effects that other American artists would achieve in landscape technique. As a documentarian, his careful studies of Indian artifacts, paintings, and costumes attest to an extraordinary ethnological knowledge. A journalist once remarked of him that he knew the Sioux so well he could "read the private history of a chief or brave by the ornaments which decorate his person."[39] Although this kind of knowledge may have differed only in degree from that of many another sensitive army officer in the West, Eastman's ability to preserve this knowledge in paint and in the descriptive notes he attached to each finished canvas sets him and his achievement apart from all others.

No less committed to preserving a record of Plains Indian life, and more explicit in her reasons for doing so, was Eastman's wife, the author Mary Eastman (1818-1880). The pattern of their joint careers suggests that she spoke for him as well. Although she achieved her greatest commercial success in 1852 with *Aunt Phillis' Cabin*, a rejoinder to Harriet Beecher Stowe,[40] she had earlier devoted years of

[37] Ibid., pp. 6ff.   [38] McDermott, *Seth Eastman*, pp. 63-78.

[39] Cited in David Lavender, *The American Heritage History of the Great West*, ed. Alvin M. Josephy Jr. (New York: American Heritage, 1965), p. 150. See also McDermott, *Seth Eastman*, pp. 90-91; Rudisill, *Mirror Image*, p. 96.

[40] McDermott, *Seth Eastman*, p. 93. See also Herbert Ross Brown, *The Sentimental Novel in America, 1789-1860* (Chapel Hill: Duke University Press, 1940), pp. 260-67.

energy to recording northern Sioux culture. Already aware by the 1840s of the parlous condition of tribes near Fort Snelling, she acquired a working knowledge of their languages as an entrance into their lives. The texts she wrote to accompany her husband's plates in *The Romance of Indian Life* (1853) and *The American Aboriginal Portfolio* (1853) stress both the red man's imminent disappearance and the value of the "faithfully depicted" record that she and her husband had compiled.[41] In their first collaboration, *Dahcotah; or, Life and Legends of the Sioux Around Fort Snelling* (1849), she specified more explicitly the reasons for their commitments:

> It will still be my endeavor to depict all the customs, feasts and ceremonies of the Sioux, before it be too late. The account of them may be interesting, when the people who so long believed in them will be no more. . . . They are receding rapidly, and with feeble resistance, before the giant strides of civilization. The hunting grounds of a few savages will soon become the haunts of densely peopled, civilized settlements. We should be better reconciled to this manifest destiny of the aborigines, if the inroads of civilization were worthy of it.[42]

This short preface intimates the pattern of the study, to be developed in the course of the following chapters: the transition from early, rushed attempts to depict and understand a disappearing native culture to somber questioning of the supplanting white culture. Of course, for all their manifest concern to record native life, the Eastmans never seriously doubted the superiority of white culture or even shed their conventional, sentimental assumptions about the Sioux they so sympathetically fixed in colors and words. Mary Eastman's final clause above barely suggests a troubling possibility.

INDEPENDENT PAINTERS IN THE 1850S

Although the federal government was one of the few reliable employers of artists in the West before the Civil War, hiring men like Eastman for its own purposes and then allowing them to fulfill personal missions, financial considerations did not altogether prevent private individuals from pursuing similar projects. Among these, a number of Europeans, with perhaps a greater sense of the exotic or

---

[41] Mary H. Eastman, *The American Aboriginal Portfolio* (Philadelphia: Lippincott, Grambo and Co., [1853]), p. v, and *The Romance of Indian Life* (Philadelphia: Lippincott, Grambo and Co., 1853), p. xi.

[42] Mary H. Eastman, *Dahcotah; or, Life and Legends of the Sioux Around Fort Snelling* (Minneapolis: Ross and Haines, 1962), p. xvi.

a more wistful yearning, came to the North American continent expressly to document a threatened wilderness and its inhabitants.

In the case of the Prussian Prince Maximilian zu Wied, who brought the talented young Swiss artist Karl Bodmer to accompany his 1833 ethnological tour of the upper Missouri territory, financial considerations were even more obviously irrelevant. Maximilian's wealth bought a priceless record. Painting far fewer tribes than had Catlin the summer before, Bodmer achieved far more detailed portraits. Where those paintings duplicate Catlin's subjects, the advantages of Bodmer's training as a draftsman and, more important, his leisurely pace are obvious. Anthropologists and art critics consider his eighty-one paintings among the finest completed in the antebellum period. Bodmer himself left nothing in words to indicate his intentions or responses, and he apparently never looked back on that part of his career from his subsequent success in France. On the other hand, scholars have long acknowledged the surpassing historical significance of Maximilian's *Travels in the Interior of North America* (1839), in which the prince claims motives similar to those of Catlin, McKenney, and the Eastmans.[43]

Another adventurous aristocrat, Sir William Drummond Stewart, visited the Rockies half a dozen times beginning in 1833, and he commissioned the young American artist Alfred Jacob Miller to accompany his 1837 tour of the West. In *Altowan* (1846), Stewart's later fictionalized record, he too expressed appreciation for the threat to landscape and native inhabitants.[44]

Important as their records are, these European aristocrats represent only a small proportion of the committed individuals who sought out the experiences of the West. Impecunious artists drawn to wilderness scenes by imagined commissions, tourists with sketch pads in hand, missionaries with a bent for illustration as well as writing—all attempted "artistic delineations," as one observed, that might "preserve from obliteration the likenesses, habits and customs of some at least, of the unfortunate race of red men."[45] If the names Felix O. C.

[43] Maximilian zu Wied, *Travels in the Interior of North America* (1843), reprinted as vols. 22-24 of Reubon Gold Thwaites, ed., *Early Western Travels 1748-1846* (Cleveland: Arthur H. Clark Co., 1906), pp. 26-28, 70-71. See also Maximilian zu Wied, *People of the First Man: Life among the Plains Indians in Their Final Days of Glory*, ed. Davis Thomas and Karin Ronnefeldt (New York: E. P. Dutton, 1976), pp. 6-13, 50, 120; DeVoto, *Across the Wide Missouri*, p. 402.

[44] Stewart, *Altowan; or, Incidents of Life and Adventure in the Rocky Mountains by an Amateur Traveler*, ed. J. Watson Webb, 2 vols. (New York: Harper and Brothers, 1846), pp. iii, vi.

[45] Winter, *The Journals and Indian Paintings of George Winter, 1837-1839* (Indianapolis: Indian Historical Society, 1948), p. 152.

Darley, George Winter, Rudolph Friedrich Kurz, Nicolas Point, and Peter Rindisbacher elicit no recognition today, it is not because these men felt less apprehensive or committed themselves less wholeheartedly than Catlin or McKenney.[46] Rather, their anonymity reflects their lesser accomplishment. That these individuals also undertook severe privations without government aid or private financing only confirms the extent of the mid-nineteenth-century movement to paint a record of Indian life.

Evidence further suggests that Catlin's self-publicizing in the 1840s encouraged similar careers on the part of other painters, including Charles Deas, Frank Blackwell Mayer, and John Mix Stanley.[47] Among them, the Canadian Paul Kane (1810-1871) most self-consciously patterned his own ambitions on Catlin's. As an art student in Europe, he was befriended by the older painter, who had just left New York City to exhibit his collection abroad. Catlin's influence, plus Kane's reading of books that called attention to the passing wilderness, confirmed the student in his new-found mission.[48] In 1845 he returned to Toronto, impelled by the need to "see the aborigines of this country in their original state."[49] Luckily, Kane found a sympathetic patron who commissioned from him one hundred Indian

[46] Felix O. C. Darley, *Scenes in Indian Life*, 4 nos. (Philadelphia: J. R. Colon, April-July 1843); Parry, *Image of the Indian*, pp. 77-79; Winter, *Journals and Indian Paintings*, pp. 96, 98, 105-8, 111, 119-20; *Journal of Rudolph Friedrich Kurz: An Account of His Experiences among Fur Traders and American Indians on the Mississippi and the Upper Missouri Rivers During the Years 1846 to 1852*, trans. Myrtis Jarrell, ed. J.N.B. Hewitt, Smithsonian Institution, Bureau of American Ethnology, Bulletin 115 (Washington: G.P.O., 1937), pp. 2, 129; *Wilderness Kingdom—Indian Life in the Rocky Mountains: 1840-1847. The Journals and Paintings of Nicolas Point, S.J.*, trans. Joseph P. Donnelly, S.J. (New York: Holt, Rinehart and Winston, 1967); Pierre Jean de Smet, S.J., *Oregon Missions and Travels Over the Rocky Mountains, in 1845-46* (1847), illus. by Nicholas Point, S.J., reprinted as vol. 29 of Thwaites, ed., *Early Western Travels* p. 111; Alvin M. Josephy Jr., *The Artist Was a Young Man: The Life Story of Peter Rindisbacher* (Fort Worth: Amon Carter Museum, 1970); DeVoto, *Across the Wide Missouri*, pp. 393-94; McCracken, *Portrait of the Old West*; Hugh Honour, *The New Golden Land: European Images of America from the Discoveries to the Present Time* (New York: Pantheon Books, 1975), p. 238; Ewers, *Artists of the Old West*. See also Gibbs, *Indian Tribes of Washington Territory*; Bushnell, "Drawings by George Gibbs."

[47] Parry, *Image of the Indian*, pp. 77-79; McCracken, *Portrait of the Old West*, pp. 97-98; Frank Blackwell Mayer, *With Pen and Pencil on the Frontier in 1851: The Diary and Sketches of Frank Blackwell Mayer*, ed. Bertha L. Heilbron (St. Paul: Minnesota Historical Society, 1932), pp. 2-6, 14-15.

[48] For details of Kane's career, see *Paul Kane's Frontier*, ed. J. Russell Harper (Austin: University of Texas Press, 1971), pt. 1; Albert H. Robson, *Paul Kane* (Toronto: Ryerson Press, 1938), pp. 4-14.

[49] Kane, *Wanderings of an Artist among the Indians of North America from Canada to Vancouver's Island and Oregon through the Hudson's Bay Company's Territory* (1859; rpt. Toronto: Radisson Society of Canada, 1925), pp. lii-liii.

paintings. During the next two and a half years he traversed Canada, completing more than five hundred sketches, detailed portraits, and genre scenes in order to produce a finished cycle of paintings that would memorialize all phases of native life.

The careful travel journal Kane published with his sketches, *Wanderings of an Artist among the Indians of North America* (1859), sold out within a few months; three foreign-language editions followed within four years. Perhaps most strikingly, foreign reviews reveal the pervasiveness of the popular anxieties that Kane touched. The London *Athenaeum* thought he "had devoted himself to an American purpose, sketching and recording the deeds and outward forms of an unhappily vanishing race."[50] A French reviewer took twenty-three pages in the prestigious *Revue des deux mondes* to make the same point, and he particularly praised Kane's documentary presentation.[51]

The popular reception for Kane, Seth Eastman, John Mix Stanley, Karl Bodmer, and George Catlin indicates the tenor of national and international concern developing for native American life. Most whites felt indifferent to the Indian and his fate. Even the more intelligently aware welcomed western artists because they, like their less perceptive contemporaries, were simply intrigued by the configuration of the country and its inhabitants. Yet if we do no more than speculate from the kind of critical reception accorded Kane and others, their enthusiasm also issued from a more profound realization of the need to make records before opportunities passed.

Many looked to the federal government to support such efforts. Though, as we have seen, McKenney did not win enough congressional support to continue his collecting and was indeed cut off, he did for a time receive government financing. Two decades later, despite a crippling economic depression, Congress came within a hair's breadth of purchasing Catlin's large collection. By 1853, McKenney's successor in the Bureau of Indian Affairs sensed "an increasing regret that the Government has not taken more timely and efficient measures for preserving memorials of the race. A National Portrait Gallery of distinguished Indians permanently located at the seat of Government, would certainly be an object of general interest and that interest would continue to increase with the lapse of time."[52]

Private owners of paintings of Indians began near mid-century to

50 Cited in J. Russell Harper's introduction to *Paul Kane's Frontier*, p. 40.
51 Cited by Harper in ibid., p. 41.
52 Commissioner of Indian Affairs Luke Lea to W. Sebastian, cited in Viola, *Indian Legacy of Charles Bird King*, p. 115.

14. Paul Kane, *Sault Ste. Marie (Ojibwa Village)*, 1845-1848. Oil on canvas. The Royal Ontario Museum, Toronto.

give them to state and local historical societies for safe-keeping as well as for public enjoyment.[53] Joseph Henry, who by 1858 had served as secretary of the Smithsonian Institution for more than a decade, warned in his annual report for that year that the paintings and artifacts already gathered from native tribes were irreplaceable. Additionally, he "hoped that Congress will in due time purchase the portraits belonging to Mr. [John Mix] Stanley which will become more and more valuable in the progress of the gradual extinction of the race of which they are such faithful representations."[54] During the next twenty years, Henry labored assiduously to convince the owner of Catlin's collection to bequeath it to the nation.

POST-CIVIL WAR PAINTERS

Following the Civil War, spiritual descendants of Catlin, Bodmer, and Kane proliferated, encouraged by public enthusiasm for their

[53] Buck, "Lappawinzo and Tishcohan," pp. 215-18; Lockwood, "St. Memin Indian Portraits," p. 3.

[54] Joseph Henry, "Report of the Secretary for 1858," in *Annual Report of the Board of Regents of the Smithsonian Institution* (Washington: G.P.O., 1859), p. 42.

work. Perhaps that popularity itself made it unnecessary for them to express their seemingly self-evident commitment. Men like William de la Montagne Cary, Henry Farny, Edwin W. Deming, Elbridge Ayer Burbank, Ralph A. Blakelock, and Charles Schreyvogel traveled west to acquire realistic documents of tribal life.[55] Although the popular magazines that bought their illustrations demanded only colorful sketches, these artists sought both accuracy and sympathetic insight. Some, like George de Forest Brush, Charles M. Russell, DeCost Smith, and Charles Craig, spent months and years learning Indian languages or living among tribes.[56] Admiring native skills and tradition, they deplored the forces threatening them. Ironically, their finished work often appears to idealize and sentimentalize, since so often they found the Indian's already reduced circumstances less interesting, and more appalling, than his life prior to white influence. These artists hoped to preserve a record of what had already distinctly passed.

In a very few areas, traditional Indian culture managed to survive intact through the 1890s. The pueblos of the Southwest, for example, had secured themselves against European invaders and external attractions for centuries. Traditional, mysterious, peaceable even to the point of apparent passivity—these tribes treasured a land that seemed harshly unappealing, indeed, actively hostile, to immigrants bent on finding a place for permanent settlement. The Hopi, Zuni, and Rio Grande Pueblos, as well as the Navaho, Pima, and Papago, enjoyed isolation at a time when aggressive pioneers forced their brethren elsewhere to conform to white dictates. Largely ignored, they were thereby able to retain their distinctive cultures. During the late 1880s, when artists and anthropologists finally realized the extent of rich tribal experience waiting to be documented, time had not already run out.

[55] Harmsen, *Harmsen's Western Americana*, pp. 26-27, 38, 42; Curry, *American West*, p. 30; Peter Hassrick *The Way West: Art of Frontier America* (New York: Harry N. Abrams, 1977), pp. 192ff.; Taft, *Artists and Illustrators of the Old West*, pp. 214, 217-25, 227-30; McCracken, *Portrait of the Old West*; Norman A. Geske, "Ralph Albert Blakelock in the West," *American Art Review*, 3 (January-February 1976), 123-35; James D. Horan, *The Life and Art of Charles Schreyvogel: Painter-Historian of the Indian-Fighting Army of the American West* (New York: Crown, 1969), pp. 17, 27-28.

[56] George de Forest Brush, "An Artist Among the Indians," *Century Magazine*, 30 (May 1885), 54-57; Harold McCracken, *The Charles M. Russell Book: The Life and Work of the Cowboy Artist* (Garden City N.Y.: Doubleday and Co., 1957); Ewers, *Artists of the Old West*, p. 232; Harmsen, *Harmsen's Western Americana*, pp. 54, 182. See also Howard Doughty, *Francis Parkman* (New York: Macmillan Co., 1962), p. 392n; Searles R. Boynton, "The Pomo Indian Portraits of Grace Carpenter Hudson," *American West*, 14 (September-October 1977), 25.

The schools of painters that established themselves around Taos and Santa Fe shared little more than an attraction to the Southwest and a self-conscious commitment to record "what was thought of as a dying race and the grandeur of an austere landscape."[57] Joseph Sharp (1859-1953), around whom the Taos art colony later grew, first visited the pueblo in 1893. Realizing that the tribe had created a complex culture, he attempted to reproduce with ethnographic accuracy their distinctive facial structure and costumes, ceremonials and customs. Over a long career, he came to be known as "the anthropologist" by fellow artists, many of whom he had already persuaded in the early 1890s to leave eastern and European studios behind in order to settle in the region.

Like Catlin and Stanley more than half a century before, Sharp traveled throughout the Far West in order to document tribes already in their last phases as autonomous cultures. Describing an 1899 painting trip to the heart of the old Sioux country in southeastern Montana, he explained, "I went north because I realized Taos would last longer."[58] Sharp spent two years in Montana—the second year in a cabin built under President Theodore Roosevelt's authorization next to the old Custer battlefield—painting hundreds of Plains Indian studies. He returned to New Mexico in 1902 to contir 1e the work for which he and his colleagues subsequently became famous. "In the past years I have seen so many things and made studies that probably no other living artist ever saw," Sharp once claimed, "that if I do not paint none ever will."[59] Today, Sharp's scrupulously detailed studies of tribal life are considered accurate enough to justify their inclusion in university anthropology collections and in the Smithsonian's Bureau of Ethnology.

Despite the genuine accomplishments of Sharp and others, the pictorial record of Indian life undertaken after the Civil War suffers in comparison with that completed earlier. Artists of the late 1850s and 1860s in general turned away from the individually distinctive toward the characteristic gesture or type. George Catlin and Seth Eastman had strived to paint precisely what they saw; Henry Farny and Joseph Sharp attempted in larger part to *recreate* a recent past.

[57] Van Deren Coke, *Taos and Santa Fe: The Artist's Environment, 1882-1942* (Albuquerque: University of New Mexico Press, 1963), p. 9, also pp. 11-16. See also Laura M. Bickerstaff, *Pioneer Artists of Taos* (Denver: Sage Books, 1955), esp. pp. 85-87; Patricia Trenton, "Picturesque Images of Taos and Santa Fe," *American Art Review*, 1 (March-April 1974), 97-98; Harmsen, *Harmsen's Western Americana*, p. 178.

[58] Cited in Bickerstaff, *Pioneer Artists of Taos*, p. 86.

[59] Cited in Coke, *Taos and Santa Fe*, p. 16.

15. Joseph Sharp, *Taos Indian Portrait*, 1914. Oil on canvas. Museum of New Mexico, Santa Fe.

Canvases completed after the Civil War, however detailed, fully register the impact of white civilization, whether through the melancholy tone of portraits or the projected idealization of domestic and genre scenes. Attempting to do more than transcribe, these latter-day artists too often succumbed to their sympathies. By contrast, Catlin conceived of his mission as a more narrowly documentary project and rarely revealed his own feelings in his paintings.

THE FRONTIER PHOTOGRAPHER

Perhaps one reason for this shift from representational accuracy was the invention of the daguerreotype in 1839. Throughout the next half century, as rapid improvements in the photographic process encouraged hundreds to haul equipment west, the camera gradually replaced the paintbrush as the documentarian's tool of choice. The very nature of painting—demanding lengthy sessions for each canvas, the artist's conscious or unconscious conformity to conventions and innovations—prevented a complete or unbiased ethnographic record. Painters like Sharp still voiced a commitment to accuracy, but similar expressions occur far more frequently among those known to their subjects as the "shadow catchers."

Despite the bulky equipment, time-consuming processing, and unpredictable results of daguerreotype and wet-plate photography, as well as the skill and inordinate patience they required, American archaeologists and ethnologists quickly comprehended the camera's inestimable value for on-site work. The early photographic successes of Seth Eastman, Frederick Catherwood, and Henry Rowe Schoolcraft encouraged the first tentative use of photographic equipment on western expeditions. Secretary of the Smithsonian, Joseph Henry, in his 1858 annual report, added his enjoinder that photography be used particularly to document tribes yet unchanged.[60] For those sensitive to such developments, the replacement of the survey artist by the staff photographer seemed only a matter of a few technological improvements to aid portability. Even prior to such improvements, individuals like A. Zeno Shindler, C. M. Bell, and Alexander Gardner took off in the late fifties to work on their own as professional photographers among the western tribes.[61]

The corps of photographic teams equipped by Matthew Brady during the Civil War provided a training ground for many western

[60] Henry, "Report of the Secretary for 1858," pp. 41-42. See also Henry, "Circular Relating to Collections in Archaeology and Ethnology," *Smithsonian Miscellaneous Collections*, 8 (1868), pp. 1-2; Viola, *Indian Legacy of Charles Bird King*, p. 114.

[61] For background, see Chapters Two and Three above; Robert Taft, *Photography and the American Scene: A Social History, 1839-1889* (New York: Macmillan Co., 1938), pp. 282-283; Joanna Cohan Scherer, *Indians: The Great Photographs that Reveal North American Indian Life, 1847-1929* . . . (New York: Crown, 1973), esp. pp. 12-21; Gen. William J. Palmer, *Report of Surveys Across the Continent in 1867-'68 on the 35th and 32nd Parallels for a Route extending the Kansas Pacific Railway* (Philadelphia, 1869), esp. plates 16, 17.

practitioners. As well, wartime improvements transformed the camera into an efficient, reliable, and extremely accurate instrument. By the 1870s, an established group of well-trained, well-equipped photographers was available to act on the deepening concern for documenting vanishing tribes. Ironically, however, improvements in photography at the same time added pounds of equipment and demanded proportionately greater skill. Moreover, the kind of account that the camera might have provided of folk and subcultures in Europe and America was no longer possible by the time it was invented. Scholars have regretted that "as the technical means for providing a brilliant and vivid record of Indian life finally became available to the photographer, conditions of Indian life had so deteriorated that what remains is, for the most part, a visual record of a harassed, defeated, and degraded people."[62] Indeed, the very technology that could enable the most accurate depiction of native American cultures had already, in pernicious manifestations of gun, barbed wire, and windmill, hastened the decline of those cultures.

The peace at Appomattox that released dozens of accomplished photographers also released dozens of well-trained army battalions for western service. Making the West safe for settlement meant at best dislocation, at worst extermination of relatively defenseless tribes. Thus, despite the unquestionably superior objectivity of photography, most post-Civil War practitioners lacked the opportunity to surpass or even equal the insights into Indian culture gained by the pre-Civil War painters. Catlin's depiction of the vital coherence of the complex Mandan culture alone makes his series of paintings more valuable than most photographic records made only a half century later.

Of course, many photographers themselves, especially those aware of the diminished possibilities, felt the same documentarian motives as painters before them. In 1866 one Ridgeway Glover reportedly planned a photographic excursion specifically "to illustrate the life and character of the wild men of the prairie."[63] He hardly traveled alone. In the next fifteen years, more Indian photographs of historical and ethnological value were produced than ever before or since.[64]

62 Robert A. Weinstein and William Webb, *Dwellers at the Source: Southwestern Indian Photographs of A. C. Vroman, 1895-1904* (New York: Grossman, 1973), p. 10, also p. 14. See also Susan Sontag, *On Photography* (New York: Farrar, Straus and Giroux, 1977), pp. 15-16, 65, 76.

63 Cited in Russell E. Belous and Robert A Weinstein, *Will Soule: Indian Photographer at Fort Sill, Oklahoma, 1869-74* (Los Angeles: Ward Ritchie Press, 1969), p. 14.

64 Ibid., p. 15, also pp. 13-14. See also Taft, *Photography and the American Scene*, pp. 282-83.

Government survey photographers were joined by independents who packed their gear west to open studios and galleries. The works of E. A. Bonine in Arizona, Major G. W. Ingalls and Will Soule in Oklahoma, Major Horatio Nelson Rust in southern California, Laton Huffman and Frank Haynes in the Dakotas confirm their commitments to documentation, though, again, not one verified that commitment in writing.[65] Their reasons for photographing Indians, however mixed, would not have been financial, since studio work offered little profit and excursions to tribal grounds even less.

After the Civil War, as before, and for similar reasons, federally sponsored expeditions made possible the most extensive records of the West. Even in the 1850s, expedition artists—John Mix Stanley on Governor Isaac Stevens's Northwest survey and Samuel Carvalho on General John C. Frémont's Southwest expeditions—packed daguerreotyping equipment to record native tribes.[66] Three of the finest postwar photographers, John K. Hillers, Timothy H. O'Sullivan, and William Henry Jackson, were hired by western surveys that produced major published reports. Although O'Sullivan and Hillers never wrote of their responses to the native Americans at whom they so frequently pointed cameras, Major John Wesley Powell did. Leader of the 1872 Colorado River Survey and other important expeditions throughout the decade, he had hired Hillers in the explicit belief that the threatened western tribes cried out for immediate documentation.[67]

[65] E. A. Bonine collection of photographs, Huntington Library, San Marino, California; Gary F. Kurutz, "Pictorial Resources: The Henry E. Huntington Library's California and American West Collections," *California Historical Quarterly*, 54 (Summer 1975), esp. 178; Belous and Weinstein, *Will Soule*, esp. pp. 11-20; Horatio Nelson Rust Collection, Huntington Library, San Marino; Mark H. Brown and W. R. Felton, *The Frontier Years: L. A. Huffman, Photographer of the Plains* (New York: Bramhall House, 1955), esp. p. 238; Brown and Felton, *Before Barbed Wire: L. A. Huffman, Photographer on Horseback* (1956; rpt. New York: Bramhall House, 1961), pp. 12, 19-21; Freeman Tilden, *Following the Frontier with F. Jay Haynes: Pioneer Photographer of the Old West* (New York: Alfred A. Knopf, 1964), pp. 197ff.; F. Jay Haynes, *Indian Types of the North West* (New York: Adolph Wittemann, ca. 1885), esp. p. 3. See also "Photographic Portraits of North American Indians in the Gallery of the Smithsonian Institution," *Smithsonian Miscellaneous Collections*, 14 (1867), 1-42.

[66] Pipes, "John Mix Stanley," p. 255; Sturhahn, *Carvalho* pp. 68-70. Susan Sontag, in *On Photography*, p. 76, has claimed: "From the start, photographers not only set themselves the task of recording a disappearing world but were so employed by those hastening its disappearance." See also ibid., pp. 64-65.

[67] Wallace Stegner, *Beyond the Hundredth Meridian: John Wesley Powell and the Second Opening of the West* (Boston: Houghton Mifflin Co., 1954), p. 130. Powell's own energetic efforts will be examined in the following chapter; see here *"Photographed All the Best Scenery": Jack Hillers' Diary of the Powell Expeditions, 1871-1875*, ed. Don D. Fowler (Salt Lake City: University of Utah Press, 1972); Julian H.

16. Timothy H. O'Sullivan, "Aboriginal Life among the Navajoe Indians near Old Fort Defiance, New Mexico," 1873. Stereoptican photograph. Collection of Alfred L. Bush.

The frontier photographer who traveled farthest throughout the continent, achieved the greatest popularity and respect, and left the most comprehensive written record of his intentions and responses was William Henry Jackson (1843-1942). After a short stint in Nebraska as a free-lance photographer following the war, he accepted Ferdinand Vandeveer Hayden's offer to join his 1870 survey of the western territories. Perhaps Hayden first persuaded the young cameraman of the historical value of photographing native tribes. The commander already felt convinced of the logic of preserving vast tracts of wilderness as they were, and he vigorously encouraged documentation of wilderness scenes and frontier life as well as ethnographic studies of the waning Indian tribes.[68] His dramatic example, in fact, probably influenced Jackson's 1870 studies of the famous Shoshone chief Washakie and the tepee village at South Pass, Wyoming, which are among the earliest photographs of indigenous tribes prior to reservation conditions.[69]

Jackson's 1868 photographs of Indians near Omaha, as well as his later career, suggest that he needed little urging. Openly regretting missed opportunities on his first expedition, he nevertheless felt relieved at having obtained illustrations of native peoples and archaeological sites before they succumbed to white devastation. Jackson continued to travel throughout the West, and by 1877 he had compiled an extensive catalogue of available photographs—his own as well as those of others—of twenty-five tribes made over as many years. The short preface that his old mentor wrote enthusiastically described the collection as "undoubtedly the largest and most valu-

Steward, "Notes on Hillers' Photographs of the Paiute and Ute Indians Taken on the Powell Expedition of 1873," *Smithsonian Miscellaneous Collections*, 98 (1939), esp. p. 2. See also James D. Horan, *Timothy O'Sullivan, America's Forgotten Photographer* (Garden City, N.Y.: Doubleday and Co., 1966), pp. 153, 239; Beaumont and Nancy Newhall, *T. H. O'Sullivan: Photographer* (Rochester: George Eastman House, 1966); Taft, *Photography and the American Scene*, pp. 284-92.

[68] Ferdinand Vandever Hayden, *Sun Pictures of Rocky Mountain Scenery* (New York: Julius Bien, 1878), pp. 32-33; Hayden, *The Great West: Its Attractions and Resources* (Philadelphia: Franklin Publishing Co., 1880) p. 36; Hayden, prefatory note to Washington Matthews, *Ethnography nd Philology of the Hidatsa Indians*, U.S. Geological and Geographical Survey, Miscellaneous Publications, no. 7 (Washington: G.P.O., 1877), pp. iii-iv.

[69] Taft, *Photography and the American Scene*, pp. 293-94. For details of Jackson's career, see Clarence S. Jackson, *Picture Maker of the Old West: William H. Jackson* (New York: Bonanza Books, 1947); William Henry Jackson, *Time Exposure: The Autobiography of William Henry Jackson* (New York: G. P. Putnam's Sons, 1940); *The Diaries of William Henry Jackson: Frontier Photographer*, ed. LeRoy R. and Ann W. Hafen (Glendale, Calif.: Arthur H. Clark Co., 1959). Useful but untrustworthy is Beaumont Newhall and Diana E. Edkins, *William H. Jackson* (Fort Worth: Amon Carter Museum, 1974).

17. William Henry Jackson, "Crow Eyes. Pawnee," 1869. Albumen photograph. Amon Carter Museum, Fort Worth, Texas.

able one extant."[70] Notably, Hayden valued the collection not only for the usual general reasons but also because it preserved evidence of specific artifacts, a consideration that was gaining importance among ethnographers. In his own prefatory note, Jackson tersely concurred.[71]

THE PASADENA EIGHT

Nowhere in the last two decades of the century were artifacts so well preserved or, as mentioned earlier, tribal cultures so richly intact as in the Southwest. Serious photographers wandered through the region in an active, explicit commitment to compiling ethnographic records. Unlike the similarly motivated paintings of Joseph Sharp and the Taos and Santa Fe schools, their work attracted only moderate attention from the general public. Though the scientific community embraced such efforts, it lacked the means to support them. Their tepid public reception almost ensured that these craftsmen would be loners, existing on limited funds, searching out remote tribes and scenes, and transporting heavy chemical supplies and fragile view camera equipment on their own by wagon.

A singular anomaly in this general pattern of loner photographers was a small group of far-sighted southern Californians who became so closely associated that students still confuse their work. Chapter Three described Charles Lummis's and George Wharton James's spearheading of a movement in the 1890s to preserve California's Spanish missions. Outside the state, they directed another project: the preservation of a record of the tribes of the Southwest. Others from Pasadena shared their commitment, including a former book-dealer, Adam Clark Vroman, the studio and expedition photographers C. J. Crandall, Frederick I. Monsen, and Carl Moon, and two dealers in Indian artifacts, Horatio Rust and Grace Nicholson. Each of these eight people appears to have known all the others, and some were close friends. From the 1870s, each made photographic trips to the pueblos of Arizona and New Mexico, sometimes annually and sometimes in the company of other members of the group. They produced tens of thousands of photographs over a span of forty years out of the recognized need to preserve "for future generations

---

[70] F. W. Hayden, prefatory note to William Henry Jackson, *Descriptive Catalogue of Photographs of North American Indians*, United States Geological and Geographical Survey of the Territories, Miscellaneous Publications, no. 9 (Washington: G.P.O., 1877), p. iii.

[71] Ibid., p. v. See also Terry William Mangan, *Colorado on Glass: Colorado's First Half-Century as Seen by the Camera* (Denver: Sundance Ltd., 1975), p. 112.

18. Carl Moon, "Navaho Weaver, Canyon de Chelly," ca. 1907-1914. Photograph. The Henry E. Huntington Library and Art Gallery, San Marino, California.

a picture-history which will show what these most interesting early Americans were like."[72]

In their acknowledged motives, an additional reason appears frequently: the need to understand these mysterious cultures on their own terms. Surely this is also implied in the excited note Adam Clark Vroman scrawled on the back of a photograph taken at his first Hopi Snake Dance in 1895:

> . . . the Dance is Over.
>
> Words cannot picture it at all. The location, the surroundings, the costumes which are beautiful, the bodies of Dancers died a rich brown with the entire chin *white*, making [the] face look almost hideous.
>
> My first thought was after it was all over was to see it again and know more about it, why it was and how it is planned. I felt I could spend a year right there, be one of them, and learn their ways and beliefs. It is a sacred rite with them and carried out to the letter and they believe it.[73]

Vroman expresses a common feeling among those entranced by the southwestern cultures. Yet like Catlin's paintings, his photographs— "unexpressive, uncondescending, unsentimental"[74]—resist the easy conversion of subject matter into sentimental plea.

[72] Frederick I. Monsen, "Picturing Indians with the Camera," *Photo-Era*, 25 (October 1910), 165. For additional such statements, plus background information on these people, see: Ruth I. Mahood, ed., *Photographer of the Southwest: Adam Clark Vroman, 1856-1916* (n.p.: Ward Ritchie Press, 1961), esp. pp. 9-10, 17-19, 222-24; Webb and Weinstein, *Dwellers at the Source*; A. C. Vroman's Diary, Hopi Indians, Huntington Library, San Marino; Frederick Monsen's Ethnographic Indian Photographs, 13 vol., Huntington Library; Frederick Monsen, *With A Kodak in the Land of the Navajo* (Rochester: Eastman Kodak, 1907?), esp. pp. 16-26; Kristina Wilkinson, "Frederick Monsen, F.R.G.S.: Explorer and Ethnographer," *Noticias*, Summer 1969, pp. 16-23; Frederick Monsen, "The Destruction of our Indians: What Civilization Is Doing to Extinguish an Ancient and Highly Intelligent Race by Taking Away its Arts, Industries, and Religion," *Craftsman*, 11 (March 1907), 683-91; Carl Moon, "A Brief Account of the Making of This Collection of Indian Pictures," typescript, 1924, Huntington Library; Carl Moon, "Photographing the Vanishing Red Man," *Leslie's Illustrated*, March 10, 1914; Carl Moon, "American Indians of the Southwest," *Century Magazine*, 74 (October 1907), 923-27; W. Jerome, "Karl Moon's Indian Photographs," *Craftsman*, 20 (April 1911), 24-32; Horatio Nelson Rust Collection, Huntington Library, esp. boxes 4, 6, 12, 13, 16; Grace Nicholson Collection, Huntington Library; Jane Apostol, "The Indian Summers of Miss Grace Nicholson," typescript, Huntington Library; Winifred Starr Dobyns, "A Treasure House," *Woman Citizen*, 56, old ser. (December 1927), 12-14; Kurutz, "Pictorial Resources," pp. 175-82. See also Gar and Maggy Packard, *Southwest 1880: With Ben Wittick, Pioneer Photographer of Indians and Frontier Life* (Santa Fe: Packard Publications, 1970), esp. pp. 3, 46.

[73] A. C. Vroman's Diary, no. 14

[74] Sontag, *On Photography*, p. 62. Sontag further observes about them: "They are not moving, they are not idiomatic, they do not invite sympathy; they make no propaganda for the Indians."

19. Adam Clark Vroman, "Gathering Snakes at the End of the Ceremony," Walpi," 1897. Photograph. The Natural History Museum of Los Angeles County.

20. Frederick I. Monsen, "Snake Dance, Oraibi, Hopi," ca. 1889-1894. Photograph. The Henry E. Huntington Library and Art Gallery, San Marino, California.

The careers of Vroman and his Pasadena housemate, Frederick I. Monsen (1865-1929), best represent the commitment made by countless other western photographers. Monsen, a young immigrant Norwegian, already had Geological Survey field experience under his belt when he discovered pueblo life in the late 1880s. Intrigued, he studied the Hopi and then the Navaho in an earnest attempt to adapt himself to their alien worlds, "so far as was possible for a white man,"[75] and began photographing the first of more than ten thousand scenes. From the turn of the century, Monsen gained a reputation as an authority on Pueblo life and was acclaimed as photographer, anthropologist, and lecturer. An unusual insight into his career can be found in his account of early enthusiasm for that work:

> It seemed to me that any truthful record of the lives and customs of the people of the Pueblos, made while they were yet unspoiled, would have an ethnological and historical value even greater than the quality of picturesqueness that is now coming to to be of such keen interest to artists. The only way to gain the true impression that alone would be of value, instead of merely gathering a collection of unusual and attractive pictures, was to become intimate with the people, to understand them and be understood by them, to gain their friendship and so coax them by imperceptible degrees to forget to be watchful and conscious in the presence of a stranger, and to live and pursue their daily occupations as if no camera or sketch-block had ever been brought within the borders of the Great Desert.[76]

In 1879, the same year that Monsen took his first photographs of the Hopi, George Eastman perfected the portable roll-film camera. Half a dozen years later, Adam Clark Vroman came west, hiring on as a Kodak dealer along with Monsen; they worked closely together, supplemented each other's ideas, and contributed to each other's collections.[77] The new Kodaks kept the pair solvent even as the cameras offered them invaluable photographic possibilities, allowing Monsen in particular to take more candid pictures than before and to complete them with far less trouble. Unfortunately, the San Francisco earthquake and fire of 1906 destroyed most of his vast collection of negatives. The few hundred that survive attest to the extraordinary range of his interests in native life, his excellent handling of the

[75] Monsen, "Destruction of Our Indians," p. 684.
[76] Ibid., pp. 683-84.
[77] See letter from Monsen's son, Courtenay, to Gary F. Kurutz, June 17, 1973, Huntington Library.

camera, and his honest, unsentimental view. Of course, Monsen lost a distinct edge in the quality of his prints to those who persisted with the more precise view cameras. On the other hand, he gained immeasurably in the range of cultural experiences available for photographic preservation; that is, he could achieve pictures that, because unposed, revealed less of the photographer's necessary preconceptions than of the native's characteristic habits and modes. In Monsen's own words, "the unconscious expression of daily life and character was what I had set my heart on obtaining."[78]

EDWARD CURTIS AND THE END OF AN ERA

As has already been noted, camera technology developed to the point where a close transcription of native life could be considered at just the time when native life was being seriously eroded. The camera itself confirmed that decline in what has been characterized as "the colonization through photography."[79] Eastman had succeeded by the turn of the century in making snapshot photography generally available; at the same time, Thomas Edison had created a popular demand for motion picture films of exotic activities. Discreet amateurs like Monsen and Vroman, respectful of their subjects, signaled the advent of a horde of tourists rudely eager for a "good shot." Poking their noses into holy places and their unwelcome cameras at native ceremonials, unflappable whites crassly paid for poses, and in some cases forever altered ceremonials whose strength inhered in their secrecy. Technological progress in the form of the camera brought a rapid end to the very experiences it was employed to preserve.

Neither Monsen nor his colleagues possessed the resources, and perhaps not the energy or inclination, to transform extensive photographic collections into published documents. At their deaths, what remained of their collections fell into disarray, remembered only by friends. In some cases, it was decades before they were rediscovered, reassembled, and published—to reveal a commitment focused intensively on only a few southwestern tribes. The usefulness of these unexcelled collections is diminished, however, by their creators' failure to leave a written record explaining the scenes they had photographed.

Only one man in the post-Civil War era surpassed the Pasadena group in his ambitions, though Edward S. Curtis (1868-1952) accomplished little in his first thirty years that might have presaged his later

[78] Monsen, "Destruction of Our Indians," p. 686.
[79] Sontag, *On Photography*, p. 64; see also p. 65.

career. As a young photographer in the vigorous Seattle of the 1890s, he specialized in portraits of the socially elite, a lucrative profession that gave him the freedom to explore the surrounding mountains during the summers. In 1898, on an excursion up Mount Rainier, Curtis stumbled upon a party of lost climbers and guided them down safely. That party happened to include George Bird Grinnell and Gifford Pinchot, both of whom took an immediate liking to the resourceful guide. Young Pinchot had yet to establish his formidable reputation as dean of American foresters. Grinnell, on the other hand, was already the recognized leader of the new movement concerned with conservation, wildlife management, and Indian ethnography. Two years later Grinnell invited Curtis on a trip to the Blackfoot reservation in Montana, which Curtis's daughter long after described as the "pivotal experience" of his life. The older admirer of Blackfoot culture and collector of Indian tales imparted his enthusiasm to the young photographer. "He often spoke of it afterward. To most people it would have been just a bunch of Indians. To him it was something that soon would never be seen again."[80] During this trip, Curtis finally committed himself to an idea he had been quietly mulling over for two years: photographing and studying all the Indian tribes still remaining west of the Mississippi River. Grinnell warmly encouraged him to turn his skills to the mammoth task and within ten days after returning to Seattle from Montana, Curtis was in southern Arizona photographing the Hopi.

Seven years later, in the introduction to the first volume of what would become a twenty-volume photographic record, Curtis asserted that he had been working arduously since the first trip "in accumulating the data necessary to form a comprehensive and permanent record of all the important tribes of the United States and Alaska that still retain to a considerable degree their primitive customs and traditions."[81] He further acknowledged that "it represents the result of personal study of a people who are rapidly losing the traces of their aboriginal character and who are destined ultimately to become assimilated with the 'superior race.' "[82] Curtis readily appreciated how late his commitment had come, late enough to throw into question the very completion of his project. In terms that reiterate the apprehensions of many before him, he emphasized this theme:

[80] Florence Curtis Graybill and Victor Boesen, *Edward Sheriff Curtis: Visions of a Vanishing Race* (New York: Thomas Y. Crowell, 1976), p. 12.

[81] Curtis, *The North American Indian: Being a Series of Volumes Picturing and Describing the Indians of the United States, and Alaska*, ed. Frederick Webb Hodge, 20 vols. (Cambridge, Mass.: Harvard University Press, 1907-30), 1:xiii.

[82] Ibid.

The great changes in practically every phase of the Indian's life that have taken place . . . have been such that had the time for collecting much of the material . . . been delayed, it would have been lost forever. The passing of every old man or woman means the passing of some tradition, some knowledge of sacred rites possessed by no other; consequently the information that is to be gathered, for the benefit of future generations . . . must be collected at once or the opportunity will be lost for all time. It is this need that has inspired the present task.[83]

Within a year after he committed himself to his life's task, in 1900, Curtis received widespread public encouragement. Early exhibits of his work in San Francisco drew reviews attesting to its "immense ethnological value,"[84] and Grinnell persuaded his old friend President Roosevelt to support the photographer. By Roosevelt's second term Curtis had won substantial encouragement from America's art and financial communities. As one important New York reviewer wrote in 1905, "the undertaking is the most remarkable artistic and historical work thus far attempted by photography in America."[85] In that same year, partly through Roosevelt's special efforts, J. P. Morgan agreed to subsidize the costly publication of Curtis's complete works. This extraordinary alliance of political and financial support secured his reputation as the most acclaimed of Indian photographers.

The weaknesses of Curtis's studies are more clearly apparent today, analogous to those of the Indian paintings of Charles Russell or of the Taos school. Instead of attempting realistic photographs of the contemporary lives of the tribes he visited, Curtis invariably portrayed a Hopi or a Crow or a Tlingit "as he moved about before he ever saw a paleface."[86] Predictably, many of these photographic studies suffer from sentimentality and stylization. They reflect what Monsen warned against as the "photographer's idea" rather than portraying the native experience. To compound the well-meant distortions, Curtis frequently carried costumes for his intended models and posed them in stereotypical groupings or sentimental actions.

Nonetheless, Curtis's fundamental motives were admirable. No one since Catlin had conceived so comprehensive a plan for preserving

[83] Ibid., 1:xvi-xvii.

[84] Arnold Genthe, review essay in *Camera Craft*, 11 (February 1901), 310, cited in Mahood, ed., *Photographer of the Southweast*, p. 18.

[85] John Tennent, review essay in *Photo-Miniaturem* 6 (September 1905), 663, cited in Mahood, ed., *Photographer of the Southwest*, p. 19. See also Theodore Roosevelt's foreword to Curtis, *North American Indian*, vol. 1.

[86] Curtis, cited in Graybill and Boesen, *Edward Sheriff Curtis*, p. 13.

21. Edward S. Curtis, "Kotsuis and Hohhuq—Nakoaktok," Kwakiutl, 1914. Photogravure from Curtis, *The North American Indian*, portfolio X.

the image of a vanishing race or had visited so many tribes.[87] In the inclusiveness of his intentions, indeed, Curtis far exceeded even Catlin.[88] More systematically than any painter or photographer before or since, he collected a massive fund of ethnological information, which he published in volumes accompanying his photographic portfolio. Yet he sadly recognized, like other serious students to be discussed in the following chapter, that "the years of a single life are insufficient for the task of treating in minute detail all the intricacies of the social structure and the arts and beliefs of many tribes."[89] Curtis's particular achievement, setting him worlds apart from those who may have shared this knowledge, lay in making the Indian's worlds more generally available through the medium of photography.

Within four years after Curtis first published his exhaustive studies, Ishi, the last "wild Indian" uninfluenced by white civilization, wan-

[87] See, however, Frederick Starr, *Indians of Southern Mexico: An Ethnographic Album* (Chicago: privately published, 1899); Starr, *Notes upon the Ethnography of Southern Mexico*, 2 vols. (Davenport, Ia.: Putnam Memorial Publication Fund, 1900-1902), esp. pp. 2-3.

[88] Curtis, *North American Indian*, 1:xvi-xvii.

[89] Ibid., 1:xvi.

dered fearfully into tiny Oroville, California, only to be forced into trousers and handcuffs by an equally bewildered sheriff.[90] In less than a century, nearly two hundred indigenous tribes had disappeared entirely or had been harried, deceived, and beaten into acceptance of white rule. Their various ways of life manifested fewer and fewer distinctive characteristics as they now imitated the clothes, hair styles, work habits, and manners of the culture that had displaced them.

CLEARLY, Catlin does not stand alone in his commitment to compiling a permanent pictorial record of the western tribes. Yet most of the painters who preceded him and many of the painters and photographers who followed never fully appreciated the work completed by their contemporaries. Catlin inspired others to the task, but for the most part artists worked in isolation and learned little from one another. A tradition of artists committed to preserving such records never existed, any more than a consistent, self-conscious pattern came to define those committed to recording the passing wilderness landscape or the disappearance of wildlife. Through a century of displacement, acculturation, and extinction, however, an increasing number came with increasing urgency to realize that much of value was being consigned to oblivion. This "mournful vision of loss,"[91] according to one historian, defines a fundamental strain of American photography. The West specifically, and the Indian in particular, emblematized all that was changing. In the many documentary photographs made through the course of the century, a "vision of loss" confronts the viewer.[92]

Before the end of the nineteenth century, pictorial records drew the serious attention of ethnologists and historians. The drawings, sketches, oils, and photographs of tribes completed years earlier and in many cases long since forgotten acquired significance for the very reasons that the original artists had claimed.[93] For tribes that had disappeared, the earlier pictorial evidence proved as helpful as it was accurate. Yet, despite the information that such records contained, they could by their very nature provide accounts of no more than physical design, the visible form, the dramatic gesture. Questions of

90 Theodora Kroeber, *Ishi in Two Worlds: A Biography of the Last Wild Indian in North America* (1961; rpt. Berkeley: University of California Press, 1971).

91 Sontag, *On Photography*, p. 67; see also pp. 56, 76.

92 Hallowell, "Backwash of the Frontier," pp. 248, 250.

93 Ewers, "Fact and Fiction," esp. pp. 79-82; Herman J. Viola, "How *Did* an Indian Chief Really Look?" *Smithsonian*, 8 (June 1977), 100-104; Weitenkampf, "Early Pictures of North American Indians," pp. 591-614; Herman Ten Kate, "On Paintings of North American Indians and Their Ethnographical Value," *Anthropos*, 7 (1911), 521-45.

meaning, of belief, of value required the efforts of individuals committed to more than vanishing appearances. So just as artists had been drawn westward by the idea of saving an image of native life, those more scientifically inclined endured similar privations in order to secure records of Indian cultural experiences.

Despite their similar missions, artists and scientists rarely worked together. Whether or not the artist would have helped the scientist to see his subject more clearly, it seems likely that the scientist might well have helped the artist. For it was first the Indian biographer, then the ethnologist, and finally the anthropologist who came to appreciate the complexity of all cultural structures. Those who rescued tribal vocabularies and ceremonial descriptions early in the century often found more than they had suspected. Nathaniel Hawthorne may have regretted never finding an "Indian story" interesting, but others turned their ears attentively and in the process not merely salvaged remnants from the ruins but came to recognize a previously rich autonomy to tribes now sadly dependent.

CHAPTER SIX

THEIR TRIBAL LORE
PRESERVED

As a race they have withered from the land. Their arrows are broken, their springs are dried up, their cabins are in the dust. . . . Ages hence, the inquisitive white man, as he stands by some growing city, will ponder on the structure of their disturbed remains, and wonder to what manner of persons they belonged. They will live only in the songs and chronicles of their exterminators. Let these be faithful to their rude virtues as men, and pay due tribute to their unhappy fate as a people.

—McGuffey's *Newly Revised*
Rhetorical Guide (1853)

Give not, give not the yawning graves their plunder;
    Save, save the lore, for future ages' joy;
The stories full of beauty and of wonder
    The songs more pristine than the songs of Troy,
The ancient speech forever to be vanished—
    Lore that tomorrow to the grave goes down!
All other thought from our horizon vanished,
    Let any sacrifice our labor crown.

—*John Peabody Harrington*
(1884-1961)

ON DECEMBER 20, 1819, an Episcopal minister stepped before the New-York Historical Society to present a "Discourse on the Religion of the Indian Tribes of North America." The Reverend Samuel Farmar Jarvis could claim firsthand knowledge neither of the Indians he chose to speak of that day nor of their religion. Yet his speech, culled mostly from published sources and printed by the society the following year, reveals an unusually sensitive mind and presages some of the major issues that would trouble Americans throughout the rest of the century. Declaring that woodland Indians had long since ceased to inspire fear among settled white communities, Jarvis added: "In the room of fear, should now arise a sentiment of pity. The red men are melting, to borrow the expressive metaphor of one of their most celebrated warriors—'like snow before the sun'; and we should be anxious, before it is too late, to copy the evanescent features of their character, and to perpetuate them on the page of history."[1] Of course, Jarvis acknowledged, those eastern tribes in closest contact with expansion-minded whites had long since abandoned the beliefs and manners most worth preserving and studying: "When a race of men are mingled with others, who consider them as inferiors, they inevitably become so."[2] Instead of the specimen that Cooper would soon portray as Mohegan John—reduced by rum to basket weaving—Jarvis demanded that historians search out the still "uncivilized" and undegraded Chingachgook: "if we wish to see him in his original character, we must follow him to his native forests.— There, surely, he is worthy of our attention."[3] Once there, however, white researchers should not recklessly leap to facile conclusions or mistake reticence for ignorance.

> The Indians themselves are not communicative in relation to their religion; and it requires a good deal of familiar, attentive, and I may add, unsuspected observation, to obtain any knowledge respecting it. Hence, many who have been transiently resident among them, have very confidently pronounced, that they have no religion; an assertion, which subsequent and more accurate travellers have shown to be entirely unfounded.

[1] Jarvis, *A Discourse on the Religion of the Indian Tribes of North America . . .* (New York: C. Wiley and Co., 1820), p. 6. See also Elémire Zolla, *The Writer and the Shaman: A Morphology of the American Indian* (1969), trans. Raymond Rosenthal (New York: Harcourt Brace Jovanovich, 1973), p. 173.

[2] Jarvis, *Discourse*, p. 6.

[3] Ibid., p. 7.

Those, also, on whom we rely for information, have either been too little informed to know what to observe, or they have been influenced by peculiar modes of thinking, which have given a tinge to all they have said on the subject.[4]

Jarvis developed these ideas in some detail before concluding with the conventional exhortation that Americans had a duty to "civilize" and "Christianize" the "scanty remnants" of Indian tribes.[5]

Jarvis's encouragements and caveats to some of New York City's most respected citizens express insights far removed from the notions generally current in 1819. He proposed that indigenous populations were rapidly declining, that their religions, "character," and cultures remained unrecorded, and that only a willing suspension of disbelief plus patient study might reveal these complex subjects. No more than a few other Americans—notably Thomas L. McKenny—had actively responded to these issues in the first decades of the nineteenth century. McKenney's and King's documentation in paint, however, differed radically from the kind of effort Jarvis demanded of the student of culture. The artist ought to transcribe appearances; the student needed to press beneath them. Only then could he comprehend native assumptions at their most resonant levels.

That Charles Bird King and Karl Bodmer, Adam Clark Vroman and Frederick I. Monsen knew little about native values, sometimes after years of familiarity with tribes, hardly detracts from their records. As were many others, they were motivated by the prospect of physical rather than ideational loss. Jarvis's supposition that cultural values were imperiled found less immediate endorsement than the call for preservation of exotic scenes and artifacts that seemed to be disappearing. Exceptional figures such as George Catlin and Seth and Mary Eastman worked to preserve both physical image and cultural experience in paint and words. But before mid-century most considered these separate, sometimes even mutually exclusive activities.

Individual painters who hurried in the 1830s and 1840s to document indigenous tribes were largely unaffected by earlier sentimental representations of the Indian. Abstract painterly norms and contemporary aesthetic theory influenced them far more than reductive assumptions about native cultures. Clearly, however, those who recognized a more compelling value in disappearing vocabularies and myths, traditions and customs were too often influenced by such assumptions. To understand why whites, almost without exception, fell victim to simplistic interpretations of native cultures requires a

4 Ibid., pp. 7-8.   5 Ibid., pp. 63-64.

quick review of intellectual history. Only against the backdrop of received ideas about race and culture can one appreciate the actual achievement of those in the nineteenth century who attempted to preserve a record of disappearing tribal cultures.

The tribes peopling the Western Hemisphere descended from successive bands of Asiatic nomads that migrated via a land bridge across the Bering Strait at least ten thousand years before Christ. Subsequent isolation ensured genetic uniformity, while tribal exchanges over the millenniums assured similar social, economic, even religious characteristics. Despite these similarities, however, the groups of "Indians" observed by Columbus and subsequent explorers proved to be far more various than whites imagined.[6] They differed radically in cultural assumptions and, in 1492, spoke between one and two thousand separate languages. The diversity suggested by this figure was compounded by European conquerors and colonials, who altered native life in obvious ways and in others more subtle, including trading and settlement patterns.[7]

This broad spectrum of cultural variation had little effect upon successive waves of European explorers and settlers, who continued generation after generation to project assumptions onto "the Indian."[8] In the earliest years, colonists admired the natives' communal ownership, simple fashions in dress, and apparently lax sexual morality.[9]

[6] On this point, see William Brandon, *The Last American: The Indian in American Culture* (New York: McGraw-Hill, 1974); Alfred W. Crosby Jr., *The Columbian Exchange: Biological and Cultural Consequences of 1492*, Contributions in American Studies, no. 2 (Westport, Conn.: Greenwood Publishing Co., 1972), esp. pp. 21ff.; John C. Ewers, "When Red and White Men Meet," *Western Historical Quarterly*, 2 (April 1971), 133-35; Edward H. Spicer, *Cycles of Conquest: The Impact of Spain, Mexico, and the United States on the Indians of the Southwest, 1533-1960* (Tucson: University of Arizona Press, 1962); Robert F. Berkhofer Jr., *The White Man's Indian: Images of the American Indian from Columbus to the Present* (New York: Alfred A. Knopf, 1978), esp. pp. 5-29; Wilbur R. Jacobs, "The Tip of an Iceberg: Pre-Columbian Indian Demography and Some Implications for Revisionism," *William and Mary Quarterly*, 3d ser., 31 (January 1974), 123-32; Wilcomb E. Washburn, *The Indian in America* (New York: Harper and Row, 1975), esp. pp. xv-xvii; Philip Borden, "Found Cumbering the Soil: Manifest Destiny and the Indian in the Nineteenth Century," in Gary B. Nash and Richard Weiss, eds., *The Great Fear: Race in the Mind of America* (New York: Holt, Rinehart and Winston, 1970), pp. 78-79; Stuart Levine, "*Sacred Circles*: Native American Art and American Culture," *American Quarterly*, 30 (Spring 1978), 108-23.

[7] See Oscar Lewis, *The Effects of White Contact upon Blackfoot Culture, with Special Reference to the Role of the Fur Trade*, monograph of the American Ethnological Society, vol. 6 (New York: J. J. Augustin, 1942); Spicer, *Cycles of Conquest*, pp. 1-5.

[8] Roy Harvey Pearce, *Savagism and Civilization: A Study of the Indian and the American Mind*, rev. ed. (Baltimore: Johns Hopkins University Press, 1965); Berkhofer, *White Man's Indian*.

[9] Brandon, *The Last Americans*, pp. 4-6.

Disaffected European intellectuals may have idealized this "natural" state through the eighteenth century, but American colonials abandoned the convention far earlier.[10] Indeed, the 1622 Jamestown massacre confirmed a racism in the southern colonies equal to that of the Massachusetts religious settlements. The need to justify displacement or extermination, to vindicate a sense of westward mission, steeled contemptuous colonists to dismiss "savage" ways. Of course, this kind of uninformed racism only mirrors the earlier idealization: both responses essentially ignored tribal cultures by reducing them to a single, limited group of values.

Exceptional figures resisted such stereotypes. John Smith and Roger Williams, for two early examples, studied local tribes with critical admiration and recorded their religious practices.[11] Others traveling among eastern tribes in the next two centuries also awoke to their unexpectedly rich cultural life. Missionaries in particular—John Eliot, Joseph Lafitau, and Gabriel Sagard, for example—attempted to understand those whom they intended to convert. They lived with woodland tribes and made extensive ethnographic studies of "their dances, songs, and other silly ceremonies," as Father Sagard entitled a chapter of his subsequent account.[12] Yet for all of their tolerant interest in native life, that description dramatically betrays the condescending air that most whites shared toward Indians.

Though some eighteenth-century European intellectuals were considering issues of culture and civilization, relatively few travel accounts of the period evince appreciation for indigenous tribes on their own cultural terms. The variously bedaubed and bedecked subjects

10 Gary B. Nash, "The Image of the Indian in the Southern Colonial Mind," *William and Mary Quarterly*, 3d ser., 29 (April 1972), 217; Nash, "Red, White and Black: The Origins of Racism in Colonial America," in Nash and Weiss, eds., *The Great Fear*, pp. 4-9; Berkhofer, *White Man's Indian*, pp. 23-25; Bordon, "Found Cumbering the Soil," pp. 72ff.; Wilbur R. Jacobs, *Dispossessing the American Indian: Indians and Whites on the Colonial Frontier* (New York: Charles Scribner's Sons, 1972), esp. pp. 2-5; Winthrop D. Jordan, *White Over Black: American Attitudes toward the Negro, 1550-1812* (Chapel Hill: University of North Carolina Press, 1968), pp. ix, 26-27; Frank Shuffelton, "Indian Devils and Pilgrim Fathers: Squanto, Hobomok, and the English Conception of Indian Religion," *New England Quarterly*, 49 (March 1976), 108-16; Benjamin Keen, *The Aztec Image in Western Thought* (New Brunswick: Rutgers University Press, 1971), esp. pp. 55, 307-9, 352-56.

11 Nash, "Image of the Indian," pp. 215, 223; Thomas F. Gossett, *Race: The History of an Idea in America* (Dallas: Southern Methodist University Press, 1963), p. 19.

12 Sagard, *The Long Journey to the Country of the Hurons* (1639), trans. H. H. Langton, ed. George M. Wrong (Toronto: Champlain Society, 1939), p. 115. See also Zolla, *The Writer and the Shaman*, pp. 41ff.; Brandon, *The Last Americans*, p. 5; John Hopkins Kennedy, *Jesuit and Savage in New France* (New Haven: Yale University Press, 1950), esp. pp. 103-9.

sometimes peer through an imposed mask of primitiveness to claim their humanity; but these examples were too few to effect even subtle change in the European conception of the Indian as deficient. He required conversion, sacred and secular. Individuals such as the Virginia planter Robert Beverley or John Heckewelder, the Moravian missionary in Pennsylvania, may have admired elements of tribal life, just so long as these did not counter their own Christian assumptions.[13]

This inability to see native Americans without prejudice persisted well into the nineteenth century. Again, the intentions of those hoping to educate and Christianize childlike primitives differed little in effect, if not motive, from the determination of those bent on destroying brute savages.[14] Kindness, as Indians soon discovered, could kill as effectively as bullets. Nineteenth-century activists attracted far more support in efforts to reform native tribes than had their few philanthropical predecessors a century earlier. Yet even they held little more informed estimations of the tribes they proposed to help.[15] Archaeologists claimed that indigenous peoples were incapable of constructing the earthwork mounds that dotted the landscape east of the Mississippi River; the structures seemed too complex, their treasures too wonderful. Instead, they devised theories of glorious mound builders destroyed in some distant past by ravaging hordes, the ancestors of present Indian tribes.[16] Ethnologists created elaborate proofs for Indian inferiority based on skull size and house structure.[17]

13 Nash, "Image of the Indian," pp. 222, 226; Nash, "Red, White and Black," p. 9; Zolla, *The Writer and the Shaman*, pp. 63-77. For Heckewelder's nonetheless incisive descriptions, see *30,000 Miles with John Heckewelder*, ed. Paul A. W. Wallace (Pittsburgh: University of Pittsburgh Press, 1958), esp. pp. v-vii, 44-45, 331-33.

14 Bernard W. Sheehan, *Seeds of Extinction: Jeffersonian Philanthropy and the American Indian* (New York: W. W. Norton, 1973). See also Michael Rogin, review of Sheehan, *Seeds of Extinction*, and Slotkin, *Regeneration through Violence*, in *Journal of Ethnic Studies*, 2 (Spring 1974), 93-104.

15 Francis Paul Prucha, S.J., ed., *Americanizing the American Indians: Writings by the "Friends of the Indian," 1880-1900* (Cambridge, Mass.: Harvard University Press, 1973), esp. pp. 1-8, 45; Prucha, "Indian Policy Reform and American Protestantism, 1880-1900," in Ray Allen Billington, ed., *People of the Plains and Mountains*, Contributions in American History, no. 25 (Westport, Conn.: Greenwood Press, 1973), pp. 120-45; Robert A. Trennert Jr., *Alternative to Extinction: Federal Indian Policy and the Beginnings of the Reservation System, 1846-51* (Philadelphia: Temple University Press, 1975); Robert Winston Mardock, *The Reformers and the American Indian* (Columbia: University of Missouri Press, 1971), esp. pp. 1-3, 87; Henry E. Fritz, *The Movement for Indian Assimilation, 1860-1890* (Philadelphia: University of Pennsylvania Press, 1963).

16 Robert Silverberg, *Mound Builders of Ancient America: The Archaeology of a Myth* (Greenwich, Conn.: New York Graphic Society, 1968), pp. 6ff., 97-103, 170.

17 William Stanton, *The Leopard's Spots: Scientific Attitudes toward Race in America, 1815-59* (Chicago: University of Chicago Press, 1960), esp. pp. 25-45, 85-86; Gossett, *Race*, esp. pp. 54ff., 228ff.

McGuffey readers and other popular grade-school texts rationalized extermination of tribes on religious and philosophical grounds.[18] Professional historians rarely quarreled with this view. As Thoreau observed in his journal, "though he professes more humanity than the trapper, mountain man, or gold digger, who shoots one as a wild beast, [the historian] really exhibits and practices a similar inhumanity to [the Indian], wielding a pen instead of a rifle."[19]

Nevertheless, against this essentially static background of cultural thought, one can discern a swelling undercurrent of concern to record native life, an undercurrent that finally surfaced in the 1820s.[20] Earlier chapters have noted the anxiety that impelled the documenting of landscapes and wildlife. A similar feeling spurred similar attempts on behalf of native tribes. As well, eastern white communities felt relatively secure from tribal retaliation at just the time when the romantic movement encouraged the sentimentalization of the primitive. Whatever the constellation of causes, interest in recording threatened vocabularies, myths, and traditions followed a pattern similar to that of the earlier concern for documenting the native American's physical world. That urge to preserve visual representations of the Indian as the prime human constituent of a vanishing wilderness led first to vague sketches and random portraits and then grew into efforts at systematic, comprehensive pictorials. Similarly, concern to fix on record not only the painted or photographed "exterior" but also the more complex "interior" forms evolved from upsophisticated adjurations among a smattering of enthusiasts into a chorus of serious ethnographic efforts.[21]

[18] Richard D. Mosier, *Making the American Mind: Social and Moral Ideas in the McGuffey Readers* (New York: Columbia University Press, 1947), pp. 148-51; Ruth Miller Elson, *Guardians of Tradition: American Schoolbooks of the Nineteenth Century* (Lincoln: University of Nebraska Press, 1964), pp. 71-79.

[19] Thoreau, *Journal*, cited in Jacobs, *Dispossessing the American Indian*, p. 19. See also Louise K. Barnett, *The Ignoble Savage: American Literary Racism, 1790-1890*, Contributions in American Studies, no. 18 (Westport, Conn.: Greenwood Press, 1975), p. 190; David Levin, *History as Romantic Art: Bancroft, Prescott, Motley, and Parkman* (Stanford: Stanford University Press, 1959), esp. pp. 136-38.

[20] Cf. Guillaume T. F. Raynal, *Histoire philosophique des Indes* (1773), cited in Kennedy, *Jesuit and Savage in ·New France*, p. 191. See also Nash, "Image of the Indian," p. 222. For a contrary opinion, see Berkhofer, *White Man's Indian*, pp. 88-89.

[21] In part, this effort may have reflected a general response to the widespread assumption of Indian extinction. See Robert F. Sayre, *Thoreau and the American Indians* (Princeton: Princeton University Press, 1977), p. 27; Berkhofer, *White Man's Indian*, pp. 88-89; Brian William Dippie, "The Vanishing American: Popular Attitudes and American Indian Policy in the Nineteenth Century" (Ph.D. diss., University of Texas, Austin, 1970), p. v; Richard Slotkin, *Regeneration through Violence: The Mythology of the American Frontier, 1600-1860* (Middletown, Conn.: Wesleyan University Press, 1973), p. 357.

Once again, little coherent thinking on the issue, much less a consolidated movement, ever developed. Few knew of like-minded enthusiasts in archaeology and archival collecting, linguistic ethnology and cultural anthropology. Yet taken together, the concerns of these men and women define a growing unrest with the state of knowledge of native tribes. Most important, that unrest forms more than an interesting strand in American intellectual history, for it fostered extensive, systematic study of numerous nonwhite cultures.

FRONTIER JOURNALS AND INDIAN BIOGRAPHIES

At its most elementary level, apprehension for vanishing tribes revealed itself in diaries, memoirs, and informal travel accounts. Such expressions, which continued nearly to the present day, consist of no more than vague laments. Joshua Clark, for example, noted in 1849 that "Indian tradition, with all its vivacity and interest, is fearfully becoming extinct. A few short years and nothing new can possibly be gleaned."[22] Reiterating this motive, frontiersmen kept journals that bracket useful accounts of native habits with predictions of their decline. Others fed a popular appetite for such material by bringing together anecdotes collected either directly from natives or from manuscripts and books.[23] Indians themselves sometimes used acquired

[22] Joshua V. H. Clark, *Onondaga; or, Reminiscences of Earlier and Later Times . . .*, 2 vols. (Syracuse: Stoddard and Babcock, 1849), 1:xiv. See also *Biblical Repertory and Princeton Review*, 10 (October 1838), 513; Abbé Emmanuel Domenech, *Seven Years' Residence in the Great Deserts of North America*, 2 vols. (London: Longman, Green, Longman, and Roberts, 1860), 1:vii-xi, 439, 461; James Buchanan, *Sketches of the History, Manners and Customs of the North American Indians* (London: Black, Young, and Young, 1824), pp. vii-ix, 1, 9, 13; Peter Skene Ogden, *Traits of American-Indian Life and Character by a Fur Trader* (London: Smith, Elder and Co., 1853), p. xi; *Peter Skene Ogden's Snake Country Journal, 1826-27*, ed. K. G. Davies, intro. by Dorothy O. Johansen, Publications of the Hudson's Bay Record Society, 23 (London: Hudson's Bay Record Society, 1961), pp. lxxi, 35, 68; John Dunn, *History of the Oregon Territory* (London: Edwards and Hughes, 1844), pp. 54-57; George Frederick Ruxton, *Life in the Far West* (1848), ed. LeRoy R. Hafen (Norman: University of Oklahoma Press, 1951), pp. 90-91, 99-100, 105-6; *Ruxton of the Rockies*, ed. LeRoy R. Hafen (Norman: University of Oklahoma Press, 1950), p. 46; John C. Cremony, *Life Among the Apaches* (San Francisco: A. Roman and Co., 1868), pp. 11-12, 310-13.

[23] See Alfred Benjamin Meacham, *Wigwam and War-Path; or, The Royal Chief in Chains*, rev. ed. (Boston: John P. Dale and Co., 1875), intro. by Wendell Phillips, p. iv; Fannie Reed Giffen, *Oo-Mah-Ha Ta-Wa-Tha (Omaha City)* (Lincoln, Nebr.: n.p., 1898), p. 7; Walter McClintock, *Old Indian Trails* (Boston: Houghton Mifflin Co., 1923), p. viii; George Wharton James, *Indian Basketry* (Pasadena: n.p., 1901), pp. 9-10, 16; review of John Dunn Hunter, *Memoirs of a Captivity among the Indians of North America*, and James Buchanan, *Sketches of the History, Manners and Customs of the North American Indians*, in *Quarterly Review*, 31 (1825), 76-77.

skills to preserve an accurate memory of their experiences. As one Pawnee chief regretfully noted in the 1880s, "Already the old things are being lost, and those who knew the secrets are many of them dead. If we had known how to write, we would have put all these things down, and they would not have been forgotten. . . . It may be that they have changed as they passed from father to son, and it is well that they should be put down, so that our children, when they are like the white people, can know what were their fathers' ways."[24] George Copway, the great Ojibwa chief and later Wesleyan missionary, prefaced his *Traditional History and Characteristic Sketches of the Ojibway Nation* (1850) with a rationale at once similar and yet more profound: "I feel incompetent for my work, but am impelled forward by the thought that the nation whose history I here feebly sketch seems passing away, and that unless a work like this is sent forth, much, very much, that is interesting and instructive in that nation's actions, will with it pass away."[25] He added that the remaining Indians "hold a key which will unlock a library of information, the like of which is not. It is for the present generation to say, whether the last remnants of a powerful people shall perish through neglect, and as they depart bear with them that key."[26] The notion that whites held an obligation to themselves as well as to posterity—that Indian experience could be valuable in and of itself, learned from as well as documented—appears increasingly throughout the nineteenth century and forms a recurrent theme in this and following chapters.

White and native self-consciousness about the need for records lends an ironic continuity to the efforts of the Eastman family. In the 1840s, Mary Eastman asked her friend Caroline Kirkland to compose a preface for her collection of Dakota Sioux myths. Attempting to explain Mrs. Eastman's project, the popular novelist declared that the Indian is "our own, and passing away—while we take no pains to arrest their fleeting traits or to record their picturesque traditions. . . . We are continually reproached by British writers for the obtuse carelessness with which we are allowing these people . . . to go into the annihilation which seems their inevitable fate as civilization advances, without

---

[24] Cited in George Bird Grinnell, *Pawnee Hero Stories and Folk-Tales with Notes on the Origin, Customs and Character of the Pawnee People* (New York: Charles Scribner's Sons, 1890), p. vi, also pp. vi-xvii, 406-8.

[25] George Copway, *The Traditional History and Characteristic Sketches of the Ojibway Nation* (London: Charles Gilpin, 1850), p. vii. See also Copway, *The Life, History, and Travels of Kah-Ge-Ga-Gah-Bowh* (Albany: n.p., 1847), pp. 7, 55.

[26] Copway, *Traditional History*, p. viii.

an effort to secure and record all that they are able to communicate respecting themselves."[27] Little could she have guessed at the double edge to her words. One of painter Seth Eastman's intimate contacts with the Dakota Sioux prior to his marriage would result in a grandson, Charles Eastman, who would write prolifically of his Sioux childhood before receiving a Dartmouth and medical education.[28] Dr. Eastman's various reminiscences did not pretend to scientific exactitude any more than had Copway's. Yet, as his white grandfather had been motivated to paint, he intended his autobiographies to preserve a history that few others could hope to know and record.[29]

Earlier in the nineteenth century, Indian biography, not autobiography, enjoyed wide popularity, analogous in many ways to the public enthusiasm for studio portraits of tribal chieftains. Consisting of European literary conventions stalely imposed upon native materials, these works rather crudely combine extensive passages of tribal history with narratives of exemplary figures. Nevertheless, impelling their authors was a desire "not merely to introduce to the reading public the Leading Men of the Indian Territory their laws and customs, etc.," as one practitioner stumblingly announced, "but to perpetuate for all time the memories of the most illustrious among the great American aborigines."[30]

Catlin's patron, publisher William Stone, had planned a comprehensive six-volume history of the famous Iroquois Confederacy long before he met the obsessed young painter. So strong was the biographical convention, however, that the two volumes he completed

[27] C. M. Kirkland, preface to Mary Eastman, *Dahcotah; or, Life and Legends of the Sioux Around Fort Snelling* (1849; rpt. Minneapolis: Ross and Haines, 1962), pp. vi, viii.

[28] John Francis McDermott, *Seth Eastman: Pictorial Historian of the Indian* (Norman: University of Oklahoma Press, 1961), p. 18.

[29] Charles Alexander Eastman, *Indian Boyhood*, illus. by E. L. Blumenschein (1902; rpt. Boston: Little, Brown and Co., 1918), esp. pp. 1, 181; Eastman, *The Soul of the Indian: An Interpretation* (Boston: Houghton Mifflin Co., 1911), foreword; Eastman, *From the Deep Woods to Civilization: Chapters in the Autobiography of an Indian* (1916; rpt. Boston: Little, Brown and Co., 1917), esp. pp. 166-67.

[30] Harry F. O'Beirne, *Leaders and Leading Men of the Indian Territory*, vol. 1, *Choctows and Chickasaws* (Chicago: American Publishers' Association, 1891), p. i. See also Minnie Myrtle, *The Iroquois; or, The Bright Side of Indian Character* (New York: D. Appleton and Co., 1855), pp. 12, 14-15, 24-25, 298; Zolla, *The Writer and the Shaman*, pp. 183-84. Roy Harvey Pearce discusses this subject in *Savagism and Civilization*, esp. p. 118, concentrating on the two best-known antiquarian scholars, Benjamin Thatcher and Samuel Gardner Drake. In contrast to Pearce's conclusions, see an anonymous review of Thatcher's *Indian Biography* (1833) in *Knickerbocker*, 2 (August 1833), 139, and Benjamin Drake, *The Life and Adventures of Black Hawk* (1838), 7th ed. rev. (Cincinnati: E. Morgan and Co., 1850).

before his death in 1844 each focused on a famous Indian leader.[31] Inspiring him was the explicit fear that the events, traditions, and myths that he had learned as a boy, and that still lived in the memories of local natives, were disappearing with old-timers into the grave.[32] For his efforts in searching out yellowing manuscripts and graying survivors, Stone won plaudits from whites and an honorary chieftainship from the Seneca tribe.

VOCABULARIES AND GRAMMARS

Although praiseworthy in intent, Stone's and others' ventures achieved little of value. More sharply focused, deliberate, and even scientific attempts to preserve the facts of Indian cultural life had been undertaken since before the turn of the century. For the most part, these efforts were directed at recording vocabularies and grammars. Thomas Jefferson, for example, lamented in his *Notes* the loss to history even by 1782 of linguistic accounts of "so many of the Indian tribes."[33] But he did more than lament. As he observed in 1809 to a like-minded friend, "I have now been thirty years availing myself of every possible opportunity of procuring Indian vocabularies to the same set of words; my opportunities were probably better than will ever occur again to any person having the same desire."[34] One of those opportunities had been the expedition on which he sent Meriwether Lewis and William Clark half a dozen years earlier. Subsequent surveys were also encouraged to collect ethnological information and were joined in these efforts by private historical and antiquarian societies.[35]

---

[31] William L. Stone, *Life of Joseph Brant—Thayendanegea, Including the Indian Wars of the American Revolution*, 2 vols. (New York: George Dearborn and Co., 1838); Stone, *The Life and Times of Red-Jacket, or Sa-Go-Ye-Wat-Ha; Being the Sequel to the History of the Six Nations* (New York: Wiley and Putnam, 1841).

[32] See William L. Stone Jr., "Memoir," in the 1866 edition of *The Life and Times of Red-Jacket*, p. 74.

[33] Cited in Paul Russell Cutright, *Lewis and Clark: Pioneering Naturalists* (Urbana: University of Illinois Press, 1969), p. 7. Henry R. Schoolcraft liked this statement also, invoking it in his *Archives of Aboriginal Knowledge*, 6 vols. (Philadelphia: J. B. Lippincott and Co., 1860), 5:viii. See also Pearce, *Savagism and Civilization*, pp. 78ff.

[34] Cited by Cutright, *Lewis and Clark*, p. 7.

[35] See Rev. Jedidiah Morse, *A Report to the Secretary of War of the United States on Indian Affairs* . . . (New Haven: S. Converse, 1822), esp. pp. 31-32, 66-67; Lt. Amiel Weeks Whipple, *Reports on Explorations and Surveys* . . . , Senate Executive Documents, 33d Cong., 2d sess., 185?, vol. 3, no. 78, esp. pt. 3, pp. 43ff.; Gibbs, *Indian Tribes of Washington Territory: Pacific Northwest Letters of George Gibbs* (1854; rpt. Fairfield, Wash.: Ye Galleon Press, 1976). See as well Constantin F. C. Volney, *A View of the Soil and Climate of the United States of America* (London: J. Johnson, 1804), pp. 488-89. For a curiously opposite contemporary

Amateur linguistic ethnologists began to appear in significant numbers only in the 1820s. There were exceptions, of course, including most singularly Jefferson. Two centuries earlier, Christian missionaries had collected word lists as aids to conversion and in rare cases had made extensive notes explicitly to preserve languages imperiled by their missionary efforts.[36] By the mid-1840s, the indefatigable Reverend Stephen R. Riggs was self-consciously following the example of early ethnographers in his admirable series of grammars and vocabularies of northern Plains tribes.[37] Enthusiastic and sometimes talented, these self-styled linguists—army personnel, boundary commissioners, frontiersmen, doctors, even a Canadian magistrate—worked diligently against time with little hope of reward.[38] Near midcentury, one of them regretted how little of Indian life remained in characteristic tones. "What was once an easy attainment, was then neglected," he observed, deploring the inadequate word lists made earlier by those with greater opportunity. "Such as it is, however, we feel very grateful for it; though small, still it is precious. . . ."[39] This alternation between regret at the loss and relief at what had been

response, see the anonymous review of Morse's *Report* in *North American Review*, 16 (January 1823), esp. 30-33, 39-40. See also Pearce, *Savagism and Civilization*, pp. 112ff.

[36] Edmund De Schweinitz, *The Life and Times of David Zeisberger: The Western Pioneer and Apostle of the Indians* (Philadelphia: J. B. Lippincott and Co., 1870), pp. 161-62, 189, 253, 686; Kennedy, *Jesuit and Savage in New France*, esp. pp. 97ff., 191.

[37] See Leslie A. White's introduction to Lewis Henry Morgan, *The Indian Journals, 1859-62*, ed. White (Ann Arbor: University of Michigan Press, 1959), pp. 7-8; William Goetzmann, *Exploration and Empire: The Explorer and the Scientist in the Winning of the American West* (New York: Alfred A. Knopf, 1966), p. 232; Stephen R. Riggs, *Dakota-English Dictionary* (1852), Contributions to North American Ethnology, no. 7 (Washington: G.P.O., 1897), p. 1. See also Rev. Marie Charles Pandosy, *Grammar and Dictionary of the Yakima Language*, trans. and ed. George Gibbs and J. G. Shea (New York: Cramoisy Press, 1862), p. 1.

[38] John Russell Bartlett, *Personal Narrative of Explorations and Incidents in Texas, New Mexico, California, Sonora, and Chihuahua, Connected with the United States and Mexican Boundary Commission, During the Years 1850, '51, '52, and '53*, 2 vols. (New York: D. Appleton and Co., 1854), esp. 1:vi; Robert V. Hine, *Bartlett's West: Drawing the Mexican Boundary* (New Haven: Yale University Press, 1968), esp. pp. 54, 63-65; Joshua V. H. Clark, *Lights and Lines of Indian Character and Scenes of Pioneer Life* (Syracuse: E. H. Babcock and Co., 1854), pp. iii-iv; Myrtle, *The Iroquois*, pp. 13-14; Joseph Barrett, *The Indian of New-England and the North-Eastern Provinces* (Middletown, Conn.: Charles H. Pelton, 1851), esp. p. 2; Gilbert Malcolm Sproat, *Scenes and Studies of Savage Life* (London: Smith, Elder and Co., 1868), p. 10; *The Journals of Captain Nathaniel J. Wyeth* (Fairfield, Wash.: Ye Galleon Press, 1969), pp. 106-9, 118-20, 129-31. On Wyeth, see Joseph Kastner, *A Species of Eternity* (New York: Alfred A. Knopf, 1977), pp. 277-80.

[39] Barrett, *Indian of New-England*, p. 2.

salvaged forms a basic rhythm to statements by collectors throughout the century.

To repeat, then, the urgent need for a comprehensive linguistic study of Indian tribes was apparent by the 1820s. Albert Gallatin, Jefferson's illustrious secretary of the Treasury and Monroe's minister to France, began in 1823 to collect word lists. Retiring from public life eight years later, he turned fully to the project. By 1843, he had published the most exhaustive contemporary study of native vocabularies, helped to found and become the first president of the American Ethnological Society of New York, and achieved the reputation of "father of American ethnology."[40] Others similarly anxious and similarly interested in comparative philology set out near mid-century to rescue vocabularies collected earlier but forgotten.[41] At the end of the century, however, sophisticated studies in linguistic anthropology were still operating under the premises of early, amateur efforts. Franz Boas's linguistic analyses and Gallatin's tribal word lists, separated by more than seventy years, share a common belief that language, like a master key, would open a series of locked cultural doors.

Though linguistic interpretation advanced relatively little in the nineteenth century, the number of those collecting tribal vocabularies grew dramatically. Confirming the heightened consciousness of a need for haste is the incidence of such phrases as "yet attainable," "while we may," "none too soon," and "will be too late."[42] Moreover, collectors recognized that the task required greater ingenuity. Horatio Hale, America's most distinguished nineteenth-century linguist after Gallatin, effected a dramatic coup in 1870 by seeking out "the lone centurion surviving fullblood" of the Tutelo tribe and patiently transcribing the Tutelo language.[43] Other vocabularies would be snatched

[40] Henry Adams, *The Life of Albert Gallatin* (Philadelphia: J. B. Lippincott, 1880), p. 644. See also *Selected Writings of Albert Gallatin*, ed. E. James Ferguson (New York: Bobbs-Merrill, 1967); Albert Gallatin, "A Synopsis of the Indian Tribes of North America," *Archaeologica Americana: Transactions and Collections of the American Antiquarian Society*, 2 (1836), 1-422; Gallatin, "Notes on the Semi-Civilized Nations of Mexico, Yucatan, and Central America," *Transactions of the American Ethnological Society*, 1 (1845), 1-352; Pearce, *Savagism and Civilization*, p. 114n.

[41] See Hermann E. Ludewig, *The Literature of American Aboriginal Languages*, ed. Nicolas Trübner (London: Trübner and Co., 1858), pp. vi, xi.

[42] See John Wesley Powell, *Introduction to the Study of Indian Languages with Words Phrases and Sentences to be Collected* (1877), 2d ed. (Washington: G.P.O., 1880), p. v.

[43] William N. Fenton, introduction to Horatio Hale, ed., *The Iroquois Book of Rites* (1883), ed. Fenton (Toronto: University of Toronto Press, 1963), p. xii.

from the grave by other ethnologists struggling alone, motivated by a similar sense of personal mission.[44]

The federal government, led by Secretary of the Smithsonian Institution Joseph Henry, increasingly recognized its responsibility for preserving and studying information on the western tribes. The institution's first thirty years chronicle a pattern of continual official pleading for ethnological collecting.[45] Under pressure from the forceful, far-sighted John Wesley Powell (1834-1902), Congress finally established the Bureau of American Ethnology as a branch of the Smithsonian in 1879.[46] Powell, who pursued careers enough for three men, all aimed at intelligent settlement of western lands, directed the newly formed bureau into two decades of large-scale, well-funded, expert compiling of vocabularies "of those languages which can still be successfully studied."[47] During his very first year in office, he publicly pleaded for American scholars to devote themselves to such work.[48] Accomplished scientists, including Washington Matthews, James C. Pilling, and George A. Dorsey, heeded his call, often out of explicit agreement with Powell's forebodings.[49] Even though much

[44] See, for instance, Albert Gatschet, "The Karankawa Indians, the Coast People of Texas," *Archaeological and Ethnological Papers of the Peabody Museum*, 1, no. 2 (1891), 69-70.

[45] Henry, "Circular Relating to Collections in Archaeology and Ethnology," *Smithsonian Miscellaneous Collections*, 8 (1868), 1-2; Henry, "Circular in Reference to American Archaeology," ibid., 15 (1878), 1. See also Pearce, *Savagism and Civilization*, pp. 129-30; William Henry Holmes, *Archaeological Studies among the Ancient Cities of Mexico*, Field Columbian Museum Publication, 8, 16 (Chicago, 1895), p. 15; Edgar L. Hewitt, "The Groundwork of American Archaeology," *Papers of the School of American Archaeology*, 1 (1908), reprinted in *American Anthropologist*, 10 (October-December 1908), 595.

[46] Neil M. Judd, *The Bureau of American Ethnology: A Partial History* (Norman: University of Oklahoma Press, 1967), pp. 2-4.

[47] John Wesley Powell, "Preface," *Bureau of Ethnology: Annual Reports*, 2 (1880-81), xx. See also William Culp Darrah, *Powell of the Colorado* (Princeton: Princeton University Press, 1951), esp. pp. 194, 255-56, 259, 262; Wallace Stegner, *Beyond the Hundredth Meridian: John Wesley Powell and the Second Opening of the West* (Boston: Houghton Mifflin Co., 1954), esp. pp. 256-60; John Upton Terrell, *The Man Who Rediscovered America: A Biography of John Wesley Powell* (New York: Weybright and Talley, 1969), pp. 162ff. See also Judd, *Bureau of American Ethnology*, p. 19; Brian M. Fagan, *Elusive Treasure: The Story of Early Archaeologists in the Americas* (New York: Charles Scribner's Sons, 1977), 285-95; Goetzmann, *Exploration and Empire*, pp. 530-76.

[48] Powell, *Study of Indian Languages*, p. viii.

[49] Washington Matthews, *Ethnology and Philology of the Hidatsa Indians*, U.S. Geological and Geographical Survey, Miscellaneous Publications, no. 7 (Washington: G.P.O., 1877), pp. 30-31; George A. Dorsey, *The Arapaho Sun Dance: The Ceremony of the Offerings Lodge*, Field Columbian Museum Publication 75 (Chicago, 1903), p. 2; Dorsey, *Traditions of the Osage*, Field Museum Publication 88 (Chicago, 1904), p. v; Dorsey, *The Cheyenne*, vol. 1, *Ceremonial Organization*, Field Columbian Museum

of the best anthropology at the century's end narrowed its focus to linguistic considerations, it did not ignore the contexts newly provided by cultural and physical anthropologists. "A language is best understood," Powell admonished, "when the habits, customs, institutions, philosophy,—the subject-matter of thought imbodied in the language are best known. The student of language should be a student of the people who speak the language."[50]

CUSTOMS AND LORE

Half a century before Powell espoused his ethnographic principle, others with little sense for the possibilities of linguistic anthropology dismissed the supposedly narrow assumptions of word-list gatherers. Such simplistic efforts, they thought, misrepresented the complexity of native languages; even worse, these enthusiasts ignored other, more valuable materials equally imperiled.[51] Crèvecoeur in 1800 was certainly not the first layman, nor Edmund Wilson in 1947 the last, enthralled enough by native myths and rituals to want to transcribe them.[52] In the nineteenth century, however, the sheer number of amateurs who set down native folklore and traditions represents a striking testament to white apprehension. Their efforts—those of Mary Eastman with Dakota tribes in the 1840s and of George Bird Grinnell among the Montana Pawnee and Blackfoot in the 1870s— derived almost entirely from a consciousness of imminent loss.[53] Simi-

Publication 99 (Chicago, 1905), p. v; Dorsey, *The Ponca Sun Dance*, Field Columbian Museum Publication 102 (Chicago, 1905), p. 67; James Constantine Pilling, *Bibliography of the Siouan Languages*, Bureau of American Ethnology, Bulletin no. 5 (Washington: G.P.O., 1887); Pilling, *Bibliography of the Chinookan Languages* (Washington: G.P.O., 1893), p. vi.

50 Powell, *Study of Indian Languages*, p. vi.

51 See, for instance, Caleb Atwater's animadversions on missionary vocabularies as fundamentally simplistic, in *Remarks Made on a Tour to Prairie Du Chien; Thence to Washington City, in 1829* (Columbus: Isaac N. Whiting, 1831), pp. 78-81.

52 Michel-Guillaume St. Jean de Crèvecoeur, *Journey into Northern Pennsylvania and the State of New York* (1801), trans. Clarissa Spencer Bostelmann, 3 vols. in 1 (Ann Arbor: University of Michigan Press, 1964), pp. 221-35; Edmund Wilson, *Red, Black, Blond and Olive—Studies in Four Civilizations: Zuni, Haiti, Soviet Russia, Israel* (New York: Oxford University Press, 1956), pp. 23ff.

53 Grinnell, *Pawnee Hero Stories*, p. x; Eastman, *Dahcotah*, p. xvi; Eastman, *The American Aboriginal Portfolio* (Philadelphia: Lippincott, Grambo and Co., [1853]), pp. v, xi, xii, 80. See also George Bird Grinnell, *Blackfoot Lodge Tales: The Story of a Prairie People* (1903?; rpt. Lincoln: University of Nebraska Press, 1962), pp. ix, xii-xv; *The Passing of the Great West: Selected Papers of George Bird Grinnell*, ed. John T. Rieger (New York: Winchester Press, 1972), esp. pp. 2, 65, 69. Missionaries also transcribed native myths out of similar apprehensions. See, for example: Pierre Jean De Smet, S.J., *Oregon Missions and Travels Over the Rocky Mountains, in 1845-46* (1847), rpt. in vol. 29 of Reubon Gold Thwaites, ed., *Early Western Travels: 1748-*

larly, the popular essayist Charles Godfrey Leland attempted to transcribe all he could of the surprisingly rich oral tradition still extant in the 1880s among the Algonquin Passamaquoddy. In resisting interpretive comment, he nicely expressed what many responsible ethnographers also felt: "when the Indian shall have passed away there will come far better ethnologists than I am, who will be much more obliged to me for collecting raw material than for cooking it."[54] Leland was right not only in maintaining this cautious critical stance but also in recognizing the cumulative value of his and others' work. Whether or not his pleas for broad public participation in such efforts converted his contemporaries, many were already attempting to track down "every scrap of information" before "the Indians shall have departed."[55]

Leland's appreciation of native life preceded his initiation into the Kaw tribe of Kansas. Other whites awoke to the value of recording the knowledge they had gained of native tribes only after they had spent many years in close contact with them. Initiation itself spurred their sense of responsibility for preserving otherwise forgotten lore.[56]

1846 (Cleveland: Arthur H. Clark Co., 1904), p. 111; Nicolas Point, S.J., *Wilderness Kingdom—Indian Life in the Rocky Mountains: 1840-1847. The Journals and Paintings of Nicolas Point, S.J.*, trans. Joseph P. Donnelly, S.J. (New York: Holt, Rinehart and Winston, 1967), pp. 120-21; Rev. Gideon H. Pond, "Dakota Superstitions," *Collections of the Minnesota Historical Society*, 2 (1860-67), 215; Gregory Mengarini, S.J., *Recollections of the Flathead Mission*, trans. and ed. Gloria Ricci Lothrop (Glendale, Calif.: Arthur H. Clark Co., 1977); Slotkin, *Regeneration through Violence*, p. 211.

54 Leland, *The Algonquin Legends of New England, or Myths and Folk Lore of the Micmac, Passamaquoddy, and Penobscot Tribes* (Boston: Houghton, Mifflin and Co., 1884), p. iv, also pp. iii, 5, 8, 13. See also Zolla, *The Writer and the Shaman*, pp. 148, 175-77, for a useful discussion of Leland.

55 Ernest Whitney, *Legends of the Pike's Peak Region: The Sacred Myths of the Manitou* (Denver: Chain and Hardy Co., 1892), pp. 12, 52; Harriet Maxwell Converse, "Myths and Legends of the New York State Iroquois," *New York State Museum Bulletin* (Albany: University of the State of New York, 1908), pp. 14, 27, 31ff. See also Zolla, *The Writer and the Shaman*, p. 179.

56 James Athearn Jones, *Traditions of the North American Indians*, 3 vols. (1830; rpt. Upper Saddle River, N.J.: Literature House, 1970), 1:ix-xi, xv; *The Journal of Major John Norton, 1816*, ed. Carl F. Klinck and James J. Talman (Toronto: Champlain Society, 1970), pp. xvii-xxiv; Sarah Winnemucca Hopkins, *Life Among the Piutes: Their Wrongs and Claims*, ed. Mrs. Horace [Mary] Mann (Boston: n.p., 1883), p. 3; George P. Belden, *Belden, The White Chief; or Twelve Years Among the Wild Indians of the Plains*, ed. Gen. James S. Brisbin (1870; rpt. Cincinnati: E. W. Starr and Co., 1875); Mary Ellicott Arnold and Mabel Reed, *In the Land of the Grasshopper Song: A Story of Two Girls in Indian Country in 1908-09* (New York: Vantage Press, 1957), pp. 3-5; C. D. Willard, "The New Editor [Charles F. Lummis]," *Land of Sunshine*, (December 1894), 12; Edwin Thompson Denig, *Five Indian Tribes of the Upper Missouri*, ed. John C. Ewers (Norman: University of Oklahoma Press, 1961), p. xxix; Jean Louis Berlandier, *The Indians of Texas in 1830*, trans. Patricia Reading Leclercq, ed. John C. Ewers (Washington: Smithsonian Institution, 1969), pp. 22-24, 153ff.

Before the Civil War, those expressing such concern tended to be frontiersmen on close terms with individual tribes. After the late 1860s, the ones to volunteer records were often military personnel who had come to feel sympathy for the very peoples they had been ordered to force onto reservations.[57]

The recognition that tribal lore needed to be preserved did not itself encourage the development of cultural tolerance, much less pluralism. Henry Rowe Schoolcraft (1793-1864), for example, the single most important ethnographer before the Civil War, empathized with Indian tribes enough to have learned a number of native dialects, spent a lifetime studying tribal lore, and married the granddaughter of an Ojibwa chief. But, to repeat, his ethnocentrism colored his views so thoroughly that the very data his monumental studies provide frequently refute his conclusions.

At the age of twenty-seven, Schoolcraft accompanied an 1820 government expedition to the Lake Superior copper region as geologist and geographer. Soon less interested in topography than in local tribes, he developed that interest during the next four decades into a career as the first ethnologist of American Indian life. Rocks, Schoolcraft felt, might wait another century or two; native cultures would not.[58] He returned to the Lake Superior region the following year as a federal Indian agent, a role that perfectly clarifies the conflict informing Schoolcraft's attitude toward indigenous tribes: the post facilitated his gathering of native materials even as it required him to negotiate against native tribes. Schoolcraft himself never appreciated the contradiction, applying the same pedantic meticulousness of his scholarship to shrewd treaties for white expansion.[59] In that regard, he exemplifies the thesis of this chapter, laboring anxiously against the loss of materials that were threatened by his own official actions.

[57] Ewers, "When Red and White Men Meet," pp. 144-45. Ewers first suggested this revisionist reading, one developed well by Thomas Leonard in *Above the Battle: War-Making in America from Appomattox to Versailles* (New York: Oxford University Press, 1978), chap. 3. See, for two instances, John G. Bourke, *On the Border with Crook* (New York: Charles Scribner's Sons, 1891), pp. 112-14; Bourke, "The Medicine-Men of the Apaches," in Bureau of American Ethnology, *Ninth Annual Report, 1887-88* (Washington: G.P.O., 1892), p. 451; Frederic Webb Hodge, "In Memoriam—John Gregory Bourke," *Journal of American Folk-Lore*, 9 (1896), esp. p. 141; Col. Randolph Barnes Marcy, *Thirty Years of Army Life on the Border* (New York: Harper and Brothers, 1866), pp. 97ff. See also Garrick Mallery, *Picture Writing of the American Indians*, 2 vols. (1893; rpt. New York: Dover Publications, 1972).

[58] Henry Rowe Schoolcraft, *Narrative Journal of Travels Through the Northwestern Regions of the United States . . .* (1821), ed. Mentor Williams (East Lansing: Michigan State College Press, 1953), p. 203.

[59] See Zolla, *The Writer and the Shaman*, pp. 148-62; Pearce, *Savagism and Civilization*, pp. 120-28.

In studies over thirty years, resulting in a series of encyclopedic published collections, Schoolcraft kept returning to the legends of his wife's Algonquin-speaking tribe, always for the same reasons. *Algic Researches* (1839), his first collection of mythological tales and, in a later version, Longfellow's source for *Hiawatha* (1855), offers "General Considerations" for the undertaking.

Every year is diminishing [the Indians'] numbers and adding to the obscurity of their traditions. Many of the tribes and languages are already extinct, and we can allude to at least one of the still existing smaller tribes who have lost the use of their vernacular tongue and adopted the English. Distinct from every benevolent consideration, weighty as these are, it is exceedingly desirable that the record of facts, from which they are to be judged, should be completed, as early as possible. It is conceived that, in rescuing their oral tales and fictitious legends, an important link in the chain has been supplied. But it is believed that still higher testimony remains.[60]

Throughout his distinguished career, Schoolcraft circled back to this theme, rededicating himself to ensuring a record of Indian life and tradition.

Not surprisingly, his Ojibwa wife, Jane, shared this concern and may even have helped him to define it more clearly. A visitor once described this European-educated woman as having "a melancholy and pity in her voice, when speaking of [her people], as if she did indeed consider them a doomed race."[61] She joined her husband in recording and translating tribal myths, but she failed to help him break through a narrow assessment of Indian cultures. Schoolcraft's lifelong study of what he referred to as the "mental character" and "interior man" of native life gave him no more than a bare inkling of the complexity of his subjects.[62] Never moving beyond the stereotypical Indian-agent cast of thought, he deplored the failure of natives to adopt white habits of industry, thrift, and cleanliness, and his occasional translations of Indian poetry confirm European, not native,

[60] *Schoolcraft's Indian Legends*, ed. Mentor Williams (East Lansing: Michigan State University Press, 1956), pp. 10-11, also p. 302. See also Hodges, *Carl Wimar*, p. 10.

[61] Mrs. Anna Brownell Jameson, *Winter Studies and Summer Rambles in Canada*, 2 vols. (New York: Wiley and Putnam, 1839), 2:148. See also Charles S. and Stellanora Osborn, *Schoolcraft—Longfellow—Hiawatha* (Lancaster, Pa.: Jacques Cattell Press, 1942), pp. 520-39.

[62] Henry Rowe Schoolcraft, *The Myth of Hiawatha and Other Oral Legends* (Philadelphia: J. B. Lippincott and Co., 1856), pp. viii, x; Schoolcraft, *Archives of Aboriginal Knowledge*, 1:vi.

conventions.[63] Nevertheless, Schoolcraft's exhaustive research remains invaluable. Completed at the very moment tribes were disappearing, his collection of myths, legends, and narratives attests to a richness and diversity of native experience that he himself could not appreciate.

By mid-century, a national reputation helped Schoolcraft to persuade others of the need for last-minute collecting of cultural documents. Amateurs and professionals alike felt a new urgency to compile such materials and came almost to resent the seemingly constitutional reserve of their informants. "This reticence on the part of the Indian may finally disappear," one prominent anthropologist wrote in 1892, reiterating a judgment made for decades; "still, it is quite time that their myths and traditions were collected, lest with the breaking up of customs on which that reticence is founded the memory of the past will be lost."[64] Of course, reticence itself betokened cultural strength, testifying to the continuing vitality of norms and taboos. The paradox here—that traditions could be transcribed only when dead, when their function and full meaning had become obsolete—was hardly lost upon recorders. Like the photographers who discovered this same truth, they nonetheless continued to work toward a cultural image as accurate as possible. By the 1890s, even popular magazines touted such efforts in patriotic terms. An article in *Harper's Monthly* announced:

> Old traditions, old customs, old aspirations, are fading swiftly and surely in the presence of the white man. It is humiliating not only for an American, but for any educated human being, to realize that in this great, rich, powerful United States, boasting ever of its general enlightenment, there is neither the intelligent public spirit nor the sustained private devotion to the wider aspects of science to secure the myths and traditions and lore of those wonderful people before this page now open upon the Story of Man shall be closed forever. For nowhere else upon this planet does this particular illumining phase of human life exist, nor will it come again. There are many fields of science in which it does not make very much difference if the work which is waiting

[63] In this context, see also Lewis Cass, *Inquiries, Respecting the History, Traditions, Languages, Manners, Customs, Religion, &c. of the Indians, Living within the United States* (Detroit: Sheldon and Reed, 1823), pp. 2ff.; Cass, "Indians of North America," *North American Review*, 22 (1826), 54-58.

[64] Adolph F. Bandelier, "Final Report of Investigations among the Indians of the Southwestern United States, Carried on Mainly in the Years from 1880 to 1885," pt. 2, *Papers of the Archaeological Institute of America, American Series*, 4 (1892), 6.

to be done shall wait a little longer. A decade more or less is of little importance in the end. But here delay is fatal.[65]

Perhaps as clearly as anywhere, this declaration evinces how an exuberant nationalism may thinly veil the uncertainties about vanishing native cultures that troubled increasing numbers of Americans toward the end of the century.

RECOVERING EARLY RECORDS

The most dramatic instances of rescued traditions involved the discovery of unique manuscripts by happenstance. It was as if a Mayan codex had been seized from the flames of Bishop Landa's sixteenth-century bonfire. Horatio Hale, an eminent ethnologist, accomplished such a feat by transcribing the sole copy of *The Iroquois Book of Rites* and publishing it in 1883. In the process, he reclaimed the cultural heritage of that great woodland confederacy, thoroughly transformed by long contact with European culture. As Hale recognized, the book's value lay in just this point, in having been "framed long before [the Iroquois] were affected by any influences from abroad."[66]

In 1884 Daniel Brinton, who achieved a correspondingly eminent reputation in linguistics, similarly resurrected "one of the most curious records of ancient American history," the *Walam Olum*.[67] Supposedly lost to history, this chronicle of the Delaware tribe now stands as a great epic poem and an invaluable anthropological document. A year later, Brinton prefaced his *Annals of the Cakchiquels* (1885) with a statement strikingly similar to Hale's evaluation of the *Book of Rites*.[68]

Such dramatic coups were rare, however—the result less of diligence than of serendipity. From the 1840s, individuals more commonly devoted themselves to collecting a literature transcribed long before, sometimes even published, but abandoned in attics or forgotten in library alcoves. They were motivated by the same concerns that prompted others to search dusty shelves for word lists and grammars, but they ranged more widely and organized more extensive ma-

---

[65] T. Mitchell Prudden, "An Elder Brother to the Cliff-Dwellers," *Harper's Monthly Magazine*, 95 (June 1897), 57.

[66] Hale, ed., *Iroquois Book of Rites*, ed. Fenton, p. 82.

[67] Brinton, *The Lenâpé and Their Legends* (1885; rpt. New York: Ams Press, 1969), p. v.

[68] Brinton, *The Annals of the Cakchiquels* (1885; rpt. New York: Ams Press, 1969), p. v. See also Franz Boas, *Chinook Texts*, Bureau of American Ethnology (Washington: G.P.O., 1894), pp. 5-6; Pilling, *Bibliography of the Chinookan Languages*, pp. v-vi.

terials in order to reconstruct a history. Hiram Beckwith, for example, described his own antiquarian efforts as a synthesis of "gleanings over a wide field of antiquated books of travel and maps long since out of print, or copies of manuscript-correspondence of a private or official character, little of which is accessible to the general reader."[69] He deplored the current state of knowledge of eastern woodland tribes. "The little information that has been preserved concerning them is so scattered through the volumes of authors who wrote from other motives, or at different dates, or of different nations, without taking thought to discriminate, that no satisfactory account of any particular tribe is now attainable. The best that may be done is to select such of these disjointed scraps as bear evidence of being the most reliable, and arrange them in something like chronological order."[70]

Statements of regret, compilations of "gleanings," and rueful observations on the appalling lack of documentary evidence might be multiplied almost indefinitely.[71] Thoreau himself—who, according to one scholar, "had Indians on the brain" as early as the 1840s[72]— spent the decade before his death in 1862 working almost exclusively on eleven manuscript notebooks that comprise more than a thousand pages of materials on North American Indians. Thoreau wanted merely to preserve, and educate himself, in materials fast fading away.

This impulse reverberated across the continent. Hubert Howe Bancroft, the eccentric San Francisco book dealer, had become an energetic collector of Americana in 1859. He stated one of the reasons that persuaded him to become a professional historian in *The Native Races of the Pacific States*: "To gather and arrange in systematic com-

[69] Hiram W. Beckwith, *The Illinois and Indiana Indians* (Chicago: Fergus Printing Co., 1884), p. v.

[70] Ibid.

[71] For a sampling, see: *Graphic Sketches from Old and Authentic Works, Illustrating the Costume, Habits, and Character of the Aborigines of America* (New York: J. and H. G. Langley, 1841), p. 3; John W. De Forest, *History of the Indians of Connecticut from the Earliest Known Period to 1850* (Hartford: William James Hamersley, 1853), pp. 1-2; William T. Corbusier, *Verde to San Carlos: Recollections of a Famous Army Surgeon and His Observant Family on the Western Frontier, 1869-1886* (Tucson: Dale Stuart King, 1969); Samuel Asahel Clarke, *Pioneer Days of Oregon History*, 2 vols. (Portland: J. K. Gill Co., 1905), 1:iii, 84ff.; James Buchanan, *Sketches of the History, Manners, and Customs of the North American Indians with a Plan for Their Melioration*, 2 vols. (New York: W. Borradaile, 1824), 1:ix, 13; John Halkett, *Historical Notes Respecting the Indians of North America . . .* (London: Archibald Constable and Co., 1825).

[72] Sayre, *Thoreau and the American Indians*, p. 97. See also Albert Keiser, "Thoreau's Manuscripts on the Indians," *Journal of English and Germanic Philology*, 27 (April 1928), esp. 198-99.

pact form all that is known of these people; to rescue some facts, perhaps, from oblivion, to bring others from inaccessible nooks, to render
all available to science and to the general reader. . . ."[73] More traditional, thorough, and accomplished historians, including Francis Parkman and William Hickling Prescott, also attempted to weave together
forgotten native materials into solid but readable works. Among nineteenth-century historians of America, those devoted to the Indian experience seem to have felt the burden and urgency of documentation
most heavily.[74]

A thin line divided the writing of history from that of belles-lettres
in the mid-nineteenth century. The height of romanticism in America
encouraged an outpouring of sentimental poems, novels, plays, and
even operas with Indian themes, Longfellow's *Hiawatha* being only
the best-known example. "Writers of frontier romances," one student
of the genre has observed, "believed that Indians would soon exist
only in their pages."[75] More serious artists, including James Fenimore Cooper, responded to the hopes expressed by Hawthorne and
Margaret Fuller, that "there might be some masterly attempt to reproduce in art or literature what is proper to them."[76] Surprising as
it may appear to readers of, say, *The Deerslayer*, Cooper was among
the first devoted to faithful fictional portraits of native tribes. Never
troubling to travel among the tribes he described, he nonetheless
read extensively in missionary reports, histories, and government surveys in order to authenticate narrative depictions of tribes declining
or extinct by the time he wrote.[77]

Some authors self-consciously resisted the trend toward adapting

[73] Bancroft, *The Native Races of the Pacific States of North America*, 5 vols.
(New York: D. Appleton and Co., 1875-1876), 1:x-xi.

[74] See, for example, the discussion of Francis Parkman in Chapter Two above.
See also Howard Doughty, *Francis Parkman* (New York: Macmillan, 1962), pp. 390-
91. Parkman, *The Jesuits in North America in the Seventeenth Century* (1867),
vols. 3-4 of the Champlain ed. of *The Works of Francis Parkman* (Boston: Little,
Brown and Co., 1897), 3:vi-vii; Edward G. Mason, "Francis Parkman," *Dial*, 1
(December 1880), 150. For useful discussions of Parkman, see Pearce, *Savagism
and Civilization*, pp. 162-68; Zolla, *The Writer and the Shaman*, pp. 139-43.

[75] Barnett, *Ignoble Savage*, p. 39. See also Keen, *Aztec Image*, p. 363. For one
explicit example of this, see Mrs. Mary H. Eastman, *The Romance of Indian Life*
(Philadelphia: Lippincott, Grambo and Co., 1853), p. xi.

[76] *The Writings of Margaret Fuller*, ed. Mason Wade (New York: Viking, 1941),
p. 88.

[77] See Gregory Lansing Paine, "The Indians of the Leather-Stocking Tales,"
Studies in Philology, 23 (1926), 20-21, 30, 39; John T. Frederick, "Cooper's
Eloquent Indians," *Publications of the Modern Language Association*, 71 (1956),
1006; Paul A. W. Wallace, "Cooper's Indians," *New York History*, 35 (October
1954), 424-27; Henry Nash Smith, introduction to Cooper, *The Prairie* (New York:
Holt, Rinehart and Winston, 1950), pp. vi-viii.

fiction to documentary ends.[78] Too many others followed Cooper's romantic lead without bothering to imitate even his second hand scholarship.[79] Not surprisingly, many frontier romancers were, in one scholar's words, "men on whom a great deal was lost."[80] But even had they been more sensitive, more intelligent, better informed, they would likely have failed in their portrayals, since no treatment that satisfies western European literary conventions could have adequately encompassed the native experience. In a vain attempt to compensate for the perceived deficiency, authors in the last decade of the century completed works that barely sustain a fictional life. Adolph Bandelier's *The Delight Makers* (1890), for instance, and Edna Dean Procter's poem *The Song of the Ancient People* (1893) are riddled with anthropological data.[81] Such efforts frequently demonstrated little more sensitivity, and often less cultural tolerance, than might have been gained from straightforward scientific accounts. They can only be praised for attempting to break from the powerful sentimentalizing influence of Longfellow and his imitators. Longfellow himself had wanted merely to romanticize Schoolcraft's Ojibwa legends in his *Song of Hiawatha* and never shared Bandelier's or Procter's concern for preservation or authenticity. Nonetheless, the poem's spectacular popularity sparked numerous attempts to collect native legends and oral traditions before time ran out.[82] Perhaps this, for all the expressed hopes of other writers, remains the single notable legacy of nineteenth-century imagings of the Indian.[83]

[78] Cf. Charles Dickens, *American Notes and Pictures from Italy* (1842; rpt. New York: E. P. Dutton, 1908), pp. 163-64.

[79] See, for example, George H. Colton, *Tecumseh; or, The West Thirty Years Since. A Poem* (New York: Wiley and Putnam, 1842), preface (unpaginated).

[80] Barnett, *Ignoble Savage*, pp. 189-90.

[81] Zolla, *The Writer and the Shaman*, pp. 166-72; Barnett, *Ignoble Savage*, pp. 191-95.

[82] Ellwood Parry, *The Image of the Indian and the Black Man in American Art, 1590-1900* (New York: George Braziller, 1974), p. 125.

[83] Unlike Longfellow, many frontier romancers did want to preserve an accurate image of native history and lore. See, among others: Rev. James Wallis Eastburn, *Yamoyden, A Tale of the Wars of King Philip: In Six Cantos* (New York: n.p., 1820), esp. pp. 3-4, 27ff.; Sir William George Drummond Stewart, *Altowan; or, Incidents of Life and Adventure in the Rocky Mountains by an Amateur Traveler*, ed. J. Watson Webb, 2 vols. (New York: Harper and Brothers, 1846), 1:iv-v; Rev. J. J. Methvin, *Andele, or The Mexican-Kiowa Captive: A Story of Real Life Among the Indians* (Louisville: Pentecostal Herald Press, 1899), p. 3; Homer F. Barnes, *Charles Fenno Hoffman* (New York: Columbia University Press, 1930), pp. 216, 315; Lewis Leary, *That Rascal Freneau: A Study in Literary Failure* (New Brunswick: Rutgers University Press, 1941), pp. 260-61. See also William H. Gardiner, review of Cooper, *The Spy*, in *North American Review*, 15 (1822), 257-58. See also Keen, *Aztec Image*, pp. 373ff.

ARCHAEOLOGY

Just as renewed collecting of myths and legends inspired fictional treatments and was inspired by them, fascination with archaeology was spurred by popular romances about the extinct mound builders.[84] Increasing numbers of enthusiasts in the 1850s, impelled by romances or scientific rationales, posed a considerable threat to sites not already destroyed by farmers' plows and the spades of artifact hunters. The innumerable earthwork mounds dotting the eastern and southern landscape of America had always attracted the curiosity of men like Henry Brackenridge and Thomas Jefferson (who made the first study of one).[85] In the nineteenth century, however, as people came to view the mounds less as mere obstacles to be demolished, interest increased markedly. As one expert has remarked, "In 1800, an Ohioan with a mound on his property was likely to level it so he could plant his crops; in 1840 it was probable that he would conduct a careful excavation and fill his house with an array of ancient artifacts."[86] Obviously, this new attitude posed almost as many problems to the emerging professional as did the old one.

In September 1820, an anonymous letter to the editor of the newly established *Detroit Gazette* asserted: "The origin and history of our Aborigines can only be discovered by a minute investigation of their numerous works of art. This investigation is rendered the more necessary as the rapidly increasing population and cultivation of our country have already occasioned the destruction of many monuments of Indian labor, and it is greatly to be feared, that other of our antiquarian relics will soon suffer the same fate. We ought to urge the more enlightened part of our comunity to draw correct plans and describe the various circumvallatory ramparts which still exist. . . ."[87] Whether or not this particular letter touched other than local sympathies, a wide variety of people—showmen, lawyers, artifact hunters, missionaries, naturalists and scientists, Governor DeWitt Clinton of New York, and Lewis Cass, governor of the Michigan Territory—

[84] Silverberg, *Mound Builders*, esp. pp. 6ff.

[85] Ibid., pp. 97ff.; Cutright, *Lewis and Clark*, p. 6; C. W. Ceram [Kurt W. Marek], *The First American: A Story of North American Archaeology* (New York: Harcourt Brace Jovanovich, 1971), pp. 4-9; Gordon R. Willey and Jeremy A. Sabloff, *A History of American Archaeology* (London: Thames and Hudson, 1974), pp. 33, 36-38; Fagan, *Elusive Treasure*, pp. 94-99.

[86] Silverberg, *Mound Builders*, p. 97.

[87] "Letters to the Editor, on Indian Antiquities. Letter I," *Detroit Gazette*, September 1, 1820, p. 1.

expressed equal concern.[88] Few committed their lives to the tasks they so energetically proclaimed. Nor did many assume that the mound builders were the direct ancestors of present tribes. A handful of devoted archaeologists, however, usually concluded just such a relationship.

Caleb Atwater, Ephraim Squier, and Cyrus Thomas—professionals whose careers neatly span the nineteenth century—attempted to compile accurate records of mounds everywhere being looted and ravaged. Early in his career, in 1820, Atwater had predicted that the mounds at Circleville, Ohio, "will entirely disappear in a few years." He "used the only means within my power, to perpetuate their memory," a drawing and a brief description.[89] For the next two decades, Atwater, and then Squier for twenty years after him, prepared accurate maps and reports of the thousands of mounds still visible. Over and over, these two rued their inadequate means and the enormity of their task.[90]

In the 1880s, Cyrus Thomas, with the funds of the Archaeological Institute of America at his disposal, was faced with the problem of how best to make a comprehensive survey of the earth structures. He rejected the idea of mapping first and investigating later. Private collectors and impatient farmers might have left nothing by the time he could return to a particular site. But if he thoroughly investigated a select few, as Robert Silverberg has noted, "the constant destruction

[88] Constantine Samuel Rafinesque, *The Ancient Monuments of North and South America*, 2d ed. (Philadelphia: n.p., 1838), p. 12; Rafinesque, *A Life of Travels and Researches in North America and South Europe* (Philadelphia: n.p., 1836), p. 62; Kastner, *A Species of Eternity*, pp. 240-53; Alexander W. Bradford, *American Antiquities and Researches into the Origin and History of the Red Race* (New York: Dayton and Saxton, 1841), pp. 1, 12-13; Chauncey Wales Riggs, *How We Find Relics: A Series of Letters* (Chicago: W. B. Conkey Co., 1893), pp. 20-21, also pp. 78-79; Bishop [Henry Benjamin] *Whipple's Southern Diary, 1843-1844*, ed. Lester B. Shippee (Minneapolis: University of Minnesota Press, 1937), pp. 147-48; Bela Hubbard, "Ancient Garden Beds of Michigan," *American Antiquarian*, 1 (April 1878), 1, 8-9; "[Thomas] Nuttall's Travels into the Old Northwest: An Unpublished 1810 Diary," ed. Jeannette E. Graustein, *Chronica Botanica*, 14 (Autumn 1951), 66-67; DeWitt Clinton, *A Memoir on the Antiquities of the Western Parts of the State of New York* (Albany: I. W. Clark, 1818), pp. 3-4; [Lewis Cass], *Ontwa, the Son of the Forest. A Poem* (New York: Wiley and Halsted, 1822), pp. 116-20. See also Curtis Dahl, "Mound-Builders, Mormons, and William Cullen Bryant," *New England Quarterly*, 34 (June 1961), 180ff.; Willey and Sabloff, *History of American Archaeology*, pp. 31-63; Silverberg, *Mound Builders*.

[89] Quoted in Silverberg, *Mound Builders*, p. 64.

[90] Caleb Atwater, *The Writings of Caleb Atwater* (Columbus: n.p., 1833), p. 6; Silverberg, *Mound Builders*, p. 61; Willey and Sabloff, *History of American Archaeology*, pp. 38-39, 43-49; Ephraim G. Squier, *The Serpent Symbol*, American Archaeological Researches, no. 1 (New York: George P. Putnam, 1851), preface (unpaginated), pp. 13-14; Squier, *Antiquities of the State of New York* (Buffalo: George H. Derby and Co., 1851), pp. 7-8, 11, 14. See also Fagan, *Elusive Treasure*, pp. 109-14, 118, 214-24; Ceram, *The First American*, pp. 201-2.

of mounds by natural erosion, private excavation, and public ignorance would remove from study many of the most interesting monuments, no matter which zone was chosen first for intensive exploration."[91] Thomas finally decided on the narrower, but more definitive,
choice and in the process set a model for other workers in the field.

Most of the century's swelling group of archaeologists realized the
concomitant needs for accuracy and haste, whether they studied
eastern mounds or southwestern pueblos, and the inaugural report
of the Archaeological Institute of America expressed this collective
purpose in 1879.[92] More than thirty years earlier, however, a popular
travel writer had garnered enduring fame by practicing and popular-
izing these principles in his studies of Central American archaeology.
John Lloyd Stephens's "great eyes" had long excited the young Herman Melville with the wonders they had seen in Europe and the
Levant.[93] But not until he was sent as a minister to Guatemala in
1839 did Stephens find his true mission. Accompanied by the English
draftsman Frederick Catherwood, Stephens soon became fascinated
with the ruins near Belize and with the native peoples themselves.
The arduous trek he made with Catherwood to Copan and Tikal,
followed by explorations and further study of all other known sites,
led to his reputation as "the father of Mayan archaeology."

The two books that Stephens published from his careful notes and
from the drawings of his companion remain standard texts on their
subject. His motives, explained in 1843, sound remarkably similar to
those of other observers, amateur and professional: "In a few generations, great edifices, their facades covered with sculptured ornaments,
already cracked and yawning, must fall, and become mere shapeless
mounds. It has been the fortune of the author to step between them
and the entire destruction to which they are destined; and it is his
hope to snatch from oblivion these perishing but still gigantic memorials of a mysterious people."[94] Indeed, Stephens and Catherwood
did "snatch from oblivion" the first, in some cases the only, accurate

91 Silverberg, *Mound Builders*, p. 203. See also Wiley and Sabloff, *History of
American Archaeology*, pp. 49-50; Fagan, *Elusive Treasure*, pp. 293-300.

92 See Charles Eliot Norton, Francis Parkman, and Alexander Agassiz, "First
Annual Report of the Executive Committee, with Accompanying Papers. 1879-80,"
in *Archaeological Institute of America* (Cambridge, Mass.: John Wilson and Co.,
1880), p. 20. See also Willey and Sabloff, *History of American Archaeology*, pp.
48-49.

93 Melville, *Redburn: His First Voyage* (1849; rpt. New York: Doubleday and
Co., 1957), p. 4.

94 Stephens, *Incidents of Travel in Yucatan*, 2 vols. (1843; rpt. New York: Dover
Publications, 1963), 1:v. For biographical information, consult Victor Von Hagan,
Maya Explorer: John Lloyd Stephens (Norman: University of Oklahoma Press,
1947).

record of numerous Mayan ruins. Moreover, Stephens's earnestness and his fine literary talents combined to awaken his countrymen, including eminent scientists and historians, to the eroding possibilities of archaeological and anthropological study.[95]

ETHNOLOGICAL SOCIETIES

The voices of Stephens, Atwater, Squier, and Thomas were only four among hundreds clamoring for the immediate collecting of indigenous materials.[96] As mentioned earlier, state governments had been organizing historical societies as repositories for all kinds of artifacts and records since the 1790s. The "Circular Letter" establishing the first of these, in Boston, dispassionately expressed the special importance of native materials among items to be collected: "Monuments and relicks of the ancient Indians; number and present state of any remaining Indians among you."[97] In 1831, in less fragmentary syntax, a tone of disquietude entered the Maine Historical Society's adjuration. Americans must transcribe Indian histories, since they "will be likely to excite higher interest as they recede more and more from future ages."[98] Little more than forty years later, excited urgency had displaced uneasy premonitions, as the "General Circular" stating the principles of the Michigan Pioneer Society reveals: "The interesting traces of the prehistoric races . . . are fast disappearing. The aboriginal tribes, our more immediate ancestors, are fast passing away, and with them the traces of their ancestors, and all traditions of the more recent events in their own unwritten history. . . . these should not be lost, but should be recorded, and that history be carefully preserved."[99]

Also in the period 1830-1880, numerous anthropological societies and museums, public and private, were founded with the purpose of collecting and preserving native materials. The federal government

[95] Richard L. Predmore, introduction to Stephens's *Incidents of Travel in Central America, Chiapas, and Yucatan* (1841), ed. Predmore, 2 vols. (New Brunswick: Rutgers University Press, 1949), 1:xviii; Willey and Sabloff, *History of American Archaeology*, pp. 64-65; Fagan, *Elusive Treasure*, pp. 138-204.

[96] Silverberg, *Mound Builders*, p. 97.

[97] "Circular Letter of the Historical Society," *Proceedings of the Massachusetts Historical Society*, 8 (1791-1835), 1. Henry Nash Smith provides a sharper historical focus to this phenomenon: "Thirty-five local and state historical societies were established between 1820 and 1850 (only three, Massachusetts, New York, Pennsylvania, had been established before 1820). In the same period collectors like John Carter Brown of Providence and James Lennox of New York began to form libraries of Americana" (Smith, "The Widening of Horizons," in Robert E. Spiller et al., eds., *Literary History of the United States: History*, 3d ed. rev. [New York: Macmillan Co., 1963], pp. 644-45).

[98] Cited in Pearce, *Savagism and Civilization*, p. 113.

[99] "General Circular Issued by the State Librarian," *Pioneer Collections: Report of the Pioneer Society of the State of Michigan*, 1 (1877), 3.

demonstrated its own increasing commitment in the programs authorized first by the Smithsonian and later by the Bureau of American Ethnology. More than any other individual, John Wesley Powell was responsible for the coordination of many scattered efforts. His dramatic initial exploration of the Colorado River in 1869 had brought him into contact with remote tribes unaware of the existence of whites. Returning to Zuni Pueblo ten years later with a larger team plus a staff photographer, he felt almost consumed by the need for active, extensive anthropological efforts. "The field of research is speedily narrowing because of the rapid change in the Indian population now in progress," he announced. "All habits, customs, and opinions are fading away; even languages are disappearing; and in a very few years it will be impossible to study our North American Indians in their primitive condition, except for recorded history. For this reason ethnologic studies in America should be pushed with the utmost vigor."[100] Acting on these principles, Powell turned the Bureau of American Ethnology away from its authorized study of historical sites and toward more encompassing ethnological efforts among living tribes.[101] An extraordinary administrator able to attract and hold together a variety of talented scholars, Powell organized the first systematic research in American Indian ethnology.

By the 1880s and 1890s, the federal government had clearly assumed responsibility for concerted, large-scale collecting of indigenous materials. Individuals convinced of the need for such work joined government-funded expeditions or submitted their work for publication in government periodicals. Again, as was true half a century earlier, only a few prominent individuals could afford not to consider government sponsorship, among them some who financed institutions and brought together collections on their own. The expatriate investment banker George Peabody, one of the richest Americans at the time, provides a spectacular example. He gave $150,000 to Harvard University in 1866 to establish the Peabody Museum of Archaeology and Ethnology, "to be devoted wholly to the acquirement and preservation of the fast disappearing material relating to primitive man."[102]

---

[100] Cited in Darrah, *Powell of the Colorado*, p. 255, also pp. 262, 278, 359. For expressions by Powell of similar sentiments, see his *Study of Indian Languages*, pp. v, vi, viii, and "Preface," p. xx. See also Stegner, *Beyond the Hundredth Meridian*, p. 130, and Carl Resek, *Lewis Henry Morgan: American Scholar* (Chicago: University of Chicago Press, 1960), pp. 142, 150.

[101] Judd, *Bureau of American Ethnology*, esp. pp. 4, 19-20; Darrah, *Powell of the Colorado*, pp. 258ff.; Terrell, *The Man Who Rediscovered America*, pp. 209-10, 226ff.

[102] Charles C. Willoughby, "The Peabody Museum of Archaeology and Ethnology, Harvard University," *Harvard Graduates' Magazine*, 31 (June 1923), 495. See also "Letter of Gift, October 8, 1866," *Reports of the Peabody Museum of*

Twenty years later, the Reverend Sheldon Jackson established a small museum in Sitka, Alaska, for similar reasons.[103] Just after the turn of the century, a young engineer, George Heye, the son of a successful Standard Oil executive, set out on his own to acquire artifacts and information from tribes of the Southwest. The endeavor resulted in the Heye Museum of the American Indian in New York City, which organized one of the largest collections of American tribal materials in the world.[104]

These enterprises were the direct descendents of McKenney's "Archives" and Catlin's "Gallery," though undertaken with scientific standards that neither of those men considered necessary. Following the Civil War, the growing appreciation of the link between artifact and ritual, art and world view dictated caution even among commercial collectors. Although relics, tools, and art pieces had excited popular interest well before the Civil War, only toward the end of the century did white observers realize the complex role such artifacts played in Indian cultural life. Recognition of the need for care and accuracy more and more tempered the urgency with which individuals approached collecting.

The single most important artifact in educating white collectors to native culture was the woven basket.[105] Shapes, styles, colors, and intricate reed patterns represented an integration of the sacred, social, ceremonial, and aesthetic values of the culture that produced them. In the process of cultural dissolution, however, weavers abandoned old methods of construction for more profitable ones. Metal proved cheaper than reed and was more durable. White collectors, sensitive to such inexorable developments, compiled voluminous notes and

American Archaeology and Ethnology with Harvard University, 1 (1868-76), 25-26; Charles Schuchert and Clara Mae LeVene, *O. C. Marsh: Pioneer in Paleontology* (New Haven: Yale University Press, 1940), pp. 76-93; Franklin Parker, *George Peabody: A Biography* (Nashville: Vanderbilt University Press, 1971), pp. 139-56.

103 Sheldon Jackson Museum pamphlet and leaflet, Sheldon Jackson Museum (est. 1888), Sitka, Alaska. See also Rev. Sheldon Jackson, *Alaska, and Missions on the North Pacific Coast* (New York: Dodd, Mead and Co., 1880), esp. pp. 86ff.

104 J. Alden Mason, *George J. Heye, 1874-1957* (New York: American Indian Heye Foundation, 1958), esp. pp. 10-12. Another notable instance is the Massachusetts philanthropist Mary Hemenway, who in 1886 financed the Hemenway Southwestern Archaeological Expedition, which brought together Adolph Bandelier, Frank H. Cushing, and others. See Fagan, *Elusive Treasure*, p. 248.

105 C. H. Green, "Brief History of Cliff Dwellers, Their Relics and Ruins," in *Catalogue of a Unique Collection of Cliff Dweller Relics* (Chicago: Art Institute, 1891), p. 19; Horatio Nelson Rust Collection, Huntington Library, San Marino; Charles F. Lummis, "The Palmer Collection," *Land of Sunshine*, 2 (February 1895), 69; J.B.B., "The Yates Collections," *Land of Sunshine*, 2 (May 1895), 98.

made extensive photographic records of both artisans and artifacts.[106] In certain cases they encouraged natives to resurrect old methods and patterns or sought out practitioners who still recalled the significance of the rich basket symbolism.[107] Commercial collectors, in other words, sometimes became good amateur ethnologists, helping professionals and museums to preserve the best still available.

THE RISE OF THE PROFESSIONAL ANTHROPOLOGIST

This chapter has so far sketched the transition from simple concern for native words to a progressively more varied, more anxious, more complex valuation of native modes of thought. Such a well-defined, linear transition never actually occurred, yet the outline characterizes the general tenor of altering assumptions. From memoirs, journal entries, and Indian biographies to more studied attempts at word lists and vocabularies, to active collection of tribal legends and lore, to rediscovery of materials already transcribed or preservation of Indian experiences through fictional means—the thematic sequence suggests an increasing concern for, if not greater understanding of, the felt experience of native cultures. As the outer form of Indian cultures came to be appreciated, many realized that the inner life also demanded attention. Even the act of collecting, preserving, and displaying physical artifacts took on a greater respect for the total cultural life. More and more, amateur and professional collectors learned to view native experience as a complexly integrated whole, larger than the sum of its variously preservable parts.[108]

[106] Livingston Farrand, "Basketry Designs of the Salish Indians," in Franz Boas, ed., *Memoirs of the American Museum of Natural History: Jesup North Pacific Expedition*, 1 (1898-1900), 391-92; James, *Indian Basketry*, pp. 9-10, 16; Otis Tufton Mason, "Aboriginal American Basketry: Studies in a Textile Art Without Machinery," in *Smithsonian Institution Annual Report, 1902* (Washington: G.P.O., 1904), esp. pp. 312-13, 315, 538-40; Frank G. Speck, *Decorative Art of Indian Tribes of Connecticut*, no. 10 Anthropological Series, Canada Department of Mines (Ottawa: G.P. Bureau, 1915), p. 6.

[107] J. Torrey Connor, "Confessions of a Basket Collector," *Land of Sunshine*, 5 (June 1896), 3, 10. See the Grace Nicholson Collection, Huntington Library, San Marino. See esp. Box 1, letter from Mary M. Bradford, November 18, 1906; Box 4; Box 5, letter from Otis T. Mason, July 1, 1902; Box 16, Nicholson's 1906 diary; Nicholson Photograph Album "B," pp. 60-90. See also Apostol, The Indian Summers of Miss Grace Nicholson, pp. 1-3; Winifred Starr Dobyns, "A Treasure House," *Woman Citizen*, 56, old ser. (December 1927), 13-14.

[108] For just two examples, see Myrtle, *The Iroquois*, p. 30; and Joseph K. Dixon, *The Vanishing Race: The Last Great Indian Council* (Garden City N.Y.: Doubleday, Page and Co., 1913), pp. xv, 5, 9-10. See as well Brandon, *The Last Americans*, p. 20.

As early as 1826, one prominent westerner declared: "Of the external habits of the Indians, if we may so speak, we have the most ample details. But of the moral character and feelings of the Indians, of their mental discipline, of their peculiar opinions, mythological and religious, and of all that is most valuable to man in the history of man, we are about as ignorant, as when Jacques Cartier first ascended the St. Lawrence."[109] Of course, a culturally prescribed ethnocentrism too often prevented those similarly committed from seeing what was in front of them. Nonetheless, some diligently tried not merely to collect materials but also to make interpretive sense of them. In part, again, they wanted to verify what complementary materials needed to be preserved before time ran out.

The greatest of these nineteenth-century ethnographers, Lewis Henry Morgan (1818-1881), established American anthropology on true professional grounds. In the 1840s, the young lawyer from Rochester, New York, began to study the social organization of the nearby Iroquois. In fact, the Seneca so fascinated him that his legal career faltered until he found a way to combine avocation and profession. The federal government had been threatening this westernmost tribe of the Iroquois confederates with removal from their attractive reserves, and in the mid-1840s Morgan joined the legal fight to allow them to stay. Success appeared far from imminent, and in the following years Morgan worked ever more urgently to preserve a record of imperiled Iroquois customs, enjoining others to similar efforts.[110]

Morgan's failing law practice finally convinced him to publish the voluminous notes he had collected and to abandon further study. His careful elucidation of social organization, written up in six hectic months as *The League of the Iroquois* (1851), achieved what John Wesley Powell praised as "the first scientific account of an Indian tribe ever given to the world."[111] Morgan's plans to salvage his legal career ended rather than began with the book's completion. That delightfully lively work confirmed him in his continuing avocation, and in the next thirty years, his intensive researches and radical theories established him as the "father of American anthropology."[112]

[109] Cass, "Indians of North America," pp. 54-55.

[110] Resek, *Lewis Henry Morgan*, p. 18. See also, for background information on Morgan, Leslie A. White's introduction to Morgan, *Indians Journals*, ed. White, pp. 3-12.

[111] Powell, "Sketch of Lewis Henry Morgan," *Popular Science Monthly*, November 1880, p. 115.

[112] For useful discussions of Morgan, see: Pearce, *Savagism and Civilization*, pp. 130-34; Berkhofer, *White Man's Indian*, pp. 52-54; Zolla, *The Writer and the Shaman*, pp. 162-68; Dwight W. Hoover, *The Red and the Black* (Chicago: Rand

More important even than Morgan's own efforts were his adjurations to contemporaries to record and systematize information on the American Indian everywhere. In a famous review of Hubert Howe Bancroft's *Native Races of the Pacific States,* he claimed:

> The question is still before us, as a nation, whether we will undertake the work of furnishing to the world a scientific exposition of Indian society, or leave it as it now appears, crude, unmeaning, unintelligible, a chaos of contradictions and puerile absurdities. With a field of unequalled richness and of vast extent . . . more persons ought to be found willing to work upon this material for the credit of American scholarship. It will be necessary for them to do as Herodotus did in Asia and Africa, to visit the native tribes at their villages and encampments, and study their institutions as living organisms, their condition, and their plan of life.[113]

A year later, Morgan lamented that time was too short to complete the necessary work, that Indian institutions and traditions were disappearing ever more rapidly, and that the efforts of American ethnologists were inadequate.[114] The very ease with which he was gaining information manifested the degree of demoralization among the Iroquois; ceremonies once carefully guarded had become performances.

Morgan's particular genius lay in his recognition of the need for more than careful description. He wanted to turn ethnology into a comparative science in which institutions might be classified and societies evaluated. Like many of his notable colleagues, including Powell and Daniel Brinton, Morgan never conceded to native cultural institutions a value comparable to that of white ones. Yet, his patronizing assumptions notwithstanding, he exactingly defined structural links between tribes, using information gathered from western field trips and from a seven-page questionnaire sent in 1859 to thirty western informants. Morgan's subsequent work, his monumental *Systems of Consanguinity* (1871), transformed responsible thinking about native peoples. He not only collated a mass of invaluable data but

McNally, 1976), pp. 97-100, 157-60; Idus L. Murphree, "The Evolutionary Anthropologists: The Progress of Mankind. The Concepts of Progress and Culture in the Thought of John Lubbock, Edward B. Tylor, and Lewis H. Morgan," *Proceedings of the American Philosophical Society,* 105 (June 1961), 272, 291-97; Keen, *Aztec Image,* pp. 380-410.

113 Morgan, "Montezuma's Dinner," *North American Review,* 122 (1876), 268-69.

114 Morgan, *Ancient Society, or Researches in the Lines of Human Progress from Savagery through Barbarism to Civilization* (New York: Henry Holt and Co., 1877), pp. vii-viii.

also created the science of kinship in what has been termed "perhaps the most original and brilliant single achievement in the history of anthropology."[115] What most considered curious facts or exotic traditions could no longer be accepted as less than the warp and woof of an entire cultural fabric. Morgan helped fellow intellectuals to understand how native societies functioned. Before him, for example, Indian tribes had been described in specious terms of kingship and feudalism. Morgan, on the other hand, authenticated their fundamentally socialist character. Though he never freed himself from a rigid cultural absolutism, he nonetheless created the possibility that others could do so and through rigorously objective standards helped to reveal native societies for what they were.

Morgan was by far the most influential person to appreciate the complex integrity of native cultures and their institutions. Beginning in the 1870s, his work achieved international recognition, inspiring Frederick Engels, for instance, to radically new socioeconomic speculations.[116] In America, he gained ardent disciples impressed by the caliber of his theorizing and converted by his urgings of haste. His classic study of *Ancient Society* (1877), which applied questionable evolutionary theory to primitive cultures, eloquently pleaded the case of native studies. Morgan directly challenged his contemporaries, whom he described as "workmen [who] have been unequal to the work. Moreover, while fossil remains buried in the earth will keep for the future student, the remains of Indian arts, languages and institutions will not. They are perishing daily, and have been perishing for upwards of three centuries. . . . After a few more years, facts that may now be gathered with ease will become impossible of discovery. These circumstances appeal strongly to Americans to enter this great field and gather its abundant harvest."[117]

Among those stimulated by Morgan was his most outstanding student, Adolph Bandelier (1840-1914). Nearly commanded by his paternal mentor to study the pueblo cultures of the Southwest, Bandelier traveled to Santa Fe in 1882, where he commenced more than a decade of painstaking study that would establish anthropology in the Southwest. In his voluminous journals and thorough manuscripts, he coordinated archaeological, ethnological, and historical evidence into

[115] George P. Murdock, *Social Structure* (New York: Macmillan Co., 1949), pp. 4-5, cited in Leslie A. White, introduction to Morgan, *Indian Journals*, ed. White, p. 10. See also Brandon, *The Last Americans*, pp. 6-7.

[116] Friedrich Engels, *The Origin of the Family, Private Property and the State in the Light of the Researches of Lewis H. Morgan* (1884), trans. Ernest Untermann (New York: International Publishers, 1942), pp. 5-6, 25-27.

[117] Morgan, *Ancient Society*, p. viii.

an integrated picture of culture. Ever Morgan's student, his work is informed throughout by the sense that much was soon to be lost.[118]

During the next twenty years, numerous serious ethnographers labored in the field explicitly to preserve what was clearly threatened. John Dunbar among the Pawnees; James Owen Dorsey among the Ponca, Osage, and Omaha tribes; George Dorsey among the Cheyenne, Arapaho, and Hopi; Frederick Starr in Mexico; J. A. Costello, James G. Swan, and Franz Boas in the Pacific Northwest; Edward Nelson among the Eskimos; Alexander Stephen with the Hopi; Washington Matthews among the Navaho; Matilda Coxe Stevenson and J. Walter Fewkes among the Zuni[119]—these are only a few of the dedicated professionals who feared that even strenuous ethnological efforts could not save enough of what was threatened. By the century's end, precipitate changes were engulfing the little that was left of Indian life. The elegiac sentiments of the early years of the century had by the 1880s evolved into large-scale, systematic, and imaginative interdisciplinary research.[120]

[118] See Leslie A. White, ed., *Pioneers in American Anthropology: The Bandelier-Morgan Letters, 1873-1883*, 2 vols. (Albuquerque: University of New Mexico Press, 1940). More particularly, see Bandelier, "Historical Introduction to Studies among the Sedentary Tribes of New Mexico," *Papers of the Archaeological Institute of America, American Series*, 1, pt. 1 (1883), 28-29; Bandelier "Final Report," pp. 3, 6.

[119] John B. Dunbar, "The Pawnee Indians: Their Habits and Customs," *Magazine of American History*, 8 (November 1882), 751; J. A. Costello, *The Siwash, Their Life, Legends and Tales* (Seattle: Calvert Co, 1895), preface (unpaginated); James G. Swan, *The Northwest Coast; or, Three Years' Residence in Washington Territory* (1857; rpt. Seattle: University of Washington Press, 1969), pp. ix, xvii, 110; Edward William Nelson, "The Eskimo About Bering Strait," in *Bureau of American Ethnology Annual Report 1896-97* (Washington: G.P.O., 1899), pp. 20-21; *Hopi Journal of Alexander M. Stephen*, ed. Elsie Clews Parson, 2 vols. (New York: Columbia University Press, 1936), 1:xlviii; Matthews, *Ethnography and Philology of the Hidatsa Indians*, pp. 30-31; *A Journal of American Ethnology and Archaeology*, ed. J. Walter Fewkes, 5 vols. (Boston: Houghton, Mifflin and Co., 1891-1908), 1:1; Matilda Coxe Stevenson, *The Zuñi Indians: Their Mythology, Esoteric Fraternities, and Ceremonies* (1905; rpt. New York: Johnson Reprint Corp., 1970), p. 608, also p. 18; Capt. John G. Bourke, *The Snake-Dance of the Moquis of Arizona* . . . (New York: Charles Scribner's Sons, 1884), pp. 14ff.; Sylvester Baxter, "The Father of the Pueblos," *Harper's New Monthly Magazine*, 65 (June 1882), 72-73; James Mooney, *The Ghost-Dance Religion and the Sioux Outbreak of 1890* (1896), ed. Anthony F. C. Wallace (New York: Dover Publications, 1972), pp. 1-2.

[120] It was with this enterprise in view that the *Journal of American Folk-Lore* announced in its inaugural issue a claim many had come to learn by heart: the need for concerted eleventh-hour anthropological efforts ("Preface," *Journal of American Folk-Lore*, ed. W. W. Newell et al., 1 [1888], 5-6). See also Justin Winson, ed., *Narrative and Critical History of America*, 8 vols. (New York: Houghton, Mifflin and Co., 1889), 1:438; Leslie W. Dunlap, *American Historical Societies, 1790-1860* (Madison, Wis.: privately printed, 1944), p. 19.

Public respect for deliberate scientific examinations grew, as it had for the work of similarly motivated painters, photographers, and writers. Popular magazines catered to this new enthusiasm, and universities followed the trend by establishing departments of anthropology in the late 1880s and 1890s. Museums flourished, especially after inaugurating changes modeled on Franz Boas's daring curatorial success at Chicago's Columbian Exposition in 1893. By the beginning of the twentieth century, a tremendous salvage operation was underway. Individuals would sacrifice careers and families, in some cases risk their lives, in order to preserve information. "All other thought from our horizon banished, / Let any sacrifice our labor crown."[121] And yet, much of the enormous amount of information preserved by these professionals has in turn "vanished" in unread manuscripts and academic monographs. Having once saved them, researchers too often failed either to study or to enjoy native traditions and lore.

By 1900, the wilderness seemed to have vanished. The Wild West of the cowboy and rancher, the army scout, miner, and trapper, the frontier and Indian communities existed only as shades of their former selves, when extant at all. What many had long prophesied had come to pass. Scientists still hastened west, but they found themselves forced to deal with information collected earlier. Artists became either elegiac or mythic in their treatments of western history. Yet the passing of the wilderness helped to effect fundamental changes in attitudes and assumptions. With surprising frequency, especially toward the end of the century, Americans found their national complacency challenged. The heavy costs that a technologically progressive civilization entailed, especially vivid in the western landscape, tested cultural allegiances.

Among those who traveled west, the initial urge to document what was passing often developed into a strong inclination to question what would replace it. At its most sentimental, the question turned on the issue of progress. Did factories, cities, and farms improve upon plains and forests or impoverish them? And what of those who lived or worked in them? Few at mid-century gave more than cursory attention to Thoreau's challenging contrast of the Indian shelter and the village house. Far more listened in patriotic agreement to Senator Thomas Hart Benton in his enthusiasm for unrestrained national expansion. Yet, later in the century, cooler and more sensible heads began to view skeptically the claim that America's manifest destiny

---

[121] John Peabody Harrington, quoted in Carobeth Laird, *Encounter with an Angry God: Recollections of My Life with John Peabody Harrington* (New York: Ballantine, 1975), p. v.

was desirable, however fated. Those who hastened to preserve tribal experiences were especially beset with doubts about the arbitrary premises of their own western European heritage. Was white civilization measurably more satisfying, more intelligent, more humane, than Indian cultures? Did it offer a greater, more significant sense of participation in social and religious endeavors? The Reverend Samuel Farmar Jarvis would have been jolted to the tips of his Episcopal whiskers at the very notion. How could he guess that those who answered his call in 1819 "to copy the evanescent features of [the Indian] character" would in time believe these questions possible. Chapter Eight will demonstrate that many did come to share this belief—or, at least, this suspension of disbelief. Perhaps the best introduction to their uncertainties is the work of an artist still in the cradle when Jarvis spoke that winter day. By the time he was thirty, though, he would have explored the issues suggested above as well as anyone and, in the process, helped to define the terms by which cultural relativism might be considered.

CHAPTER SEVEN

MELVILLE'S CANNIBALS
AND CHRISTIANS

We are all of us—Anglo-Saxons, Dyaks,
and Indians—sprung from one head, and
made in one image. And if we regret this
brotherhood now, we shall be forced to
join hands hereafter. A misfortune is not
a fault; and good luck is not meritorious.
The savage is born a savage; and the
civilized being inherits his civilization,
nothing more.
> —*Melville* review of Parkman,
> *The California and Oregon Trail*
> (March 1849)

"It's a mutual, joint-stock world, in all
meridians. We cannibals must help these
Christians."
> —*Moby-Dick* (1851)

HERMAN MELVILLE's *Moby-Dick* (1851) either stimulates or stymies its reader with its plethoric display of knowledge about whales. From its opening "Etymology" and "Extracts" of whaling quotations, through its long disquisitions on cetology and its taxonomy of species and hunting tools, to its catalogue of whaling paintings, the book aspires to exhaust the possibilities of its material. Critics have rightly interpreted this exhaustiveness in thematic terms: in spite of all one can learn about whaling, the whale itself forever evades the harpoon of definition.[1]

The impressive array of facts marshaled in this metaphysical quest also presents another aspect: a genre picture of an imperiled way of life. Melville could not have predicted Daniel Drake's success in drilling for petroleum in August 1859 at Titusville, Pennsylvania, or guessed at its consequences for the whaling industry. Yet by the time he had completed *Moby-Dick* the sperm whale industry was already sinking into its long decline, while extinction itself threatened right and gray whales. Confident Ishmael answers the question titling one chapter, "—Will He Perish?" by invoking a contrast with the extermination of buffalo in Illinois: "the far different nature of the whale-hunt peremptorily forbids so inglorious an end to the Leviathan" (383). Perhaps thematic necessity dictated so sanguine a conclusion. Without full consciousness of the need for such a record, Melville nonetheless labored to document the business of whaling as thoroughly as possible. Few others possessed such knowledge. Though Melville was hardly the harpooner of two and a half years' experience he sometimes whimsically claimed to be, still, as for Ishmael, a whaleship was his Yale College and his Harvard. It provided him with experiences other authors might envy and made him one of the few capable of documenting the whaling industry in its heyday of the 1840s. His efforts compare strikingly with, say, those of George Caleb Bingham on the Missouri frontier.

Four of the five novels Melville wrote prior to *Moby-Dick* document contemporary cultures. *Typee* (1846) and *Omoo* (1847) proclaim themselves accurate records of Polynesian life at the very

1 Or, as Ishmael remarks, in trying merely to comprehend the whale's tail: "The more I consider this mighty tail, the more do I deplore my inability to express it. . . . Dissect him how I may, then, I but go skin deep; I know him not, and never will. But if I know not even the tail of this whale, how understand his head? much more, how comprehend his face, when face he has none?" Melville, *Moby-Dick; or, The Whale*, ed. Harrison Hayford and Hershel Parker (New York: W. W. Norton, 1967), pp. 317-18. All subsequent references are to this edition.

moment that Christian missionaries and white sailors threatened it. Melville hurriedly finished *Redburn* (1849) for needed advance, roughly sketching out his initial experiences at sea of a decade earlier and incidentally documenting merchant-marine life in the North Atlantic. *White-Jacket* (1850), also more or less autobiographical, claims scholarly accuracy in illustrating shipboard life on an American man-of-war. Midway through his narrative Melville reflects that he feels himself "actuated by the same motive which has prompted many worthy old chroniclers, to set down the merest trifles concerning things that are destined to pass away entirely from the earth, and which, if not preserved in the nick of time, must infallibly perish from the memories of man. Who knows that this humble narrative may not hereafter prove the history of any obsolete barbarism? Who knows that, when men-of-war shall be no more, *White Jacket* may not be quoted to show to the people in the Millennium what a man-of-war was?"[2] This sentiment informs much of the energy of *Moby-Dick* as well.

Melville possessed, as critics like to remind us, the most thoroughly symbolic as well as the most "appropriative" imagination ever nurtured by American soil and salt water. His densely textured world is firmly rooted in mid-century social life, boldly anchored in contemporary factual currents.[3] Yet as keen an observer as he was, he serves representatively here for other reasons. Factualism was, after all, not unique; others, especially James Fenimore Cooper, had already devoted themselves to recording ways of life evanescently American. Melville's experiences propelled him farther, in part because, unlike Cooper, he had encountered at firsthand supposedly primitive life. He anticipated ways of thinking about vanishing tribes, as well as questions of progress and culture, that others adopted only much later. George Catlin's preservationist crusade made him a representative figure for issues examined earlier; his career combined so many allied commitments. A far greater artist, Melville was at the same time far less programmatically narrow in his manipulation of a fictional wilderness. In this regard, he provides a profound entrance into issues others would explore only later.

At twenty, lacking other employment, Herman Melville (1819-1891) shipped as a cabin boy from the economically depressed Amer-

2 Melville, *White-Jacket, or The World in a Man-of-War*, ed. Harrison Hayford, Hershel Parker, and G. Thomas Tanselle (Evanston: Northwestern University Press and The Newberry Library, 1970), p. 282. All subsequent references are to this edition.

3 See Warner Berthoff, *The Example of Melville* (1962; rpt. New York: W. W. Norton, 1972), pp. 21-22.

ica of the late 1830s. By the time he was discharged at Boston five years later, he had served in the merchant marine, the American navy, and aboard Pacific whalers; he had seen the Atlantic and the North and South Pacific; he had jumped ship, been held captive by a tribe of Polynesian cannibals, and spent time as a vagabond in both Tahiti and Hawaii. These five most active years of his life provided him with an admiral's knot of experiences to unravel. Like Henry Rowe Schoolcraft after his first frontier expedition, converted from geology to ethnology; like George Catlin and Lewis Henry Morgan, who abandoned portrait painting and a legal career, respectively, for anthropology—Melville returned from the South Seas with a fund of adventures that would dictate the course of his life. He had little inclination to pursue the staid professions his family might have hoped for him. Instead, he began a narrative about Polynesian natives, one that branded him with the vexing reputation of a "man who lived among the cannibals."[4]

Melville had certainly not hurried to the "West" intending to document its passing, however much his early fiction may suggest such a purpose.[5] Yet he had quickly realized the importance of his experiences as an early visitor to a still unaltered native environment. By combining observations made during four years in the Pacific with exhaustive reading of contemporary accounts, he created an invaluable ethnographic record. Moreover, he explored an intellectual pattern that many others would trace more firmly later in the century among American Indians. Polynesian and Indian cultures were threatened with extinction by white encroachment, and both sets evoked similar responses from concerned white Americans.

Of course, Melville later achieved far more in his career than relates to our purposes. His maturing as an artist in the ten years from the publication of *Typee* and *Omoo* through *Moby-Dick* to the completion of *The Confidence-Man* in 1856 entailed a progressive disengagement from purely cultural questions and an increasing devotion to issues metaphysical and moral. Naturally, with his memories of them receding, the distinctive elements of his South Seas adventures seem less and less fresh where they appear in later work. But this de-

[4] Melville to Nathaniel Hawthorne, June 1?, 1851, in *The Letters of Herman Melville*, ed. Merrill R. Davis and William H. Gilman (New Haven: Yale University Press, 1960), p. 130.

[5] See Melville, *Typee: A Peep at Polynesian Life*, ed. Harrison Hayford, Hershel Parker, and G. Thomas Tanselle (Evanston: Northwestern University Press, 1968), p. xiii; *Omoo: A Narrative in the South Seas*, ed. Harrison Hayford, Hershel Parker, and G. Thomas Tanselle (Evanston: Northwestern University Press, 1968), pp. xiv, 184. All subsequent references are to these editions.

velopment also resulted from Melville's more deliberately symbolic characterizations. Although *Typee*, "Benito Cereno" (1855), and *The Confidence-Man*, for example, share relevant themes, the last two handle the subject of racial variations in highly charged, highly allusive modes. Much of the present chapter concentrates on *Typee* and *Omoo* in order to define more straightforwardly the effect that native peoples had on Melville. Later works will warrant attention precisely to the extent that they form incisive, if highly symbolic, examinations of truths that Melville discovered in first reflecting upon his stay among the Marquesans and Tahitians.

One of Melville's most persistent fictional themes concerns man's imposing of belief upon experience, a theme that first appears in *Typee*, predictably in cultural garb. It is best typified in an early passage describing the island reception awaiting the narrator and his mates:

> How often is the term "savages" incorrectly applied! None really deserving of it were ever yet discovered by voyagers or by travellers. They have discovered heathens and barbarians, whom by horrible cruelties they have exasperated into savages. It may be asserted without fear of contradiction, that in all the cases of outrages committed by Polynesians, Europeans have at some time or other been the aggressors, and that the cruel and blood-thirsty disposition of some of the islanders is mainly to be ascribed to the influence of such examples. (27)

Melville tracks this theme through the rest of *Typee* and *Omoo* and tightens it to its fullest resonances in *Moby-Dick*. Following his frightening encounter with the kindly cannibal Queequeg, Ishmael might agree with Tommo: "Thus it is that they whom we denominate 'savages' are made to deserve the title" (26).[6]

The notion that primitive peoples often become what they were labeled finds its best formulation in *The Confidence-Man*, in those chapters devoted to "The Metaphysics of Indian-Hating." But by now, Melville treats the Indian so symbolically as to render the fiction an

----

[6] One of the valuable sources Melville researched prior to composing this passage claimed a similar provenance for native antagonism toward whites. According to Charles S. Stewart, "It has principally been in resentment for some real or supposed outrage on the part of civilized man" (Stewart, *A Visit to the South Seas in the U.S. Ship Vincennes, During the Years 1829 and 1830*, 2 vols. [1831; rpt. New York: Praeger Publishers, 1970], 1:317). Earlier, Stewart had angrily charged that "it is in such aggression and barbarity on the part of civilized and nominally Christian men, that more than half the reputed savageness of the heathen world has its origin" (ibid., p. 298).

allegorical satire on the evil that Christians do in the name of good.[7] Indian-hating, epitomized by John Moredock, reduces the white to the very evils he has vowed to eradicate. The creed that Christ preached, taken too narrowly to heart, degenerates to its most wretched inversion in the hands of its most vigorous proponents.

One must approach these chapters with caution, however, for it is easy to gloss over their inner complexities, ignoring the clues that suggest the story be read as one more instance in the book's catalogue of self-deception and misplaced confidence. Though Melville's Indians loom as mere symbolic grotesques, the fearful embodiment of irrational, ineluctable evil, the Moredock story may also be read in the light of Tommo's statement that "they whom we denominate 'savages' are made to deserve the title." The Indian fills for the Indian-hater a projected role as Devil, in other words, just as Moby Dick does for Captain Ahab; both apparently become what their adversaries expect of them.

Chapter Twenty-six on "The Metaphysics of Indian-Hating" provides a description of "backwoods education," an education obsessively devoted to "histories of Indian lying, Indian theft, Indian double-dealing, Indian fraud and perfidy, Indian want of conscience, Indian blood-thirstincss, Indian diabolism" (126). The narrator reveals the perspective from which to interpret the chapter in his caveat: "Still, all this is less advanced as truths of the Indians than as examples of the backwoodsman's impression of them" (127). Obsession blinds the backwoodsman to any interpretation but his own. Some Indians may stoop to treachery, but the Indian-hater cannot distinguish the many who do not. Pointedly, the narrator implies that native treachery represents a predictable response to evils perpetrated by whites. Mocmohoc, for instance, the alleged epitome of savage vengeance, is chief of "a dwindled tribe" (128). We are left to infer that the tribe has dwindled for the usual melancholy reasons connected with white settlement of adjacent lands. The question that more broadly demands our consideration, though, is put by the narrator: "But are all Indians like Mocmohoc?" (129). According to the backwoodsman, whether or not all act alike, they should be treated alike.

The original Moredock party was massacred by "a band of twenty renegades from various tribes, outlaws even among Indians" (133). The action sets off John Moredock on an obsessed career, namely, the destruction of this small band, followed by vengeance on the entire

---

[7] See Hershel Parker, "The Metaphysics of Indian-Hating," *Nineteenth-Century Fiction*, 18 (September 1963), reprinted in Herman Melville, *The Confidence-Man: His Masquerade*, ed. Hershel Parker (New York: W. W. Norton, 1971), p. 330.

race. He vows to exterminate the very tribes that had originally banished the twenty renegades. Ignoring his own inconsistencies, the
Indian-hater acts constantly so as to provoke a predictable native
response. Stressing Moredock's self-dehumanization, the satire exposes him as an armed paranoiac, compelling from others precisely
the actions he most fears. More to the point, he resembles the South
Seas sailors whose unprovoked aggressions Melville had vividly
described.

Of course, the notion that primitives respond as they are treated
illuminates little about relative cultural development. Yet the issue
of cultural imposition necessarily involved for Melville a contrast in
values between the supposedly civilized and the primitive. His narrator in *Typee* asks, in respect of a resplendently attired admiral and
a naked savage, "may not the savage be the happier man of the two?"
(29). If he lacks the comforts bestowed by material progress, the
Typee native is also free of its concomitant problems. As facile as this
Rousseauistic comparison may seem, Melville pressed through its conventional sentiment to a troubling series of judgments. Informed
sympathy for Polynesian societies allowed him to see what others
would only later begin to approach, that every culture represents just
one of many expressions of a common humanity. Western European
institutions could maintain no claim to inherent superiority.

Melville's development of these issues hardly followed a logical
progression and must be assessed in the terms used in earlier chapters
to define whole eras: moving from apprehensive concern for a preserved record, to tolerant understanding of what was recorded, to
incipient cultural relativism. In beginning with Melville's rationale
for his first two novels, one finds that it duplicates in part the motivation of artists discussed earlier. Though he never confessed an intention to record Marquesan culture before it changed irrevocably, he
called strongly and persistently for an accurate record of it while deploring its imminent loss. That desire for accuracy led Melville to
confirm firsthand experience with research.[8] He had spent a mere four
weeks among the Typees, not the four months claimed by Tommo—

[8] For corroboration of Melville's accounts, see H. Bruce Franklin, *The Wake of the
Gods: Melville's Mythology* (Stanford: Stanford University Press, 1963), pp. 106-7;
Charles Roberts Anderson, *Melville in the South Seas* (1939; rpt. New York: Dover
Publications, 1966), pp. 190, 270; James Baird, *Ishmael: A Study of the Symbolic
Mode in Primitivism* (New York: Harper and Brothers, 1956), pp. 9, 109; *Typee*, pp.
291-93; *Omoo*, pp. 322-25. When Melville occasionally strays from faithful renderings
to embellish his account—as, for instance, in his "Characteristic Anecdote of the
Queen of Nukuheva" or his description of boating excursions with the beautiful
Fayaway—he does so to epitomize conditions, not to distort them.

hardly time to learn so difficult a language or to understand so complex a tribe. To refresh his memory, then, and to supplement his partial knowledge, he read "almost every available account of the Marquesas."[9] Indeed, Melville borrowed freely from the works of Charles S. Stewart, Captain David Porter, William Ellis, and Georg H. von Langsdorff, though he maintained a shrewd distrust of any single account, even his own. He knew too well how Western observers grossly misinterpreted "primitive" behavior out of familiar preconceptions, unconfirmed assumptions, or religious or cultural narrowness. *Typee*, in fact, deftly satirizes the complacent ethnologist and the agreeably imaginative native respondent, whose "powers of invention increase with the credulity of his auditors. He knows just the sort of information wanted, and furnishes it to any extent" (170).

Melville conscientiously refused to extrapolate from cultural data, as he states explicitly in *Typee* and *Omoo* and acknowledges tacitly in the premises informing episodes in his later fiction.[10] The humor of Ishmael's "unwarrantable prejudices" on first seeing the cannibal Queequeg; the near-tragedy of Captain Amasa Delano's blithe presumptions about Babo and the black slaves in "Benito Cereno"; and the dark satire of Moredock's obsessive hatred of Indians in *The Confidence-Man*—each of these perspectives on cultural interpretation stresses its dangers, suggesting that even at best it is always in part projection. Each perspective derives by contrast from Melville's own tolerant, even open-ended, reading of cultural behavior.

This concern for pure description hinged upon Melville's sense that the Typee culture would soon pass beyond the possibility of accurate recording. The cause of its degeneration appeared to him in part internal, more largely external. Native religion had seemed to be declining even prior to the advent of whites, as Tommo notes: "In truth, I regard the Typees as a back-slidden generation. They are sunk in religious sloth, and require a spiritual revival. A long prosperity of bread-fruit and cocoa nuts has rendered them remiss in the performance of their higher obligations" (179). True, Melville is enjoying his sly ironies at the expense of a god-haunted and insistently pious American society.[11] Nevertheless, he did intuit a cultural

---

[9] Franklin, *Wake of the Gods*, p. 9. Melville commented on the difficulty of the Typee language in *Typee*, pp. 24-25. See also Anderson, *Melville in the South Seas*, p. 146.

[10] *Typee*, p. xiii; *Omoo*, p. xiv. Charles Anderson, in *Melville in the South Seas*, pp. 108, 137, 167-68, discusses the author's intelligent caution in such matters.

[11] See *Typee*, p. 174. See also Baird, *Ishmael*, pp. 103-4; Anderson, *Melville in the South Seas*, p. 175; Stewart, *Visit to the South Seas*, 1:292.

decline confirmed by later, more scientific studies. Cultural dissolution from within allowed whites more quickly to undermine social values, but even this process was less appalling than the threat to the very existence of the native population. In both *Typee* and *Omoo* Melville deplored the sharp drop in island numbers, attributing it to irreversible causes that made extinction no longer inconceivable.[12] *Omoo*, in fact, deliberately exaggerates the decline in population in order to dramatize Melville's apprehensions. This decline resulted entirely from the enforced adoption of Western modes, which proved meaningless to a native population. Only their own culture could sustain the Marquesans: "Nay, as a race, they can not otherwise long exist" (190). Even as late as an 1858-1859 lecture on "The South Seas," Melville reiterates this concern: "So the result of civilization, at the Sandwich Islands and elsewhere, is found productive to the civilizers, destructive to the civilizees. It is said to be compensation—a very philosophical word; but it appears to be very much on the principle of the old game, 'You lose, I win': good philosophy for the winner."[13] A dozen years earlier, he had written more bluntly: "Their prospects are hopeless."[14]

As imminent as the destruction of Polynesian cultures and peoples seemed, especially in Tahiti and Hawaii, much of the vigorous life on remoter islands continued in the 1840s. Melville cherished his opportunity as perhaps the last white, certainly the last to write an account, with direct knowledge of Marquesan culture prior to the encroachment of Western civilization.[15] The islands were still "tenanted by beings as strange and barbarous as ever."[16] This remark appears in *Omoo* as well, and even the later lecture refers to island enclaves "yet uncontaminated by the contact of civilization."[17] Melville seized upon just such threatened occasions, as early reviewers knew, congratulating him for having plucked from the Pacific Ocean accurate records of an uncorrupted, but sinking, native culture.[18]

[12] *Typee*, pp. 154-56, 188-89, 191-93, 195; *Omoo*, p. 125. See also, Louise K. Barnett, *The Ignoble Savage: American Literary Racism, 1790-1890*, Contributions in American Studies, no. 18 (Westport, Conn.: Greenwood Press, 1975), p. 173.

[13] Merton M. Sealts Jr., *Melville as Lecturer* (Cambridge, Mass.: Harvard University Press, 1957), p. 179. Although Melville never published this or other public lectures, Sealts has reconstructed as much as can be known of them from contemporary newspaper accounts.

[14] *Omoo*, p. 192.

[15] Compare William Ellis's similar response a quarter century before Melville, in *Polynesian Researches: Polynesia*, 2d ed. (1831; rpt. Rutland, Vt.: Charles E. Tuttle, Co., 1969), p. xiv.

[16] *Typee*, p. 5, also p. 11. See also Stewart, *Visit to the South Seas*, 1:212.

[17] *Omoo*, p. 265; Sealts, *Melville as Lecturer*, p. 180. See also *Typee*, pp. 5, 11.

[18] Hugh W. Hetherington, *Melville's Reviewers: British and American, 1846-1891* (Chapel Hill: University of North Carolina Press, 1961), pp. 34ff.

Yet the abandonment of indigenous ways troubled Melville far less because it deprived history of an account than because natives were losing a vital, autonomous culture. In diametrical opposition to many contemporaries who "sighed for the beginning of missionary instruction among them,"[19] the novelist felt, in James Baird's words, "that no affront to primitive man exceeds the missionary's intent to strip him of his native symbolism and leave him naked in the world, save for the ill-fitting habiliments of a misunderstood Christianity."[20] Melville admired the healthy integrity of Marquesan institutions, which had already resulted in an apparently ideal society in which government remained at a minimum and economic and social equality extended to all.[21] Of course, his enthusiasm echoed what had been considered "enlightened" sentiment since the eighteenth century. Yet his was an informed enthusiasm; personal experience allowed him to substantiate a realistic account of coherent native culture.

In *Typee* Melville presents an entire society living together peacefully and productively. "These islanders were heathens! savages! ay, cannibals! and how came they, without the aid of established law, to exhibit, in so eminent a degree, that social order which is the greatest blessing and highest pride of the social state?" (200). Taboo, the immediate answer, hardly satisfies the broader implications of the question. That Typee culture seemed incomprehensible to Western whites was no reason to assume that it functioned less adequately for its members than did western European culture.

Another, related point deserves mention here. Melville never forgot the extent to which he remained an outsider in Polynesia. It was notably astute of him to recognize the implications of that fact so early, and the insight explains one major motif in *Typee*, that of the alien confused by a culture whose rules and values are inaccessible to him. Repeatedly, Tommo observes native behavior without being able to comprehend its meaning. Though he vows to record "their practical every-day operation" (173), religion and its rites prove "a complete mystery" to him. Typee culture retains a vitality, despite signs of decay, that is best evident in its impenetrability. "I was utterly at a loss how to account for their singular conduct," Tommo confesses in one form or another throughout the narrative.[22] In part, his hesitation merely confirms Melville's initial refusal to venture unverifiable in-

19 Stewart, *Visit to the South Seas*, 1:295.

20 Baird, *Ishmael*, p. 99. For a larger view of Melville's attitude toward culture and society, see Harry B. Henderson III, *Versions of the Past: The Historical Imagination in American Fiction* (New York: Oxford University Press, 1974), p. 129.

21 Anderson, *Melville in the South Seas*, pp. 132, 140, 169-70.

22 *Typee*, pp. 120, 166, 169, 173, 177, 186-87, 189, 200, 221, 224, 232, 236.

ferences. In larger part, Tommo's bewilderment attests to the extraordinary complexity of Polynesian cultures. Even so astute an observer as he cannot penetrate their workings, as his lengthy, but self-consciously inadequate, appraisals of taboo demonstrate.[23]

That quality of mystery thwarting the alien observer of cultural behavior converts "Benito Cereno" from a mere grotesquerie to a subtle examination of guilt, evil, and epistemology. Melville, as he freely concedes, took the basic plot from the first-person narrative of Amasa Delano, an American sea captain who spent a bewildered and anxious day on board a Spanish slave ship. As Melville transforms the story, its vaguely threatening power emerges through Delano's misunderstanding of the enigmatic poses taken by the blacks: picking oakum, polishing rusty hatchets, scraping a wooden platter, dipping rope strands into pitch. More vividly developed is Delano's confrontation with enigmas that hint at a life wholly unknown to him. The nursing black mothers, for example, or the royally unyielding bearing of the slave king Atufal suggest a mysterious social ethic at work.

This story exaggerates the tendency evident in Melville's later prose toward the syntactically ambiguous and ambivalent. Locutions like "seems," "as if," and "he thought . . . but" further create the ambience achieved at times in *Typee*. Babo, Atufal, and the other blacks—like Kory-Kory, Mehevi, and other Polynesians in *Typee*—act in ways incomprehensible to the white observer. But whereas Tommo consciously refuses to interpret the Typees' taboo behavior, Delano indulges in facile, myopic assumptions. Melville transformed the actual Delano into a naive racist, one who poses a telling contrast to the more restrained, perceptive example provided by Tommo.[24] That Tommo tolerantly allows the alien phenomena of native culture to remain mysterious in their irreducible complexity finally redeems his efforts; that Delano interprets them reductively according to his own narrow lights almost proves his undoing.

From the beginning, Melville cast a skeptical eye on the progressive values his white contemporaries unquestioningly assumed. Tolerant admiration of Polynesian cultures prompted him to condemn the supposedly civilizing influence of such values, whether introduced by whalers, merchantmen, or French missionary expeditions. *Omoo* illustrates the devastation of Tahitian and Hawaiian cultures over half a century by religious and commercial solicitation, illustrations that pulse even more damningly in juxtaposition with the record of

---

[23] *Typee*, pp. 91, 221-23. See also Anderson, *Melville in the South Seas*, pp. 166-68.
[24] Henderson, *Versions of the Past*, p. 150.

unspoiled Marquesan life provided only a year before in *Typee*.[25] The "semi-civilization" of Tahiti, as Melville reveals it in the later book, exemplifies the worst of both worlds. At its least harmful, this transitional state elicits merely ridiculous behavior. A half-understood code pressures native churchgoers, for example, into wearing outlandish costumes, so that at one service there appear "half-a-dozen strapping fellows, in white shirts and no pantaloons" (171). Those who strutted awkwardly in European suits, hats, and petticoats had abandoned native costumes "graceful in the extreme, modest to all but the prudish, and peculiarly adapted to the climate" (182).

More insidiously, Christian civilization renders the natives defenseless against the corruption, diseases, and brutal exploitation introduced by the whites. They had coerced natives into abandoning old customs without offering a viable cultural system in return. The subsequent "amazing decrease" (191) in population seems less cruel, ironically, than the "physical degeneracy" (128) of the survivors. Stable native societies based on polyandrous family units gave way to an anarchy of self-destructive licentiousness. "In view of these things, who can remain blind to the fact, that, so far as mere temporal felicity is concerned, the Tahitians are far worse off now, than formerly" (192).

Responsibility for much of this destruction, of course, lies with the least respectable elements of white civilization. In the very beginning of *Typee*, Tommo describes the greeting given his ship by native girls upon its arrival at Nukuheva. The natives' kindness, openness, and generous welcome are met by the crew's licentiousness and "most shameful inebriety." He continues bitterly, "Alas for the poor savages when exposed to the influence of these polluting examples! Unsophisticated and confiding, they are easily led into every vice, and humanity weeps over the ruin thus remorselessly inflicted upon them by their European civilizers. Thrice happy are they who, inhabiting some yet undiscovered island in the midst of the ocean, have never been brought into contaminating contact with the white man" (15). This description would have surprised few readers, as it differs little from the accounts of Captain Cook or, more contemporaneously, J. Ross Browne, Captain David Porter, and Charles S. Stewart.[26] But Melville alone pursued the theme. Moving well beyond an exposition of out-

25 Melville thought the Marquesans destined to the exploitative pattern of their island counterparts. See *Typee*, pp. 6, 188-89, 195. See also, for confirmation, Anderson, *Melville in the South Seas*, p. 175; Baird, *Ishmael*, p. 103; *Omoo*, pp. 184-89.

26 Anderson, *Melville in the South Seas*, pp. 37-38, 96; Stewart, *Visit to the South Seas*, 1:298.

rages committed by rough sailors and unscrupulous traders, he came to see such incidents as symptomatic of, not marginal exceptions to, western European civilization.[27]

The true representatives of a tolerant Christian civilization in Polynesia should have been the missionaries, both French and English. Yet neither nationality tolerates the other, each pursuing its own narrow notions of native policy. These "saviors of the heathen" dismiss Polynesian customs and beliefs out-of-hand, complacently assuming the benefits to be gained from their cultural imperialism. Deeply racist, they segregate schooling for their children and introduce rickshaw taxi service, with natives "civilized into draught horses, and evangelized into beasts of burden" (196). A line of these vehicles stands at the same mission churches where they preach the democratizing love of Christ.[28] Hypocrisy aside, this scene best symbolizes native enslavement to a class-structured, work-driven culture. More than a decade after writing Omoo, Melville still felt his old animus, revealed in the conclusion to his lecture on "The South Seas." "I hope that these Edens of the South Seas . . . will long remain unspoiled in their simplicity, beauty, and purity. And as for annexation, I beg to offer up an earnest prayer—and I entreat all present and all Christians to join me in it—that the banns of that union should be forbidden until we have found for ourselves a civilization morally, mentally, and physically higher than one which has culminated in almshouses, prisons, and hospitals."[29]

Exercised as he continued to be by this issue, Melville must have appreciated what an easy target it offered for criticism. All human societies bear flaws, surely; neither vice nor corruption is a sufficient argument against fundamental institutions. Yet, for Melville, civilized vices, however destructive, proved less insidiously damaging than the enforced virtues. Appropriate as Western ways may have been for whites, they only incapacitated Polynesians. As the narrator of Omoo states after hearing a missionary's sermon, "In fact, there is, perhaps, no race upon earth, less disposed, by nature, to the monitions of Christianity, than the people of the South Sea" (174). Even when "the missionaries were prompted by a sincere desire for good . . . the effect has been lamentable." Forced to think abstractly, to work diligently, to forgo games and celebrations in favor of more "serious" employment, to worship with studied restraint rather than with emotional abandon, the natives found the very bases of an individualistic,

27 See especially Typee, pp. 188-89, and Omoo, p. 127.

28 Franklin, Wake of the Gods, p. 15.

29 Sealts, Melville as Lecturer, p. 180.

success-oriented, materialistic Western culture dissatisfying. These cultural values need not prove ultimately inadequate; but they are not simply transportable truths, to be rudely imposed on any or all societies.

By the same token, Tommo feels no more comfortable with the equally rigorous, arbitrary, and mystifying beliefs of the natives. Despite certain manifest advantages to their way of life, the Typees display as blind an intolerance and as unyielding a disposition as the missionaries. They listen to their wooden idol, Moa Artua, and interpret his godly message as "generally of a complimentary nature" (176). Standing outside such belief, Tommo can only wonder at the degree of communal projection laid bare here, the self-deception characterizing not only primitive religion but also, by extension, all such rituals. He treats this religious myopia rather lightheartedly at first; the natives, at least, unlike the missionaries, do not seem to proselytize. Yet when every one of the Typees vigorously supports Karky in his demand to tattoo Tommo, the captive sailor perceives that the basis of their desire is to make a conversion as complete as that which the missionaries plan in their turn. None of the Typees comprehends Tommo's refusal, his evident rejection of their values. Like the white sailors and missionaries against whom they are thematically posed, the natives cannot move beyond a cultural absolutism.

To be sure, two natives—the beautiful Fayaway and the gentle old man Marheyo—seem able to transcend their culture's values, at least a little. "Of all the natives," Tommo remarks of his island consort, "she alone seemed to appreciate the effect which the peculiarity of the circumstances in which we were placed had produced upon the minds of [Toby] and myself. In addressing me, . . . there was a tenderness in her manner which it was impossible to misunderstand or resist" (108). Similarly, Marheyo, in the midst of Tommo's dramatic escape from his kindly captors, comes to his side. "He placed his arm upon my shoulder, and emphatically pronounced the only two English words I had taught him—'Home' and 'Mother.' I at once understood what he meant" (248). Marheyo then commands his son to carry Tommo to the beach and to freedom. These two instances, however, seem so thoroughly colored by romantic sentimentality that they only reinforce the original contention respecting any culture's narrow angle of vision.

Nevertheless, the possibility that cultural limits can give way to a shared humanity, that absolutism and intolerance of whatever stripe might moderate, persistently attracted Melville. Tommo's desperate escape at the end of the novel represents resistance to all cultural absolutes. He must if need be put a boathook into the throat of his erstwhile friend, the one-eyed chief Mow-Mow. In doing so, of course, he defends his threatened life and his Western identity. But he also puts a boathook into all one-eyed, one-sided interpretations of experience, all cultural absolutes. He gains freedom to return to a sea world where at least the possibility of contingent relationships and cultural relativity still exists.

Clearly, Melville rejected the notion that a particular culture or race can hold a warrant on truth. "What plays the mischief with the truth," he wrote in a famous letter to Hawthorne as he was finishing *Moby-Dick* in 1851, "is that men will insist upon the universal application of a temporary feeling or opinion."[30] One could easily extend this thought, without misconstruing Melville's meaning, to include "or the universal application of particular cultural patterns or goals." Melville denied that certain races were inherently depraved or, conversely, that others were superior. Captain Delano's blindness to circumstances aboard the *San Dominique*, for instance, largely results from his bland racism, his willingness truly to believe that "Most negroes are natural valets and hairdressers . . . [with] a certain easy cheerfulness, harmonious in every glance and gesture" (306, 314). In *Typee* Melville most clearly states the need for an open attitude toward cross-cultural variations:

> Civilization does not engross all the virtues of humanity: she has not even her full share of them. They flourish in greater abundance and attain greater strength among many barbarous people. The hospitality of the wild Arab, the courage of the North American Indian, and the faithful friendships of some of the Polynesian nations, far surpass any thing of a similar kind among the polished communities of Europe. If truth and justice, and the better principles of our nature, cannot exist unless enforced by the statute-book, how are we to account for the social condition of the Typees? (202-3)

His belief that genuinely complex systems structured non-Western cultures distinguishes Melville from most of his contemporaries. He seems to have understood that cultures form indigenous patterns both expressive of and responsive to communal needs. This approximation of cultural relativism, derived almost by definition from Melville's informed tolerance, is revealed nicely in the description of Wooloo

---

[30] *Letters of Herman Melville*, ed. Davis and Gilman, p. 131. See also Louise Barnett's discussion of this theme in *Ignoble Savage*, pp. 173-80.

the Polynesian in *White-Jacket*. "In our man-of-war, this semi-savage, wandering about the gun-deck in his barbaric robe, seemed a being from some other sphere. His tastes were our abominations: ours his. Our creed he rejected: his we. We thought him a loon: he fancied us fools. Had the case been reversed; had we been Polynesians and he an American, our mutual opinion of each other would still have remained the same. A fact proving that neither was wrong, but both right" (118). Among Melville's contemporaries, Hawthorne most closely characterized the man he had yet to meet in his review of *Typee*. He particularly praised the author's "freedom of view—it would be too harsh to call it levity of principle—which renders him tolerant of codes of morals that may be little in accordance with our own."[31]

More than just "freedom of view," which can be cultivated in Salem as readily as in the South Seas, Melville stressed the need for intimate exposure to native life. Only then can true cultural tolerance be tested. The most striking development of this idea occurs in *Typee* when Tommo confronts cannibalism. From the beginning, Tommo invokes the natives' reputed love of human flesh as a source of awful suspense. This theme alters during his stay, however, from a melodramatic one to one more profound. Despite his fears, Tommo finds the Typees enchanting, and when, after a week among them, his companion remarks on their anthropophagic tastes, he replies, "Granted, . . . but a more humane, gentlemanly, and amiable set of epicures do not probably exist in the Pacific" (97). He later compares their "epicurism" favorably with countless "examples of civilized barbarity" even as he deprecates the charge of cannibalism by dismissing exaggerated accounts. Only toward the end of his stay is he again plagued by fears. This alternation in narrative perspective hardly demonstrates Tommo's reversion to the usual contemporary response, however.[32] It is one thing to contemplate cannibalism with equanimity; it is quite another to face being eaten oneself! Intimate exposure had allowed Tommo to judge this communion ceremony more tolerantly; but his "freedom of view" did not extend to partaking himself, or being partaken of.

Typee's development of the subject of cannibalism reveals the depth of Melville's tolerance for alien cultures. Although *Moby-Dick* propounds issues at once more symbolically ambitious, more metaphysical, and correspondingly less cultural, it also focuses on a cannibal in elaborating its major themes. That elaboration best reveals

[31] Cited in Hetherington, *Melville's Reviewers*, p. 51.
[32] See, for another reading, Anderson, *Melville in the South Seas*, p. 110.

discoveries Melville had made in *Typee* and best anticipates those that others would make more than a generation later. On a rather simple level, as already suggested, the entire novel is committed to documenting a major mid-century enterprise. Yet understated symbols throughout the narrative enforce the sense of irrecoverability, of experiences beyond the possibility of recording. The *Pequod* itself is named for "a celebrated tribe of Massachusetts Indians, now extinct as the ancient Medes" (67). That the ship emblematizes the questing, cannibalistic spirit of industrial society also links white predatory success with native decline. Similarly, quiet Tashtego, the second harpooner, represents the only Indian among the "Anacharsis Clootz deputation from all the isles of the sea" (108) that constitutes the *Pequod*'s crew. He comes from "Gay Head . . . where there exists the last remnant of a village of red men" (107). These descriptions serve as quiet reminders of the human costs dictated by white America's western progress.[33]

Structurally, *Moby-Dick* splits into two sections usually identified according to the dominant characters: Ishmael in the opening third; Ahab thereafter. The split might be more fruitfully identified, however, as one between Queequeg and Ahab, each of whom educates Ishmael in alternative responses to experience. When Ahab appears, the limits to his dramatic vision have already been identified by contrast to Queequeg's tolerance, generosity, and responsiveness. Ahab's gesture against the white whale is Promethean, but Queequeg has made it possible for Ishmael to realize the self-projecting nature of Ahab's torment, "that vulture the very creature he creates" (175). The captain heaps on the "dead wall" of Moby Dick's brow his own angry burden of hate, as the backwoodsman did to the Indian and as Tommo, in a less defiant, more fearful way, initially did to the Typees. Melville masterfully develops the dramatic possibilities of Ahab's moral absolutism, his fierce conversion of belief into truth. Yet the severest challenge to that absolutism comes not from those who openly resist his monomaniacal hunt for Moby Dick but from Queequeg's example.

Thrown into the strange bed of a tattooed Polynesian near the opening of the novel, Ishmael finds his fears instantly aroused by "unwarrantable prejudices." He watches Queequeg carefully, first in his preparations for bed and the next morning during his ablutions, and describes every action with an almost ethnological care. His initial response to Queequeg's "strange antics" and "queer proceed-

---

[33] See Barnett, *Ignoble Savage*, pp. 170, 176, 180, for a similar discussion of these issues.

ings" (30) resembles Captain Delano's reductive interpretation of mysteries aboard the *San Dominique*. Unlike Delano, he grows wide-eyed with fear in anticipation of some cannibal violence. In the very midst of his paralysis, nonetheless, he counsels himself to tolerance. "What's all this fuss I have been making about, thought I to myself—the man's a human being just as I am: he has just as much reason to fear me, as I have to be afraid of him" (31). Queequeg, in fact, soon bears out this confidence.

As he becomes a "bosom friend" of Queequeg, Ishmael learns to respect more fully those mysterious, unacculturated aspects of behavior beyond his ken. Queequeg's oblations to his idol, Yojo; his curious notions about sickness, death, and friendship; his daylong Ramadan—all define a system of beliefs completely outside Ishmael's cultural inheritance. Of course, they pique his curiosity and encourage his "rational" adjurations. But Melville thoroughly rejects any moral absolutism, even Ishmael's kindly sort.

> After all, I do not think that my remarks about religion made much impression upon Queequeg. Because, in the first place, he somehow seemed dull of hearing on that important subject, unless considered from his own point of view; and, in the second place, he did not more than one third understand me, couch my ideas simply as I would; and, finally, he no doubt thought he knew a good deal more about the true religion than I did. He looked at me with a sort of condescending concern and compassion, as though he thought it a great pity that such a sensible young man should be so hopelessly lost to evangelical pagan piety. (82)

The ironies here compound one another. Ishmael's arch tone, meant to puncture Queequeg's complacency, ends in self-deflation as well. Assessing the shortcomings of an intolerant Polynesian religion, he reveals his own mild intolerance. Ishmael's saving grace is his appreciation of the irony of their mutually condescending proselytizings.

Religion in particular divides within and between cultures by enforcing formal barriers to a common humanity. Recognizing this, Ishmael offers a mock-humorous rationalization for joining Queequeg in his worship:

> I was a good Christian; born and bred in the bosom of the infallible Presbyterian Church. How then could I unite with this wild idolator in worshipping his piece of wood? But what is worship? thought I. Do you suppose now, Ishmael, that the magnani-

mous God of heaven and earth—pagans and all included—can possibly be jealous of an insignificant bit of black wood? Impossible! But what is worship?—to do the will of God—*that* is worship. And what is the will of God?—to do to my fellow man what I would have my fellow man to do to me—*that* is the will of God. Now, Queequeg is my fellow man. And what do I wish that this Queequeg would do to me? Why, unite with me in my particular Presbyterian form of worship. Consequently, I must then unite with him in his; ergo, I must turn idolator. So I kindled the shavings. . . . (54)

Later, Queequeg's outraged exclamation on nearly losing his hand to the still-snapping jaws of a dead shark illustrates the ultimate insignificance of all cultural labels: "Queequeg no care what god made him shark, . . . wedder Fejee god or Nantucket god; but de god wat made shark must be one dam Ingin" (257).

The "sharkish world" sometimes breaks down cultural patterns to reveal a shared humanity. More often, cultural patterns alone articulate complex human impulses. When Queequeg "pressed his forehead against mine, clasped me round the waist, and said that henceforth we were married" (53), he expresses affection in the only way he knows how—wonderfully strange to Ishmael, yet unmistakable. Remarkably, Melville could stand slightly aside from his own culture as well and see it *as* a culture with its own distinct prescriptions. This "negative capability" meant that Melville could see Western behavior from a Polynesian perspective as both strangely arbitrary and understandable. Tommo and his companion, Toby, for instance, first enter the Typee Valley at once afraid and stalwart. Their demeanor—fully understandable from a Western perspective—ironically evokes nearly identical fears from the first Typees they see, who are scared off because the two act like "white cannibals" (69). Later, the sailors are invited to try a dish of poee-poee. Melville inverts the convention of the natives unable to cope with the civilization of fork and spoon by having the pair's unpracticed attempts to eat with their fingers "convulse the bystanders with uncontrollable laughter" (73). Once again, *Moby-Dick* best explores the theme of culturally fixed patterns when Queequeg recounts his first ignorant handling of a wheelbarrow. Carrying it on his back, he found, attracted condescending attention. But his ignorance differed little from that of a merchant captain who, visiting Queequeg's native island, had mistaken a punch bowl for a finger dish. " 'Now,' said Queequeg, 'what you tink now?—Didn't our people laugh?' " (59).

Melville never developed his thinking about cultural forms beyond this anecdotal and rather mechanical level. But perhaps that level was best suited to revealing their fundamental arbitrariness. Queequeg looks ridiculous as an "undergraduate" in western civilization, as did the Tahitians and Hawaiians in *Omoo*. He crawls under the bed in only his top hat to put on the boots that New Bedford society demands. "He was just enough civilized to show off his outlandishness in the strangest possible manner" (34). Yet his example, here as elsewhere, exposes the strict dogmatism of Western fashion, of dress codes, as well as of considerations of modesty. Moreover, Queequeg's attempt to conform to Western codes debilitates rather than enhances him morally. In providing the biography of this Polynesian prince, Ishmael describes his reason for emigrating: "at bottom—so he told me—he was actuated by a profound desire to learn among the Christians, the arts whereby to make his people still happier than they were; and more than that, still better than they were" (57). He soon learned "that even Christians could be both miserable and wicked; infinitely more so, than all his father's heathens" (57). In an ironic twist to the stereotypical tale of lapsed Christian morality, Queequeg can no longer return to inherit his kingship: "he was fearful Christianity, or rather Christians, had unfitted him for ascending the pure and undefiled throne of thirty pagan Kings before him" (57).

In earlier novels Melville attacked Western practices by juxtaposing them with native practices commonly condemned by whites, especially cannibalism. In *Moby-Dick* he remonstrated against cruel and wasteful consumption in a similar fashion:

> Go to the meat-market of a Saturday night and see the crowds of live bipeds staring up at the long rows of dead quadrupeds. Does not that sight take a tooth out of the cannibal's jaw? Cannibals? who is not a cannibal? I tell you it will be more tolerable for the Fejee that salted down a lean missionary in his cellar against a coming famine; it will be more tolerable for that provident Fejee, I say, in the day of judgment, than for thee, civilized and enlightened gourmand, who nailest geese to the ground and feastest on their bloated livers in thy paté-de-foie-gras. (255-56)

This question of true and false cannibalism informs the entire novel. The *Pequod*, on a predatory mission, is itself described in cannibalistic terms. Queequeg alone can educate Ishmael to considerations of tolerance, generosity, and selflessness. Later, Ahab will educate him to the contrasted terms of Western society, terms that Melville had hinted at in his earlier fiction. The whaling ship *Dolly*, for example, rejected by Tommo in the opening chapter of *Typee*, symbolizes Western civilization at its most blindly exploitative. Like the *Pequod*, its contempt for more elementary levels of natural and animal life, its scorn for native societies, finally becomes grotesquely cannibalistic. The story of the ship *Perseverance*, whose skipper simply touched port for replenishments and then headed back to whaling grounds, suggests an entire civilization ever questing and taking, eternally unsatisfied. The *Dolly* will also continue to sail until the last reminder of land and animal life, Pedro the rooster, is devoured. Only then will the ship return to land, taking more provisions for life it never replenishes. This coldly rational, power-impelled civilization is epitomized in Ahab's quest, his brutal social domination for private ends. He heroically perfects his society's assumptions. In *Israel Potter* (1855) Melville developed this indictment of Western "cannibalism" into a searching question, one at once less sententious and less easily dismissed than the "meat-market" passage quoted above: "What separates the enlightened man from the savage? Is civilization a thing distinct, or is it an advanced stage of barbarism?"[34]

Melville's later reflections on his experiences among Polynesian cultures convinced him of more than their autonomous vitality. Compared with his society, they seemed in surprising respects genuinely superior. Their democratic, fraternal nature delighted him, as did such socially reinforced characteristics as a "sense of delicacy," politeness, and the serene self-sufficiency that Queequeg representatively manifests. Indeed, if "the contemporary view of Christian civilization toward Oceania and Asia" was, in James Baird's words, "as *the regions of darkness*," then for Melville, by a radical inversion, those areas were "to become the only regions of light." For him, Baird goes on to claim, "the achievement of persuading an agreeable people (those of Tahiti, for example), to give up a traditional symbolism in answer to vague mumblings of peace, where peace and good will were already known, was an act of sacrilege, suspect in itself of 'civilized' evil. This feat of persuasion was a virtual token of the symbolic impoverishment in which the zeal of the missions originated."[35]

Beyond such improvishment, however, Melville saw nineteenth-century Western civilization in actively, humanly destructive terms. London, its symbol, appeared to him "the City of Dis," with emissaries convincingly more barbaric than those whom they deemed "barbarians."[36] In *White-Jacket*, his young narrator queries rhetorically:

[34] Melville, *His Fifty Years of Exile (Israel Potter)*, ed. Lewis Leary (New York: Sagamore Press, 1957), p. 186, also p. 170.
[35] Baird, *Ishmael*, p. 99, also p. 16. See also Barnett, *Ignoble Savage*, pp. 168ff.
[36] *Israel Potter*, p. 225.

"Are there no Moravians in the Moon, that not a missionary has yet visited this poor pagan planet of ours, to civilize civilization and Christianize Christendom?" (267). Earlier, in *Typee*, Tommo had not even phrased it as a question: "The term 'Savage' is, I conceive, often misapplied, and indeed when I consider the vices, cruelties, and enormities of every kind that spring up in the tainted atmosphere of a feverish civilization, I am inclined to think that so far as the relative wickedness of the parties is concerned, four or five Marquesan Islanders sent to the United States as Missionaries might be quite as useful as an equal number of Americans despatched to the Islands in a similar capacity" (125-26).

A more compellingly bitter articulation of this attitude occurs in Melville's later lecture, where he describes the efforts of actual missionaries:

> I am sorry to say we whites have a sad reputation among many of the Polynesians. The natives of these islands are naturally of a kindly and hospitable temper, but there has been planted among them an almost instinctive hate of the white man. They esteem us, with rare exceptions, such as *some* of the missionaries, the most barbarous, treacherous, irreligious, and devilish creatures on the earth. This may of course be a mere prejudice of these unlettered savages, for have not our traders always treated them with brotherly affection? Who has ever heard of a vessel sustaining the honor of a Christian flag and the spirit of the Christian Gospel by opening its batteries in indiscriminate massacre upon some poor little village on the seaside—splattering the torn bamboo huts with blood and brains of women and children, defenseless and innocent.[37]

Little of Cooper's ambivalence regarding the spread of "civilization" along the frontier is evident here. Already, the disillusionment savors of the sort that later spiced Mark Twain's writings. A decided shift has taken place along the spectrum of attitudes outlined earlier in the discussion of Crèvecoeur and Cather.

Melville enjoyed resounding popularity with his first two books—more than he ever again received. Some pious critics found his strictures on missionaries blasphemous; most enjoyed the lively view he presented of Polynesia. Yet, with regard to other exotic captivity and travel narratives popular at the time, none matched Melville's easy

[37] Sealts, *Melville as Lecturer*, pp. 168-69. See also Anderson, *Melville in the South Seas*, p. 447; Richard Slotkin, *Regeneration through Violence: The Mythology of the American Frontier, 1600-1860* (Middletown, Conn.: Wesleyan University Press, 1973), p. 550.

sophistication with other cultures or his correspondingly severe cross-cultural critiques and reverse comparisons. He anticipated a constellation of attitudes toward primitive cultures that became commonplaces only near the end of the century: the need for broad tolerance, for a recognition of a culture's autonomy as well as of its mysterious inner complexity. The question remains whether his contemporaries tacitly endorsed the controversial views expressed in *Typee, Omoo,* and, had they read it, *Moby-Dick*.

To judge only by some of the quotations offered in preceding chapters, many shared at least some of these attitudes. They too had learned to appreciate complex values in tribal life, though they were unable to integrate them as Melville had. To what extent was Melville at mid-century only one among the avant-garde? The answer to that question will require a full examination of those who, whether or not they began by commiting themselves to records of imperiled indigenous cultures, discovered nonetheless an authentic and autonomous value to them. The intellectual history of their explorations matches, in striking ways, the template offered by Melville's fictions. Moreover, they would subscribe to profound new assumptions about cultural life at which he had only hinted.

CHAPTER EIGHT

TOWARD CULTURAL RELATIVISM

It is related by Æsop, that a forester once meeting with a lion, they travelled together for a time, and conversed amicably without much differing in opinion. At length a dispute happening to arise upon the question of superiority between their respective races, the former, in the absence of a better argument, pointed to a monument, on which was sculptured, in marble, the statue of a man striding over the body of a vanquished lion. "If this," said the lion, "is all you have to say, let us be the sculptors, and you will see the lion striding over the vanquished man."

The moral of this fable should ever be borne in mind when contemplating the character of that brave and ill-used race of men, now melting away before the Anglo-Saxons like the snow beneath a vertical sun—the aboriginals of America. The Indians are no sculptors.
  —*Col William L. Stone*
  Life of Joseph Brant (1838)

The data of ethnology prove that not only our knowledge, but also our emotions are the result of the form of our social life and of the history of the people to whom we belong. If we desire to understand the development of human culture we must try to free ourselves of these shackles. This is possible only to those who are willing to adapt themselves to the strange ways of thinking and feeling of primitive people.
  —*Franz Boas*
  "The Aims of Ethnology" (1888)

Aɴ ᴇᴍɪɴᴇɴᴛ ᴍᴏᴅᴇʀɴ ᴀɴᴛʜʀᴏᴘᴏʟᴏɢɪsᴛ has provided a simple touchstone for studies by his fellow practitioners. "Know what he thinks a savage is," Clifford Geertz claims, with a gleam in his eye, "and you have the key to his work."[1] Despite his assurances, such a simple key aids more surely in theory than in practice. In part, this is because the concept of the "savage"—the "primitive" or the "wild man"—masks such a welter of attitudes as to render the label inadequate to those it purports to define. Melville, for a prime instance, explored the concept in ways unmatched in the mid-nineteenth century, the result of unique personal adventures, exhaustive reading, and a searching artistry. He therefore exposes most convincingly the limits to Geertz's attractive dictum. Although Melville's idea of the savage might well be found in *Typee*, it can hardly be reduced to less than the narrative whole. No simple key to his work exists. Geertz realizes this, of course, as his elaboration confirms: "You know what he thinks he himself is and, knowing what he thinks he himself is, you know in general what sort of thing he is going to say about whatever tribes he happens to be studying. All ethnography is part philosophy, and a good deal of the rest is confession."[2] Whatever one believes of the savage invokes the fullest conceptions of oneself and one's culture.

Impelled by greater self-consciousness about their own value systems, twentieth-century anthropologists have abandoned their predecessors' absolutist perspectives. Yet that rejection itself represents only one more step in a history of increasingly sophisticated perspectives, all rejected in their own turn. Most people in the eighteenth century lacked the experience that might have encouraged them to move beyond contemporary stereotypes to relative judgments of other societies. Nevertheless, significant numbers began in the nineteenth century to treat exotic cultures more circumspectly. Some of the writers, artists, and photographers introduced in Chapters Five and Six, for example, discerned in the records they had preserved a challenge to their assumptions about tribal life. The realization that Indians might well be valued for more than pictorial or antiquarian reasons in turn brought into question received opinion on the issue of culture itself—a development so controversial that it continues to shake conventional assumptions.[3]

[1] Clifford Geertz, *The Interpretation of Cultures: Selected Essays* (New York: Basic Books, 1973), p. 346.
[2] Ibid.
[3] For background, see: David Bidney, "The Concept of Value in Modern Anthropology," in A. L. Kroeber, ed., *Anthropology Today: An Encyclopedic Inventory*

This chapter elaborates a sequence intimated in the preceding discussion of Melville, tracing four progressively more complex understandings of Indian tribes. Those who recognized an autonomous value to native cultures frequently stopped at that, incapable of pressing insight further. A more perceptive group appreciated as well their mystery and warned against easy hypotheses about these "closed" social worlds. Others went on to stress the need for intimate and protracted association. To comprehend the native, they realized, required learning to live and to think like one. Finally, one group won its way to an acceptance of primitive societies as comparable, and in many ways superior, to their own—a cultural relativism that in turn fueled inquiries into the concepts of advanced civilizations and material progress. These four lines of thought hardly developed as a distinct historical progression, nor are they necessarily linked. It is difficult nonetheless to conceive of the emergence of later, more complex forms of appreciation without the insights brought about by increasingly respectful tolerance.

The word *culture* itself underwent a remarkable transformation through the nineteenth century, acquiring new meanings at the same time that it crept into common parlance. Fuller understanding of this change may be gained here from a review of attitudes that Europeans initially held toward Indians, a review that risks sounding reductive only because European attitudes generally were so. From the sixteenth century on, most whites could not help but distort information about native life. One example is the imposed notion of kingship, as in the case of the misnamed King Philip's War. In fact, virtually no tribe lived under anything resembling a monarchy. In other respects, the long-developed European concept of wildness—defined by Hayden White as part of a "set of culturally self-authenticating devices which includes, among many others, the ideas of 'madness' and 'heresy' "[4]—

(Chicago: University of Chicago Press, 1953), pp. 682-99; Bidney, "The Idea of the Savage in North American Ethnohistory," *Journal of the History of Ideas*, 15 (April 1954), 322-27; F. R. Cowell, *Culture in Private and Public Life* (London: Thames and Hudson, 1954), esp. pp. 235ff.; Marvin Harris, *Culture, People, Nature: An Introduction to General Anthropology*, 2d ed. (New York: Thomas Y. Crowell, 1975), esp. pp. 146-47; George W. Stocking Jr., *Race, Culture, and Evolution: Essays in the History of Anthropology* (New York: Free Press, 1968); Raymond Williams, *Culture and Society: 1780-1950* (Harper and Row, 1958), pp. xiv, 58-65; Geertz, " 'From the Native's Point of View': On the Nature of Anthropological Understanding," in Keith H. Basso and Henry A. Selby, eds., *Meaning in Anthropology* (Albuquerque: University of New Mexico Press, 1976), pp. 221-37; David M. Schneider, "Notes toward a Theory of Culture," in ibid., pp. 197-220.

[4] Hayden White, "The Forms of Wildness: Archaeology of an Idea," in Edward Dudley and Maximillian E. Novak, eds., *The Wild Man Within: An Image in Western Thought from the Renaissance to Romanticism* (Pittsburgh: University

provided ready-made categories for defining the denizens of this paradigmatic wilderness.

Historians have offered compelling reasons for the persistence of this narrow, negative view of indigenous tribes. The strength of certain Christian mores predisposed Europeans to see Indians as a kind of negative definition of themselves, as deficient whites. Settling the land according to European economic practice in any case meant dispossessing native tribes, which further encouraged dehumanizing assumptions as a way of absolving guilt. Through the eighteenth century, then, ethnocentrism fostered an image of the Indian composed of largely Western patterns of intention and desire.

Even those intellectuals who professed a kind of moral tolerance rarely considered making inductive observations. They merely conceived of the Indian as the "other." The "noble savage" fathered by Diderot, Rousseau, Freneau, and Franklin was little more than a twin to wretched Caliban, both of whom had been delivered without aid of the midwife culture. Only the values ascribed to their births differed. Instead of damning him, Enlightenment intellectuals comforted the primitive child as a way of reflexively criticizing their own civilization. This reaction, itself an impressive development, allowed them to recognize some of their own society's arbitrary modes. As early as 1582, Montaigne shrewdly observed "that everyone gives the title of barbarism to everything that is not according to his usage; as, indeed, we have no other criterion of truth and reason than the example and pattern of the opinions and customs of the country where-

---

of Pittsburgh Press, 1972), p. 4, also pp. 3-38. See also Peter S. Thorslev Jr., "The Wild Man's Revenge," in ibid., pp. 281-307; Gary B. Nash, "Red, White and Black: The Origins of Racism in Colonial America," in Nash and Richard Weiss, eds., *The Great Fear: Race in the Mind of America* (New York: Holt, Rinehart and Winston, 1970), pp. 1-26; Nash "The Image of the Indian in the Southern Colonial Mind," *William and Mary Quarterly*, 3d ser., 29 (April 1972), 197-230; Roy Harvey Pearce, *Savagism and Civilization: A Study of the American Mind*, rev. ed. (Baltimore: Johns Hopkins University Press, 1965); Henri Baudet, *Paradise on Earth: Some Thoughts on European Images of Non-European Man* (1959), trans. Elizabeth Werthoff (New Haven: Yale University Press, 1965), esp. pp. vii, 5-25; Richard Slotkin, *Regeneration through Violence: The Mythology of the American Frontier, 1600-1860* (Middletown, Conn.: Wesleyan University Press, 1973), esp. pp. 116ff.; Robert F. Berkhofer Jr., *The White Man's Indian: Images of the American Indian from Columbus to the Present* (New York: Alfred A. Knopf, 1978), esp. pp. 5-7, 10-11, 25-27; Elémire Zolla, *The Writer and the Shaman: A Morphology of the American Indian* (1969), trans. Raymond Rosenthal (New York: Harcourt Brace Jovanovich, 1973), esp. pp. 5-27; Benjamin Keen, *The Aztec Image in Western Thought* (New Brunswick: Rutgers University Press, 1971), pp. 217-309; Michael Paul Rogin, "Liberal Society and the Indian Question," *Politics and Society*, 1 (May 1971), 269-312; Hoxie Neale Fairchild, *The Noble Savage: A Study in Romantic Naturalism* (New York: Columbia University Press, 1928).

in we live."[5] Two centuries later, Benjamin Franklin could add little, despite firsthand knowledge the French philosopher could not claim: "Savages we call them, because their Manners differ from ours, which we think the Perfection of Civility. They think the same of theirs."[6]

The tolerance that grew in America as threats of Indian attack on eastern colonies diminished probably reflected little more than that abeyance. Certainly, the old ethnocentric ideas died hard even among those few closely acquainted with tribal life. Though missionaries and traders, explorers and Indian captives had always been capable of sympathetic assessments of specific native societies, they did not abandon a secure confidence in white superiority. Appreciation of a complex tribal diversity rarely developed into more profound attempts to understand native cultures on their own terms, much less into more penetrating assessments of the issue of culture itself.[7] More to the point, such appreciation, even when it existed, seldom extended beyond a select group.

Well into the nineteenth century, Americans continued to subscribe to fixed cultural assumptions. Polygenesis, the dominant scientific concept in this era, offered a rational defense for longstanding racism. Government policy, though occasionally deflected or softened, rarely abandoned the reductive premise that Indians were children unable to appreciate their beleaguered past or their circumscribed future. This hoary notion found spokesmen among people as tolerant as Carl Schurz, President Hayes's secretary of the Interior Department. "We must not expect them, therefore, to evolve out of their own consciousness what is best for their salvation," Schurz counseled.

---

[5] *Montaigne: Selected Essays*, ed. Blanchard Bates (New York: Random House, Modern Library, 1949), p. 77.

[6] Benjamin Franklin, "Remarks Concerning the Savages of North America," Papers of Benjamin Franklin, Library of Congress microcopy (1941), 2d ser., vol. 10, no. 2334-2344, p. 1. See as well, for outstanding instances of this form of Enlightenment relativism: [Joseph Addison], *The Spectator*, April 27, 1711, pp. 1-2; *Captain Cook's Journal . . . 1768-71*, ed. Captain W.J.L. Wharton (London: Elliott Stock, 1893), p. 232; Alan Moorehead, *The Fatal Impact: An Account of the Invasion of the South Pacific, 1767-1840* (New York: Harper and Row, 1966), p. 70; *The Prose of Philip Freneau*, ed. Philip M. Marsh (New Brunswick: Scarecrow Press, 1955), pp. 332-42; *The Western Journals of Washington Irving*, ed. John Francis McDermott (Norman: University of Oklahoma Press, 1944), pp. 103-4; John Francis McDermott, "Up the Wide Missouri: Travelers and Their Diaries, 1794-1861," in McDermott, ed., *Travelers on the Western Frontier* (Urbana: University of Illinois Press, 1970), pp. 21-23; Pearce, *Savagism and Civilization*, pp. 138-41; Stocking, *Race, Culture, and Evolution*, p. 37; Robert F. Sayre, *Thoreau and the American Indians* (Princeton: Princeton University Press, 1977), Leslie Fiedler, *The Return of the Vanishing American* (New York: Stein and Day, 1968), pp. 41ff.

[7] Gary B. Nash, "Red, White and Black," p. 9; Nash, "Image of the Indian," pp. 222, 225, 229; Berkhofer, *White Man's Indian*, p. 49; Pearce, *Savagism and Civilization*, p. 91.

"We must in a great measure do the necessary thinking for them, and then in the most humane way possible induce them to accept our conclusions."[8] Apart from his sheer patronization, Schurz reveals the inability of most otherwise sympathetic individuals to recognize the extraordinary variety of Indian cultures.[9]

Yet if this overview illustrates in large brushstrokes the attitudes generally shared by whites, it also paints over the emergence of significant resistance to and revision of those attitudes. In the nineteenth century, many of those who ventured west not only experienced revelations about Indian tribes shared by relatively few others for centuries, but they also stumbled into radically new ways of thinking about them. This development coincided in the 1860s with the emergence of anthropology as a central intellectual issue in an age rocked by geological, biological, and religious controversies.[10] To be sure, the ensuing mood of unsettled questioning was an international phenomenon, in large part the result of theoretical breakthroughs unconnected with the North American continent. Nonetheless, countless travelers on the western frontier contributed to this reassessment of notions of culture. Tourists, explorers, and amateur and professional ethnologists began during the second quarter of the nineteenth century to see native cultures as rich, vital, and autonomous, the evidence of their experiences among western tribes having patently contradicted longstanding theory and pressed them to more adequate interpretations. Ironically, acknowledgment of the viability of indigenous cultures—and with it, attitudes of respect, tolerance, even cultural relativism—gained acceptance just as Americans finally undermined most of those cultures.

The broad transition outlined in the following pages, then, is from cultural absolutism and ethnocentrism to cultural relativism. These terms, briefly discussed in Chapter One, reflect a progressively less complacent, more self-conscious appraisal of cultural thought and

[8] Carl Schurz, "Present Aspects of the Indian Problem," *North American Review*, 133 (July 1881), 19. For background to this paragraph, see: Stocking, *Race, Culture, and Evolution*, p. 39; Philip Borden, "Found Cumbering the Soil: Manifest Destiny and the Indian in the Nineteenth Century," in Nash and Weiss, eds., *The Great Fear*, p. 96.

[9] Borden, "Found Cumbering the Soil," p. 78; Wilcomb E. Washburn, *Red Man's Land/White Man's Law: A Study of the Past and Present Status of the American Indian* (New York: Charles Scribner's Sons, 1971), pp. 60-75; Alan Heimert, "Puritanism, the Wilderness, and the Frontier," *New England Quarterly*, 26 (September 1953), 371ff.; Richard Drinnon, *White Savage: The Case of John Dunn Hunter* (New York: Schocken Books, 1972), p. 241.

[10] Stocking, *Race, Culture, and Evolution*, p. 74; H. Bruce Franklin, *The Wake of the Gods: Melville's Mythology* (Stanford: Stanford University Press, 1963), pp. 3-4; Borden, "Found Cumbering the Soil," p. 92.

behavior. Historically, the shift has been from an initial belief in the exclusive worth of one's institutions to a hierarchical theory. Known as cultural evolutionism, this view grudgingly concedes value to other societies insofar as they share supposedly earlier or incipient forms of one's own institutions. This social-stages-of-history theory, given fictional garb by James Fenimore Cooper, in turn bowed to a pluralistic one: that cultures can not be evaluated against absolute norms, because each one intrinsically may warrant as much respect as another. Whether this sort of pure tolerance can ever be achieved, it forms an admirable goal, and the development of that recognition forms a fascinating history.

AWARENESS OF CULTURAL AUTONOMY

To reiterate, the majority of white Americans in the nineteenth century accepted a legacy of racial stereotypes: the good and bad Indian, the noble savage and unconscionable devil. In the nineteenth century, however, for reasons already discussed, the number of those who rejected that legacy grew significantly for the first time. They began to regard natives as complex human beings, as diverse as whites and equally admirable though differing radically in thought and behavior. Offering greatest impetus for this more widespread altering of attitudes were those who had actually lived among tribes, including Indian captive John Dunn Hunter, fur trapper Osborne Russell, and painter-ethnologist George Catlin.[11] Many others adopted their tolerance—but without following their example—through the next half century. In the 1870s, individuals as different as General George Crook and anthropologist James Mooney would feel the need to reiterate to an ever more receptive public what Commissioner of Indian Affairs Jedidiah Morse had perceptively remarked in the 1820s: "There is as visible a difference of character among the different tribes, as there is in our own population; few general observations, therefore, will apply to them as a body."[12] Perhaps the best articulation of this view ap-

[11] John Dunn Hunter, *Memoirs of a Captivity Among the Indians of North America* (1824), ed. Richard Drinnon (New York: Schocken Books, 1973), pp. xiv-xv, xxii-xxiii, 207, 210-12; Osborne Russell, *Journal of a Trapper* (1914), ed. Aubrey L. Haines (Portland: Oregon Historical Society, 1955), pp. 113, 121; George Catlin, *Letters and Notes on the Manners, Customs, and Conditions of the North American Indians*, 2 vols. (1844; rpt. New York: Dover Publications, 1973), 1:23; Oliver M. Spencer, *Indian Captivity* (1835; rpt. Ann Arbor: University Microfilms, 1966), esp. pp. 72-93, 102-7, 120-23.

[12] Cited in *A Collection of Indian Ancedotes* (Concord, N.H.: William White, 1838), p. xi; Gen. George Crook, *General George Crook: His Autobiography*, 2d ed., ed. Martin F. Schmitt (Norman: University of Oklahoma Press, 1960), p, 271;

peared in a letter written to *Century Magazine* in July 1889, criticizing
Frederic Remington's painted Indians:

> There are Indians and Indians, and he who should form his
> general impression of the Indian from a glimpse of the savagery
> of individual Apaches would find it necessary to discard his work
> and begin anew in the presence of the peaceful and skillful Zuni.
> . . . Those who have studied the question on the ground are
> agreed that while the Army view, the view of the frontiersman,
> and the view of the philanthropist are each true in individual
> cases, none of them contains the whole truth. The Indian char-
> acter is as varied as the character of the white man who sits in
> judgment upon him.[13]

Yet the concepts of human variety and even tribal diversity proved
less difficult to grasp than that of cultural complexity. Observers
were repeatedly astonished at the degree to which Iroquois, Kwakiutl,
Sioux, Algonquin, Papago, and Cherokee tribal life constituted whole
and extensive cultures, with idiosyncratic institutions shaping nearly
every facet of human behavior. Far from simple collectives, these and
other native cultures comprised intricate structures. Each aspect of
tribal life—religious, linguistic, political, artistic, economic, and social
—meshed into a mutually reinforcing whole, altogether unlike the
divisive strains of white society.[14]

Confirming this profound social integrity, redeemed white captives
sometimes described their experiences in terms very much like those
Melville invoked in *Typee*.[15] Others provided an even more sympa-

---

James Mooney, *The Ghost-Dance Religion and the Sioux Outbreak of 1890* (1896),
ed. Anthony F. C. Wallace (New York: Dover Publications, 1972), p. ix. See also Rev.
Jedidiah Morse, *A Report to the Secretary of War of the United States on Indian
Affairs* . . . (New Haven: S. Converse, 1822), pp. 66-67, 82; Col. Richard Irving Dodge,
*Our Wild Indians: Thirty-Three Years' Personal Experience Among the Red Men
of the Great West* . . . (Hartford, Conn.: A. D. Worthington and Co., 1883), pp. 53-54;
Ewers, "When Red and White Men Meet," *Western Historical Quarterly*, 2 (April
1971), 134. For a more general, and contradictory, reading of the period, see Pearce,
Savagism and Civilization, pp. 108-9; Berkhofer, *White Man's Indian*, pp. 19-11, 26,
71 ff.

[13] Hamilton Wright Mabie, "Indians, and Indians," *Century Magazine*, 38 (July
1889), 471.

[14] For suggestions of this novel insight, see: Robert V. Hine, *Bartlett's West:
Drawing the Mexican Boundary* (New Haven: Yale University Press, 1968), pp. 63-
65; Charles Granville Johnson, *History of the Territory of Arizona*, 3 vols. (San
Francisco: Vincent Ryan and Co., 1868), 1:11; Charles G. Leland, *The Algonquin
Legends of New England, or Myths and Folk Lore of the Micmac, Passamaquoddy,
and Penobscot Tribes* (Boston: Houghton, Mifflin and Co., 1884), pp. 3-5, 13. See
also Stocking, *Race, Culture, and Evolution*, esp. p. 87.

[15] The earliest such description is "The Narrative of Alvar Nunez Cabeza de Vaca,"
trans. (Thomas) Buckingham Smith, ed. Frederick W. Hodge, in *Spanish Explorers*

thetic gloss on their experience by freely returning to native life without published comment. Their actions stood as judgment on their "captivities."[16] Former compatriots dismissed these eccentrics out-of-hand, of course, for voluntarily sacrificing "civilized" restraints for "savage freedom." Others, however, recognized the attraction of the highly socialized, if alien, character of tribal life. John Dunn Hunter's case is the most celebrated. In the early 1820s he caused a minor national uproar with the publication of his *Manners and Customs of the Indian Tribes Located West of the Mississippi* (1823), the record of his captivity, adoption, and training since childhood among woodland tribes. His eloquent ambivalence about white society, his generous validation of native life, his sympathy for people whom he characterized in fully human terms—all divided readers sharply into those supporting him and those charging fraud.[17]

Being held captive, of course, was no prerequisite for appreciating native cultures. Near mid-century, James Swan voluntarily chose to live among the Chehalis and Chinook Indians of the Pacific Northwest in order to study their complex societies. This somewhat eccentric frontiersman, who served as translator for Isaac Stevens's exploring expeditions, argued forcibly against the territorial governor's efforts toward "civilizing and Christianizing the Indians."[18] Speaking of the tribes' willingness to trade with the whites, he countered:

> They neither wish to adopt the white man's style of living, or his language, or religion.
>   They feel as we would if a foreign people came among us, and attempted to force their customs on us whether we liked them or

in the Southern United States, 1528-1543, Original Narratives of Early American History Series (New York: Charles Scribner's Sons, 1907), pp. 1-126. See also John R. Jewitt, *A Narrative of the Adventures and Sufferings of John R. Jewitt During a Captivity of Nearly Three Years Among the Savages of Nootka Sound* (1815), 3d ed. (New York, 1816), esp. pp. 34-35, 197; Edwin James, ed., *A Narrative of the Captivity and Adventures of John Tanner . . .* (1830; rpt. Minneapolis: Ross and Haines, 1956); Pearce, *Savagism and Civilization*, pp. 116-18; Slotkin, *Regeneration through Violence*; Michael J. Colacurcio, review of Slotkin, *Regeneration*, in *Early American Literature*, 9 (Winter 1975), 336.

[16] J. Norman Heard, *White into Red: A Study of the Assimilation of White Persons Captured by Indians* (Metuchen, N.J.: Scarecrow Press, 1973), esp. pp. 1-6, 11-13, 138, 156; Slotkin, *Regeneration through Violence*, pp. 100-102.

[17] Hunter, *Memoirs of a Captivity*. See also Drinnon, *White Savage*, esp. pp. xvi-xvii, 12, 30, 37-39; [John P. Foote?], review of John D. Hunter, *Manners and Customs of the Indian Tribes Located West of the Mississippi*, in *Cincinnati Literary Gazette*, 1 (January 1, 10, 1824), 1-2, 9-10; review of Hunter, *Memoirs*, in *Quarterly Review*, 31 (1825), 76-80.

[18] James G. Swan, *The Northwest Coast, or, Three Years' Residence in Washington Territory* (1857; rpt. Seattle: University of Washington Press, 1969), p. 367.

not. We are willing the foreigners should come, and settle, and live with us; but if they attempted to force upon us their language and religion, and make us leave our old homes and take up new ones, we would certainly rebel; and it would only be by a long intercourse of years that our manners could be made to approximate.[19]

This recognition of cultural autonomy in native life constitutes perhaps the greatest strength of Swan's account. Moreover, the kind of argument he made had numerous advocates by mid-century.[20] John Wesley Powell spoke for a large segment of the educated population of 1878 when he asserted "Savagery is not inchoate civilization; it is a distinct status of society with its own institutions, customs, philosophies, and religion."[21] Like other cultural evolutionists who believed in a historical progression through increasingly more advanced social organizations, Powell could not accept an equation between "savagery" and "civilization." But he demonstrated the kind of respect for native tribes that formed a prerequisite to such acceptance.

Only recently have anthropologists exposed the fallacy common to all of the above statements, that culture supposedly reduces to man-

[19] Ibid., p. 368, also pp. ix, xi.

[20] See, for instance, John Beeson, *A Plea for the Indians* . . . (New York: J. Beeson, 1857), preface (unpaginated), pp. 112-14; William Watts H. Davis, *El Gringo; or, New Mexico and Her People* (New York: Harper and Brothers, 1857), esp. pp. 133-34; "Mrs. J. E. De Camp Sweet's Narrative of Her Captivity in the Sioux Outbreak of 1862," *Collections of the Minnesota Historical Society*, 6 (1894), 382-84; *Captivity and Adventures of John Tanner*, ed. James, pp. xvii-xviii, xxviii-xxix, xxxi. See also, Edward P. Dozier, "Resistance to Acculturation and Assimilation in an Indian Pueblo," *American Anthropologist*, 53 (January-March 1951), 56-66.

[21] Cited by William Culp Darrah, *Powell of the Colorado* (Princeton: Princeton University Press, 1951), p. 256. For similar statements, see Henry A. Boller, *Among the Indians. Eight Years in the Far West: 1858-1866* (Philadelphia: T. Ellwood Zell, 1868), p. 54; Daniel G. Brinton, *Essays of an Americanist* (Philadelphia: David McKay, 1890), p. 103; Brinton, *The Myths of the New World: A Treatise on the Symbolism and Mythology of the Red Race of America* (1868), 3d ed. (Philadelphia: David McKay, 1896), p. 15; Capt. John G. Bourke, *The Snake-Dance of the Moquis of Arizona* . . . (New York: Charles Scribner's Sons, 1884), p. 14; Catlin, *Letters and Notes*, 1:11, 26; Edward S. Curtis, *The North American Indian; Being a Series of Volumes Picturing and Describing the Indians of the United States, and Alaska*, ed. Frederick Webb Hodge, 20 vols. (Cambridge, Mass.: Harvard University Press, 1907-30), 1:xv-xvi; George Bird Grinnell, *Pawnee Hero Stories and Folk-Tales with Notes on the Origin, Customs and Character of the Pawnee People* (New York: Charles Scribner's Sons, 1890), pp. xii-xv; George Frederick Ruxton, *Ruxton of the Rockies*, ed. LeRoy R. Hafen (Norman: University of Oklahoma Press, 1950), p. 46; Matilda Coxe Stevenson, *The Zuñi Indians: Their Mythology, Esoteric Fraternities, and Ceremonies* (1905; rpt. New York: Johnson Reprint Corp., 1970), pp. 20, 607-8; Charles F. Lummis, *Bullying the Moqui*, ed. Robert Easton and Mackenzie Brown (Flagstaff: Prescott College Press, 1968), esp. pp. 3-4, 30ff.

ners and that human nature remains the same independent of time and place. Similar desires do not, like common physiques, appear under different cultural garbs. In fact, "cultural universal" suggests a contradiction, since human nature emerges only in particular contexts. "Culture," Clifford Geertz observes, "is not just an ornament of human existence but . . . an essential condition for it. . . . To be human here is thus not to be Everyman; it is to be a particular kind of man, and of course men differ."[22] Ironically, Geertz here defines the very terms of an older understanding of culture against which the best-intentioned ethnologists in the nineteenth century so stridently fought. Experiences with western tribes had led these more sensitive observers to honor various cultures as manifestations of identical human capacities; different conditioning seemed merely to give expression to a common human nature. The sole premise Geertz shares with their formulations—a significant one—is a fundamental respect for all cultural forms.

Those few times that writers ventured it in fiction, cultural relativism offered a clumsy perspective. Cooper's Leatherstocking tales represent a partial exception, defining whites and Indians in a roughly cultural fashion according to the repeated distinction between "gifts" and "natur'." In *The Deerslayer* (1841), Natty Bumppo provides the best definitions of these terms for Judith Hutter:

> "You find different colors on 'arth, as anyone may see, but you don't find different natur's. Different gifts, but only one natur'."
>
> "In what is a gift different from a nature? Is not nature itself a gift from God?"
>
> "Sartain; that's quick-thoughted and creditable, Judith, though the main idee is wrong. A natur' is the creatur' itself; its wishes, wants, idees, and feelin's, as all are born in him. This natur' never can be changed in the main, though it may undergo some increase or lessening. Now, gifts come of sarcunstances. Thus, if you put a man in a town, he gets town gifts; in a settlement, settlement gifts. . . . All these increase and strengthen until they get to fortify natur', as it might be, and excuse a thousand acts and idees. Still, the creatur' is the same at the bottom. . . ."[23]

[22] Geertz, *Interpretation of Cultures*, pp. 46, 53.

[23] Cooper, *The Deerslayer; or, The First War-Path* (New York: W. A. Townsend and Co., 1859), p. 477. (All further references to Cooper's works will be to this collected edition known as the Author's Revised Edition, illustrated by F.O.C. Darley and printed between 1859 and 1861.) Cooper has Bumppo provide this, his most thorough explanation, largely in order to elucidate a distinction that had been mired in vague contradiction since its initial presentation fifteen years earlier in *The Last of the Mohicans* (1826). Nevertheless, the hunter-philosopher has

Despite glaring inconsistencies in Bumppo's "gifts" thesis, Cooper achieved a remarkable assessment of cultural values. For the first time in American fiction, Iroquois and Sioux, Delaware and Pawnee move in relatively authentic native contexts, not just in worlds defined negatively by white standards. Within the limitations of his art and his conservative theories of evolutionary social history, Cooper represented Indians as complex beings in authentic cultures. He could never detail those cultures, nor could he believe them equal to European civilization. Yet his Indian was no longer a stock primitive, either mere savage negation or noble epitome, though both types do appear in his pages.

Cooper established a rough system of native values counter to those that whites wanted to impose. The novels declare that every person must be measured against the standards of behavior inculcated by his own society; behavior thereby deemed appropriate for one person may not be so for another. According to Natty, Indians differ as radically from whites in their conception of an afterlife as in that of battlefield courage; both concepts, however, pose acceptable alternatives to European notions of redemption and chivalry. Throughout the novels, the native is expected to be grudgingly implacable, his white counterparts forgiving. The former's culture values the laconic and reserved; the latter's, a genial openness and sociability. The Indian's alertness and shrewd deceptiveness contrast with the white's mean, complaining manner. Within what he posits as the framework of a common humanity, Cooper allows for workable variations in behavior. Or, as Natty remarks at one point, "In my judgment, every man is to be esteemed or condemned according to his gifts."[24]

Culture ever takes precedence, determining the ethical context within which to judge personal behavior. Natty Bumppo tells Chingachgook that "no christianizing will ever make even a Delaware a white man, nor any whooping and yelling convart a paleface into a redskin."[25] Underlying the implicit racism of these contrasted ex-

---

invoked the terms throughout the tales with reference to such a medley of idiosyncrasies, prejudices, habits, and culturally sanctioned customs, and mixed them so frequently (in the final two tales, an average of once every ten pages), as to render this concluding explanation nearly meaningless.

24 *The Pathfinder*, p. 100. See also ibid., pp. 37, 41, 53, 67, 72, 81-82, 133, 338, 435, 476, 479; *The Last of the Mohicans*, pp. 174, 243, 259, 263; *The Deerslayer*, pp. 48, 91, 162, 226. Edwin Fussell, in *Frontier: American Literature and the American West* (Princeton: Princeton University Press, 1965), pp. 63-67, comments intelligently on such supposed racial differentiation.

25 *The Pathfinder*, p. 130. See also ibid., pp. 242, 338; *The Deerslayer*, p. 87. For an interpretation of this line that is at odds with my own, see Joel Porte, *The Romance in America: Studies in Cooper, Poe, Hawthorne, Melville, and James* (Middletown, Conn.: Wesleyan University Press, 1969), p. 16.

amples—Christianity versus "whooping and yelling"—is an elementary recognition of cultural integrity. Despite his lack of firsthand experience, despite the thoroughgoing romanticism of his plots, with however little intellectual sophistication and in however contradictory a fashion, Cooper produced a fictional testament to his conditional respect for other cultures on their own terms.

Cooper stood with a distinct minority in the 1830s and 1840s. Contemporaries had as much difficulty in conceding the cultural terms of his fictions as they did, say, in accepting that the great ancient American cultures were indigenous, not introduced. Only in the 1880s would John Wesley Powell and Cyrus Thomas finally dispel the myth of a supposedly white-skinned race—the mound builders—exterminated by Indian savages. Yet George Catlin and Albert Gallatin had authoritatively declared half a century earlier that the very ancestors of nineteenth-century Indians had built the impressive ruins.[26] Similarly, their perceptive contemporaries, Alexander Bradford and Theodore Parker, had been quick to recognize the sophistication of the great civilizations of Central and South America, the Toltecs, Aztecs, and Incas. Parker, in fact, quarreled at length with William Hickling Prescott's monumental *History of the Conquest of Mexico* (1843) for its bland defense of Cortez's vile depredations and its patronizing attitude toward an Aztec civilization Parker considered the equal of Spain's.[27]

As mentioned in Chapter Six, the most successful popularizer of these radical concepts, John Lloyd Stephens, discovered and described many ancient Mayan ruins in the early 1840s. But he did far more. His boldly documented and marvelously illustrated claim for the autonomy of a native Indian civilization, its superb complexity and high sophistication, refuted the notion of Indians as simple, primitive, or barbarically savage. In the first of his two Mayan books, *Incidents of Travel in Central American, Chiapas, and Yucatan* (1841), he described his response to the massive temple at Copan, the first site he uncovered:

[26] Catlin, *Life Among the Indians* (London: Gall and Inglis, 187?), p. 21; Albert Gallatin, "A Synopsis of the Indian Tribes in North America," *Archaeologica Americana: Transactions and Collections of the American Antiquarian Society*, 2 (1836), 6, 147. See above, Chapter Six, p. 157, for a discussion of nineteenth-century interest in the mound builders.

[27] Alexander W. Bradford, *American Antiquities and Researches into the Origin and History of the Red Race* (New York: Dayton and Saxton, 1841), p. 72; Theodore Parker, "Prescott's Conquest of Mexico" (1849), reprinted in Theodore Parker, *The American Scholar*, ed. George Willis Cooke (Boston: American Unitarian Association, 1907), pp. 248-49, 265.

America, say historians, was peopled by savages; but savages never reared these structures, savages never carved these stones. When we asked the Indians who had made them, their dull answer was "Quién sabe? (Who knows?)" There were no associations connected with the place. . . . But architecture, sculpture, and painting, all the arts which embellish life, had flourished in this overgrown forest; orators, warriors, and statesmen, beauty, ambition, and glory had lived and passed away, and none knew that such things had been, or could tell of their past existence. Books, the records of knowledge, are silent on this theme.[28]

Stephens went on to offer persuasive reasons why this culture had to have been indigenous and to show its approximation to the glory of ancient Greece and Egypt. Indeed, his sensitivity to the ruins was as important, finally, as his documentation of them.

Yet the idea that *contemporary* Indian tribes also had intricate cultures gained popular acceptance far less readily, despite increasing numbers of individual proponents. Before mid-century, most ridiculed native cultures as at best a fiction of romantic sensibilities, at worst, an impediment to quick acculturation.[29] Institutions like the Carlisle School for Indians (and its counterpart, Hampton Institute for blacks) persisted in turning their charges into motivated bourgeois. At the same time, however, whites were increasingly recognizing Indian cultures for what they actually were and not merely for what they initially appeared to be. Their mysteriously complex structures began at last to demand fuller respect.

THE NEED FOR INTELLIGENT CAUTION

By the time Melville sardonically inveighed against the complacent ethnologist to a broad popular readership, others were also refusing to slip into the trap of unverifiable hypotheses. This cautious response became commonplace only late in the nineteenth century; even today, the full extent of necessary caution continues to trouble anthropologists. Yet Stephens, Melville, and other careful students of alien cultures established for ethnologists a pattern of continuous, self-conscious uncertainty that Clifford Geertz regards as basic to the science:

[28] Stephens, *Incidents of Travel in Central America, Chiapas, and Yucatan* (1841), ed. Richard L. Predmore, 2 vols. (New Brunswick: Rutgers University Press, 1949), 1:80-81. See also Victor Von Hagan, *Maya Explorer: John Lloyd Stephens* (Norman: University of Oklahoma Press, 1947), pp. 195-96.

[29] See, for a good description of these attitudes, Pearce, *Savagism and Civilization*, pp. 96-97; see also pp. 105ff.

"Cultural analysis is intrinsically incomplete. And, worse than that, the more deeply it goes the less complete it is. It is a strange science whose most telling assertions are its most tremulously based, in which to get somewhere with the matter at hand is to intensify the suspicion, both your own and that of others, that you are not quite getting it right. But that, along with plaguing subtle people with obtuse questions, is what being an ethnographer is like."[30] The very fact of recognizing one's informants as "subtle people" "plagued" by one's questions suggests a perspective too sensitive by half for ethnographers to appreciate until late in the nineteenth century.

Yet long before Geertz, many observers suffered honest, intelligent confusion about the peoples they studied, recognizing a more startling complexity to native life than any proposed in the fictions of alleged authorities. Captain James Cook, that most intrepid of eighteenth-century explorers, repeatedly acknowledged the inadequacy of his observations made in the Pacific. As James Boswell noted after breakfasting with the celebrated voyager, "He candidly confessed to me that he and his companions who visited the South Sea Islands could not be certain of any information they got, or supposed they got, except as to objects falling under the observation of the senses; their knowledge of the language was so imperfect they required the aid of their senses, and anything which they learnt about religion, government, or traditions might be quite erroneous."[31] As in so many other respects, Cook stood nearly alone, his exemplary caution imitated by few contemporaries.

By 1819, Reverend Jarvis, in his speech before the New-York Historical Society, could set forth certain ethnographic principles for those pursuing field research:

> If we wish to see him in his original character, we must follow him to his native forests. —There, surely, he is worthy of our attention.
>
> The Indians themselves are not communicative in relation to their religion; and it requires a good deal of familiar, attentive, and I may add, unsuspected observation, to obtain any knowledge respecting it. Hence, many who have been transiently resident among them, have very confidently pronounced, that they have no religion, an assertion, which subsequent and more accurate travellers have shown to be entirely unfounded.

[30] Geertz, *Interpretation of Cultures*, p. 29.
[31] James Boswell, *Boswell: The Ominous Years, 1774-1776*, ed. Charles Ryskamp and Frederick Pottle (New York: McGraw-Hill, 1963), p. 341.

Those, also, on whom we rely for information, have either been too little informed to know what to observe, or they have been influenced by peculiar modes of thinking, which have given a tinge to all they have said on the subject.[32]

Jarvis, more deliberately than Cook and long before Geertz, encouraged intelligent respect for tribal cultures. Only the dull and insensitive would assume easy access to them.

By the mid-1830s, even someone as inexperienced as Washington Irving espoused these principles. Rewriting the notes of fur magnate John Jacob Astor into *Astoria* (1836), he at one point remarked, "The religious belief of these people was extremely limited and confined," but quickly added, "or rather, in all probability, their explanations were but little understood by their visitors."[33] Having never seen the tribes, Irving nonetheless assumed their integrity and therefore the inaccuracy of the traders' reports. In spite of such isolated statements on the one hand, however, or the widely popular example of John Lloyd Stephens on the other, this attitude took hold only in the period following the Civil War, when it received the encouragement of professionals such as Powell, Grinnell, Hale, and Bandelier.[34]

One major pitfall of ethnographic research, then, was to assume too little, reducing native behavior to barely more than irrational impulse. Another danger, more problematic because less readily discernible, was to assume too much. As the painter Frederic Remington counseled about tribes of the Southwest, "The searching of the ethnologist must not penetrate his thoughts too rapidly, or he will find that he is reasoning for the Indian, and not with him."[35] Lewis Henry Morgan, the father of American anthropology, best articulated this resistance to facile ethnological interpretation in 1876. He flailed earlier recorders for succumbing to imaginative sentimentality: "Ig-

[32] Samuel Farmar Jarvis, *A Discourse on the Religion of the Indian Tribes of North America. Delivered Before the New-York Historical Society, Dec. 20, 1819* (New York: C. Wiley and Co., 1820), pp. 7-8.

[33] Irving, *Astoria, or Anecdotes of an Enterprise Beyond the Rocky Mountains*, ed. Edgeley W. Todd (Norman: University of Oklahoma Press, 1964), p. 334.

[34] Darrah, *Powell of the Colorado*, p. 255; Grinnell, *Pawnee Hero Stories*, pp. xi-xii; Horatio Hale, ed., *The Iroquois Book of Rites* (1883), ed. William N. Fenton (Toronto: University of Toronto Press, 1963), p. 37; Adolph F. Bandelier, "Final Report of Investigations among the Indians of the Southwestern United States," pt. 1, *Papers of the Archaeological Institute of America, American Series*, 3, (1890), 316. See also Gilbert Malcolm Sproat, *Scenes and Studies of Savage Life* (London: Smith, Elder and Co., 1868), p. 203; Stevenson, *Zuñi Indians*, pp. 607-8.

[35] Frederic Remington, "On the Indian Reservations," *Century Magazine*, 38 (July 1889), 400. See also the entry for October 30 in C. F. Saunders, Pocket Diary for 1909 Tour, Box 9, Saunders Collection, Huntington Library.

norant of its [Indian culture's] structure and principles, and unable to comprehend its peculiarities, they invoked the imagination to supply whatever was necessary to fill out the picture. When the reason, from want of facts, is unable to understand and therefore to explain the structure of a given society, imagination walks bravely in and fearlessly rears its glittering fabric to the sky."[36]

Morgan's caveat made eminent sense to increasing numbers of Americans in the next thirty years, who learned for themselves what Thoreau, Catlin, and Melville had discovered at least thirty years before.[37] One absolutely had to maintain cautious respect, to withhold judgment, neither assuming little nor imagining much, in order to come to understand the far more profound imaginative reaches of the people under study. Increasing familiarity with certain tribes led whites to remark with increasing frequency an indefinable, even recondite quality. A whole array of curiously implicit laws dictated social behavior. Particular occasions could not be isolated; they were enmeshed in a web of cultural assumptions that vibrated at every point when touched at one. As an army colonel later admitted about his fascination with Plains Indian religions in the 1870s, "One peculiarity of a people grows out of or is involved in, other peculiarities, and I soon found that I could give no explanation of the Indian religion which would be satisfactory even to myself, without a thorough knowledge of all his other characteristics and peculiarities. From the study of his religion I began to study the man."[38] Though frustration in this case led to renewed efforts, in many others it produced only a deepened sense of inadequacy.

By the early 1890s, the finest early anthropologist to work among the Hopi had lost nearly all confidence in his ability to understand

---

[36] Morgan, "Montezuma's Dinner," *North American Review*, 122 (1876), 268.

[37] Thoreau, *The Maine Woods* (1864), ed. Joseph J. Moldenhauer (Princeton: Princeton University Press, 1972), pp. 178-79; Catlin, *Life Among the Indians*, p. 9. See also Brinton, *Essays of an Americanist*, pp. iii-iv, 103; John C. Ewers, "Jean Louis Berlandier: A French Scientist among the Wild Comanches of Texas in 1828," in McDermott, ed., *Travelers on the Western Frontier*, esp. pp. 296-99; *Selected Prose of John Wesley Powell*, ed. George Crossette (Boston: David R. Godine, 1970), p. 115; Curtis, *North American Indian*, 1:xv-xvi.

[38] Dodge, *Our Wild Indians*, p. 40. See also John T. Flanagan, introduction to William Joseph Snelling, *Tales of the Northwest* (1830; rpt. Minneapolis: University of Minnesota Press, 1936), pp. xviii-xix; William Philo Clark, *The Indian Sign Language, with Brief Explanatory Notes . . .* (Philadelphia: L. R. Hamersly and Co., 1884), pp. 13-17; Col. Randolph B. Marcy, *Thirty Years of Army Life on the Border* (New York: Harper and Brothers, 1866), pp. 101ff.; Francis Parkman, *The Conspiracy of Pontiac and the Indian War after the Conquest of Canada* (1851), vols. 16-18 of the Champlain Edition of *The Works of Francis Parkman* (Boston: Little, Brown and Co., 1898), 16:43; Alfred Robinson, *Life in California* (New York: Wiley and Putnam, 1846), pp. 235-36.

them. "The *Journal* is primarily a record of the ceremonial life," observes the editor of Alexander Stephen's *Hopi Journal*, "which is so full and so elaborated that it causes the Journalist to exclaim in despair that it is beyond the compass of a man's lifetime to understand and that it argues the possession of a sixth sense in the townspeople whom he finds at times very dull, i.e. unresponsive to his own terms of thought. It is the integration of the ceremonial life with the general life which is his despair, and ours."[39] Naturally, part of this mysteriousness in Indian behavior was due to the native's fear that by explaining activities he would expose to the white outsider not just himself, in the sense of personal privacy, but his source of being, his access to divine power. Among others, James Swan and Lieutenant Amiel Weeks Whipple had inferred this motive behind what the photographer Edward Curtis termed "the deep-rooted superstition, conservatism, and secretiveness so characteristic of primitive people, who are ever loath to afford a glimpse of their inner life to those who are not of their own."[40] Furthermore, only privileged figures—the sachems, society priests, and chiefs—fully understood sacred rituals or had access to the most cherished of cultural secrets.

Captain John G. Bourke, stationed in the Southwest for fifteen years, also discovered fierce native resistance to the inquiries he pursued in his spare time among local tribes. The research that proved unusually difficult for him, later published as *The Snake-Dance of the Moquis of Arizona* (1884), describes one of the most famous of all tribal ceremonies, during the most compelling moments of which dancers hold rattlesnakes in their mouths. Explaining the Moqui (or Hopi) tribe's animus toward him, Bourke vividly recalls the explanation offered by an "unusually bright Indian" named Nanahe:

> "You must not ask me to give you any information about that order. I am a member of it. It is a secret order, and under no circumstances can any of its secrets be made known. Very few

39 Elsie Clews Parsons, introduction to *Hopi Journal of Alexander M. Stephen*, ed. Parsons, 2 vols. (New York: Columbia University Press, 1936), 1:xlviii. See also *David Thompson's Narrative of His Explorations in Western America, 1784-1812*, ed. Joseph Burr Tyrrell (Toronto: Champlain Society, 1916), pp. 81-82; Charles Alexander Eastman, *Indian Boyhood* (1902; rpt. Boston: Little, Brown and Co., 1918), p. 181.

40 Curtis, *North American Indian*, 1:xiv. See also Swan, *The Northwest Coast*, pp. 151-52; Lt. Amiel Weeks Whipple, *Reports on Explorations and Surveys . . .*, Senate Executive Documents, 33d Cong., 2d sess., 185?, vol. 3, no. 78, p. 104; Bourke, *Snake-Dance of the Moquis*, p. 14; Catlin, *Letters and Notes*, 1:8-9; Charles G. Leland, "Legends of the Passamaquoddy," *Century Magazine*, 28 (September 1884), 676; J. Walter Fewkes, "Summer Ceremonials at Zuni Pueblo," *Journal of American Ethnology and Archaeology*, 1 (1891), 1n; Bandelier, "Final Report," pt. 1, p. 6.

people, even among the Moquis, know anything about it, and its members would be more careful to keep its affairs from the knowledge of the Moquis, not members, than they would from you. . . . We tell all sorts of stories to outsiders, even in Moqui.

"Of course that is lying, but if we adopted any other course our secrets wouldn't be kept very long. You must not get angry at me for speaking thus to you, but I cannot tell you what you want to know, and I don't want to deceive you."[41]

Momentarily, Nanahe's apologetic explanation shifts in tone as he severely rebukes Bourke's apparent lack of consideration for Hopi values and beliefs:

"We saw you writing down everything as you sat in the Estufa, and we knew that you had all that man could learn from his eyes. We didn't like to have you down there. No other man has ever shown so little regard for what we thought, but we knew that you had come there under orders, and that you were only doing what you thought you ought to do to learn all about our ceremonies. So we concluded to let you stay.

"No man—no man"—(with much emphasis) "has ever seen what you have seen—what you have seen—and I don't think that any stranger will ever see it again. One of our strictest rules is never to shake hands with a stranger while this business is going on, but you shook hands with nearly all of us, and you shook them very hard too. There never was a man who took notes of the dance while it was going on until you did; any one who says he did tells a lie."[42]

As any reader will discover, Bourke conveys extreme sensitivity, especially for Hopi efforts to defend the integrity of their sacred institutions. His very recounting of this reproach bears out that impression.

Wordsworth's phrase, "We murder to dissect," might have seemed an apt characterization of Bourke's and others' efforts. The information they acquired could never evoke the ineffable sense of the living social organism. Yet without their attempts, which themselves threatened cultural integrity, native traditions would have fallen into the grave of unrecorded history. If tribal resistance spurred them to haste,

---

[41] Bourke, *Snake-Dance of the Moquis*, pp. 180-81.

[42] Ibid., pp. 181-82. See also Bourke, "The Medicine-Men of the Apaches," in Bureau of American Ethnology, *Ninth Annual Report, 1887-88* (Washington: G.P.O., 1892), p. 451; Frederick Webb Hodge, "In Memoriam—John Gregory Bourke," *Journal of American Folk-Lore*, 9 (1896), 141. For a similar exclamation from a native, see Margaret Mead, *Ruth Benedict* (New York: Columbia University Press, 1974), pp. 31-32.

however, it also encouraged a more intelligent spirit of inquiry, tempered by renewed respect. Early in the twentieth century, Dr. Charles Eastman listed his reasons for describing his religious life prior to his conversion to Christianity. He felt as George Copway had half a century earlier: haste alone would not help whites to acquire a record of sacred lore.

> The religion of the Indian is the last thing about him that the man of another race will ever understand.
>
> First, the Indian does not speak of these deep matters so long as he believes in them, and when he has ceased to believe he speaks inaccurately and slightingly.
>
> Second, even if he can be induced to speak, the racial and religious prejudice of the other stands in the way of his sympathetic comprehension.
>
> Third, practically all existing studies on this subject have been made during the transition period, when the original beliefs and philosophy of the native American were already undergoing rapid disintegration.[43]

Deeper significances than met the eye required, paradoxically, both haste and caution from white observers desiring to understand tribal cultures as they truly persisted.

THE NEED FOR INTIMATE ASSOCIATION

That tribal life would ever elude simple, straightforward attempts at understanding led to the corollary recognition of the need to suspend cultural bias. Only by adopting a native perspective, or coming as close to it as possible, could one comprehend the strength of tribal culture. By 1884, the observation by a student of native sign languages that "one must train the mind to *think* like the Indians" before drawing conclusions may well have seemed commonplace.[44] More than half a century earlier, in 1830, a redeemed Indian captive had noted even more pointedly, "It is quite impossible that any one, who has not been among and 'of' the North American Indians, should be able to form even a tolerable idea of the extent to which they are acted upon by their superstitions."[45] During the years spanned by these

43 Eastman, *The Soul of the Indian: An Interpretation* (Boston: Houghton Mifflin Co., 1911), foreword (unpaginated); George Copway, *The Life, History, and Travels of Kah-Ge-Ga-Gah-Bowh* (Albany: n.p., 1847), p. 55.

44 Clark, *Indian Sign Language*, p. 17, also pp. 18-19.

45 James Athearn Jones, *Traditions of the North American Indians*, 3 vols. (1830; rpt. Upper Saddle River, N.J.: Literature House, 1970), 1:x-xi. See also Jean Louis

two statements, scores of ethnographers and historians sought to unravel the mysteries of tribal life.

Of course, many refused to consider the native perspective, among them William Hickling Prescott: as his *Conquest of Mexico* suggests, their work suffered for that refusal.[46] On the other hand, some put aside an initial skepticism to find themselves deeply moved by native customs and modes. Dr. Washington Matthews, one of America's finest field ethnographers, came to cherish a particular admiration for the Southwest Pueblo tribes, and he revealed their complexity in a series of careful studies to a scientific community still beset with monographs dismissing native art and religion as puerile. For more than eight years in the 1880s and 1890s, Matthews devoted all his spare time to studying native life near Fort Wingate in the heart of Navaho country. Initially delighted with weaving and silverwork, his interest in physical anthropology gave way to a fascination with the impressive Navaho chants that his best later work examines. Matthews discovered that his sensibilities grew more refined as he attended more carefully and that what he first took for a "succession of grunts" revealed themselves to an educated ear as an extraordinarily sophisticated body of lore: "thousands of significant songs—or poems as they might be called—which have been composed with care and handed down, for centuries perhaps, from teacher to pupil, from father to son, as a precious heritage."[47]

Understandably, chants presented an almost impenetrable experience for white listeners, however fully they wanted to cross cultural boundaries. Musical conventions are far more arbitrary than representational artistic modes, far less satisfying to any but initiates, and even Matthews could cultivate little more than an intellectual appreciation. The account Alice C. Fletcher offered of the Omaha is all the more surprising, then, in its encompassingly emotional quality. A brilliant anthropologist devoted to the study of Indian music, Miss Fletcher long afterwards recalled her initial work in the early 1880s:

> My first studies were crude and full of difficulties, difficulties that I afterward learned were bred of preconceived ideas, the

Berlandier *The Indians of Texas in 1830*, trans. Patricia Reading Leclercq, ed. John C. Ewers (Washington: Smithsonian Institution, 1969), pp. 11, 22; Edwin Thompson Denig, *Five Indian Tribes of the Upper Missouri*, ed. John C. Ewers (Norman: University of Oklahoma Press, 1961), pp. xxxi-xxxii.

[46] See Keen, *Aztec Image*, p. 363. Harry B. Henderson III, in *Versions of the Past: The Historical Imagination in American Fiction* (New York: Oxford University Press, 1974), p. 32, offers an alternative interpretation.

[47] Actually, these are the words of a Dr. Jona Letherman in an 1856 report, revised and published by Dr. Washington Matthews as "Songs of the Navajos" in *Land of Sunshine*, 5 (October 1896), 197; see also p. 201.

influence of generally accepted theories concerning "savage" music. . . . For a considerable time I was more inclined to distrust my ears than my theories, but when I strove to find facts that would agree with these theories I met only failure. . . . During these investigations I was stricken with a severe illness and lay for months ministered to in part by Indian friends. While I was thus shut in from the rest of the world . . . they would often at my request sing for me. They sang softly because I was weak, and there was no drum, and then it was that the distraction of noise and confusion of theory were dispelled, and the sweetness, the beauty and meaning of these songs were revealed to me.[48]

Matthews's and Fletcher's famous contemporary in American anthropology, Daniel G. Brinton, spoke more generally along these lines in 1890: "Savage symbolism is rich and is expressed both in object and word; and what appears cruelty, puerility or obscenity assumes a very different aspect when regarded from the correct, the native, point of view, with a full knowledge of the surroundings and the intentions of the myth-makers themselves."[49] At the same time, the only way to learn "the correct, the native, point of view" was to move in their closed world for extended periods. Or, in the words of one amateur ethnologist as early as 1830, "a man must live, emphatically, *live*, with Indians; share with them their lodges, their food, and their blankets, for years, before he can comprehend their ideas, or enter into their feelings."[50] The implicit corollary to this injunction is that only by living with them can the white alien be trusted enough for natives to open up to him. George Belden among the Plains tribes, Henry Boller with the Minnetarees, James G. Swan among the Pacific Northwest Chinooks, George Bird Grinnell among the Pawnee, and Adolph Bandelier, Captain John G. Bourke, Alexander M. Stephen, and in particular, Frank Hamilton Cushing with the Southwest Pueblo tribes—these are only some of the more notable among a wide variety of people who forsook white ways, if only temporarily, in order to gain more complete access to native modes.[51]

[48] Alice C. Fletcher, "A Study of Omaha Indian Music," *Archaeological and Ethnological Papers of the Peabody Museum*, 1, no. 5 (June 1893), 8.

[49] Brinton, *Essays of an Americanist*, p. 103. See also Dwight W. Hoover, *The Red and the Black* (Chicago: Rand McNally, 1976), p. 162; Thoreau, *The Maine Woods*, ed. Moldenhauer, p. 237.

[50] Snelling, *Tales of the Northwest*, p. 3.

[51] George P. Belden, *Belden, The White Chief; or Twelve Years Among the Wild Indians of the Plains*, ed. Gen. James S. Brisbin (1870; rpt. Cincinnati: E. W. Starr and Co., 1875), pp. 90ff.; Boller, *Among the Indians*, p. 48; Swan, *The Northwest Coast*, p. 148; Grinnell, *Pawnee Hero Stories*. See as well Thomas P. Wentworth, *Early*

In his flamboyant yet mysterious fashion, Cushing best embodies the different strains of this chapter. More brilliantly than any person before and most since, he comprehended the inner life of a native American culture, experiencing it as few others had from within. Curiously, the career he forged for himself precisely fits the famous definition Crèvecoeur offered for an American: *"He* is an American, who, leaving behind him all his ancient prejudices and manners, receives new ones from the new mode of life he has embraced."[52] Cushing's new "prejudices and manners" made him, in a way the eighteenth-century farmer-philosopher could never have imagined, the most extraordinary figure in the history of American anthropology.

Born in western New York State in 1857, Cushing suffered frail health all his life and died prematurely in 1900. By the time he was fourteen, he owned an impressive collection of pre-Columbian arrowheads; at seventeen, he published his first article on Indian folklore. Though largely self-taught, he was appointed a year later to the Smithsonian as an assistant in ethnology. By the age of twenty, Cushing had already gained an enviable reputation among anthropologists. Joining the Bureau of American Ethnology in 1879, he accompanied an expedition that fall to the Southwest, where he became fascinated with the secretive Zuni tribe. A decade after John Wesley Powell had seen them, the Zuni remained of all tribes the least influenced by white settlers. Others in the expedition collected artifacts and took photographs and notes. (A *Harper's* journalist reported their efforts in the long familiar terms of loss, necessity of haste, and danger of naiveté.)[53] But Cushing quickly chafed against the tribe's close-lipped resistance in matters of apparent internal importance. "Much dis-

---

Life Among the Indians: Reminiscences from the Life of Benjamin G. Armstrong (Ashland, Wis.: A. W. Bowron, 1891), esp. p. 147; James Willard Schultz, *My Life as an Indian: The Story of a Red Woman and a White Man in the Lodge of the Black-feet* (1906-07; rpt. Boston: Houghton Mifflin Co., 1914), pp. iii, 6, 45; Daniel W. Jones, *Forty Years Among the Indians* (Salt Lake City: Juvenile Instructor Office, 1890), pp. 363-64; Walter Hough, *The Moki Snake Dance* (Chicago: Passenger Department, Santa Fe Route, 1898), pp. 50-51.

[52] Crèvecoeur, *Letters from an American Farmer* (1782; rpt. New York: E. P. Dutton, 1957), p. 39.

[53] Sylvester Baxter, "The Father of the Pueblos," *Harper's New Monthly Magazine*, 65 (June 1882), 75. Baxter's two articles on Cushing—this one and "An Aboriginal Pilgrimage," *Century Magazine* 24 (August 1882), 526-36—are the best contemporary accounts. For the most judicious biography of Cushing, see Jessie Green's introduction to *Zuni: Selected Writings of Frank Hamilton Cushing*, ed. Green (Lincoln: University of Nebraska Press, 1979), pp. 3-34. The following account was written prior to my reading of Green but has been partially revised according to his findings. See also Fagan, *Elusive Treasure*, pp. 248-55.

couraged," he later wrote of his first months there, "at last I determined to try living with the Indians."[54]

Surprising both his white colleagues and the Zuni, Cushing decided to move into the pueblo, remaining as anthropology's first "participant observer" after the expedition completed its two-month investigation. "Until I could overcome the suspicion and secure the full confidence of the Indians," he noted, "it would be impossible to gain any knowledge of importance regarding their inner life."[55] Despite his fears of being reduced to a "doomed exile," Cushing took an increasing part in tribal activities and doggedly learned to speak the difficult language. The Zuni accepted him, but only on their own terms, expecting to make him one of them. They were dismayed by Cushing's ever present sketchbook—just as Bourke's notebook had alienated the Hopi—and finally decided to use physical means to oppose this crude invasion of their cultural life. The sacred dance called the Kca-k'ok-shi was about to begin when Cushing found himself cornered in his room:

> "Leave your books and pencils behind, then," said they.
>
> "No, I must carry them wherever I go."
>
> "If you put the shadows of the great dance down on the leaves of your books to-day, we shall cut them to pieces," they threatened.
>
> Suddenly wrenching away from them, I pulled a knife out from the bottom of my pouch, and, bracing up against the wall, brandished it, and said that whatever hand grabbed my arm again would be cut off, that whoever cut my books to pieces would only cut himself to pieces with my knife. It was a doubtful game of bluff, but the chiefs fell back a little, and I darted through the door. Although they followed me throughout the whole day, they did not again offer to molest me, but the people gathered so closely around me that I could scarcely find opportunity for sketching.[56]

After the Zuni's initial wariness passed, Cushing acquired close friends, assumed full Zuni costume, and accepted foster parents. Similarly, when he set aside his own notions of taboo and allowed his ears to be pierced, he was adopted into the Macaw clan and given the name Ténatsali, or Medicine Flower, a name that "only one man in a

---

[54] Cushing, "My Adventures in Zuni," *Century Magazine*, 25 (December 1882), 199.

[55] Ibid., p. 204.

[56] Ibid., p. 205.

generation could bear."[57] For four and a half years Cushing lived in full acceptance among the tribe, participating in sacred ceremonies, serving on the tribal council, and even gaining admittance to a secret medicine fraternity. His most notable distinction came in 1881, with his initiation into the Priesthood of the Bow, one of the most esoteric orders and the most powerful. According to his biographer, "As he improved his knowledge of the language and assimilated the complexities of the Zuni social order, he assumed an influential role in the government of the tribe. And, a gifted raconteur, he became not only a recognized authority in matters of Zuni history, myth, and ceremony but a favorite among the tribal storytellers, making contributions of his own to the collective story."[58] Perceptive, intelligent, and sensitive, Cushing achieved far greater participation than any other white, even more than most Zuni, advancing in the priesthood to assistant chief. Ultimately, after taking the requisite enemy scalp—probably the only scientist to do so in the line of duty—he was made head war chief.

Suddenly, in early 1894, Cushing left Zuni without public explanation, never to return. White Americans were both fascinated and confused by this long-haired, earringed man, the only person in history to justifiably identify himself, as he once officially did, with the double title "1st War Chief of Zuni, U.S. Asst. Ethnologist."[59] In fact, Cushing had been officially recalled for having successfully defended Zuni land rights against powerful federal interests, thereby jeopardizing the Bureau of American Ethnology itself. But these circumstances were unknown to readers of *Century* and *Atlantic*, whose interest had been excited by Cushing's descriptions of his exotic experiences. Nor was the public aware of his recurrent illnesses, which only confirmed his chronic inability to complete written reports. All they knew was that he seemed voluntarily to refrain from publishing everything but a score or so of pieces from his vast collection of materials. He never organized that collection, never catalogued his many masks and dolls, and never completed his fine study of Zuni mythology. The volumes he did publish, along with his manuscripts, suggest Cushing's profound insight into Zuni culture. They also underscore the painful loss to anthropology of a wealth of unrecorded knowledge and experiences. It was as if a door had been shut firmly on the finest five years of nineteenth-century ethnology.

[57] Cushing, "My Adventures in Zuni. II.," *Century Magazine*, 26 (February 1883), 511.

[58] Green, introduction to Cushing, *Zuni*, ed. Green, p. 10.

[59] Ibid., pp. 5-6.

During the next two years, Cushing pursued archaeological investigation along the Gila and Salt Rivers in Arizona, before ill health in the winter of 1888-1889 forced him to leave the region forever.[60] He never again achieved the acceptance he had won among the Zuni in the early 1880s. Thomas Eakins's famous 1895 portrait of the thirty-eight-year-old ethnologist reveals a lanky, melancholy figure apparently locked in memories evoked by the Zuni fetishes that surround him. Eakins's biographer has written that the painting "celebrates a disappearing culture and the dying man who devoted his life to studying it. Tragic possibility is written in Cushing's face, in an understanding that is beyond solace and in the emaciated figure of the man. . . . The man exists alone and in the broader experience of the age, expressing his reverence for a civilization being engulfed and destroyed in nineteenth-century America."[61]

This interpretation somewhat sentimentalizes Cushing's actual response to the Zuni, whom he did not think were declining, either numerically or culturally. (He even subscribed to a mild form of cultural evolutionism, and thought a more advanced white culture should eventually assimilate the Zuni.) Yet like other ethnologists, he found much in native culture superior to his own, including ethical, spiritual, and even agricultural knowledge. He wanted to make available to his white contemporaries the system of Zuni philosophy within its cultural context, but his inability to reveal so much of what his intelligent, persistent efforts had unveiled may have been owing to more than merely constitutional reasons.[62] Informed speculation leads to the conclusion that he may consciously have refused to publicize important materials. Like the priests who attempted to prevent him from taking notes during his first months in Zuni, he certainly came to appreciate the intricate, fragile balance of belief with mystery, significant gesture with sacred knowledge. True cultural relativism may never be attainable, as modern anthropologists affirm. To the extent that Cushing chose between the alternatives of white openness and native secrecy, he embraced the latter.

For other ethnologists, if apparently not for Cushing, tribal life hardly could support theories of progressive social stages in an evolutionary spectrum of cultures. Increasingly, it appeared structured by

[60] For a description of Cushing's contributions to archaeology in these years, see Gordon R. Willey and Jeremy A. Sabloff, *A History of American Archaeology* (London: Thames and Hudson, 1974), pp. 59-60, 114.

[61] Sylven Schendler, *Eakins* (Boston: Little, Brown and Co., 1967), p. 137; see also p. 136.

[62] See, for evidence supporting the claims of this paragraph, Cushing, *Zuni*, ed. Green, pp. 145, 166, 184, 218, 252-54, 427-28.

22. Thomas Eakins, *Frank Hamilton Cushing*, 1894-1895. Oil on canvas. The Thomas Gilcrease Institute of American History and Art, Tulsa, Oklahoma.

institutions whose complexity rivaled and surpassed that of institutions in supposedly more advanced societies. Though less flexible, perhaps less "intelligent" or "rational" than that of western Europe, native American cultures could also manifest an integrity, a significance, a value for their members in ways more satisfying. As Melville had discovered, those whites who allowed themselves to accept that possibility and to share that perspective found that the tables might be turned. "Indian tribes look upon the whites as an inferior race," observed one midwesterner in 1868 after having lived with the Minnetaree tribe, "pretty much in the same light that we formerly regarded plantation negroes."[63]

THE PROSPECT OF CULTURAL RELATIVISM

The notions that native Americans could make serious judgments on white institutions and patterns and that, by extension, white Americans might assess western European civilization from the perspective of native ones set the terms for a fourth way of looking at culture. Before the nineteenth century, expressions such as Benjamin Franklin's on the "Savage" perspective reflect a certain abstract admiration for native life.[64] Yet this incipient relativism had negligible influence, in part because real tolerance for particular native institutions was too wholly constrained by Western assumptions. Circumspect questions about cultural variations would rarely be posed until well into the nineteenth century, much less answered. Even then, recognition of the complex autonomy of native cultures developed slowly and uncertainly among the most perceptive and willing of whites. Since the perspective that true cultural relativism allows depends upon a prior acknowledgment of cultural autonomy, insights more informed than Franklin's had to wait half a century.

An assortment of important discoveries encouraged this new attitude, especially those in the fields of comparative religion and mythology. Such investigations, along with those in biology and geography, "turned much of Western Scripture from historical fact into metaphorical or psychological fact—or, perhaps, mere fancy."[65] That the psychological bases for Western civilization differed little from those for any other culture was one of the most radical ideas to emerge in the late nineteenth century. Again, the implication is not what many liberal thinkers have often believed, that beneath outer

[63] Boller, *Among the Indians*, p. 54.
[64] See above, p. 218.
[65] Franklin, *Wake of the Gods*, p. 3.

cultural forms all humans share a common psychological nature: "No
two languages are ever sufficiently similar to be considered as rep-
resenting the same social reality," Edward Sapir noted in a different
context half a century ago. "The worlds in which different societies
live are distinct worlds, not merely the same world with different
labels attached."[66] On the other hand, differences between societies reveal nothing about differences in supposed racial capacities or pre-
dispositions.

More than a few came to suspect that savagery and civilization
were not absolute conditions but relative states, or, as one man described them in 1843, matters of "taste."[67] Partly, this suspicion grew
as people recognized "the weakness of arbitrary technological criteria
of cultural progress."[68] The San Francisco bibliophile and amateur
historian Hubert Howe Bancroft attacked Lewis Henry Morgan's
deprecatory assessment of the Aztecs on these very terms. What, he
asked in 1883, was meant by "half-civilization, or quarter-civiliza-
tion, or wholly civilized? A half-civilized nation is a nation half as
civilized as ours. But is our civilization fully civilized?"[69] Others also
recognized, some more pointedly and in detail, that whites could by no
means claim sole possession of superior knowledge and that native
tribes had often served as instructors. "It is the common cry among us,"
declared one historian in 1825, "that the savage must now at length be
taught to till the ground, to sow, and to reap; we all the while forget-
ting that it was the same savage who actually taught the European
emigrant how to cultivate the American soil, to clear the stubborn forest by degrees, and to grow that valuable grain, the maize, or Indian
corn; and that the farmers even of the present day . . . do little more
than follow the agricultural lessons taught to their progenitors by the
Indians."[70]

Alfred W. Crosby and Virgil J. Vogel have detailed the enormous
debt incurred by European settlers to native Americans, especially in

[66] Sapir, "Linguistics," *Language*, 5 (1929), epigraph, cited in Drinnon, *White
Savage*, p. 125.

[67] Felix O. C. Darley, *Scenes in Indian Life*, 4 nos. (Philadelphia: J. R. Colon,
April-July 1843), no. 2, May 1843.

[68] Keen, *Aztec Image*, p. 391.

[69] Hubert Howe Bancroft, *The Early American Chroniclers* (San Francisco: A. L.
Bancroft and Co., 1883), p. 10. See also Kevin Starr, *Americans and the California
Dream, 1850-1915* (New York: Oxford University Press, 1973), p. 125; Keen, *Aztec
Image*, pp. 403ff.; John Walton Caughey, *Hubert Howe Bancroft, Historian of the
West* (Berkeley: University of California Press, 1946), pp. 122ff.

[70] John Halkett, *Historical Notes Respecting the Indians of North America* . . .
(London: Archibald Constable and Co., 1825), p. 325, also pp. 2, 26, 338.

medicine and agriculture.[71] Cooper dramatized this debt from a more sardonic perspective in his first Leatherstocking novel. *The Pioneers* early presents the Mohican healer Chingachgook and Dr. Elnathon Todd jointly attending the wounded young hero. Not only are Todd's ministrations revealed as patently ineffective, but he unashamedly steals the Indian's medicinal ointments. As the narrator observes, "It was fortunate for Dr. Todd that his principles were so liberal, as, coupled with his practice, they were the means by which he acquired all his knowledge, and by which he was gradually qualifying himself for the duties of his profession."[72] Less wryly, but no less aware of equivalent cultural differences, Thoreau remarked in the late 1850s, "One revelation has been made to the Indian, another to the white man. I have much to learn of the Indian, nothing of the missionary. I am not sure but all that would tempt me to teach the Indian my religion would be his promise to teach me *his*."[73]

This recognition paralleled, perhaps even contributed to, an increasing circumspection about the national policy of "civilizing" the Indian. "The Choctaws and Chickasaws will not long retain such a knowledge of *astronomy* and *surveying*," charged the scientist Edwin James in 1830, "as would be useful to guide their wanderings, or make out their possessions in those scorched and sterile wastes to which it is our fixed intention to drive them. The giving to a few individuals of a tribe an education which, as far as it has any influence, tends directly to unfit them for the course of life they are destined to lead, with whatever intention it may be undertaken, is certainly far from being an act of kindness."[74]

A quarter century later, James Swan expressed similar sympathy for the Chinooks, who were resisting white cultural patterns. A half century after Swan, the Pasadena Eight grew to cherish a profound respect for the Hopi and Navaho. "Only to be among these Indians," Frederick Monsen once declared of the Hopi, "to hear them talk, and to observe their treatment of one another and of the casual stranger that is within their gates, is to have forced upon one the realization that here is the unspoiled remnant of a great race, a race of men who have, from time immemorial, lived quiet, sane, whole-

---

[71] Alfred W. Crosby Jr., *The Columbian Exchange: Biological and Cultural Consequences of 1492*, Contributions in American Studies, no. 2 (Westport, Conn.: Greenwood Publishing Co., 1972); Virgil J. Vogel, *American Indian Medicine* (Norman: University of Oklahoma Press, 1970).

[72] Cooper, *The Pioneers*, p. 95.

[73] Thoreau, *The Maine Woods*, ed. Moldenhauer, p. 239.

[74] James, ed., *Captivity and Adventures of John Tanner*, p. xxviii, also p. xxxi.

some lives very close to Nature."[75] Appreciating the integrity of Hopi life and its religious strength, Monsen deplored its destruction by a "too-benevolent white race."[76] Sadly, he conceded that "the world is losing something of pure beauty because it knows no better than to thrust aside these things. . . . Some day when it is too late, we may realize what we have lost by 'educating' the Indian, and forcing him to accept our more complex but far inferior standards of life, work and art."[77]

Now perhaps we are in a better position to recognize a strain that has been present intermittently, incompletely throughout these chapters. Crèvecoeur half entertained it; in Melville it is mockingly explicit. From Washington Irving and George Catlin near the beginning of the century, to translator William Philo Clark and painter Charles M. Russell near the end, commentators on the effects of white attempts to civilize Indian tribes took an increasingly critical view of the value system offered in place of native modes, and they later scrutinized it ever more carefully from the native perspective itself.[78] Far from assisting natives, material progress seemed actually to unfit both Polynesians and Indians for life either in their own communities or in the white one. As one amateur ethnologist observed in 1909, "true philanthropy is to make way for them the path of development along the lines which they themselves have started and wonderfully continued till Washington discovered them."[79]

From this critical outlook, it was only a slight step to the suggestion that the intrinsic value of native cultures might even excel that of Western civilization. So radical a notion, naturally, persuaded few but the most disaffected or the most perceptive. Still, the very fact that it was considered at all reflects the extent of appreciation for native

[75] Frederick I. Monsen, "Picturing Indians with the Camera," Photo-Era, 25 (October 1910), 170.

[76] Frederick Monsen, "The Destruction of Our Indians: What Civilization Is Doing to Extinguish an Ancient and Highly Intelligent Race by Taking Away Its Arts, Industries, and Religion," Craftsman, 11 (March 1907), 688.

[77] Ibid., p. 691.

[78] Irving, Western Journals, ed. McDermott, pp. 103-4; Catlin, Letters and Notes, 1:245, 272; Catlin, Life Among the Indians, p. 19; Clark, Indian Sign Language, pp. 18-20; Harold McCracken, The Charles M. Russell Book: The Life and Work of the Cowboy Artist (Garden City, N.Y.: Doubleday and Co., 1957), pp. 130-31. See also Parker, "Prescott's Conquest," p. 263; Mrs. Anna Brownell Jameson, Winter Studies and Summer Rambles in Canada, 2 vols. (New York: Wiley and Putnam, 1839), 2:335, also 2:231-33.

[79] Charles Francis Saunders, Pocket Diary for 1909 Tour of the Pueblos, Box 9, November 26. With less restraint, he had earlier quipped, "Let 'em go to hell their own way—I think anyhow they have as good a chance of keeping out of hell as I have" (ibid., entry for August 1).

societies.[80] Fur traders of the 1830s, for example, recognized some truth in native assertions that their community life put that of whites to shame.[81] More tellingly, assorted individuals began in the 1820s to trouble over the alarming rate of recidivism among redeemed white captives.[82] Whether more former captives returned to their captors than remained in civilized society is an issue still debated. Of greater importance is the question "why individuals of both races who experienced both civilizations so frequently preferred the Indian life style. It would appear that Indian family life offered much to the fulfillment of the individual that was lacking in the more advanced civilization."[83] Another historian has hypothesized that these "white Indians" discovered "a kind of unity of thought and action and a kind of social cohesion which deeply appealed to them, and which they did not find with the whites, especially not with the pioneers."[84] Some of those who chose to remain with their "own kind" expressed just such comparative judgments, casting serious doubts on the premises of Western society even as they praised the possibilities defined in native ones.

In this light, we can understand nineteenth-century scientists' energetic theorizing about these questions. Britain's John Lubbock and Edward Tylor and America's Lewis Henry Morgan, for instance, independently grappled with issues that others had been content merely to brush up against, and they defined thereby fuller possibilities for the science of anthropology. Matthew Arnold's celebrated *Culture and*

80 See Father Gabriel Sagard, *The Long Journey to the Country of the Hurons* (1639), trans. H. H. Langton, ed. George M. Wrong (Toronto: Champlain Society, 1939), pp. 58, 138, 213; Mrs. John H. Kinzie, *Wau-Bun, The "Early Day" in the North-West* (New York: Derby and Jackson, 1856), pp. vii, 340-42, 363; Charles Alexander Eastman, *From the Deep Woods to Civilization: Chapters in the Autobiography of an Indian* (1916; rpt. Boston: Little, Brown, and Co., 1917), pp. 143, 194; Robert F. Berkhofer Jr., *Salvation and the Savage: An Analysis of Protestant Missions and American Indian Response, 1787-1862* (Louisville: University of Kentucky, 1965), pp. 107-11.

81 Lewis O. Saum, *The Fur Trader and the Indian* (Seattle: University of Washington Press, 1965), pp. 244-45, also pp. 110, 113, 197, 223.

82 See, among others, *Letters and Other Writings of James Madison*, 4 vols. (Philadelphia: J. B. Lippincott and Co., 1865), 3:64-65; Halkett, *Historical Notes Respecting the Indians*, p. 316; John F. Meginess, *Biography of Frances Slocum, the Lost Sister of Wyoming* (1891; rpt. New York: Arno Press, 1974), pp. 68ff.; Kinzie, *Wau-Bun*, p. 287; Drinnon, *White Savage*, pp. 11-12, 37.

83 Heard, *White into Red*, p. 13. See also Slotkin, *Regeneration through Violence*, pp. 100-101, 265.

84 Erwin H. Ackerknecht, " 'White Indians': Psychological and Physiological Peculiarities of White Children Abducted and Reared by North American Indians," *Bulletin of the History of Medicine*, 15 (January 1944), 34, also pp. 19-21, 28-31. See also John R. Swanton, "Notes on the Mental Assimilation of Races," *Journal of the Washington Academy of Sciences*, 16 (November 1926), 493-502.

Anarchy (1869) educated his age to a humanist meaning of culture that was quickly adopted by anthropologists. Yet Arnold "could never have called a work *Primitive Culture*," as George Stocking has shrewdly noted about Tylor's masterwork, which appeared two years later; "the very idea would have been to him a contradiction in terms. To argue that culture actually existed among all men, in however 'crude' or 'primitive' a form, may be viewed as a major step toward the anthropological concept."[85] Despite the breakthrough they pioneered in notions of primitive culture, neither Tylor nor Morgan could move beyond the dominant paradigm of their time—an ethnocentric cultural evolutionism.[86]

The truly radical assessments of the concept of culture occurred among those working in the field. Firsthand experience led the more tolerant to challenge the finely phrased assumptions of even so brilliant a theorist as Tylor, sometimes only implicitly, sometimes in a rather rough-and-ready fashion. More than any other single person, Franz Boas (1858-1942) made this challenge explicit, far-ranging, and convincing. His experiences among native American tribes in the 1880s led him to theoretical interpretations of a kind that Melville could only guess at. His long subsequent career forced him back repeatedly to field work for confirmation of these extraordinary speculations. Moreover, his life's work defines a decisive curve in the idea of culture as it has come to be accepted. Like Frank Hamilton Cushing, the other figure representative of this chapter, Boas was shocked into respect for the intense cultural life of supposedly "primitive" societies. Unlike Cushing, he transformed that realization into a brilliant set of ideas and went on to train some of the finest anthropologists America has produced.[87]

Again in contrast to Cushing, young Boas had not started out with any particular interest in anthropology. German-born and raised, having studied physics and geography for a doctorate, he had every intention of spending his life in the German academic world of "hard

[85] Stocking, *Race, Culture, and Evolution*, p. 87. See also Idus L. Murphree, "The Evolutionary Anthropologists: The Progress of Mankind. The Concepts of Progress and Culture in the Thought of John Lubbuck, Edward B. Tylor, and Lewis H. Morgan," *Proceeding of the American Philosophical Society*, 105 (June 1961), 265-300.

[86] See Stocking, *Race, Culture, and Evolution*, pp. 81-82; Bidney, "Concept of Value," pp. 687ff.; Saum, *Fur Trader and the Indian*, pp. 198-223.

[87] For background, see: Stocking, *Race, Culture, and Evolution*, pp. 148, 156-59, 200-209, 228-30; Berkhofer, *White Man's Indian*, pp. 62-65; Keen, *Aztec Image*, pp. 404-5; Hoover, *The Red and the Black*, pp. 211-17; Willey and Sabloff, *History of American Archaeology*, pp. 86-87, 89, 91; Margaret Mead and Ruth L. Bunzel, eds., *The Golden Age of American Anthropology* (New York: Braziller, 1960), pp. 306, 400, 461, 577ff.

science." Like Melville, Schoolcraft, Catlin, and Morgan, however, he discovered in his early twenties the absolute irrelevance of the first career on which he had set his life. On a scientific expedition to Baffin Island in the mid-1880s, he lived for some weeks with local Eskimos. Intrigued by their culture, he turned to the larger idea of culture itself. Boas never turned back, and, more remarkably, over the decades in which he then gave himself to that idea, his thought shows astonishing consistency. There is little of the changing, progressive sweep of ideas building out of or contradicting early discoveries that so often characterizes great innovative thinkers. His finest, most incisive ideas were there at the beginning, only waiting to be fully developed. In that first winter of 1883-1884, for instance, Boas complimented his Eskimo hosts with certain seminal observations in his notebook:

> I often ask myself what advantages our "good society" possesses over that of the "savages." The more I see of their customs, the more I realize that we have no right to look down on them. Where amongst our people would you find such true hospitality? . . . We have no right to blame them for their forms and superstitions which may seem ridiculous to us. We "highly educated people" are much worse, relatively speaking. . . . As a thinking person, for me the most important result of this trip lies in the strengthening of my point of view that the idea of a "cultured" individual is merely relative and that a person's worth should be judged by his *Herzenbildung*.[88]

This observation cut through the thick flesh of evolutionary bias to the bones of a radical theory that Boas would spend his entire career articulating. The special value of this observation for anthropology was that, unlike others who made similar comments, Boas had a rigorous scientific background, which forced him to more than mere tolerant conjecture.

By 1888, Boas had emigrated to America and become an accomplished anthropologist. However narrowly focused his essays on those Pacific Northwest tribes he considered his special province, his writings implicitly espouse the view of culture he first glimpsed on Baffin Island. "At least by implication," one noted historian has observed about an early essay, "On Alternating Sounds" (1888), "it sees cultural phenomena in terms of the imposition of conventional meaning on the flux of experience. It sees them as historically conditioned and transmitted by the learning process. It sees them as determinants of our very perceptions of the external world. And it sees them in

88 Cited in Stocking, *Race, Culture, and Evolution*, p. 148.

relative rather than in absolute terms. Much of Boas' later work, and that of his students after him, can be viewed simply as the working out of implications present in this article."[89] Instead of moving from conventional premises to specific interpretations, Boas worked inductively; he wanted not to define culture in the singular and abstract but rather to understand in their particularity a variety of autonomous tribal cultures.

The consistency of Boas's career may best be illustrated through his celebrated accomplishments in the special field of museum arrangements. In 1887 he wrote an astonishing series of letters to John Wesley Powell and Otis Mason, the Smithsonian Institution's curator of ethnology. Boas clarified his resistance to Mason's arrangement of specimens according to commonly accepted practice, that is, by alleged cultural stages operating regardless of time or place. Boas thought materials should be arranged by ethnological, not typological, connections—by tribe, not function. Rather than placing, say, all baskets together, he thought it far more important to show how baskets from a particular tribe fitted in with its other cultural artifacts. Only then could the tribe's integrity, to say nothing of its uniqueness, be appreciated. Boas was given a chance to put his theory into practice half a dozen years later, when he was appointed chief assistant in anthropology at Chicago's World Columbian Exposition of 1893. Supervising the ethnology arrangement that was later converted into the Field Museum of Natural History, he established a model that transformed museum collections the world over. Boas deeply believed in a concept of total culture, one that placed human activities within a specific cultural context and stressed as well the need for "study of the thoughts, emotional life, and ethical standards of the common people"[90] more than those of the select classes of priests and chiefs.

The prerequisite to such knowledge, manifestly, was study carried out according to strict scientific rules of observation and evidence. In such work lay Boas's true genius. Prolific as a scholar, indefatigable as a field researcher, innovative as a curator, he could have secured fame in any one of these fields alone. His most substantial contribution, however, was to attract and train an entire generation of talented scholars. With his appointment to Columbia University in the mid-1890s, he began to establish the world's finest graduate program in anthropology. As one of his students later wrote, "He brought to anthropology rigorous standards of proof, a critical skepticism toward all generalization, and the physicist's unwillingness to accept any gen-

[89] Ibid., p. 159.

[90] Franz Boas, "The Ethnological Significance of Esoteric Doctrines," in Boas, *Race, Language and Culture* (New York: Macmillan Co., 1940), p. 315.

eralization or explanation as anything more than a useful hypothesis until it has been clearly demonstrated that no other explanation is possible."[91] Boas demanded much from his students—like Morgan, sometimes dictating professional, even private, decisions—but he also inculcated by stern example the possibilities of his considered view of culture.

Boas's own work in the 1890s among the Pacific Northwest Coast tribes only confirmed his early dismissal of cultural absolutism. His contributions to linguistic anthropology, including the countless native texts he collected, demonstrated that "primitive" languages equaled, even surpassed Indo-European varieties in their formal complexity. His rejection of simple anthropological evolution opened the possibility of a diverse body of cultures, none to be shunted under specious eveluative rubrics. To turn away from the dominant comparative method, Boas asserted, was to turn away from belief in any fixed standard of judgment. The strength of anthropology was in its ability "to impress us with the relative value of all forms of culture," as he claimed in 1904, "and thus serve as a check to an exaggerated valuation of the standpoint of our own period, which we are only too liable to consider the ultimate goal of human evolution."[92] Precisely because other cultures differed so radically from one's own, the very notion of objective scientific valuation of them was invalidated. In Boas's simple assertion. "There is no absolute progress."[93] The western European prejudice for rationality, for instance, was no better than the modes of thought peculiar to other cultures, nor was it any less determined by cultural tradition.

It is somewhat difficult for us to recognize that the value which we attribute to our own civilization is due to the fact that we participate in this civilization, and that it has been controlling all our actions since the time of our birth; but it is certainly conceivable that there may be other civilizations, based perhaps on different traditions and on a different equilibrium of emotion and reason which are of no less value than ours, although it may be impossible for us to appreciate their values without having grown up under their influence.[94]

[91] Ruth L. Bunzel, in Mead and Bunzel, eds., *Golden Age of Anthropology*, p. 403.
[92] Boas, "The History of Anthropology," in *The Shaping of American Anthropology, 1883-1911: A Franz Boas Reader*, ed. George W. Stocking Jr. (New York: Basic Books, 1974), p. 36.
[93] Boas, *The Mind of Primitive Man* (1911), rev. ed. (New York: Macmillan Co., 1938), p. 206.
[94] Ibid., p. 225. For a discussion of this passage, see Stocking, *Race, Culture, and Evolution*, pp. 103-4. See also Bidney, "Concept of Value," pp. 687-88.

Boas thrust through to an entirely new way of thinking about issues long discussed and consequences long conceded. Moreover, the orientation he provided remains standard in principle among anthropologists. Most Americans did not share his assessments of native tribes at the time; perhaps few more do so today. Yet others had come to a roughly similar point of view. That is to say, by the last third of the nineteenth century, a broad spectrum of Americans sympathized with Indian tribes in ways altogether different from earlier attitudes.[95]

It should be noted that modern anthropologists consider cultural relativism a suspect concept.[96] Acculturated beings ourselves, they argue, we cannot help rendering value judgments. Boas himself assumed certain tenets as absolutely good, including freedom, tolerance, rationality, and mutual respect. By theoretical definition, however, true cultural relativism would be completely neutral. The important point historically is not that true cultural relativism is inherently unattainable. Rather, it is how that belief affected people at the time —that so many white Americans, from the most humane of motives, dismissed ethnocentrism to embrace a larger view. They could hardly realize the psychological depths of the assumptions they made in their attempt to be open-minded toward aliens. But they had nevertheless taken the first steps toward such a realization.

Once again in the nineteenth century, a vanishing wilderness altered Americans' sense of themselves. In each of the preceding cases—landscape and wild game, white frontiersmen, native tribes seen first as merely exotic, then as intrinsically worthy of respect—Americans had

[95] See, for instance, Parker Gillmore, *A Hunter's Adventures in the Great West* (London: Hurst and Blackett, 1871), pp. 4-5; Beeson, *Plea for the Indians*; Helen Hunt Jackson, *Glimpses of California and the Missions* (1883; rpt. Boston: Little, Brown and Co., 1903), esp. pp. 32, 97, 101, 173; Jackson, *A Century of Dishonor: The Early Crusade for Indian Reform* (1881) ed. Andrew F. Rolle (New York: Harper and Row, 1965), pp. 9-11, 27, 64, 102, 118, 185; Henry Benjamin Whipple, *Lights and Shadows of a Long Episcopate: Being Reminiscences and Recollections of The Right Reverend Henry Benjamin Whipple, Bishop of Minnesota* (New York: Macmillan Co., 1899), esp. pp. 34ff. See, in a slightly different context, William Graham Sumner, *Folkways: A Study of the Sociological Importance of Usages, Manners, Customs, Mores, and Morals* (1906; rpt. New York: New American Library, 1940), esp. pp. 27-28, 30-31. See also Robert Winston Mardock, *The Reformers and the American Indian* (Columbia: University of Missouri Press, 1971); Willey and Sabloff, *History of American Archaeology*, pp. 86-87; George W. Stocking Jr., "Introduction: The Basic Assumptions of Boasian Anthropology," in Boas, *Shaping of American Anthropology*, ed. Stocking, pp. 18-20.

[96] Geertz, *Interpretation of Cultures*, pp. 37, 40, 43-44, 53; Stocking, *Race, Culture, and Evolution*, pp. 88, 231; Bidney, "Idea of the Savage," p. 326; Bidney, "Concept of Value," pp. 687-94; Fiedler, *Return of the Vanishing American*, p. 170; Mead and Bunzel, eds., *Golden Age of American Anthropology*, p. 403; Hoover, *The Red and the Black*, pp. 214, 297-98, 366.

felt the tremendous costs entailed by their conquest of the wilderness. Before the century's end, few counted the cost too high. But a significant number gradually, grudgingly wondered how their own allegedly more advanced civilization so often failed at what native tribes so eminently succeeded in doing. Melville's condemnation in *Typee* of the smug complacency of French missionaries and American sailors found many unconscious analogues during the rest of the century. The sole difference would be in the degree of their progressively more damning criticisms of American civilization.

CHAPTER NINE

WEIGHED, MEASURED, AND FOUND WANTING

"Ye see, Hinnissy, th' Indyun is bound f'r to give way to th' onward march iv white civilization. You 'an me, Hinnissy, is th' white civilization. . . . Th' on'y hope f'r th' Indyun is to put his house on rollers, an' keep a team hitched to it, an', whin he sees a white man, to start f'r th' settin' sun. . . . Th' onward march iv th' white civilization, with morgedges an' other modhern improvements, is slowly but surely, as Hogan says, chasin' him out. . . ."

—*Finley Peter Dunne*
"On the Indian War" (1898)

October 12, the Discovery. It was wonderful to find America, but it would have been more wonderful to miss it.

—*Mark Twain*
"Pudd'nhead Wilson's Calendar" (1894)

In 1845 a popular southern author explained the reasons for "our blinding prejudices against the [Indian] race—prejudices which seem to have been fostered as necessary to justify the reckless and unsparing hand with which we have smitten them in their habitations, and expelled them from their country. We must prove them unreasoning beings, to sustain our pretensions as human ones—show them to have been irreclaimable, to maintain our own claims to the regards and respect of civilization."[1] Or, as Melville allowed Tommo to consider a year later, "they whom we donominate 'savages' are made to deserve the title." Sardonic puncturings of white complacency were hardly new to the nineteenth century. Directed not against their society itself but at its dramatic depredations and self-justifying logic, such reformist protests had a long history, if to little effect. Increasingly respectful admiration for native tribes, however, prompted many in the nineteenth century to a more profoundly disturbing outrage at the very terms of their culture itself. As Clifford Geertz reminds us, one's notion of the savage necessarily invokes one's self-conception. To see others as no longer savage negations is not necessarily to deny the contrast with one's own culture but to raise the prospect that that contrast might be reversed, that one's society might itself be fundamentally "savage." Cultural relativism, then, more than inspiring envious admiration of native tribes, encouraged a devastating indictment of American society from the very perspective offered by tribal life.

At its least telling, reflexive critiques of this sort merely challenged the effect of sacred and secular efforts to "redeem" native souls and to "advance" their societies. Such efforts had achieved little more than the corruption of both. Deploring the natives' wretched treatment, some travelers shrewdly noted that behind the policy of removing Indian tribes westward lay the paradoxical premise that contact with whites would only drive them to further depths of supposed savagery. Others, more outraged if less sophisticated, scathingly indicted a history of broken treaties, fraud, and corruption in the federal government's displacement of the Indian.[2] George Catlin, the most vocal

[1] William Gilmore Simms, *Views and Reviews in American Literature, History and Fiction, First Series* (1845), ed. C. Hugh Holman (Cambridge, Mass.: Harvard University Press, 1962), p. 142.

[2] See Count de Pourtalès, *On the Western Tour with Washington Irving: The Journal and Letters of Count de Pourtalès*, ed. George F. Spaulding (Norman: University of Oklahoma Press, 1968), p. 62; George Frederick Ruxton, *Life in the Far West* (1848), ed. LeRoy R. Hafen (Norman: University of Oklahoma Press, 1951), pp. 99-100; Bishop [Henry B.] *Whipple's Southern Diary, 1843-1844*, ed. Lester B. Shippee (Minneapolis: University of Minnesota Press, 1937), p. 63; Frederic Remington,

protestor before the Civil War, formulated the issue well but never more succinctly or more forcefully than did Lewis Henry Morgan in his conclusion to *League of the Iroquois*: "It cannot be forgotten, that in after years our Republic must render an account, to the civilized world, for the disposal which it makes of the Indian. It is not sufficient, before this tribunal, to plead inevitable destiny."[3]

By the mid-1860s, even someone who shared as fully in his society's prejudices as did the youthful Mark Twain could satirize missionary efforts among the Hawaiians: "The contrast is so strong—the wonderful benefit conferred upon this people by the missionaries is so prominent, so palpable, and so unquestionable, that the frankest compliment I can pay them, and the best, is simply to point to the condition of the Sandwich Islanders of Captain Cook's time, and their condition today. Their work speaks for itself."[4] Twain later exposes the deadly effectiveness of missionaries' work in alluding to the statistical condition of the Hawaiian race: "Doubtless this purifying is not far off, when we reflect that contact with civilization and the whites has reduced the native population from *four hundred thousand* (Captain Cook's estimate) to *fifty-five thousand* in something over eighty years!"[5]

Within the next third of a century, such cuts and thrusts at white civilization slashed through a large body of public expression, though the notion that manifest destiny merely meant genocide was never welcome. True, Americans had long satirized the deplorable treatment of Indian tribes; but in the past these excesses had seemed necessary evils, the predictable exceptions to a humane rule. More and more widely through the nineteenth century, however, the rule of Western civilization itself seemed suspect, and respect for indigenous cultures spurred further doubts about continental platitudes. Even in the instances of less facile white assumptions, those invoking the scales

---

"Artist Wanderings Among the Cheyennes," *Century Magazine*, 38 (August 1889), 541; Capt. D. C. Poole, *Among the Sioux of Dakota: Eighteen Months' Experience as an Indian Agent* (New York: D. Van Nostrand, 1881), pp. 225-28; Benjamin Drake, *The Life and Adventures of Black Hawk* (1838), 7th ed. rev. (E. Morgan and Co., 1850), p. 5. For a calmer statement directed at this same issue, see Young Joseph, "An Indian's Views of Indian Affairs," *North American Review*, 128 (1879), esp. 432-33.

[3] Morgan, *League of the Ho-De-No Sav-Nee or Iroquois* (1851), rpt. 2 vols. in 1 (New Haven: Human Relations Area Files, 1954), 2:123.

[4] *Mark Twain's Letters from Hawaii*, ed. A. Grove Day (New York: Appleton-Century, 1966), pp. 54-55; see also pp. 52-53, 129-30.

[5] Samuel Clemens [Mark Twain], *Roughing It*, ed. Franklin R. Togers (Berkeley: University of California Press, 1972), pp. 423-24; see also pp. 411-13, 423ff. For background, see Justin Kaplan, *Mr. Clemens and Mark Twain: A Biography* (New York: Simon and Schuster, 1966), p. 30; Walter Francis Frear, *Mark Twain and Hawaii* (Chicago: Lakeside Press, 1947), pp. 33-34, 128-32, 490-500.

of cultural contrast weighed, measured, and found them also wanting.[6] When Theodore Parker and Alexander Bradford suggested as early as the 1840s that Cortez's destruction of the Aztec empire was the act of a barbarian, they sounded a note that would echo down the century. Montezuma's civilization, however militaristic, turned on less inherently destructive modes than those the Spanish conquistadors introduced; in other ways, it seemed superior. As Parker and Bradford sharply observed, contemporary America's self-complacent faith in its institutions was similarly unwarranted, similarly deplorable.[7]

Albert Gallatin opposed President Polk's expansionist administration during the 1840s by likewise arguing vigorously, in his editor's words, against the "white-man's burden argument that justified annexation as conferring the benefits of higher civilization upon the backward Mexicans."[8] A decade later, Mary Eastman would conclude her elegiac lament for the vanishing Sioux with the weighted profession: "We should be better reconciled to this manifest destiny of the aborigines, if the inroads of civilization were worthy of it."[9] In each of these and other cases, doubts about the tenets and practices of western European culture had evolved out of admiration for those of native American ones. By the end of the century, Boas could even reverse the intellectual sequence, warning in dire terms against cultural absolutism precisely because it fed a nationalistic arrogance.[10]

Of course, other domestic and foreign issues aroused Americans, certainly by the time Boas spoke. Resistance to militant missionizing

6 See Mrs. Anna Brownell Jameson, *Winter Studies and Summer Rambles in Canada*, 2 vols. (New York: Wiley and Putnam, 1839), 2:231-33; James F. Rusling, *Across America: Or, The Great West and the Pacific Coast* (New York: Sheldon and Co., 1874), p. 138.

7 Theodore Parker, "Prescott's Conquest of Mexico" (1849), reprinted in Parker, *The American Scholar*, ed. George Willis Cooke (Boston: American Unitarian Association, 1907), pp. 246-51, 261-67; Alexander W. Bradford, *American Antiquities and Researches into the Origin and History of the Red Race* (New York: Dayton and Saxton, 1841), pp. 72, 82-83, 160-61.

8 *Selected Writings of Albert Gallatin*, ed. E. James Ferguson (New York: Bobbs-Merrill, 1967), p. 456; see also p. v.

9 Mrs. Mary H. Eastman, *Dahcotah; or, Life and Legends of the Sioux Around Fort Snelling* (1849; rpt. Minneapolis: Ross and Haines, 1962), p. xvi. For similar statements, see Francis Parkman, "Preface to the Illustrated Edition" (September 16, 1892), and "Preface to the Fourth Edition" (March 30, 1872), both in *The Oregon Trail: Sketches of Prairie and Rocky Mountain Life*, ed. E. N. Feltskog (Madison: University of Wisconsin Press, 1969), pp. vii, ix, xi-xii; Ben Merchant Vorpahl, ed., *My Dear Wister: The Frederic Remington–Owen Wister Letters*, ed. Ben Merchant Vorpahl (Palo Alto, Calif.: American West Co., 1972), pp. 95-96; and Daniel G. Brinton, *Races and Peoples: Lectures on the Science of Ethnography* (Philadelphia: David McKay, 1901), pp. 289-300.

10 See David Bidney, "The Concept of Value in Modern Anthropology," in A. L. Kroeber, ed., *Anthropology Today: An Encyclopedic Inventory* (Chicago: University of Chicago Press, 1953), pp. 687-88.

had swollen into a flood tide of public opinion, and alienation from contemporary society expressed itself most outspokenly against America's ruthless imperialism in the Philippines, in China, in Central America, and, not least, in the American West, where the frontier was closing. A collective sense of powerlessness, of victimization by forces that might otherwise have been converted to beneficent ends, led to a reexamination of American society's basic tenets. Although the larger terms of this revaluation do not figure here, they offer a context of revulsion from arrogant Western assumptions that was shared most readily by individuals willing to adopt a native perspective.[11]

COMPELLED by an uneasiness, then a disillusionment with white American institutions, Cooper explored the terms of this perspective more profoundly than any other author besides Melville in the first half of the nineteenth century. He certainly failed in his Leatherstocking tales to do justice to native societies or psychology. Dissatisfied with what he saw America becoming, however, he adopted the native point of view in later novels of the series as a means of censuring white society. Both Dew of June, the kindly Tuscarora in *The Pathfinder*, and Rivenoak, the wise Huron in *The Deerslayer*, deliver scathing, irrefutable indictments of whites. In response to the Huron chief's criticisms, simple-minded Hetty Hutter pleads to her friend Wah-ta!-Wah, "there can't be two sides to truth." Wah-ta!-Wah ruefully responds, "Well, to poor Injin girl it seem everything *can* be to palefaces. . . . One time 'ey say white, and one time 'ey say black. Why *never can be?*"[12] Melville's description of Shakespeare here applies to Cooper: in the mouths of his characters he puts terrific truths that would be madness to utter in his own person.

[11] For nineteenth-century assumptions about progress, see: Arthur Alphonse Ekirch Jr., *The Idea of Progress in America, 1815-1860*, Studies in History, Economics and Public Law, no. 511 (New York: Columbia University Press, 1944); David Levin, *History as Romantic Art: Bancroft, Prescott, Motley, and Parkman* (Stanford: Stanford University Press, 1959), pp. 27ff.; Fred Somkin, *Unquiet Eagle: Memory and Desire in the Idea of American Freedom, 1815-1860* (Ithaca: Cornell University Press, 1967); David W. Noble, *The Paradox of Progressive Thought* (Minneapolis: University of Minnesota Press, 1958); Henry F. May, *The End of American Innocence: A Study of the First Years of Our Own Time, 1912-1917* (New York: Alfred A. Knopf, 1959).

[12] Cooper, *The Deerslayer; or, The First War-Path* (New York: W. A. Townsend and Co., 1859), p. 208. (All further references to Cooper's works will be to this collected edition, known as the Author's Revised Edition, illustrated by F.O.C. Darley and printed between 1859 and 1861. See also Donald A. Ringe, *James Fenimore Cooper* (New York: Twayne Publishers, 1962), pp. 8off.; Howard Mumford Jones, "Prose and Pictures: James Fenimore Cooper" (1951), reprinted in Jones, *History and the Contemporary: Essays in Nineteenth-Century Literature* (Madison: University of Wisconsin Press, 1964), p. 76; Marius Bewley, *The Eccentric Design: Form in the Classic American Novel* (New York: Columbia University Press, 1957), p. 96.

Once sensitized to this strain, one can recognize it even in the speech of an otherwise unlikely character, Magua, from *The Last of the Mohicans*. Though, as Magua notes, all peoples are created by a godly spirit, the races display profound differences:

> "Some He made with faces paler than the ermine of the forests: and these He ordered to be traders; dogs to their women, and wolves to their slaves. He gave this people . . . appetites to devour the earth. He gave them tongues like the false call of the wild-cat; hearts like rabbits; the cunning of the hog (but none of the fox). . . . With his tongue [the white man] sops the ears of the Indians . . . and his arms inclose the land from the shores of the salt-water to the islands of the great lake. His gluttony makes him sick. God gave him enough, and yet he wants all. Such are the pale-faces!"[13]

Self-serving as it is, Magua's speech nevertheless seems corroborated by his following eulogy to his race, voiced with what one reader has characterized as "all the accents of poetic truth that Cooper can muster."[14] Ratifying this judgment is the acknowledgment offered by Tamenund, the far less vindictive Mohican chief, sometimes called a "spokesman for the novelist."[15] Indeed, the novel supports these assessments. Nearly all the respectable white characters are incompetent or tedious, while Uncas emerges as the series' hero. If his death augurs that of native experience itself, the entire novel confirms a bleaker vision that juxtaposes the loss of wilderness against the dubious gain of white civilization.

Although Cooper elsewhere vouched support for America's westward mission, his novels as a whole register a telling skepticism about its fulfillment.[16] The contradiction in his conception—social good deriving from careless greed and irresponsible anarchy—repeatedly converts a mythic rendition of pioneering into a dark prognosis for America. The Leatherstocking tales in particular express something

13 Cooper, *Last of the Mohicans*, pp. 380-81.
14 Joel Porte, *The Romance in America: Studies in Cooper, Poe, Hawthorne, Melville, and James* (Middletown, Conn.: Wesleyan University Press, 1967), p. 19.
15 Edwin Fussell, *Frontier: American Literature and the American West* (Princeton: Princeton University Press, 1965), p. 43.
16 See Henry Nash Smith, introduction to Cooper, *The Prairie: A Tale* (New York: Holt, Rinehart and Winston, 1950), pp. ix, xvi; Porte, *Romance in America*, p. 52; Jones, "Prose and Pictures," p. 74; Robert H. Zoellner, "Conceptual Ambivalence in Cooper's Leatherstocking," *American Literature*, 31 (January 1960), 397-420; Donald Ringe, "Man and Nature in Cooper's *The Prairie*," *Nineteenth-Century Fiction*, 15 (March 1961), 313-23; Charles A. Brady, "James Fenimore Cooper, 1789-1851: Mythmaker and Christian Romancer," in Harold C. Gardiner, S.J., ed., *American Classics Reconsidered: A Christian Appraisal* (New York: Charles Scribner's Sons, 1958), p. 61.

more than dramatic regret that the wilderness is fated to pass, since the drama they unfold converts that regret into tragic loss. The imagined future rarely glimmers more desirably than the lost past.[17]

Readers no more grasped this strain in the popular series than did Cooper, certainly not before mid-century. Moreover, the issues raised by a nation pulling apart tended to close off debate on such topics until after the Civil War, when despoliation of the wilderness and of wild game, abandonment of frontier patterns, and subduing of native tribes all revived at a madcap pace. "The last gun fired at Appomattox," Stewart Udall has felicitously observed, "was, in effect, the starter's gun in an intensified race for resources."[18] The nation could turn renewed energies and a sophisticated technology on the West, which is merely to say that "the peace at Appomattox meant war for the Indian."[19]

At the same time, broad-based resistance to the government's treatment of Indians rapidly began to develop. Indeed, the very men sent to impose a sentence of death often sympathized with their enemy's tragic circumstances. Even General Philip Sheridan, the renowned Indian fighter who coined the popular "good Indian, dead Indian" tag, confessed, "We took away their country and their means of support, broke up their mode of living, their habits of life, introduced disease and decay among them and it was for this and against this they made war. Could anyone expect less?"[20] The upshot of this question for those who asked was disillusionment with one's government and, finally, one's culture. "In the West," according to one army historian, "the Indian often seemed more than a worthy opponent: he cast doubt on the value of war for civilization itself. Empathizing with the red man while fighting him was an unsettling experience. . . ."[21]

[17] John Lynen, in *The Design of the Present: Essays on Time and Form in American Literature* (New Haven: Yale University Press, 1969), p. 174, has stated similarly: "In essence the action of *The Pioneers* is the process of discovering the basis of community. Cooper's regret for the passing of the wilderness is more than sentimental nostalgia; it arises from the agonizing doubt whether civilization is worth the terrible price men pay for it." See also ibid., pp. 168-200; Richard Slotkin, *Regeneration through Violence: The Mythology of the American Frontier, 1600-1860* (Middletown, Conn.: Wesleyan University Press, 1973), pp. 509-15.

[18] Stewart L. Udall, *The Quiet Crisis* (New York: Avon, 1963), p. 96.

[19] Thomas C. Leonard, *Above the Battle: War-Making in America from Appomattox to Versailles* (New York: Oxford University Press, 1978), p. 43.

[20] Cited in ibid., p. 46.

[21] Ibid. See as well Perkins, *Three Years in California: William Perkins' Journal of Life at Sonoma, 1849-1852*, ed. Dale L. Morgan and James R. Scobie (Berkeley: University of California Press, 1964), pp. 123-25; Lewis Henry Morgan, "Letter to the Editor: The Hue-&-Cry Against the Indians," *Nation*, July 20, 1876, pp. 40-41; *General George Crook: His Autobiography*, 2d ed., ed. Martin F. Schmitt (Norman: University of Oklahoma Press, 1960), pp. 15-16, 228-29, 269-71; Nelson Miles, *Personal*

Among the minority who were so unsettled, of course, none resigned his commission or otherwise resisted. Nor did those appalled by the Indian solution abandon their conviction that the price of civilization was not too high. But soldiers during the post-Civil War period, with some major exceptions, viewed themselves less and less as conquerors, more and more in the frustrating role of policemen of treaties broken by the federal government.[22] Inadequate as their divided feelings were to the devastation wrought, such disquietude was expressed with increasing, and increasingly public, stridency.

Apart from questions of the reasonableness of Indian policy, corruption permeated the Indian service in the late 1860s to a degree that outraged Americans more directly at their society's excesses. As early as 1857, one self-styled reformer attributed the Indians' squalid condition entirely to the effects of a decadent white civilization. Slavery and an impending civil war, he intimated, exposed the moral inadequacy of a society no better than the ones it was wantonly destroying.[23] Others, sharing in this self-revulsion, worked to reform the Indian service. Perhaps surprisingly, these reformers drew their greatest strength not from eastern sentimentalists but from western settlers who saw at first hand the frequently fraudulent, otherwise indifferent federal management of native affairs. Their efforts culminated in the Dawes Act of 1887, which broke up the reservations and assimilated individual Indians into white society. However dubious the achievement, especially in its devastating social effects upon the natives, the act institutionalized racial egalitarianism for the first time as federal policy.[24]

Recollections and Observations of General Nelson A. Miles . . . (New York: Werner Co., 1897), p. 88; Miles, *Serving the Republic: Memoirs of the Civil and Military Life of Nelson A. Miles . . .* (New York: Harper and Brothers, 1911), pp. 113-15, 116-17; Mrs. Margaret I. Carrington, *Absaraka, Home of the Crows* (1868), ed. Milo Milton Quaife (Chicago: R. R. Donnelley and Sons, 1950), p. 211; Edward S. Ellis, *The Indian Wars of the United States* (New York: Cassell Publishing Co., 1892), introduction (unpaginated).

[22] Leonard, *Above the Battle*, pp. 43-44. See as well, John C. Ewers, "When Red and White Men Meet," *Western Historical Quarterly*, 2 (April 1971), 141-45; Robert M. Utley, *Frontiersmen in Blue: The United States Army and the Indian, 1848-1865* (New York: Macmillan Co., 1967), pp. 110, 341, 346.

[23] John Beeson, *A Plea for the Indians; With Facts and Features of the Late War in Oregon* (New York: J. Beeson, 1857), p. 131.

[24] Henry E. Fritz, *The Movement for Indian Assimilation, 1860-1890* (Philadelphia: University of Pennsylvania Press, 1963), p. 34. See also Francis Paul Prucha, S.J., ed. *Americanizing the American Indians: Writings by the "Friends of the Indian," 1880-1900* (Cambridge, Mass.: Harvard University Press, 1973), and Prucha, "Indian Policy Reform and American Protestantism, 1880-1900," in Ray Allen Billington, ed., *People of the Plains and Mountains*, Contributions in American History, no. 25 (Westport, Conn.: Greenwood Press, 1973), pp. 120-45.

The person most successful in arousing public opinion, Helen Hunt Jackson, published *A Century of Dishonor* (1881) precisely to document the history of governmental injustice. Offering a particularly bitter indictment of treaties broken with the Delaware tribe, she concluded "Such uprooting, such perplexity, such loss, such confusion and uncertainty, inflicted once on any community of white people anywhere in our land, would be considered quite enough to destroy its energies and blight its prospects for years."[25] Her more damning statement appeared three years later. *Ramona* (1884), intended to accomplish for Indians what *Uncle Tom's Cabin* (1852) had for blacks, enjoyed resounding success and in fact garnered considerable support for reform. Unfortunately, the book encouraged the kind of improved treatment that American bureaucracy has historically provided in crises—too little and too late.[26] Despite the novel's sentimentality, Mrs. Jackson developed a telling critique of American values from what she assumed was an indigenous point of view. Against the fragile love of the Indian Alessandro and the half-Indian Ramona, the novelist depicts the rapine of land-hungry settlers. Alessandro's father is brutally murdered and his southern Californian village destroyed; nowhere can he and Ramona escape the white hordes. Finally driven insane, Alessandro is killed by a representative of the society whose winning of the land only confirms its inhumanity.

By the end of the century, the tide of factors eroding American idealism and simple-minded faith in progress—the dehumanization of industrial labor, for one notable example, and the gross inequalities between poverty and ostentatious wealth for another—had risen dangerously. Among these, the recognition of superior values in cultures not obsessed with progress and self-serving Darwinian analogies may seem less significant, but it unquestionably forms a basis for sterner judgments and bleaker disillusions.

Moreover, the ever present complement of this revulsion against traditional attitudes toward the Indian—criticism of land policy and mindless exploitation—was gaining urgency. Long before the Civil War, Thoreau, Catlin, and Cole had deplored mere utilitarian valuation of the land, as Chapter Two illustrated. Adopting a far more analytical approach in *Our Land and Land Policy* (1871), Henry George attacked his countrymen's assumptions by illustrating their

---

[25] Jackson, *A Century of Dishonor: The Early Crusade for Indian Reform* (1881), ed. Andrew F. Rolle (New York: Harper and Row, 1965), p. 64. For similar observations see her *Glimpses of California and the Missions* (1883; rpt. Boston: Little, Brown and Co., 1903).

[26] Wallace Stegner, "Western Record and Romance," in Robert E. Spiller et al., eds. *Literary History of the United States: History*, 3d ed. rev. (New York: Macmillan Co., 1963), p. 869.

mismanagement of the wilderness. "Evidently," he stated, referring to the federal government's own General Land Office figures, "if we get rid of our remaining public land at the rate which we have been . . . it will be all gone some time before the year 1890."[27] Dismayed at the bureaucratic resistance his popular ideas met, George turned more radical, finally questioning material progress itself. Civilization's advance across the continent, as he came to understand it, actually encouraged greater economic dislocation. Speaking on "The Crime of Poverty" in 1885, he asked, "What is the most astonishing thing in our civilization? Why, the most astonishing thing to those Sioux chiefs who were recently brought from the Far West and taken through our manufacturing cities in the East, was not the marvelous inventions that enabled machinery to act almost as if it had intellect . . . but the fact that amid this marvelous development of productive power, they found little children at work."[28] Despite the "marvelous inventions" industry had fostered, conditions in America were too quickly replicating European ones. According to George, "the general condition of the working classes is becoming worse instead of better."[29] Formulating a difficult but necessary question, he continued, "A very Sodom's apple seems this 'progress' of ours to the classes that have the most need to progress. We have been 'developing the country' fast enough. We have been building railroads, and peopling the wilderness, and extending our cities. But what is the gain? . . . are the masses of the people any better off?"[30]

Admirers of native cultures had come to see that white depredations were less exceptions to than expressions of their culture's basic tenets. So too those who, like George, treasured the landscape—not more than they desired the good of society, but precisely for society's good—realized that the enemy was themselves. A connection would seem to follow. At every point—wilderness conservation on the one hand and tribal preservation on the other, appreciation for the land and respect for indigenous cultures, destruction of the environment and extinction of Indian tribes—the issues seem to fall into logical, even obvious associations.[31] As if only further to conjoin the two sets of

27 George, Our Land and Land Policy (1871; rpt. New York: Doubleday Page and Co., 1904), pp. 9, 11. See also Edward T. Peters, "Evils of Our Public Land Policy," Century Magazine, 25 (February 1883), 599-601.

28 George, Moses/The Crime of Poverty (New York: International Joseph Fels Commission, 1918), p. 39, also p. 34; George, Progress and Poverty (1879; rpt. New York: Robert Schalkenbach Foundation, 1954), pp. 7-8.

29 George, Our Land and Land Policy, p. 119.

30 Ibid.

31 Wilbur R. Jacobs, in Dispossessing the American Indian: Indians and Whites on the Colonial Frontier (New York: Charles Scribner's Sons, 1972), pp. 19 20, 25, is one of the few recent scholars to have noted this interrelationship.

issues, most tribes shared a sacred respect for their regions' ecological balance and were revolted by the arrogant indifference to the natural environment that characterized successive waves of pioneers. It is a little surprising, then, that obvious thematic associations in fact do not correspond to actual historical patterns. Few whites who valued wilderness conservation were also committed to Indian rights. Still, both groups contributed to revaluating a fundamental cultural assumption, and under pressure from some of America's best minds, the postulate of inevitable human progress began to erode.

MARK TWAIN, the quintessential exponent of intricate technology and bonanza schemes for quick wealth, can hardly be expected to serve as a compelling example of these thematic strains. Perhaps for that reason, however, he illustrates a more common state of unrest in late nineteenth-century America, and in so doing, he nicely complements Cooper's uneasiness. *A Connecticut Yankee in King Arthur's Court* (1889), Twain's longest essay into cultural comparison, was meant to confute sentimental nostalgias by comparing a primitive with an industrial society, to the latter's advantage, of course. Yet in Twain's hands, the two cultures share more than salient features. The perspective of a backward society, defined by nineteenth-century standards, finally exposes the bankruptcy of those very standards. What begins as a contemptuous account of the squalor and filth of Arthurian life becomes a paean to a pastoral beauty that industrialism renders irrecoverable.

Hank Morgan, suddenly transported back hundreds of years to Arthurian Britain, sets about freeing a feudal society enslaved by monarchism, caste, ignorance, and superstition. Like Christian missionaries among native American tribes, he hopes to subvert the religious and social institutions of the rude Celts in order to convert them to his brand of industrial progress. Twain had intended along the way to excoriate the fashionable admiration for medieval life and English institutions, but, interestingly, he shifted ground in the process of writing. His opening depiction of the population as alternately "childlike" and "savage" is challenged by the later view that nobility, courage, and compassion are encouraged by feudal training. The novel switches disconcertingly between Hank's claims for progressive industrial democracy and Twain's incipient doubts about it. Nowhere else in his works does he voice such fervid hopes for the economic, political, and social progress of the American system, and yet nowhere else are his confusions as vivid. Developing the comic premise of a mechanical wizard in a backward land only exposed his deep reservations about material progress and dictated in the process a perversely uncomical novel. As he later recognized, rewriting it would require "a pen warmed-up in hell."[32]

Part of the problem is that Hank does not live up to his advance billing as the engineer of a social revolution that will truly improve Arthurian society. During his seven-year tenure as "The Boss," his technological know-how provides little more than telephones, bicycles, and explosives. More than half a century earlier, Cooper had also intended his Leatherstocking tales to demonstrate the superiority of European civilization over life on the American frontier. Just as he failed to create credible patricians illustrative of his socially progressive theory, Twain later could not endow his own allegedly superior conceptions with fictional authenticity.[33]

More distressing than the ends Hank achieves are his suspect means of instituting a capitalist, industrial American way of life. Introducing consumer goods through crass commercialism and vulgar advertising ploys only confirms his willingness to reduce everything to cost-accounting. He abruptly dismisses the Grail quest as unprofitable; instead, he orders stove-pipe hats for King Arthur's knights, better to equip them to peddle shoe polish, sewing machines, and barbed wire. The population's illiteracy hardly curbs Hank's distribution of a "Court Circular," a daily newspaper, and a prohibition journal. All these publications, of course, are meant either for comic deflation or as occasions of parody. More often than not, however, a wary reader sees the possibility of such instances cutting sharply the other way. Instead of conceiving sensitive solutions to social problems, Hank imposes useless products and services with Procrustean willfulness. He replaces jousting with "armored" baseball and converts a hermit's religious abasement into the power source for a shirt factory. Aspiring to recognition as the modern man *par excellence*—like Napoleon III in *Innocents Abroad*, "representative of the highest modern civilization, progress, and refinement"[34]—he achieves successes as trivial as Merlin's.

[32] Frederick Anderson, William M. Gibson, and Henry Nash Smith, eds., *Selected Mark Twain-Howells Letters, 1872-1910* (1960; rpt. New York: Atheneum, 1968), p. 287.

[33] See Roger B. Saloman, *Twain and the Image of History* (New Haven: Yale University Press, 1961), pp. 113, 118-19; James M. Cox, *Mark Twain: The Fate of Humor* (Princeton: Princeton University Press, 1966), pp. 216-17; Henry Nash Smith, *Mark Twain's Fable of Progress: Political and Economic Ideas in "A Connecticut Yankee"* (New Brunswick: Rutgers University Press, 1964), pp. 86-87.

[34] Samuel Clemens [Mark Twain], *The Innocents Abroad, or, The New Pilgrim's Progress* (1869; rpt. Hartford, Conn.: American Publishing Co., 1890), p. 126.

Where Hank himself fails to do so, those he attempts to civilize call his perspective into question. At first, he can join in their humor at his expense, appreciating that his actions reflect a social training as restrictive as theirs. "Inherited ideas are a curious thing, and interesting to observe and examine. I had mine, the king and his people had theirs. In both cases they flowed in ruts worn deep by time and habit, and the man who should have proposed to divert them by reason and argument would have had a long contract on his hands."[35] Hank acknowledges his dogmatism only infrequently thereafter; he even denies having been shaped by cultural patterns as constrictingly inhumane as the Arthurians'. Nonetheless, the novel displays a representative Hank with moral deficiencies more troubling than those apparent in the people he wants to raise. The novel's grim conclusion ironically exposes him as the true barbarian Arthurians first suspected. Long before the end, Twain points to the ambivalent nature of Hank's talents. The opening reference to his nineteenth-century employer, the Colt arms factory, for example, reminds us of technology's capacity for destruction as well as for material progress. And however little the novel substantiates genuine progress, it amply illustrates the machine's destructive efficiency. Early in his career as "The Boss," Hank revealingly speaks of his secret factories operating like "a serene volcano, standing innocent with its smokeless summit in the blue sky and giving no sign of the rising hell in its bowels."[36] The conclusion, perhaps the most grotesque in American literature, figures forth the appalling implications of this image in what is also the most elaborate manifestation of Hank's technology. He and his small band of boys electrocute, drown, and gun down twenty-five thousand men, only to succumb themselves to a miasma of rotting flesh. The whole gruesomely acknowledges the moral exhaustion of Hank's scientific philosophy and, by extension, of Twain's economic and political beliefs.[37]

This seemingly unintended repudiation of industrial technology was not informed by any genuine understanding of the possibilities offered by another culture. Twain's youthful excursion to the Sandwich Islands and encounters with native Hawaiians may have lent certain qualities to his basic conception in *A Connecticut Yankee*. But if so, he practiced a device differing in degree, not kind, from Enlightenment instancings of primitive peoples to measure their cul-

[35] Clemens, *A Connecticut Yankee in King Arthur's Court* (New York: Charles L. Webster and Co., 1889), p. 98.

[36] Ibid., p. 120.

[37] See Henry Nash Smith, *Fable of Progress*, pp. 6-7, and Smith, *Mark Twain: The Development of a Writer* (1962; rpt. New York: Atheneum, 1967), p. 12.

ture's inadequacies. That degree, however, was considerable, and had as much to do with the passing of the nineteenth century as with the talents of any particular writer.

More to present purposes, Twain combined in his fictional assessment three strains we have already seen emerging in the nineteenth century. Starting with a basic revaluation of primitive culture, he soon evinced deeply ambivalent feelings about his own society. Indeed, his work goes on to reveal the fundamental incompatibility of pastoral simplicity, as expressed in Sandy, with the surging volcano of technological industry. Finally, he could do nothing more than expose the moral bankruptcy of his technology, its all-embracing destructiveness. Perhaps the very fact that Twain did not intend this sequence or even fully realize its implications suggests how compelling these strains were for him and his contemporaries. He had arrived at a fictional view that many individuals by the last third of the century perceived more directly and factually: that western European civilization, particularly its American variant, might have little to redeem it from a charge of fundamental inhumanity.

Just as Rebecca Harding Davis's story "Life in the Iron Mills" (1861) presaged the muckrakers' efforts of the early 1900s, so a feature article in the popular *Harper's New Monthly Magazine* of May 1870 discreetly raised the question, "What is a Barbarian? What is a Civilized Man?" It concluded with the uncertain query: "Is civilization a good or an evil?"[38] Doubtless, neither the writer nor his readers hesitated more than a comfortable few minutes over the question. As should be all too clear by now, however, this predictable response hardly concedes what one recent historian has claimed, that "altogether what infuriated the white man was the Indians' indifference to that which was so obvious: the superiority of the white man's civilization."[39]

Increasingly toward the century's turn, those familiar with native cultures found themselves forced to challenge their civilization. By 1896 the famous anthropologist of the Ghost-Dance religion, James Mooney, could adopt the native perspective to a similar end: "The wise men tell us that the world is growing happier—that we live longer than did our fathers, have more comfort and less of toil, fewer wars and discords, and higher hopes and aspirations. So say the wise men; but deep in our own hearts we know they are wrong. . . . We

[38] Benson J. Lossing, "Our Barbarian Brethren," *Harper's New Monthly Magazine*, 40 (May 1870), 793, 811.

[39] Howard H. Peckham, "Indian Relations in the United States," in John Francis McDermott, ed., *Research Opportunities in American Cultural History* (Lexington: University Press of Kentucky, 1961), p. 31.

found the glory that had lured us onward was only the sunset glow that fades into darkness while we look, and leaves us at the very goal to sink down, tired in body and sick at heart. . . . As with men, so it is with nations."⁴⁰ Manifestly, though speaking for Indians, Mooney was also expressing a judgment on white America. Boas remarked more directly and pointedly that "greater lack of cultural values than that found in the inner life of some strata of our modern population is hardly found anywhere."⁴¹ By the time he said this, America could seem well into the later scenes of Thomas Cole's *Course of Empire.*

40 James Mooney, *The Ghost-Dance Religion and the Sioux Outbreak of 1890* (1896), ed. Anthony F. C. Wallace (New York: Dover Publications, 1972), p. 1.
41 Cited by William Brandon, *The Last Americans: The Indian in American Culture* (New York: McGraw-Hill, 1974), p. 3. See also Bidney, "Concept of Value," pp. 687-88.

CHAPTER TEN

EPILOGUE

Conservation is getting nowhere because it is incompatible with our Abrahamic concept of land. We abuse land because we regard it as a commodity belonging to us. When we see land as a community to which we belong, we may begin to use it with love and respect. There is no other way for land to survive the impact of mechanized man.

—Aldo Leopold
A Sand County Almanac (1949)

So-called primitive societies, of course, exist in history; their past is as old as ours, since it goes back to the origin of the species. . . . But they have specialized in ways different from those which we have chosen. Perhaps they have, in certain respects, remained closer to the very ancient conditions of life, but this does not preclude the possibility that in other respects they are farther from those conditions than we are.

—Claude Lévi-Strauss
Inaugural Lecture, Collège de France
(January 1960)

İT IS CUSTOMARY in literary and cultural history to see the catastrophe of World War I as closing a century of faith in rationality and progress. Perhaps so, but the state of mind associated with the young American men and women thereafter had more distant antecedents. From the vantage of 1900, glancing over figures dotting this book's landscape, we can see these latter-day doubts evolving long before 1918. Whether they were prompted by aesthetic, historical, or cultural considerations, or some mix of the three; whether they expressed their concerns through federal and institutional efforts or those characteristically private (not to say eccentric); whether they used their experiences to make knowledgeable, sometimes brilliant assessments or merely to reiterate conventional wisdom—Americans in the nineteenth century felt growing uncertainties about the possibilities foreclosed by a westering, progressive ideology. Of course, this uneasy ferment was hardly unique to America. The terrifying rapidity of industrial transformation going on throughout Western civilization also generated European equivalents—the preservation of country villages, the encouragement of nearly lost handicrafts, and so on.[1] But what invests American history with a peculiar, indeed a tragic intensity is the once compelling Edenic myth of hope, regeneration, and perfection. Nowhere else did there exist just that conjunction of magnificent wilderness, a once unparalleled plentitude of animal life, a wide variety of intrinsically self-contained alien cultures, and an energetic, pioneering intruder. Only in America, that is, were conditions quite so ready for the emergence of the strains outlined here at so many levels of awareness and intensity.

The point nonetheless bears repeating that far less than a majority ever felt the apprehensions, much less entertained the ideas, suggested above. Those who have leafed through western Americana collections can testify that every expression of concern for the physical continent, native tribes, or American society is discovered only after turning over countless volumes mindlessly effusing over the promise of westward expansion. Public opinion may have constrained some of these to write what they did not quite believe, but most remained deaf to the troubling observations of their contemporaries. Only a mildly intractable minority gave voice to the underlying uncertainties that the larger group perhaps felt but could not articulate because so at odds with the acceptable commonplaces of American life. Whether

[1] See, for example, John Ward, *Pyramids and Progress: Sketches From Egypt* (London: Eyre and Spottiswoode, 1900), p. xvii.

or not America actually experienced its most rapid transformation during the mid-nineteenth century, it is true that never before did Americans feel so intensely deracinated. "We have the St. Vitus' dance," declared Thoreau, appalled at his countrymen's frenetic westering.[2] But few thought to slow the dance that would alter the landscape seemingly overnight. Still fewer guessed to what it would lead.

By 1900, white Americans had effectively settled and "civilized" the continent. They had reduced native tribes to their weakest state, in part by reducing them to a number fewer than ever before or since.[3] The Eleventh United States Census of 1890 offered figures on which Frederick Jackson Turner three years later based his thesis of the closing of the frontier. That same document was also, ironically, "one of the most exhaustive sources of information on the American Indian ever published."[4] In other words, the census signaled both that wilderness no longer existed and that its human symbol was no longer an alien. A ward of the government, the Indian was at best a museum piece, at worst a scorned anachronism. The process that had shaped America even as it exterminated many of its indigenous populations was supposedly at an end, having confirmed what Americans both desired and feared.

The advent of the twentieth century, far from calming eight or so decades of apprehensions, meant instead their intensification. To develop an account of the further shifts in attitude during these last eight decades would require another book as long as this one. Indeed, the survey would be lengthier, since the conflicts have grown that much more complex, public and private endeavors that much more various. How shall we today reconcile these violently contradictory actions and consequences? On the one hand, there is the Alaska Native Claims Settlement Act of 1971, which deeded extraordinarily generous grants of land to native populations, set aside vast tracts for conservation, and otherwise protects against exploitation. For the first time, Congress refused to impose paternalistic terms of use on tribal recipients, abandoning solutions based on removal, reservations, and wardship. As well, it legislated respect for a fragile ecology, to be protected at all costs against the consequences of thoughtless developers and careless oil companies intent only on completing a pipe-

---

[2] Thoreau, *Walden* (1854), ed. J. Lyndon Shanley (Princeton: Princeton University Press, 1971), p. 93.

[3] Wilbur R. Jacobs, "The Indian and the Frontier in American History—A Need for Revision," *Western Historical Quarterly*, 4 (January 1973), 47.

[4] Robert Taft, in *Artists and Illustrators of the Old West 1850-1900* (New York: Charles Scribner's Sons, 1953), p. 215, speaking of the *Report on Indians Taxed and Indians Not Taxed in the United States (Except Alaska) at the Eleventh Census: 1890* (1894).

line across the state.[5] On the other hand, consider the more recent legislation authorizing what is by the Department of the Interior's own evaluation the useless damming of the Little Tennessee River. It means the dispossession of a sturdy yeomanry, the inundation of a uniquely beautiful and fertile valley, and the ruthless disregard for the archaeological sites of the Cherokees' ancestral religious center— all, so far as can be determined, for the real benefit only of certain land developers and the political fortunes of a senator.[6] The debate continues, as present jobs vie with future generations, native rights and conservation contend with a powerfully exploitative ethos.

Yet there are signs—most of them hopeful, though still tentative— and perhaps it is worth the risk of superficiality to name at least some of them. To write a history of conservation for our time would be to start with Theodore Roosevelt's friendship with Gifford Pinchot, which led to the most sustained public movement ever on behalf of conservation.[7] Special-interest and private groups, in some cases modeled after California's Sierra Club, also helped to convince Americans of the need to husband natural resources.[8] Government officials such as Steve Mather and Horace M. Albright successfully encouraged fellow countrymen to "See America First" and at the same time aggrandized power to the National Park Service.[9] According to one scholar, "It is no exaggeration to say that by 1921 the conservation of natural resources had become a well-established government function.[10]

During this period, the setting aside of large tracts of unspoiled land became a mark of good citizenship for the well-to-do, especially following the example of John D. Rockefeller.[11] An innovative land-

5 See Robert D. Arnold, *Alaska Native Land Claims* (Anchorage: Alaska Native Foundation, 1976); Wilcomb E. Washburn, *Red Man's Land, White Man's Law: A Study of the Past and Present Status of the American Indian* (New York: Charles Scribner's Sons, 1971), pp. 124ff.; John McPhee, *Coming into the Country* (New York: Farrar, Straus and Giroux, 1977), pp. 18-21, 34-36, 152, 391-93.

6 See Peter Matthiessen, "How to Kill a Valley," *New York Review of Books*, February 7, 1980, pp. 31-36.

7 William H. Harbaugh, *The Life and Times of Theodore Roosevelt*, rev. ed. (New York: Oxford University Press, 1963), pp. 304ff.

8 Douglas H. Strong, "The Sierra Club—A History. Part I: Origins and Outings," *Sierra*, October 1977, pp. 10-14; Strong, "The Sierra Club—A History. Part II: Conservation," *Sierra*, November-December 1977, pp. 16-20.

9 Donald C. Swain, *Wilderness Defender: Horace M. Albright and Conservation* (Chicago: University of Chicago Press, 1970), esp. pp. 46ff.; Robert Shankland, *Steve Mather of the National Parks* (New York: Alfred A. Knopf, 1951), pp. 4, 12-13.

10 Donald C. Swain, *Federal Conservation Policy, 1921-1933*, University of California Publications in History, 76 (Los Angeles: University of California Press, 1963), p. 5.

11 Stewart L. Udall, *The Quiet Crisis* (New York: Avon, 1963), pp. 161-64.

scape architect, Clarence Stein, popularized Olmsted's ideas in conceiving entire greenbelt towns designed in accordance with, rather than as impositions on, the natural environment.[12] In a rather crude and anarchic fashion, modern suburban sprawl has seemed to adopt this principle. Perhaps we may feel less ambiguity about the continuing popularity of *A Sand County Almanac* (1949), in which retired forester Aldo Leopold formulated an ethos of respect for the land as a community in which man is only one participant. Leopold declared that man had no more, perhaps less, inherent right to alter that environment to his ends and that we need to evolve "an ethical relation to the land" based on "love, respect, and admiration.[13] To be sure, Leopold's vision borders on the sentimental. But the degree of serious consideration given to like-minded philosophies by the 1930s and 1940s suggests a radical change in Americans' regard for the continent.

Similarly, Americans revised their opinion of Indians in the first half of this century, though the process differed in two substantial ways: fewer whites shared in this revaluation, and Indians themselves considerably shaped those altered assumptions. The Dawes Severalty Act of 1887 finally completed the process of destruction where wars, diseases, and removal had not quite succeeded. Aside from indirectly effecting the loss of more than two-thirds of the remaining reservation lands, it struck a catastrophic psychological blow at Indians. By 1928, when the Secretary of the Interior was presented with the well-researched Lewis Merriam report, the documented record of the bankruptcy of government policy came as little surprise. At least one of the report's conclusions, however, pointed to a genuine rethinking of possibilities: "He who wants to remain an Indian and live according to his old culture should be aided in doing so."[14] This idea formed the basis of the next phase of federal policy, pressed into law by perhaps the most remarkable white man to serve the federal government in the cause of Indian affairs.

Nearly a decade before the Merriam report, John Collier felt completely diseffected with post-World War I America, "its externalism

---

[12] Ada Louise Huxtable, "Clarence Stein—The Champion of the Neighborhood," *New York Times*, January 16, 1977, pp. 23, 28.

[13] Leopold, *A Sand County Almanac* (1949; rpt. New York: Ballantine, 1970), p. 261. See also Roderick Nash, ed., *The American Environment: Readings in the History of Conservation* (Reading, Mass.: Addison-Wesley, 1968), pp. 105ff.

[14] Cited in Washburn, *Red Man's Land*, p. 77. See as well Harold E. Driver, *Indians of North America*, 2d ed. rev. (Chicago: University of Chicago Press, 1969), pp. 493-95. Note the reception during this period given Ruth Benedict's *Patterns of Culture* (Boston: Houghton Mifflin Co., 1934), the most popular anthropology text ever sold.

and receptive sensualism, its hostility to human diversity, its fanatical devotion to downgrading standardization, its exploitative myopia, and that world fascism and home fascism which the boundless, all-haunting insecurity and the consequent lust for personal advantage were bringing to fatal power."[15] Moving to the Southwest in 1920, he became fascinated with the kind of life still maintained by local tribes. The election of Franklin Delano Roosevelt in 1932 brought the unexpected appointment of Collier, long a caustic critic of America's Indian policies, as Commissioner of Indian Affairs. Immediately, he set about preparing legislation that would result in the Indian Reorganization Act of 1934. Instead of attempting to assimilate natives into a supposed American melting pot, the act encouraged communal ownership of lands, separate tribal constitutions, and the revival of native arts, crafts, and education. Though the bill was Collier's inspiration, he realized that its passage into law reflected a more general change in attitudes. The 1934 act did not redress the long history of wrongs perpetrated against native tribes. It did not even mark a final stage in progressively more enlightened attitudes among white Americans, for within twenty years Congress gutted the Indian New Deal. Yet those programs for the first time registered the American government's respectful acceptance of native tribes on their own terms.

By the time Franklin Roosevelt took office, in other words, selfless efforts on behalf of the land and of native peoples had at last won a measure of nationwide respect. Curiously, the two large issues still attracted different sets of proponents, but with one notable exception: Harold L. Ickes, Roosevelt's Secretary of the Interior. A charter member of the American Indian Defense Association, Ickes deserves primary credit for the appointment of Collier as Commissioner of Indian Affairs. At the same time, his commitment to land conservation urged him to try to remake the Department of the Interior into a Department of Conservation.

Likewise, twentieth-century artists have fictionally explored the interlinked issues of the rights of indigenous natives and those of the land itself. Willa Cather, for example, whose *The Professor's House* was

15 John Collier, *The Indians of the Americas* (New York: W. W. Norton, 1947), p. 18, also pp. 244ff. See also Driver, *Indians of North America*, p. 494; Robert F. Berkhofer Jr., *The White Man's Indian: Images of the American Indian from Columbus to the Present* (New York: Alfred A. Knopf, 1978), pp. 178-88; Washburn, *Red Man's Land*, pp. 78ff.; Washburn, *The Indian in America* (New York: Harper and Row, 1975), pp. 253-54; Kenneth R. Philip, "John Collier and the Controversy over the Wheeler-Howard Bill," in Jane F. Smith and Robert M. Krasnicka, eds., *Indian-White Relations: A Persistent Paradox* (Washington: Howard University Press, 1976), pp. 171-200; Lawrence C. Kelly, "John Collier and the Indian New Deal: An Assessment," in ibid., pp. 227-41.

discussed earlier, attempted such a synthesis in her celebrated novel *Death Comes for the Archbishop* (1927). Father Jean Latour, bishop to the mid-nineteenth-century diocese of New Mexico, grows to respect the peaceable Hopi and Navaho in their relation to the land. At first, however, neither appeals to him; the people seem as formidably inaccessible as the landscape: "he was quite willing to believe that behind Jacinto," the narrator notes about the bishop's response to his Hopi guide, "there was a long tradition, a story of experience, which no language could translate to him. A chill came with the darkness."[16]

Latour first fears, then comes to respect this "kind of life out of reach." As he learns, native religion values all nature as sacred; it is not to be altered by proud man but merely "passed through."[17] Devotion to his project of a great cathedral is thematically balanced against this deepening appreciation. Near the close of his life, however, Latour recognizes the defects of his own white influence. "Men travel faster now," a Navaho comments to the dying archbishop, reflecting on the recent railroad as Thoreau had; "but I do not know if they go to better things."[18] Santa Fe's tawdry new buildings come to represent for Latour the loss of something "in the air," and he regrets not having recorded the old native legends and myths, now forever lost.[19] Most important, Cather intimates his distress at the civilized consciousness that arbitrarily isolates individual acts from spatial context, man from nature, a culture from the landscape. One scholar has probed this idea to even more troubling depths in reflecting on "the last Americans":

> The important point is that the Indian world may really have been a genuine, influential civilization worth taking seriously in American history. It may really have been a civilization so firmly committed to its strange attitudes that it nourished its own conquerors and abetted its own conquest. It may really have been a civilization so incomprehensibly foreign to Europeans that Europeans could not recognize its existence even while in mortal embrace with it, somewhat as in the case of the dark planets imagined by Alfred North Whitehead that move on a scale of space and time so radically different from our own as to be undetectable to our sense and instruments. And finally it may have been a

[16] Cather, *Death Comes for the Archbishop* (1927; rpt. New York: Random House, 1971), p. 92.
[17] Ibid., pp. 103, 233-35.
[18] Ibid., p. 291.
[19] Ibid., pp. 275, 277.

civilization affecting not only our past but still to affect our future.[20]

More than responsible scholarship is clearly involved here. As always, questions of gain and loss obtrude, of what material progress genuinely accomplishes against what it rudely sacrifices. Or, rather, during the century and a half since Americans first voiced them, these considerations have become as complex as the changing conditions of American life.

Technological progress and constant economic growth, far from shimmering in attractive prospect, have tarnished badly in the event. "The more science, technology, and the gross national product grow," one respected economist has written, "the more nasty, brutish, vile and precarious becomes human existence."[21] While extending prosperity, modern industrial economies have also compelled ever larger numbers to labor at ever less satisfying and meaningful tasks. Some observers further argue that trying to correct these unforeseen consequences of progress will only contribute to greater social enslavement.

It is no surprise that a much less vocal minority in the nineteenth century sensed this distinction between a technical and a moral ordering of experience, between their own epistemology, which was relatively indifferent to humankind, and a supposedly primitive one that encouraged individuals in responsible action.[22] Perhaps less obvious, however, are the ways in which contemporary unease with Western culture ironically mirrors that first expressed by native Americans and acknowledged by some whites. To credit what popular literature, cinema, and television inadvertently reveal, we feel about modern technology much as Indians felt about the pioneers who introduced them to its earlier forms. Sophisticated machines, computers in particular, challenge our humane values even as they offer material benefits. Their extraordinary capacity for quantitative analysis inspires awe, to be sure. But it also instills a sense of dread, since such knowledge and consequent power seem ever greater threats to human auton-

20 William Brandon, *The Last Americans: The Indian in American Culture* (New York: McGraw-Hill, 1974), p. 22. See also, for a tangential comment, Jarold Ramsey, *Coyote Was Going There: Indian Literature of the Oregon Country* (Seattle: Washington University Press, 1977), p. xxxi.

21 Leonard Silk, "Bigger Badder," review of E. J. Mishan, *The Economic Growth Debate*, in *New York Times Book Review*, February 5, 1978, p. 12.

22 Walter J. Ong, S.J., "World as View and World as Event," *American Anthropologist*, 71 (August 1969), 634-47; Robert Redfield, *The Primitive World and Its Transformations* (Ithaca: Cornell University Press, 1953), esp. pp. 22-24, 81-83, 102-10.

omy. Native tribes received pioneers no differently, regarding them with both envy and disgust. Even as they wonderingly accepted a technology of guns, traps, and textiles, Indians abhorred the day-to-day patterns that whites demanded they adopt. How could they embrace ways of life so contrary to all they cherished in life itself? How could they accept modes and mores that violated sacred knowledge? The mixed reception they gave to whites and, in turn, white Americans' growing appreciation of the reasons offer means for understanding our present circumstances.

Clearly, the issues traced here still shape attitudes and actions; in large ways and small, in public legislation as in private fears, they mold our responses. This study has not assumed an easy progression from misgivings early in the nineteenth century to our tentative resolutions of them. Nor should we make any larger claim for recent efforts than they warrant. Yet it is true that a whole array of private and government programs have lately focused public energies on endangered species and land conservation. Grants supporting preservation and revival of native lore proliferate, as do newsweekly essays encouraging them. A national constituency subscribes to such groups as the Sierra Club, the Society for Endangered Species, and the American Indian Movement, each of which is devoted to a holding action in the erosion of landscape and cultures. Predictably, scholars still claim that too little is being done too slowly and too late. Indian tribes have turned, so some allege, into what whites always imagined them: a single entity, bound together by economic necessity and social ostracism.[23] While this charge partially describes native affairs, characteristically from a white perspective, people nonetheless have tried as never before to understand, even to learn from native points of view.[24] Anthropologists now find themselves joined by historians and government officials.[25] All of these efforts only barely indicate how variously the impulse to leave a record for future generations continues to affect Americans.

Perhaps fiction, once again, offers the best touchstone, since it more concisely reveals the multiple extensions of contemporary response. By that standard, Barry Lopez's short story "The Photographer" (1977) is exemplary, summing up in all of two pages the issues we have been exploring throughout. A young man decides to make a gallery of "endangered and possibly extinct animals. He

23 Berkhofer, White Man's Indian, p. 195; Frederick Turner, " 'Tribe' Is a White Man's Concept," New York Times, January 8, 1978, Week in Review section, p. 2.

24 Wilbur R. Jacobs, Dispossessing the American Indian: Indians and Whites on the Colonial Frontier (New York: Charles Scribner's Sons, 1972), p. 25.

25 For a good review of current trends, see Francis Paul Prucha, "Doing Indian History," in Smith and Krasnicka, eds., Indian-White Relations, pp. 3-10.

would go to the places where the last of a species had been reported and he would systematically set about capturing the animals on film."[26] After spending "some years" among Plains Indians learning wilderness lore, the unnamed photographer sets out on his mission. Over nearly a decade, he patiently completes thirty-one portraits of birds, rodents, and mammals listed as extinct or endangered. In each one he achieves "exactly what he wanted. A portrait of an endangered species that would terrify."

Exhibited in New York City, the photographs garner instant acclaim. But their "unsettling" quality soon converts enthusiasm to "a sort of fear." Conservationists and art scholars decide to reproduce the invaluable portraits, since the negatives have been destroyed. Yet as they begin, the photographs start to fade and within a few hours become unrecognizable blurs. The photographer himself had refused payment, publicity, or further commission: "he thought privately that he had done what he set out to do and that in an odd way he was now free to go." Unconcerned with his photographs' fate, he abandons his camera equipment and travels to Alaska "to study the behavior of humpback whales."

The story is hardly representative of actual history, perhaps least so in the photographer's final abjuration of responsibility—so different from the fierce perseverance of contemporaries committed to so many holding actions against industrial progress. Still, the story nicely integrates the kinds of careers and many of the themes we have been studying: the concern for vanishing wildlife; the impulse to document it; the artistic preparation for the self-imposed task; the appreciation of native American lore in best comprehending the wilderness; the discovery, in compiling that record, of aspects more compelling than had been anticipated; and finally, the photographer's conclusion, despite excursions elsewhere, that "there was nothing outside North America that held his interest."

The story grips the imagination for reasons that, as with all literature, ultimately elude analysis. In part it does so, for the American reader at least, by concisely imaging a constellation of ideas and attitudes that our history has rehearsed. The constellation is a lesser one, certainly, within the galaxy of America's social, economic, and intellectual history. Yet a vanishing continental wilderness elicited apprehensions and commitments that in telling ways continue to define us as a people. Which is simply to say that whatever we may mean to evoke by the phrase "American character" must not ignore that mixed strain of regret about the process of westering that ramified so variously, so vigorously through the nineteenth century.

26 Lopez, "The Photographer," *North American Review*, 262 (Fall 1977), 66-67.

SELECTED BIBLIOGRAPHY

Manuscript Collections

Akerly, Samuel. "On the Cultivation of Forest Trees; In a Letter Addressed to Jonathan Thompson, Esq. Collector of the Customs of the Port of New York." Broadside. 1823. American Antiquarian Society. Worcester, Massachusetts.

Banks, D. C. "To the Citizens of Kentucky." Broadside. February 15, 1840. American Antiquarian Society.

Bonine, E. A. Collection of Photographs. Henry E. Huntington Library, San Marino, California.

Catlin, George. "The North Americans in the Middle of the Nineteenth Century: A Numerous and Noble Race of Human Beings fast passing to oblivion and leaving no monuments of their own behind them." Bound folio. George Catlin Collection. Huntington Library.

Hillers, Jack. Photographic Views of Ancient Ruins of Hopi Villages. 9 original photographs mounted and bound. 1880s? Huntington Library.

James, George Wharton. Photographs; stereophotos. Box 5. Huntington Library.

Kern, Edward, and Kern, Richard. *The Published Pictures, Portraits and Maps Collectively Depicting the Indians, Scenery and Topography of the Far West, Drawn by Edward Kern and Richard Kern, 1846-1851.* Fort Sutter Papers. Vol. 39. Huntington Library.

Monsen, Frederick. *Frederick Monsen's Ethnographic Indian Photographs.* 13 vols. Huntington Library.

Moon, Carl, "A Brief Account of the Making of this Collection of Indian Pictures." Typescript. Dated: Pasadena, Calif., 1924. Huntington Library.

————. Letter to Grace Nicholson. January 14, 1931. Box 6, Nicholson Collection. Huntington Library.

Nicholson, Grace. Grace Nicholson Photograph Albums "A"–"E." Huntington Library.

————. Nicholson Collection. Boxes i-xvi. Huntington Library.

————. *Nicholson (Grace) Collection: Summary Report.* Huntington Library.

Rollins, Philip. Philip Rollins Western Americana Collection. Firestone Library. Princeton University. Princeton, New Jersey.

Rust, Horatio Nelson. Horatio Nelson Rust Collection. Huntington Library.

Saunders, Charles Francis. Pocket Diary for 1909, July 31–September 5, tour of the pueblos. Box 9, Saunders (Charles Francis) Collection. Huntington Library.

———. Pocket Diary for 1909 Tour, September 25–November 18. Box 9, Saunders Collection. Huntington Library.

Vroman, A. C. A. C. Vroman's Diary, Hopi Indians. Ca. 1895. Huntington Library.

PUBLISHED SOURCES

Primary

Atwater, Caleb. *Remarks Made on a Tour to Prairie Du Chien; Thence to Washington City, in 1829.* Columbus: Isaac N. Whiting, 1831.

———. *The Writings of Caleb Atwater.* Columbus: n.p., 1833.

Audubon, John James. *Delineations of American Scenery and Character.* New York: G. A. Baker and Co., 1926.

Audubon, Maria R. *Audubon and His Journals.* 2 vols. New York: Charles Scribner's Sons, 1897.

Ayer, I. Winslow. *Life in the Wilds of America, and Wonders of the West in and beyond the Bounds of Civilization.* Grand Rapids, Mich.: Central Publishing Co., 1880.

J.B.B. "The Yates Collections." *Land of Sunshine,* 2 (May 1895), 98.

Baird, Henry S. "Recollections of the Early History of Northern Wisconsin." *Collections of the State Historical Society of Wisconsin,* 4 (1859), 197-221.

Baird, Spencer F. "Letter from the Secretary of the Smithsonian Institution." In *Annual Report of the Board of Regents of the Smithsonian Institution for the Year Ending June 30, 1887,* pp. 1-27. Washington: G.P.O., 1889.

Bancroft, Hubert Howe. *The Early American Chroniclers.* San Francisco: A. L. Bancroft and Co., 1883.

———. *The Narrative Races of the Pacific States of North America.* 5 vols. New York: D. Appleton and Co., 1875-76.

Bandelier, Adolph F. *Papers of the Archaeological Institute of America, American Series.* 5 vols. Boston: Cupples, Upham, and Co., 1883-92.

Barrett, Joseph, M.D. *The Indian of New-England and the North-Eastern Provinces.* Middletown, Conn.: Charles H. Pelton, 1851.

Bartlett, John Russell. *Personal Narrative of Explorations and Incidents in Texas, New Mexico, California, Sonora, and Chihuahua, Connected with the United States and Mexican Boundary Commission, During the Years 1850, '51, '52, and '53.* 2 vols. New York: D. Appleton and Co., 1854.

Baxter, Sylvester. "An Aboriginal Pilgrimage." *Century Magazine,* 24 (August 1882), 526-36.

———. "The Father of the Pueblos." *Harper's New Monthly Magazine,* 65 (June 1882), 72-91.

Beckwith, Hiram W. *The Illinois and Indiana Indians.* Chicago: Fergus Printing Co., 1884.

Beeson, John. *A Plea for the Indians; With Facts and Features of the Late War in Oregon.* New York: J. Beeson, 1857.

Beggs, Rev. Stephen R. *Pages from the Early History of the West and Northwest.* . . . Cincinnati: Methodist Book Concern, 1868.

Benjamin, S.G.W. *Art in America: A Critical and Historical Sketch.* New York: Harper and Brothers, 1880.

Berlandier, Jean Louis. *The Indians of Texas in 1830.* Translated by Patricia Reading Leclercq. Edited by John C. Ewers. Washington: Smithsonian Institution, 1969.

Bierstadt, Albert. "Letter from the Rocky Mountains, July 10, 1859." *Crayon,* 6 (September 1859), 287.

Bird, Robert Montgomery. *Peter Pilgrim; or, A Rambler's Recollections.* 2 vols. Philadelphia: Lea and Blanchard, 1838.

Boas, Franz. *Chinook Texts.* Bureau of American Ethnology. Washington: G.P.O., 1894.

———. *Race, Language and Culture.* New York: Macmillan Co., 1940.

———. *The Shaping of American Anthropology, 1883-1911: A Franz Boas Reader.* Edited with an introduction by George W. Stocking Jr. New York: Basic Books, 1974.

Boller, Henry A. *Among the Indians. Eight Years in the Far West: 1858-1866.* Philadelphia: T. Ellwood Zell, 1868.

Bourke, Capt. John G. *On the Border with Crook.* New York: Charles Scribner's Sons, 1891.

———. *The Snake-Dance of the Moquis of Arizona.* . . . New York: Charles Scribner's Sons, 1884.

Brace, Charles Loring. *The New West; or, California in 1867-1868.* New York: G. P. Putnam and Son, 1869.

Brackenridge, Henry Marie. *Recollections of Persons and Places in the West*. Philadelphia: James Kay, Jun. and Brother, 1834.

Bradford, Alexander W. *American Antiquities and Researches into the Origin and History of the Red Race*. New York: Dayton and Saxton, 1841.

Brinton, Daniel G. *The Annals of the Cakchiquels*. 1885. Reprint. New York: Ams Press, 1969.

———. *Essays of an Americanist*. Philadelphia: David McKay, 1890.

———. *The Lenâpé and Their Legends*. 1885. Reprint. New York: Ams Press, 1969.

———. *Races and Peoples: Lectures on the Science of Ethnography*. Philadelphia: David McKay, 1901.

Brush, George de Forest. "An Artist Among the Indians." *Century Magazine*, 30 (May 1885), 54-57.

Bryant, William Cullen. *Letters of a Traveller; or, Notes of Things Seen in Europe and America*. 1850. 4th ed. New York: G. P. Putnam and Co., 1855.

———. "A New Public Park." *New York Evening Post*, July 3, 1844, p. 2.

———. *Poems*. Philadelphia: Carey and Hart, 1848.

Buchanan, James. *Sketches of the History, Manners, and Customs of the North American Indians with a Plan for Their Melioration*. 2 vols. New York: W. Borradaile, 1824.

Buck, William J. "Lappawinzo and Tishcohan, Chiefs of the Lenni Lenape." *Pennsylvania Magazine of History and Biography*, 7 (1883) 215-18.

Carr, John. *Pioneer Days in California*. Eureka, Calif.: Times Publishing Co., 1891.

Carrington, Mrs. Margaret I. *Absaraka, Home of the Crows*. 1868. Edited by Milo Milton Quaife. Chicago: R. R. Donnelley and Sons, 1950.

Carroll, Rev. George R. *Pioneer Life in and Around Cedar Rapids, Iowa from 1839 to 1849*. Cedar Rapids: n.p., 1895.

Cass, Lewis. "Indians of North America." *North American Review*, 22 (1826), 53-119.

———. *Inquiries, Respecting the History, Traditions, Languages, Manners, Customs, Religion, &c. of the Indians, Living within the United States*. Detroit: Sheldon and Reed, 1823.

[———]. *Ontwa, the Son of the Forest. A Poem*. New York: Wiley and Halsted, 1822.

Catlin, George. *Letters and Notes on the Manners, Customs, and Conditions of the North American Indians*. 2 vols. 1844. Reprinted with an introduction by Marjorie Halpin. New York: Dover Publications, 1973.

———. *Life Among the Indians*. London: Gall and Inglis, [187?].

———. *O-kee-pa: A Religious Ceremony and Other Customs of the Mandans*. Edited by John C. Ewers. New Haven: Yale University Press, 1967.

———. *Shut Your Mouth and Save Your Life*. 1860. Reprint. London: Trübner and Co., 1875.

Chapman, Frank M. *Autobiography of a Bird-Lover*. New York: D. Appleton-Century Co., 1933.

Clark, Joshua V. H. *Lights and Lines of Indian Character and Scenes of Pioneer Life*. Syracuse: E. H. Babcock and Co., 1854.

———. *Onondaga; or Reminiscences of Earlier and Later Times*. . . . 2 vols. Syracuse: Stoddard and Babcock, 1849.

Clark, William Philo. *The Indian Sign Language, with Brief Explanatory Notes*. . . . Philadelphia: L. R. Hamersly and Co., 1884.

Clarke, Samuel Asahel. *Pioneer Days of Oregon History*. 2 vols. Portland: J. K. Gill Co., 1905.

Clinton, DeWitt. *A Memoir on the Antiquities of the Western Parts of the State of New York*. Albany: I. W. Clark, 1818.

Cole, Thomas. "The Lament of the Forest." *Knickerbocker*, 17 (June 1841), 516-19.

———. "Lecture on American Scenery, Delivered before the Catskill Lyceum, April 1st, 1841." *Northern Light*, 1 (May 1841), 25-26.

Collection of Indian Anecdotes, A. Concord, N.H.: William White, 1838.

Colton, George H. *Tecumseh; or, The West Thirty Years Since. A Poem*. New York: Wiley and Putnam, 1842.

Connor, J. Torrey. "Confessions of a Basket Collector." *Land of Sunshine*, 5 (June 1896), 3-10.

Conrad, Howard Louis. *"Uncle Dick" Wootton, the Pioneer Frontiersman of the Rocky Mountain Region*. Chicago: W. E. Dribble and Co., 1890.

Converse, Harriet Maxwell. "Myths and Legends of the New York State Iroquois." *New York State Museum Bulletin* 125. Albany: University of the State of New York, 1908.

Cook, James. *Captain Cook's Journal . . . 1768-71*. Edited by Capt. W.J.L. Wharton. London: Elliott Stock, 1893.

Cooper, Judge William. *A Guide in the Wilderness: or the History of the First Settlements in the Western Counties of New-York with Useful Instructions to Future Settlers*. 1810. Reprinted with an introduction by James Fenimore Cooper. Rochester, N.Y.: George P. Humphrey, 1897.

Copway, George. *The Life, History, and Travels of Kah-Ge-Ga-Gah-Bowh.* Albany: n.p., 1847.

————. *The Traditional History and Characteristic Sketches of the Ojibway Nation.* London: Charles Gilpin, 1850.

Costello, J. A. *The Siwash, Their Life, Legends and Tales.* Seattle: Calvert Co., 1895.

Cremony, John C. *Life Among the Apaches.* San Francisco: A. Roman and Co., 1868.

Crèvecoeur, Ferdinand F. *Old Settlers' Tales.* . . . Onaga, Kan.: n.p., 1902.

Crèvecoeur, Michel-Guillaume St. Jean de [J. Hector Saint John de Crèvecoeur]. *Journey into Northern Pennsylvania and the State of New York.* 1801. Translated by Clarissa Spencer Bostelmann. 3 vols. in one. Ann Arbor: University of Michigan Press, 1964.

Crook, George. *General George Crook: His Autobiography.* 2d ed. Edited by Martin F. Schmitt. Norman: University of Oklahoma Press, 1960.

Curtis, Edward S. *The North American Indian; Being a Series of Volumes Picturing and Describing the Indians of the United States, and Alaska.* Edited by Frederick Webb Hodge. Foreword by Theodore Roosevelt. 20 vols. Cambridge, Mass.: Harvard University Press, 1907-30.

Cushing, Frank Hamilton. "My Adventures in Zuni." *Century Magazine,* 25 (December 1882), 191-207.

————. "My Adventures in Zuni. II." *Century Magazine,* 26 (February 1883), 500-11.

————. *Zuni: Selected Writings of Frank Hamilton Cushing.* Edited and with an introduction by Jesse Green. Lincoln: University of Nebraska Press, 1979.

Darley, Felix O. C. *Scenes in Indian Life.* 4 numbers. Philadelphia: J. R. Colon, April-July 1843.

De Forest, John W. *History of the Indians of Connecticut from the Earliest Known Period to 1850.* Hartford: William James Hamersley, 1853.

Denig, Edwin Thompson, *Five Indian Tribes of the Upper Missouri.* Edited by John C. Ewers. Norman: University of Oklahoma Press, 1961.

Denny, Arthur A. *Pioneer Days on Puget Sound.* 1888. Reprint. Seattle: Alice Harriman Co., 1908.

De Schweinitz, Edmund. *The Life and Times of David Zeisberger: The Western Pioneer and Apostle of the Indians.* Philadelphia: J. B. Lippincott and Co., 1870.

De Smet, Pierre Jean, S.J. *Oregon Missions and Travels Over the Rocky Mountains, in 1845-46.* Illustrated by Nicolas Point. 1847. Reprinted in vol. 29 of Thwaites, ed., *Early Western Travels,* pp. 103-424.

Dixon, Joseph K. *The Vanishing Race: The Last Great Indian Council.* Garden City, N.Y.: Doubleday, Page and Co., 1913.

Dodge, Col. Richard Irving. *Our Wild Indians: Thirty-Three Years' Personal Experience Among the Red Men of the Great West. . . .* Hartford, Conn.: A. D. Worthington and Co., 1883.

Domenech, Abbé Emmanuel. *Seven Years' Residence in the Great Deserts of North America.* 2 vols. London: Longman, Green, Longman, and Roberts, 1860.

Donaldson, Thomas. *The George Catlin Indian Gallery in the U.S. National Museum.* Author's edition. Washington: G.P.O., 1887.

————. *The Public Domain: Its History, with Statistics.* 1880. 3d ed. Washington: G.P.O., 1884.

Dorsey, George A. *The Arapaho Sun Dance: The Ceremony of the Offerings Lodge.* Field Columbian Museum Publication 75. Chicago, 1903.

————. *The Cheyenne.* Vol. 1: *Ceremonial Organization.* Field Columbian Museum Publication 99. Anthropological Series, vol. 9, no. 1. Chicago, 1905.

————. *The Ponca Sun Dance.* Field Columbian Museum Publication 102. Anthropological Series, vol. 7, no. 2. Chicago, 1905.

Downing, Andrew Jackson, ed. *The Horticulturist and Journal of Rural Art and Rural Taste.* 1 (1846-47), 6 (1851-52).

Drake, Benjamin. *The Life and Adventures of Black Hawk.* 1838. 7th ed. rev. Cincinnati: E. Morgan and Co., 1850.

Drake, Daniel, M.D. *Discourse on the History, Character, and Prospects of the West.* 1834. Reprint. Gainesville, Fla.: Scholars' Facsimiles and Reprints, 1955.

————. *Pioneer Life in Kentucky: A Series of Reminiscential Letters from Daniel Drake, M.D., of Cincinnati, to His Children.* Edited by Charles D. Drake. Cincinnati: Robert Clarke and Co., 1870.

Dunbar, John B. "The Pawnee Indians: Their Habits and Customs." *Magazine of American History,* 8 (November 1882), 734-54.

Duval, John Crittenden. *Early Times in Texas.* Austin: H.P.N. Gammel and Co., 1892.

Dwight, Timothy. *Travels in New-England and New-York.* 4 vols. London: William Baynes and Son, 1823.

Eastman, Charles Alexander [Ohiyesa]. *From the Deep Woods to Civilization: Chapters in the Autobiography of an Indian.* 1916. Reprint. Boston: Little, Brown and Co., 1917.

———. *Indian Boyhood.* Illustrated by E. L. Blumenschein. 1902. Reprint. Boston: Little, Brown and Co., 1918.

———. *The Soul of the Indian: An Interpretation,* Boston: Houghton Mifflin Co., 1911.

Eastman, Mrs. Mary H. *The American Aboriginal Portfolio.* Illustrated by Seth Eastman. Philadelphia: Lippincott, Grambo and Co., [1853].

———. *Dahcotah; or, Life and Legends of the Sioux Around Fort Snelling.* Illustrated by Seth Eastman. 1849. Reprint. Minneapolis: Ross and Haines, 1962.

———. *The Romance of Indian Life.* Philadelphia: Lippincott, Grambo and Co., 1853.

Eggleston, Edward. *The Hoosier Schoolmaster.* 1871. Reprint. New York: Orange Judd Co., 1890.

Egleston, N. H. "What We Owe to the Trees." *Harper's New Monthly Magazine,* 64 (April 1882), 675-87.

Eliot, Charles William. *Charles Eliot: Landscape Architect.* Boston: Houghton Mifflin and Co., 1902.

Elliott, William. *Carolina Sports by Land and Water.* 1867? Reprint. Columbia, S.C.: State Co., 1918.

Farrand, Livingston. "Basketry Designs of the Salish Indians." In Franz Boas, ed., *Memoirs of the American Museum of Natural History: Jesup North Pacific Expedition,* 1 (1898-1900), 391-412.

Fernow, Bernhard Eduard. *Economics of Forestry: A Reference Book for Students of Political Economy and Professional and Lay Students of Forestry.* New York: Thomas Y. Crowell, 1902.

———. *Report upon the Forestry Investigations of the United States Department of Agriculture, 1877-1898.* Washington: G.P.O., 1899.

Fewkes, J. Walter, ed. *A Journal of American Ethnology and Archaeology.* 5 vols. Boston: Houghton Mifflin and Co., 1891-1908.

Fletcher, Alice C. "A Study of Omaha Indian Music." *Archaeological and Ethnological Papers of the Peabody Museum,* 1, No. 5 (June 1893), 231-382.

Flint, Timothy. *The Personal Narrative of James O. Pattie of Kentucky.* 1831. Reprinted in vol. 18 of Thwaites, ed., *Early Western Travels.*

————. *Recollections of the Last Ten Years Passed in Occasional Residences and Journeyings in the Valley of the Mississippi . . . In a Series of Letters. . . .* Boston: Cummings, Hilliard, and Co., 1826.

[Foote, John P.]. Review of John D. Hunter, *Manners and Customs of the Indian tribes located west of the Mississippi. Cincinnati Literary Gazette,* 1 (January 1, 10, 1824), 1-2, 9-10.

"Forests." *Hours at Home,* 3 (September 1866), 398-402.

Franchère, Gabriel. *Narrative of a Voyage to the Northwest Coast of America in the Years 1811, 1812, 1813, and 1814; or The First American Settlement on the Pacific.* 1820. Translated and edited by J. V. Huntington, 1854. Reprinted in vol. 6 of Thwaites, ed., *Early Western Travels.*

Franklin, Benjamin. "Remarks Concerning the Savages of North America." Papers of Benjamin Franklin. Library of Congress microcopy. 1941. 2d Ser., vol. 10, no. 2334-2344.

Freneau, Philip. *The Prose of Philip Freneau.* Edited by Philip M. Marsh. New Brunswick: Scarecrow Press, 1955.

Fuller, Margaret. *The Writings of Margaret Fuller.* Edited by Mason Wade. New York: Viking, 1941.

Gallatin, Albert. *Selected Writings of Albert Gallatin.* Edited by E. James Ferguson. New York: Bobbs-Merrill, 1967.

Garland, Hamlin. *Crumbling Idols: Twelve Essays on Art Dealing Chiefly with Literature Painting and the Drama.* 1894. Edited by Jane Johnson. Cambridge, Mass.: Harvard University Press, 1960.

Gatschet, Albert. "The Karankawa Indians, the Coast People of Texas." *Archaeological and Ethnological Papers of the Peabody Museum,* 1, No. 2 (1891), 65-103.

George, Henry. *Moses/The Crime of Poverty.* New York: International Joseph Fels Commission, 1918.

————. *Our Land and Land Policy.* 1871. Reprint. New York: Doubleday Page and Co., 1904. Expanded in 1878 to *Progress and Poverty.*

————. *Progress and Poverty.* 1879. Reprint. New York: Robert Schalkenbach Foundation, 1954.

Gibbs, George. *Indian Tribes of Washington Territory. Pacific Northwest Letters of George Gibbs.* 1854. Reprint. Fairfield, Wash.: Ye Galleon Press, 1967.

Giffen, Fannie Reed. *Oo-Mah-Ha Ta-Wa-Tha (Omaha City).* Lincoln, Nebr.: n.p., 1898.

Gifford, John, ed. *The New Jersey Forester: A Bi-Monthly Pamphlet Devoted to the Development of Our Forests.* 1-2 (1895-1896).

Gillmore, Parker. *A Hunter's Adventures in the Great West.* London: Hurst and Blackett, 1871.

Greeley, Horace. *Glances at Europe.* New York: Dewitt and Davenport, 1851.

Green, C. H. "Brief History of Cliff Dwellers, Their Relics and Ruins." In *Catalogue of a Unique Collection of Cliff Dweller Relics.* Chicago: Art Institute, 1891.

Grinnell, George Bird. *Beyond the Old Frontier: Adventures of Indian-Fighters, Hunters, and Fur-Traders.* New York: Charles Scribner's Sons, 1913.

———. *Blackfoot Lodge Tales: The Story of a Prairie People.* 1903? Reprint. Lincoln: University of Nebraska Press, 1962.

———. *The Passing of the Great West: Selected Papers of George Bird Grinnell.* Edited by John T. Reiger. New York: Winchester Press, 1972.

———. *Pawnee Hero Stories and Folk-Tales with Notes on the Origin, Customs and Character of the Pawnee People.* New York: Charles Scribner's Sons, 1890.

———, ed. *American Big Game Hunting in Its Haunts.* New York: Forest and Stream Publishing Co., 1904.

Hale, Horatio. *An International Idiom: A Manual of the Oregon Trade Language or "Chinook Jargon."* London: Whittaker and Co., 1890.

———, ed. *The Iroquois Book of Rites.* 1883. Edited by William N. Fenton. Toronto: University of Toronto Press, 1963. Originally no. 2 of D. G. "Brinton's Library of Aboriginal Literature" (Philadelphia).

Halkett, John. *Historical Notes Respecting the Indians of North America: With Remarks on the Attempts Made to Convert and Civilize Them.* London: Archibald Constable and Co., 1825.

Hall, James. *Legends of the West: Sketches Illustrative of the Habits, Occupations, Privations, Adventures and Sports of the Pioneers of the West.* 1832. Reprint. Cincinnati: Applegate and Co., 1857.

———. *Sketches of History, Life, and Manners in the West.* 2 vols. Philadelphia: Harrison Hall, 1835.

Hamilton, William Thomas. *My Sixty Years on the Plains: Trapping, Trading, and Indian Fighting.* 1905. Reprint. Norman: University of Oklahoma Press, 1960.

Hammond, Samuel H. *Wild Northern Scenes; or Sporting Adventures with the Rifle and the Rod.* New York: Derby and Jackson, 1857.

Hart, Col. Joseph C. *Miriam Coffin, or The Whale Fishermen: A Tale.* 1834. New ed. 2 vols. in 1. San Francisco: H. R. Coleman, 1872.

Hawthorne, Nathaniel. *The American Notebooks.* Edited by Claude M. Simpson. Columbus: Ohio State University Press, 1972.

―――. "Sketches from Memory." 1835. Reprinted in *Mosses from an Old Manse*, pp. 422-38. Vol. 10 of Centenary Ed. Columbus: Ohio State University Press, 1974.

Henry, Joseph. "Circular Relating to Collections in Archaeology and Ethnology." *Smithsonian Miscellaneous Collections*, 8 (1868), 1-2.

―――. "Report of the Secretary for 1858." In *Annual Report of the Board of Regents of the Smithsonian Institution*, pp. 13-43. Washington: G.P.O., 1859.

Hildreth, S. P. *Pioneer History: Being an Account of the First Examinations of the Ohio Valley and the Early Settlement of the Northwest Territory.* Cincinnati: H. W. Derby and Co., 1848.

Hill, Alice Polk. *Tales of the Colorado Pioneers.* Denver: Pierson and Gardiner, 1884.

Hillers, Jack. *"Photographed All the Best Scenery": Jack Hillers' Diary of the Powell Expeditions, 1871-1875.* Edited by Don D. Fowler. Salt Lake City: University of Utah Press, 1972.

Holley, Frances Chamberlain. *Once Their Home; or, Our Legacy from the Dahkotahs.* Chicago: Donohue and Henneberry, 1890.

Holmes, William Henry. *Archaeological Studies among the Ancient Cities of Mexico.* Field Columbian Museum Publication 8, 16. Anthropological Series, vol. 1, no. 1. Chicago, 1895.

Hopkins, Sarah Winnemucca. *Life Among the Piutes: Their Wrongs and Claims.* Edited by Mrs. Horace [Mary] Mann. Boston: n.p., 1883.

Hornaday, William T. *The Extermination of the American Bison.* Washington: G.P.O., 1889.

Hough, Emerson. *The Story of the Cowboy.* New York: D. Appleton and Co., 1897.

Hough, Franklin B. "On the Duty of Governments in the Preservation of Forests." *Proceedings of the American Association for the Advancement of Science*, 22, pt. 2 (1873), 1-10.

Hubbard, Bela. "Ancient Garden Beds of Michigan." *American Antiquarian*, 1 (April 1878), 1-9.

―――. *Memorials of a Half-Century.* New York: G. P. Putnam's Sons, 1887.

Hunter, John Dunn. *Memoirs of a Captivity Among the Indians of*

North America. 1824. Edited by Richard Drinnon. New York: Schocken Books, 1973.

Hurlbut, Henry H. *Chicago Antiquities.* Chicago: n.p., 1881.

Irving, John Treat, Jr. *Indian Sketches Taken During an Expedition to the Pawnee Tribes [1833].* 1835. Edited by John Francis Mc-Dermott. Norman: University of Oklahoma Press, 1955.

Irving, Washington. *The Adventures of Captain Bonneville, U.S.A., in the Rocky Mountains and the Far West.* 1837. Edited by Edgeley W. Todd. Norman: University of Oklahoma Press, 1961.

———. *Astoria, or Anecdotes of an Enterprise Beyond the Rocky Mountains.* Edited by Edgeley W. Todd. Norman: University of Oklahoma Press, 1964.

———. *The Western Journals of Washington Irving.* Edited by John Francis McDermott. Norman: University of Oklahoma Press, 1944.

Jackson, Helen Hunt. *A Century of Dishonor: The Early Crusade for Indian Reform.* 1881. Edited by Andrew F. Rolle. New York: Harper and Row, 1965.

———. *Glimpses of California and the Missions.* 1883. Reprint. Boston: Little, Brown and Co., 1903.

Jackson, Rev. Sheldon. *Alaska, and Missions on the North Pacific Coast.* New York: Dodd, Mead and Co., 1880.

Jackson, William Henry. *Descriptive Catalogue of Photographs of North American Indians.* With a prefatory note by F. W. Hayden. United States Geological and Geographical Survey of the Territories. Miscellaneous Publications, no. 9. Washington: G.P.O., 1877.

James, Edwin, ed. *A Narrative of the Captivity and Adventures of John Tanner During Thirty Years Residence Among the Indians in the Interior of North America.* 1830. Reprint. Minneapolis: Ross and Haines, 1956.

James, George Wharton. *In and Out of the Old Missions of California: An Historical and Pictorial Account of the Franciscan Missions.* Boston: Little, Brown and Co., 1905.

———. *Indian Basketry.* Pasadena: n.p., 1901.

———. *Old Missions and Mission Indians of California.* Los Angeles: B. R. Baumgardt and Co., 1895.

James, Isabella. "American Forests." *Lippincott's Magazine,* 1 (June 1868), 596-602.

James, Gen. Thomas. *Three Years among the Indians and Mexicans.* 1846. Reprint. Chicago: R. R. Donnelley and Sons, 1953.

Jameson, Mrs. Anna Brownell. *Winter Studies and Summer Rambles in Canada.* 2 vols. New York: Wiley and Putnam, 1839.

Jarvis, Samuel Farmar. *A Discourse on the Religion of the Indian Tribes of North America. Delivered Before the New-York Historical Society, Dec. 20, 1819.* New York: C. Wiley and Co., 1820.

Jerome, W. "Karl Moon's Indian Photographs." *Craftsman,* 20 (April 1911), 24-32.

Jones, James Athearn. *Traditions of the North American Indians.* 1830. 3 vols. Reprint. Upper Saddle River, N.J.: Literature House, 1970.

Journal of American Folk-Lore, The. Edited by W. W. Newell, Franz Boas, T. Frederick Crane, J. Owen Dorsey. Vol. 1. Boston: Houghton Mifflin and Co., 1888.

Kane, Paul. *Wanderings of an Artist among the Indians of North America from Canada to Vancouver's Island and Oregon through the Hudson's Bay Company's Territory.* 1859. Reprint. Toronto: Radisson Society of Canada, 1925.

Kinzie, Mrs. John H. [Juliette Augusta]. *Wau-Bun, The "Early Day" in the North-West.* New York: Derby and Jackson, 1856.

Knight, Sarah Kemble. *The Journal of Madam Knight.* Boston: Small, Maynard and Co., 1920.

Latrobe, Charles Joseph. *The Rambler in North America: 1832-1833.* 2 vols. London: R. B. Seeley and W. Burnside, 1835.

Lawrence, James H. "Discovery of the Nevada Fall." *Overland Monthly.* 2d ser., 4 (October 1884), 360-71.

Leland, Charles G. *The Algonquin Legends of New England, or Myths and Folk Lore of the Micmac, Passamaquoddy, and Penobscot Tribes.* Boston: Houghton Mifflin and Co., 1884.

———. "Legends of the Passamaquoddy." *Century Magazine,* 28 (September 1884), 668-77.

"Letters to the Editor, on Indian Antiquities. Letter I." *Detroit Gazette,* September 1, 1820, p. 1.

Lewis, James Otto. *The North American Aboriginal Port-Folio.* 1835-36. New York: J. P. Callender, 1838.

[Longstreet, Augustus Baldwin]. *Georgia Scenes, Characters, Incidents &c. in the First Half Century of the Republic.* 2d ed. New York: Harper and Brothers, 1860.

Lossing, Benson J. "Our Barbarian Brethren." *Harper's New Monthly Magazine,* 40 (May 1870), 793-811.

Ludewig, Hermann E. *The Literature of American Aboriginal Languages. Edited by Nicholas Trübner.* London. Trübner and Co., 1858.

Lummis, Charles F. "The Palmer Collection." *Land of Sunshine*, 2 (February 1895), 68-69.

Mabie, Hamilton Wright. "Indians, and Indians." *Century Magazine*, 38 (July 1889), 471-72.

McClintock, Walter. *Old Indian Trails*. Boston: Houghton Mifflin Co., 1923.

McGee, W. J. "The Conservation of Natural Resources." *Proceedings of the Mississippi Valley Historical Association*, 3 (1909-10), 361-79.

McKenney, Thomas L., and Hall, James. *The Indian Tribes of North America, with Biographical Sketches and Anecdotes of the Principal Chiefs*. 1836-44. New ed. Edited by Frederick Webb Hodge. 3 vols. Edinburgh: John Grant, 1933-34.

McKnight, Charles. *Our Western Border . . . One Hundred Years Ago*. Philadelphia: J. C. McCurdy and Co., 1875.

Mahan, Rev. Asa. *Autobiography: Intellectual, Moral and Spiritual*. London: T. Woolmer, 1882.

Marcy, Randolph Barnes. *Border Reminiscences*. New York: Harper and Brothers, 1872.

———. *Thirty Years of Army Life on the Border*. New York: Harper and Brothers, 1866.

Marsh, George Perkins. *Address Delivered Before the Agricultural Society of Rutland County, Sept. 30, 1847*. Rutland, Vt.: n.p., 1848.

———. *Man and Nature*. 1864. Edited by David Lowenthal. Cambridge, Mass.: Harvard University Press, 1965.

———. "The Study of Nature." Review of Alexander von Humboldt, *Views of Nature* (1850), and W. R. Alger, *Lessons for Mankind from the Life and Death of Humboldt* (1859). *Christian Examiner*, 5th ser., 68 (January 1860), 33-62.

Marshall, Humphrey. *The History of Kentucky*. Frankfort: n.p., 1824.

Mason, Edward G. "Francis Parkman." *Dial*, 1 (December 1880), 149-51.

Mason, Otis Tufton. "Aboriginal American Basketry: Studies in a Textile Art without Machinery." In *Smithsonian Institution Annual Report, 1902*, pp. 171-548. Washington: G.P.O., 1904.

Matthews, Washington. *Ethnography and Philology of the Hidatsa Indians*. With a preface by F. V. Hayden. United States Geological and Geographical Survey, Miscellaneous Publications, no. 7. Washington: G.P.O., 1877.

————. "Songs of the Navajos." *Land of Sunshine,* 5 (October 1896), 197-201.

Maximilian zu Wied. *People of the First Man: Life among the Plains Indians in Their Final Days of Glory.* Edited by Davis Thomas and Karin Ronnefeldt. New York: E. P. Dutton, 1976.

————. *Travels in the Interior of North America.* Translated by H. Evans Lloyd. 1843. Reprinted as vols. 22-24 of Thwaites, ed., *Early Western Travels.*

Mayer, Frank Blackwell. *With Pen and Pencil on the Frontier in 1851: The Diary and Sketches of Frank Blackwell Mayer.* Edited by Bertha L. Heilbron. Saint Paul: Minnesota Historical Society, 1932.

Meacham, Alfred Benjamin. *Wigwam and War-Path; or The Royal Chief in Chains.* Rev. ed. Boston: John P. Dale and Co., 1875.

Messiter, Charles Alston. *Sport and Adventures among the North American Indians.* London: R. H. Porter, 1890.

Methvin, Rev. J. J. *Andele, or The Mexican-Kiowa Captive: A Story of Real Life Among the Indians.* Louisville: Pentecostal Herald Press, 1899.

Miles, Nelson. *Personal Recollections and Observations of General Nelson A. Miles. . . .* New York: Werner Co., 1897.

"Mr. Remington as Artist and Author." Review of Remington, *Crooked Trails. Dial,* 25 (October 1898), 265.

Monsen, Frederick I. "The Destruction of Our Indians: What Civilization Is Doing to Extinguish an Ancient and Highly Intelligent Race by Taking Away Its Arts, Industries, and Religion." *Craftsman,* 11 (March 1907), 683-91.

————. "Picturing Indians with the Camera." *Photo-Era,* 25 (October 1910), 165-78.

Moon, Carl. "Photographing the Vanishing Red Man." *Leslie's* Illustrated, March 10, 1914.

Mooney, James. *The Ghost-Dance Religion and the Sioux Outbreak of 1890.* 1896. Edited by Anthony F. C. Wallace. New York: Dover Publications, 1972.

Morgan, Lewis H. *Ancient Society, or Researches in the Lines of Human Progress from Savagery through Barbarism to Civilization.* New York: Henry Holt and Co., 1877.

————. *The Indian Journals, 1859-62.* Edited by Leslie A. White. Ann Arbor: University of Michigan Press, 1959.

————. *League of the Ho-De-No Sav-Nee or Iroquois.* 1851. Reprint 2 vols. in 1. New Haven: Human Relations Area Files, 1954.

Morgan, Lewis H. "Letter to the Editor: The Hue-&-Cry Against the Indians." Dated Rochester, July 10, 1876. *Nation*, July 20, 1876, pp. 40-41.

———. "Montezuma's Dinner." Review of H. H. Bancroft, *Native Races of the Pacific States*. *North American Review*, 122 (1876), 265-308.

Morse, Rev. Jedidiah. *A Report to the Secretary of War of the United States on Indian Affairs Comprising a Narrative of a Tour Performed in the Summer of 1820*. New Haven: S. Converse, 1822.

Muir, John. *Our National Parks*. New York: Houghton Mifflin Co., 1901.

Myrtle, Minnie. *The Iroquois; or, The Bright Side of Indian Character*. New York: D. Appleton and Co., 1855.

Nelson, Edward William. "The Eskimo About Bering Strait." In *Bureau of American Ethnology Annual Report, 1896-97*. Washington: G.P.O., 1899.

Noble, Louis L. *The Course of Empire, Voyage of Life, and Other Pictures of Thomas Cole, N.A.* New York: Lamport, Blakeman and Law, 1853.

Norton, Charles Eliot; Parkman, Francis; and Agassiz, Alexander. "First Annual Report of the Executive Committee, with Accompanying Papers, 1879-80." In *Archaeological Institute of America*. Cambridge, Mass.: John Wilson and Co., 1880.

Norton, John. *The Journal of Major John Norton, 1816*. Edited by Carl F. Klinck and James J. Talman. Toronto: Champlain Society, 1970.

Nuttall, Thomas. *A Journal of Travels into the Arkansas Territory, During the Year 1819. . . .* 1821. Reprint as vol. 13 of Thwaites, ed., *Early Western Travels*.

O'Beirne, Harry F. *Leaders and Leading Men of the Indian Territory*. Vol. 1: *Choctaws and Chickasaws*. Chicago: American Publishers' Association, 1891.

Ogden, Peter Skene. *Peter Skene Ogden's Snake Country Journal, 1826-27*. Edited by K. G. Davies. With an introduction by Dorothy O. Johansen. Publications of The Hudson's Bay Record Society, 23. London: Hudson's Bay Record Society, 1961.

———. *Traits of American-Indian Life and Character by a Fur Trader*. London: Smith, Elder and Co., 1853.

Olmsted, Frederick Law. *The Papers of Frederick Law Olmsted*. Vol. 1: *The Formative Years, 1822 to 1852*. Edited by Charles Capen McLaughlin. Baltimore: Johns Hopkins University Press, 1977.

————. "The Yosemite Valley and the Mariposa Big Trees: A Preliminary Report (1865)." With introductory note by Laura Wood Roper. *Landscape Architecture*, 43 (October 1952), 12-25.

Pandosy, Rev. Marie Charles. *Grammar and Dictionary of the Yakama Language*. Translated and edited by George Gibbs and J. G. Shea. New York: Cramoisy Press, 1862.

Parkman, Francis. *The Conspiracy of Pontiac and the Indian War after the Conquest of Canada.* 1851. Vols. 16-18 of the Champlain Edition of *The Works of Francis Parkman*. Boston: Little, Brown and Co., 1898.

————. *The Jesuits in North America in the Seventeenth Century.* 1867. Vols. 3-4 of the Champlain Edition of *The Works of Francis Parkman*. Boston: Little, Brown and Co., 1897.

————. *The Oregon Trail: Sketches of Prairie and Rocky-Mountain Life.* 1849. Edited by E. N. Feltskog. Madison: University of Wisconsin Press, 1969.

————. "The Works of James Fenimore Cooper." *North American Review*, 74 (January 1852), 147-61.

Peters, Edward T. "Evils of Our Public Land Policy." *Century Magazine*, 25 (February 1883), 599-601.

"Petition to the Massachusetts Legislature," October, 1812. In *American Antiquarian Society Collections*, 1:17-18. Worcester, Mass., 1820.

Peyton, John Lewis. *Over the Alleghanies and Across the Prairies: Personal Recollections of the Far West*. London: Simpkin, Marshall and Co., 1869.

"Photographic Portraits of North American Indians in the Gallery of the Smithsonian Institution." *Smithsonian Miscellaneous Collections*, 14 (1867), 1-42.

Pilling, James Constantine. *Bibliography of the Chinookan Languages*. Washington: G.P.O., 1893.

————. *Bibliography of the Siouan Languages*. Bureau of American Ethnology, Bulletin 5. Washington: G.P.O., 1887.

Pourtalès, Count de. *On the Western Tour with Washington Irving: The Journal and Letters of Count de Pourtalès*. Edited by George F. Spaulding. Norman: University of Oklahoma Press, 1968.

Powell, G. W. "American Forests." *Harper's New Monthly Magazine*, 59 (August 1879), 371-74.

Powell, John Wesley. *Introduction to the Study of Indian Languages with Words Phrases and Sentences to be Collected*. 1877. 2d ed. Washington: G.P.O., 1880.

Powell, John Wesley. "Preface." *Bureau of Ethnology: Annual Reports,* 2 (1880-81).

———. *Selected Prose of John Wesley Powell.* Edited by George Crossette. Boston: David R. Godine, 1970.

———. "Sketch of Lewis Henry Morgan." *Popular Science Monthly,* November 1880, pp. 114-21.

Pratt, John Lowell, ed. *Currier and Ives: Chronicles of America.* Introduction by A. K. Baragwanath. Maplewood, N.J.: Hammond Inc., 1968.

Prudden, T. Mitchell. "An Elder Brother to the Cliff-Dwellers." *Harper's Monthly Magazine,* 95 (June 1897), 56-62.

Rafinesque, Constantine Samuel. *The Ancient Monuments of North and South America.* 2d ed. Philadelphia: n.p., 1838.

———. *A Life of Travels and Researches in North America and South Europe.* Philadelphia: n.p., 1836.

Ralph, Julian. "Frederic Remington." *Harper's Weekly,* 39 (July 20, 1895), 688.

Remington, Frederic. *Crooked Trails.* 1898. Reprint. Freeport, N.Y.: Books for Libraries Press, 1969.

———. "On the Indian Reservations." *Century Magazine,* 38 (July 1889), 394-405.

Review of "Catlin's North American Indians." *United States Magazine, and Democratic Review,* new ser., 11 (July 1892), 44-52.

Review of Exhibition of National Academy of Design. *Literary World,* May 15, 1847, pp. 347-48.

Review of Roosevelt, *Ranch Life and the Hunting Trail. Overland Monthly,* 2d ser., 28 (November 1896), 604.

Richardson, Albert D. *Beyond the Mississippi: From the Great River to the Great Ocean, Life and Adventure on the Prairies, Mountains, and Pacific Coast . . . 1857-1867.* Hartford, Conn.: American Publishing Co., 1867.

Riggs, Stephen R. *Dakota-English Dictionary.* 1852. Contributions to North American Ethnology, no. 7. Washington: G.P.O., 1897.

Robertson, S. C. "An Army Hunter's Notes on Our North-Western Game." *Outing,* 11 (January 1888), 302-09.

Robinson, Alfred. *Life in California.* New York: Wiley and Putnam, 1846.

Roehm, Marjorie Catlin, ed. *The Letters of George Catlin and His Family: A Chronicle of the American West.* Berkeley: University of California Press, 1966).

Roosevelt, Theodore. "Frontier Types." *Century Magazine,* 36 (October 1888), 832-43.

————. *Hunting Trips of a Ranchman/Hunting Trips on the Prairie and in the Mountains.* 1885. Reprint. New York: G. P. Putnam's Sons, 1905.

————. *The Letters of Theodore Roosevelt.* Edited by Elting E. Morison. 8 vols. Cambridge, Mass.: Harvard University Press, 1951.

————. "Ranch Life in the Far West." *Century Magazine*, 35 (February 1888), 495-510.

————. "The Ranchman's Rifle on Crag and Prairie." *Century Magazine*, 36 (June 1888), 200-212.

————. "Sheriff's Work on a Ranch." *Century Magazine*, 36 (May 1888), 39-51.

————, and Grinnell, George Bird, eds. *American Big-Game Hunting: The Book of the Boone and Crockett Club.* New York: Forest and Stream Publishing Co., 1893.

Ross, Alexander. *Adventures of the First Settlers on the Oregon or Columbia River . . . 1849.* Reprinted as vol. 7 of Thwaites, ed., *Early Western Travels.*

Rusling, James F. *Across America: Or, The Great West and the Pacific Coast.* New York: Sheldon and Co., 1874.

Russell, Osborne. *Journal of a Trapper. . . .* Edited by Aubrey L. Haines. Portland: Oregon Historical Society, 1955.

Ruxton, George Frederick. *Life in the Far West.* 1848. Edited by LeRoy R. Hafen. Norman: University of Oklahoma Press, 1951.

Sagard, Gabriel. *The Long Journey to the Country of the Hurons.* 1639. Translated by H. H. Langton. Edited by George M. Wrong. Toronto: Champlain Society, 1939.

Schoolcraft, Henry R. *Archives of Aboriginal Knowledge.* 6 vols. Philadelphia: J. B. Lippincott and Co., 1860.

————. *Narrative Journal of Travels Through the Northwestern Regions of the United States Extending from Detroit through the Great Chain of American Lakes to the Sources of the Mississippi River in the Year 1820.* 1821. Edited by Mentor Williams. East Lansing: Michigan State College Press, 1953.

————. *Schoolcraft's Indian Legends.* Edited by Mentor Williams. East Lansing: Michigan State University Press, 1956.

Schultz, James Willard [Apikuni]. *My Life as an Indian: The Story of a Red Woman and a White Man in the Lodge of the Blackfeet.* Boston: Houghton Mifflin Co., 1914. Serialized 1906-1907 in *Forest & Stream* as "In the Lodges of the Blackfeet."

Schurz, Carl. "Present Aspects of the Indian Problem." *North American Review*, 133 (July 1881), 1-24.

Schwatka, Frederick. "An Elk-Hunt on the Plains." *Century Magazine*, 35 (January 1888), 447-56.

Seton-Thompson, Ernest. *Wild Animals I Have Known*. New York: Charles Scribner's Sons, 1898.

Shinn, Charles Howard. "San Fernando Mission by Moonlight." *Land of Sunshine*, 2 (April 1895), 79-80.

Simms, William Gilmore. *Views and Reviews in American Literature, History and Fiction, First Series*. 1845. Edited by C. Hugh Holman. Cambridge, Mass.: Harvard University Press, 1962.

Simpson, Lt. James H. *Journal of a Military Reconnaissance from Santa Fé, New Mexico to the Navajo Country*. Philadelphia: Lippincott, Grambo and Co., 1852.

Snelling, William Joseph. *Tales of the Northwest*. 1830. Reprint. Minneapolis: University of Minnesota Press, 1936.

Speck, Frank G. *Decorative Art of Indian Tribes of Connecticut*. No. 10 Anthropological Series, Canada Department of Mines. Ottawa: G. P. Bureau, 1915.

Spencer, J. W. *Reminiscences of Pioneer Life in the Mississippi Valley*. 1872. Reprinted in Milo Milton Quaife, ed., *The Early Days of Rock Island and Davenport*, pp. 1-85. Chicago: R. R. Donnelley and Sons, 1942.

Spencer, Oliver M. *Indian Captivity*. 1835. Reprint. Ann Arbor: University Microfilms, 1966.

Sproat, Gilbert Malcolm. *Scenes and Studies of Savage Life*. London: Smith, Elder and Co., 1868.

Squier, Ephraim G. *Antiquities of the State of New York*. Buffalo: George H. Derby and Co., 1851.

————. *The Serpent Symbol*. American Archaeological Researches, no. 1. New York: George P. Putnam, 1851.

Stanley, John Mix. "Portraits of North American Indians with Sketches of Scenery, Etc." *Smithsonian Miscellaneous Collections*, 2 (1862), 1-76.

Starr, Frederick. *Notes upon the Ethnography of Southern Mexico*. 2 vols. Davenport, Ia.: Putnam Memorial Publication Fund, 1900-1902.

Stephen, Alexander M. *Hopi Journal of Alexander M. Stephen*. Edited by Elsie Clews Parsons. 2 vols. New York: Columbia University Press, 1936.

Stephens, John Lloyd. *Incidents of Travel in Central America, Chiapas, and Yucatan*. 1841. Edited by Richard L. Predmore. 2 vols. New Brunswick: Rutgers University Press, 1949.

———. *Incidents of Travel in Yucatan.* 2 vols. 1843. Reprint. New York: Dover Publications, 1963.

Stevenson, Matilda Coxe. *The Zuñi Indians: Their Mythology, Esoteric Fraternities, and Ceremonies.* 1905. Reprint. New York: Johnson Reprint Corp., 1970.

Stewart, Sir William Drummond. *Altowan; or Incidents of Life and Adventure in the Rocky Mountains by an Amateur Traveler.* Edited by J. Watson Webb. 2 vols. New York: Harper and Brothers, 1846.

Stillman, J.D.B. *Seeking the Golden Fleece; A Record of Pioneer Life in California.* San Francisco: A. Roman ad Co., 1877.

Stone, William L. *The Life and Times of Red-Jacket, or Sa-Go-Ye-Wat-Ha; Being the Sequel to the History of the Six Nations.* New York: Wiley and Putnam, 1841.

———. *Life of Joseph Brant—Thayendanegea, Including the Indian Wars of the American Revolution.* 2 vols. New York: George Dearborn and Co., 1838.

Stuart, Granville. *Forty Years on the Frontier as seen in the Journals and Reminiscences of Granville Stuart, Gold-Miner, Trader, Merchant, Rancher and Politician.* Edited by Paul C. Phillips. 2 vols. 1925. Reprint. Glendale, Calif.: Arthur H. Clark Co., 1957.

Swan, James G. *The Northwest Coast; or, Three Years' Residence in Washington Territory.* 1857. Reprint. With an introduction by Norman H. Clark. Seattle: University of Washington Press, 1969.

Sweet, Mrs J. E. De Camp. "Mrs. J. E. De Camp Sweet's Narrative of Her Captivity in the Sioux Outbreak of 1862." *Collections of the Minnesota Historical Society,* 6 (1894), 354-80.

Tallent, Annie D. *The Black Hills; or, The Last Hunting Ground of Dakotahs.* St. Louis: Nixon-Jones, 1899.

Taylor, Bayard. *At Home and Abroad: A Sketch-Book of Life, Scenery, and Men.* 2d ser. New York: G. P. Putnam, 1862.

Taylor, Joseph Henry. *Sketches of Frontier and Indian Life.* Pottstown, Pa.: n.p., 1889.

Thwaites, Reuben Gold, ed. *Early Western Travels: 1748-1846.* 32 vols. Cleveland, Ohio: Arthur H. Clark Co., 1904-07.

Turner, O. *Pioneer History of the Holland Purchase of Western New York.* Buffalo: Jewett, Thomas and Co., 1849.

Victor, Mrs. Francis Fuller. *The River of the West: Life and Adventure in the Rocky Mountains and Oregon.* Hartford, Conn.: R. W. Bliss and Co., 1869.

Vischer, Edward. *Sketches of the Washoe Mining Region: Photographs Reduced from Originals.* San Francisco: Valentine and Co., 1862.

Vischer's Pictorial of California: Landscape, Trees and Forest Scenes; Grand Features of California Scenery, Life, Traffic and Customs. 5 series of 12 numbers each. San Francisco: n.p., April 1870.

Volney, Constantin François Chasseboeuf. *A View of the Soil and Climate of the United States of America.* London: J. Johnson, 1804.

Vorphal, Ben Merchant, ed. *My Dear Wister: The Frederic Remington–Owen Wister Letters.* Palo Alto, Calif.: American West Publishing Co., 1972.

Waddle, W., Jr. "The Game Water-Fowl of America." *Harper's New Monthly Magazine,* 40 (February 1870), 433-37.

Wallace, Paul A. W., ed. *30,000 Miles with John Heckewelder.* Pittsburgh: University of Pittsburgh Press, 1958.

Whipple, Lt. Amiel Weeks. *Reports on Explorations and Surveys, To Ascertain the Most Practicable and Economical Route for a Railroad from the Mississippi River to the Pacific Ocean, 1853-4.* Senate Executive Documents, 33d Cong., 2d sess., 185?, vol. 3, no. 78, pt. 3, pp. 1-127.

White, Leslie A., ed. *Pioneers in American Anthropology: The Bandelier–Morgan Letters, 1873-1883.* 2 vols. Albuquerque: University of New Mexico Press, 1940.

Whitney, Ernest. *Legends of the Pike's Peak Region: The Sacred Myths of the Manitou.* Denver: Chain and Hardy Co., 1892.

"The Wilderness Hunter." *Atlantic Monthly,* 75 (June 1895), 826-30.

Willard, C. D. "The New Editor [Charles F. Lummis]. *Land of Sunshine,* 1 (December 1894), 12-13.

Williams, J. Fletcher. "A History of the City of Saint Paul and of the County of Ramsey, Minnesota." *Collections of the Minnesota Historical Society,* 4 (1876).

Williams, John S., ed. *The American Pioneer: A Monthly Periodical, Devoted to the Objects of the Logan Historical Society; or, To Collecting and Publishing Sketches Relative to the Early Settlement and Successive Improvement of the Country.* Cincinnati, Ohio. 1 (1842); 2 (January-October 1843).

Winter, George. *The Journals and Indian Paintings of George Winter, 1837-1839.* Indianapolis: Indiana Historical Society, 1948.

Wister, Owen. *Owen Wister Out West: His Journals and Letters.* Edited by Fanny Kemble Wister. Chicago: University of Chicago Press, 1958.

Wyeth, Nathaniel J. *The Journals of Captain Nathaniel J. Wyeth.* Fairfield, Wash.: Ye Galleon Press, 1969.

Secondary

Ackerknecht, Erwin H. " 'White Indians': Psychological and Physiological Peculiarities of White Children Abducted and Reared by North American Indians." *Bulletin of the History of Medicine,* 15 (January 1944), 15-36.

Apostol, Jane. "Francis of the Flowers: An Appreciation of Charles Francis Saunders." *California History,* 58 (Spring 1979), 38-47.

———. "Saving Grace." *Westways,* 68 (October 1976), 22-24, 71-72.

Arnold, Robert D. *Alaska Native Land Claims.* Anchorage: Alaska Native Foundation, 1976.

Baird, James. *Ishmael: A Study of the Symbolic Mode in Primitivism.* New York: Harper and Brothers, 1956.

Barlow, Elizabeth. *Frederic Law Olmsted's New York.* New York: Praeger, 1972.

Barnett, Louise K. *The Ignoble Savage: American Literary Racism, 1790-1890.* Contributions in American Studies, no. 18. Westport, Conn.: Greenwood Press, 1975.

Bartlett, Richard A. *Nature's Yellowstone.* Albuquerque: University of New Mexico Press, 1974.

Berkhofer, Robert F., Jr. *Salvation and the Savage: An Analysis of Protestant Missions and American Indian Response, 1787-1862.* Lexington: University Press of Kentucky, 1965.

———. *The White Man's Indian: Images of the American Indian from Columbus to the Present.* New York: Alfred A. Knopf, 1978.

Bickerstaff, Laura M. *Pioneer Artists of Taos.* Denver: Sage Books, 1955.

Bidney, David. "The Concept of Value in Modern Anthropology." In A. L. Kroeber, ed., *Anthropology Today: An Encyclopedic Inventory,* pp. 682-94. Chicago: University of Chicago Press, 1953.

———. "The Idea of the Savage in North American Ethnohistory." *Journal of the History of Ideas,* 15 (April 1954), 322-27.

Borden, Philip. "Found Cumbering the Soil: Manifest Destiny and the Indian in the Nineteenth Century." In Nash and Weiss, eds., *The Great Fear.*

Brandon, William. *The Last Americans: The Indian in American Culture.* New York: McGraw-Hill, 1974.

Brown, Mark H., and Felton, W. R. *Before Barbed Wire: L. A. Huffman, Photographer on Horseback.* 1956. Reprint. New York: Bramhall House, 1961.

Brown, Mark H., and Felton, W. R. *The Frontier Years: L. A. Huffman, Photographer of the Plains.* New York: Bramhall House, 1955.

Butterfield, Lyman H. "Draper's Predecessors and Contemporaries." In Donald R. McNeil, ed., *The American Collector,* p. 16. Madison: State Historical Society of Wisconsin, 1955.

Callcott, George H. *History in the United States, 1800-1860, Its Practice and Purpose.* Baltimore: Johns Hopkins University Press, 1970.

Carter, Everett. *The American Idea: The Literary Response to American Optimism.* Chapel Hill: University of North Carolina Press, 1977.

Caughey, John Walton. *Hubert Howe Bancroft, Historian of the West.* Berkeley: University of California Press, 1946.

Ceram, C. W. [Kurt W. Marek]. *The First American: A Study of North American Archaeology.* New York: Harcourt Brace Jovanovich, 1971.

Cikovsky, Nicolai, Jr. " 'The Ravages of the Axe': The Meaning of the Tree Stump in Nineteenth Century American Art." *Art Bulletin,* 61 (December 1979), 611-26.

Coke, Van Deren. *Taos and Santa Fe: The Artist's Environment, 1882-1942.* Albuquerque: University of New Mexico Press, 1963.

Cunliffe, Marcus. "American Watersheds." *American Quarterly,* 13 (Winter 1961), 480-94.

Curry, Larry. *The American West: Painters from Catlin to Russell.* New York: Viking, 1972.

Cutright, Paul Russell. *Lewis and Clark: Pioneering Naturalists.* Urbana: University of Illinois Press, 1969.

Dahl, Curtis. "The American School of Catastrophe." *American Quarterly,* 11 (Fall 1959), 380-90.

———. "Mound-Builders, Mormons, and William Cullen Bryant." *New England Quarterly,* 34 (June 1961), 178-90.

Darrah, William Culp. *Powell of the Colorado.* Princeton: Princeton University Press, 1951.

DeVoto, Bernard. *Across the Wide Missouri.* Boston: Houghton Mifflin Co., 1947.

Dippie, Brian William. "The Vanishing American: Popular Attitudes and American Indian Policy in the Nineteenth Century." Ph.D. diss., University of Texas, Austin, 1970.

Dobyns, Winifred Starr. "A Treasure House." *Woman Citizen,* 56, old ser. (December 1927), 12-14.

Doughty, Howard. *Francis Parkman.* New York: Macmillan Co., 1962.

Dozier, Edward P. "Resistance to Acculturation and Assimilation in an Indian Pueblo." *American Anthropologist*, 53 (January-March 1951), 56-66.

Drinnon, Richard. *White Savage: The Case of John Dunn Hunter*. New York: Schocken Books, 1972.

Dudley, Edward, and Novak, Maximillian E., eds. *The Wild Man Within: An Image in Western Thought from the Renaissance to Romanticism*. Pittsburgh: University of Pittsburgh Press, 1972.

Elson, Ruth Miller. *Guardians of Tradition: American Schoolbooks of the Nineteenth Century*. Lincoln: University of Nebraska Press, 1964.

Ewers, John C. *Artists of the Old West*. Garden City, N.Y.: Doubleday and Co., 1965.

―――. "Fact and Fiction in the Documentary Art of the American West." In John Francis McDermott, ed., *The Frontier Re-examined*, pp. 79-95. Urbana: University of Illinois Press, 1967.

―――. "Jean Louis Berlandier: A French Scientist among the Wild Comanches of Texas in 1828." In McDermott, ed., *Travelers on the Western Frontier*, pp. 290-300.

―――. "When Red and White Men Meet." *Western Historical Quarterly*, 2 (April 1971), 133-50.

Fagan, Brian M. *Elusive Treasure: The Story of Early Archaeologists in the Americas*. New York: Charles Scribner's Sons, 1977.

Fairbanks, Jonathan L. Introduction to *Frontier America: The Far West*, pp. 13-23. Boston: Museum of Fine Arts, 1975.

Fein, Albert. *Frederick Law Olmsted and the American Environmental Tradition*. New York: George Braziller, 1972.

Francis, Rell G. "Views of Mormon Country: The Life and Photographs of George Edward Anderson." *American West*, 15 (November-December 1978), 14-29.

Fritz, Henry E. *The Movement for Indian Assimilation, 1860-1890*. Philadelphia: University of Pennsylvania Press, 1963.

Fuess, Claude Moore. *Carl Schurz: Reformer (1829-1906)*. New York: Dodd, Mead and Co., 1932.

Geertz, Clifford. " 'From the Native's Point of View': On the Nature of Anthropological Understanding." In Keith H. Basso and Henry A. Selby, eds., *Meaning in Anthropology*, pp. 221-37. Albuquerque: University of New Mexico Press, 1976.

―――. *The Interpretation of Cultures: Selected Essays*. New York: Basic Books, 1973.

Geske, Norman A. "Ralph Albert Blakelock in the West." *American Art Review*, 3 (January-February 1976), 123-35.

Glacken, Clarence J. "Changing Ideas of the Habitable World." In William L. Thomas, ed., *Man's Role in Changing the Face of the Earth*, pp. 70-92. Chicago: University of Chicago Press, 1956.

Goetzmann, William. *Exploration and Empire: The Explorer and the Scientist in the Winning of the American West*. New York: Alfred A. Knopf, 1966.

Gordon, Dudley C. *Charles F. Lummis: Crusader in Corduroy*. Los Angeles: Cultural Assets Press, 1972.

Graybill, Florence Curtis, and Boesen, Victor. *Edward Sheriff Curtis: Visions of a Vanishing Race*. New York: Thomas Y. Crowell, 1976.

Haley, J. Evetts. *Life on the Texas Range*. With photographs by Erwin E. Smith. Austin: University of Texas Press, 1952.

Hampton, H. Duane. *How the U.S. Cavalry Saved Our National Parks*. Bloomington: Indiana University Press, 1971.

Harmsen, Dorothy. *Harmsen's Western Americana: A Collection of One Hundred Western Paintings with Biographical Profiles of the Artists*. Flagstaff: Northland Press, 1971.

Harper, J. Russell, ed. *Paul Kane's Frontier*. Austin: University of Texas Press, 1971.

Hassrick, Peter. *The Way West: Art of Frontier America*. New York: Harry N. Abrams, 1977.

Hassrick, Royal. *George Catlin Book of American Indians*. New York: Watson-Guptill, 1977.

Heard, J. Norman. *White into Red: A Study of the Assimilation of White Persons Captured by Indians*. Metuchen, N.J.: Scarecrow Press, 1973.

Hesseltine, William B. *Pioneer's Mission: The Story of Lyman Copeland Draper*. Madison: State Historical Society of Wisconsin, 1954.

Hine, Robert V. *Bartlett's West: Drawing the Mexican Boundary*. New Haven: Yale University Press, 1968.

————. *Edward Kern and American Expansion*. New Haven: Yale University Press, 1962.

Hoover, Dwight W. *The Red and the Black*. Chicago: Rand McNally, 1976.

Horan, James D. *The McKenney-Hall Portrait Gallery of American Indians*. New York: Crown, 1972.

Huth, Hans. *Nature and the American: Three Centuries of Changing Attitudes*. Berkeley: University of California Press, 1957.

————. "Yosemite: The Story of an Idea." *Sierra Club Bulletin*, 33 (March 1948), 47-78.

Jackson, Clarence S. *Picture Maker of the Old West: William H. Jackson.* New York: Bonanza Books, 1947.

Jacobs, Wilbur R. "The Indian and the Frontier in American History—A Need for Revision." *Western Historical Quarterly*, 4 (January 1973), 43-56.

————. "The Tip of an Iceberg: Pre-Columbian Indian Demography and Some Implications for Revisionism." *William and Mary Quarterly*, 3d ser., 31 (January 1974), 123-32.

Johnson, Gerald W. *Mount Vernon: The Story of a Shrine.* New York: Random House, 1953.

Judd, Neil M. *The Bureau of American Ethnology: A Partial History.* Norman: University of Oklahoma Press, 1967.

Keen, Benjamin. *The Aztec Image in Western Thought.* New Brunswick: Rutgers University Press, 1971.

Kennedy, John Hopkins. *Jesuit and Savage in New France.* New Haven: Yale University Press, 1950.

Kroeber, A. L. *Anthropology: Race, Language, Culture, Psychology, Prehistory.* Rev. ed. New York: Harcourt, Brace and Co., 1948.

Kroeber, Theodora. *Ishi in Two Worlds: A Biography of the Last Wild Indian in North America.* 1961. Reprint. Berkeley: University of California Press, 1971.

Kurutz, Gary F. "Pictorial Resources: The Henry E. Huntington Library's California and American West Collections." *California Historical Quarterly*, 54 (Summer 1975), 175-82.

Leonard, Thomas. *Above the Battle: War-Making in America from Appomattox to Versailles.* New York: Oxford University Press, 1978.

Lévi-Strauss, Claude. *The Scope of Anthropology.* Translated by Sherry Ortner Paul and Robert A. Paul. London: Jonathan Cape, 1967.

Lillard, Richard. *The Great Forest.* New York: Alfred A. Knopf, 1947.

Lopez, Barry. "The Photographer." *North American Review*, 262 (Fall 1977), 66-67.

Lowenthal, David. *George Perkins Marsh: Versatile Vermonter.* New York: Columbia University Press, 1958.

McCloskey, Maxine E., and Gilligan, James P., eds. *Wilderness and the Quality of Life.* New York: Sierra Club, 1969.

McCracken, Harold. *The Charles M. Russell Book: The Life and Work of the Cowboy Artist.* Garden City, N.Y.: Doubleday and Co., 1957.

McCracken, Harold. *Frederic Remington: Artist of the Old West.* Philadelphia: J. B. Lippincott Co., 1947.

———. *George Catlin and the Old Frontier.* New York: Bonanza Books, 1959.

McDermott, John Francis. *Seth Eastman: Pictorial Historian of the Indian.* Norman: University of Oklahoma Press, 1961.

———. *Seth Eastman's Mississippi: A Lost Portfolio Recovered.* Urbana: University of Illinois Press, 1973.

———, ed. *Travelers on the Western Frontier.* Urbana: University of Illinois Press, 1970.

Mahood, Ruth I., ed. *Photographer of the Southwest: Adam Clark Vroman, 1856-1919.* N.p.: Ward Ritchie Press, 1961.

Mardock, Robert Winston. *The Reformers and the American Indian.* Columbia: University of Missouri Press, 1971.

Mason, J. Alden. *George J. Heye, 1874-1957.* Leaflets of the American Indian Heye Foundation, no. 6. New York, 1958.

Matthiessen, Peter. "How to Kill a Valley." *New York Review of Books,* February 7, 1980, pp. 31-36.

Miller, Perry. "The Romantic Dilemma in American Nationalism and the Concept of Nature." *Harvard Theological Review,* 48 (October 1955), 239-53.

Mosier, Richard D. *Making the American Mind: Social and Moral Ideas in the McGuffey Readers.* New York: Columbia University Press, 1947.

Murphree, Idus L. "The Evolutionary Anthropologists: The Progress of Mankind. The Concepts of Progress and Culture in the Thought of John Lubbuck, Edward B. Tylor, and Lewis H. Morgan." *Proceedings of the American Philosophical Society,* 105 (June 1961), 265-300.

Nash, Gary B. "The Image of the Indian in the Southern Colonial Mind." *William and Mary Quarterly,* 3d ser., 29 (April 1972), 197-230.

———, and Weiss, Richard, eds. *The Great Fear: Race in the Mind of America.* New York: Holt, Rinehart and Winston, 1970.

Nash, Roderick. "The American Invention of National Parks." *American Quarterly,* 22 (Fall 1970), 726-35.

———. *Wilderness and the American Mind.* Rev. ed. New Haven: Yale University Press, 1973.

———, ed. *The American Environment: Readings in the History of Conservation.* 2d ed. Reading, Mass.: Addison-Wesley, 1976.

Northrop, F.S.C. "Man's Relation to the Earth in Its Bearing on His Aesthetic, Ethical, and Legal Values." In William L. Thomas, ed., *Man's Role in Changing the Face of the Earth*, pp. 1052-67. Chicago: University of Chicago Press, 1956.

Novak, Barbara. *American Painting of the Nineteenth Century: Realism, Idealism, and the American Experience*. New York: Praeger, 1969.

Olson, Victoria Thomas. "Pioneer Conservationist A. P. Hill: 'He Saved the Redwoods.'" *American West*, 14 (September-October 1977), 32-40.

Ong, Walter J., S.J. "World as View and World as Event." *American Anthropologist*, 71 (August 1969), 634-47.

Packard, Gar, and Packard, Maggy. *Southwest 1880: With Ben Wittick, Pioneer Photographer of Indian and Frontier Life*. With photographs from the Museum of New Mexico. Santa Fe: Packard Publications, 1970.

Parker, Franklin. *George Peabody: A Biography*. Nashville: Vanderbilt University Press, 1971.

Parry, Ellwood. *The Image of the Indian and the Black Man in American Art, 1590-1900*. New York: George Braziller, 1974.

Pearce, Roy Harvey. *Savagism and Civilization: A Study of the American Mind*. Baltimore: Johns Hopkins University Press, 1965.

Pinkett, Harold T. *Gifford Pinchot: Private and Public Forester*. Urbana: University of Illinois Press, 1970.

Pipes, Nellie B. "John Mix Stanley, Indian Painter." *Oregon Historical Quarterly*, 33 (September 1932), 250-58.

Poesch, Jessie. *Titian Ramsey Peale and His Journals of the Wilkes Expedition, 1799-1885*. Philadelphia: American Philosophical Society, 1961.

Pomeroy, Earl. *In Search of the Golden West: The Tourist in Western America*. New York: Alfred A. Knopf, 1957.

Prucha, Francis Paul, S.J., ed. *Americanizing the American Indians: Writings by the "Friends of the Indian" 1880-1900*. Cambridge, Mass.: Harvard University Press, 1973.

Rathbone, Perry T. *Charles Wimar, 1828-1862: Painter of the Indian Frontier*. St. Louis: City Art Museum, 1946.

Reiger, John F. *American Sportsmen and the Origins of Conservation*. New York: Winchester Press, 1975.

Resek, Carl. *Lewis Henry Morgan: American Scholar*. Chicago: University of Chicago Press, 1960.

Ringe, Donald A. *The Pictorial Mode: Space and Time in the Art of Bryant, Irving, and Cooper*. Lexington: University Press of Kentucky, 1971.

Rodgers, Andrew Denny, III. *Bernhard Eduard Fernow: The Story of North American Forestry*. Princeton: Princeton University Press, 1951.

Roper, Laura Wood. *FLO: A Biography of Frederick Law Olmsted*. Baltimore: Johns Hopkins University Press, 1973.

Rudisill, Richard. *Mirror Image: The Influence of the Daguerreotype on American Society*. Albuquerque: University of New Mexico Press, 1971.

Runte, Alfred. *National Parks: The American Experience*. Lincoln: University of Nebraska Press, 1979.

Saum, Lewis O. *The Fur Trader and the Indian*. Seattle: University of Washington Press, 1965.

Scherer, Joanna Cohan. *Indians: The Great Photographs that Reveal North American Indian Life, 1847-1929, from the Unique Collection of the Smithsonian Institution*. New York: Crown, 1973.

Shankland, Robert. *Steve Mather of the National Parks*. New York: Alfred A. Knopf, 1951.

Sheehan, Bernard W. *Seeds of Extinction: Jeffersonian Philanthropy and the American Indian*. New York: W. W. Norton, 1973.

Silverberg, Robert. *Mound Builders of Ancient America: The Archaeology of a Myth*. Greenwich, Conn.: New York Graphic Society, 1968.

Smith, Jane F., and Krasnicka, Robert M., eds. *Indian-White Relations: A Persistent Paradox*. Washington: Howard University Press, 1976.

Somkin, Fred. *Unquiet Eagle: Memory and Desire in the Idea of American Freedom, 1815-1860*. Ithaca: Cornell University Press, 1967.

Spengemann, William C. *The Adventurous Muse: The Poetics of American Fiction, 1789-1900*. New Haven: Yale University Press, 1977.

Spicer, Edward H. *Cycles of Conquest: The Impact of Spain, Mexico, and the United States on the Indians of the Southwest, 1533-1960*. Tucson: University of Arizona Press, 1962.

Stanton, William. *The Leopard's Spots: Scientific Attitudes toward Race in America, 1815-59*. Chicago: University of Chicago Press, 1960.

Starr, Kevin. *Americans and the California Dream, 1850-1915*. New York: Oxford University Press, 1973.

Steward, Julian. "Evolution and Process." In A. L. Kroeber, ed., *Anthropology Today: An Encyclopedic Inventory*, pp. 313-26. Chicago: University of Chicago Press, 1953.

Stocking, George W., Jr. *Race, Culture, and Evolution: Essays in the History of Anthropology.* New York: Free Press, 1968.

Strong, Douglas H. "The Sierra Club—A History. Part I: Origins and Outings." *Sierra,* October 1977, pp. 10-14.

———. "The Sierra Club—A History. Part II: Conservation." *Sierra,* November-December 1977, pp. 16-20.

Sturhahn, Joan. *Carvalho: Artist—Photographer—Adventurer—Patriot: Portrait of a Forgotten American.* Merrick, N.Y.: Richwood Publishing Co., 1976.

Swain, Donald C. *Federal Conservation Policy, 1921-1933.* University of California Publications in History, 76. Los Angeles: University of California Press, 1963.

———. *Wilderness Defender: Horace M. Albright and Conservation.* Chicago: University of Chicago Press, 1970.

Swanton, John R. "Notes on the Menal Assimilation of Races." *Journal of the Washington Academy of Sciences,* 16 (November 1926), 493-502.

Taft, Robert. *Artists and Illustrators of the Old West 1850-1900.* New York: Charles Scribner's Sons, 1953.

———. *Photography and the American Scene: A Social History, 1839-1889.* New York: Macmillan Co., 1938.

Ten Kate, Herman. "On Paintings of North American Indians and Their Ethnological Value." *Anthropos,* 7 (1911), 521-45.

Tilden, Freeman. *Following the Frontier with F. Jay Haynes: Pioneer Photographer of the Old West.* New York: Alfred A. Knopf, 1964.

Trennert, Robert A., Jr. *Alternative to Extinction: Federal Indian Policy and the Beginnings of the Reservation System, 1846-51.* Philadelphia: Temple University Press, 1975.

Trenton, Patricia. "Picturesque Images of Taos and Santa Fe." *American Art Review,* 1 (March-April 1974), 96-111.

Udall, Stewart L. *The Quiet Crisis.* New York: Avon, 1963.

Utley, Robert M. *Frontiersmen in Blue: The United States Army and the Indian, 1848-1865.* New York: Macmillan Co., 1967.

Viola, Herman J. "How *Did* an Indian Chief Really Look?" *Smithsonian,* 8 (June 1977), 100-104.

———. *The Indian Legacy of Charles Bird King.* Smithsonian Institution Press, 1976.

Von Hagan, Victor. *Maya Explorer: John Lloyd Stephens.* Norman: University of Oklahoma Press, 1947.

Washburn, Wilcomb E. *Red Man's Land/White Man's Law: A Study of the Past and Present Status of the American Indian.* New York: Charles Scribner's Sons, 1971.

Way, Ronald L. *Ontario's Niagara Parks: A History.* Niagara: Niagara Parks Commission, 1946.

Webb, William, and Weinstein, Robert A. *Dwellers at the Source: Southwestern Indian Photographs of A. C. Vroman, 1895-1904.* New York: Grossman, 1973.

White, G. Edward. *The Eastern Establishment and the Western Experience: The West of Frederic Remington, Theodore Roosevelt, and Owen Wister.* New Haven: Yale University Press, 1968.

Wilkinson, Kristina. "Frederick Monsen, F.R.G.S.: Explorer and Ethnographer." *Noticias,* Summer 1969, pp. 16-23.

Williams, Stanley T. *The Life of Washington Irving.* 2 vols. New York: Oxford University Press, 1935.

Willoughby, Charles C. "The Peabody Museum of Archaeology and Ethnology, Harvard University." *Harvard Graduates' Magazine,* 31 (June 1923), 495-503.

Zolla, Elémire. *The Writer and the Shaman: A Morphology of the American Indian.* 1969. Translated by Raymond Rosenthal. New York: Harcourt Brace Jovanovich, 1973.

INDEX

Library of Congress Cataloging in Publication Data

Mitchell, Lee Clark, 1957-
  Witnesses to a vanishing America.

  Bibliography: p.
  Includes index.
    1. Nature conservation—United States—History. 2. Conservation of
natural resources—United States—History. 3. Frontier and pioneer life—
United States—History. I. Title.
QH76.M54   333.95'0973   80-8567
ISBN 0-691-06461-X